LAS VEGAS
& DAY TRIPS
ARIZONA, UTAH & CALIFORNIA
2010/11

LAS VEGAS

& DAY TRIPS
ARIZONA, UTAH & CALIFORNIA

2010/11

Karen Marchbank
with Jane Anderson

foulsham
LONDON • NEW YORK • TORONTO • SYDNEY

foulsham

The Oriel, Thames Valley Court, 183–187 Bath Road, Slough, Berkshire, SL1 4AA, England

Foulsham books can be found in all good bookshops and direct from www.foulsham.com

ISBN: 978-0-572-03573-0

Look out for the latest editions of Foulsham's other travel guides:
Brit Guide to Orlando and Walt Disney World by Simon and Susan Veness
Brit Guide to Disneyland Paris by Simon and Susan Veness
Brit Guide to New York by Amanda Statham

Printed in Dubai by Oriental Press

CONTENTS

A note on the Brit Guides

This *Brit Guide* is one of an innovative series of travel guides that aim to offer practical, user-friendly guidance for the British traveller abroad. Focusing on clear, honest information, it is one British traveller's advice to another – without the jargon or sales pitch of the brochures.

What to read and watch to get you in the mood

Fear and Loathing in Las Vegas, a novel by Hunter S. Thompson and a film starring Johnny Depp
The Cold Six Thousand, a novel by James Ellroy
Bit the Jackpot, a novel by Erin McCarthy
Viva Las Vegas with Elvis Presley
Casino with Sharon Stone
21 with Kevin Spacey
Ocean's Eleven, *Twelve* and *Thirteen* with Brad Pitt and George Clooney
The Hangover with Bradley Cooper
Leaving Las Vegas with Nicolas Cage

Top Las Vegas facts and figures

How many visitors come to Las Vegas each year?	37,481,552
How many convention delegates visit?	5,899,725
How many conventions are held per year?	22,454
What is the Las Vegas Strip's gaming revenue?	$6.1b
What is the average gambling budget per trip?	$532
How long is the average visitor's stay?	3.5 nights (2008 figures)

INTRODUCTION

Sin City continues to grow and remake itself in astonishing ways, and yet it is the same old Las Vegas. Where else can mum relax in the embrace of a world-class spa treatment while dad fires golf balls about a quality nine holes? Then you meet later for a few hours of blackjack, poker or some time pulling on the 'one-armed bandits', before strolling through the fabulous plazas of Caesar's shops. Next, you stop and enjoy a romantic dinner at the two Michelin Alex at the Wynn before claiming marvellous seats for Bette Midler or Cirque du Soleil®'s new show, *Viva ELVIS*. Then it's drinks and dancing into the small hours at Paul Oakenfold's RAIN and before you know it, the sun is peeking over the horizon and you stagger off for a few moments of sleep before rising to do it all over again.

Legions of visitors descend on this isolated city in the desert to spend long, sleepless nights losing their inhibitions in an orgy of memorable good times, best confided with great prudence to family back home! In fact, it is often hard to keep track of everything, from how many glittering resorts are rising on the Strip skyline to which day it is!

Las Vegas is continuing to grow at an astonishing rate, and – in America at least – there's also been a change in Las Vegas's image. Associated in recent decades with tacky brashness, the city is now being transformed. The monstrous, themed resorts like the Venetian, Caesars Palace, Excalibur, Mandalay Bay and Bellagio are being challenged by new, even more titanic, wantonly decadent creations like Wynn Las Vegas, CityCenter, Trump International and The Cosmopolitan. Las Vegas wants to up the sophistication with the opening of plush, non-gaming hotels including Mandarin Oriental Las Vegas, Vdara Hotel and The Harmon Hotel.

Two sides to every adult

After a brief, unsuccessful flirtation with selling itself as a family destination in the 1980s, Las Vegas realised it could never compete with the massive theme parks of Orlando, Florida. Adults were the natural market for Vegas. So, with Circus Circus and Excalibur standing as notable exceptions, Las Vegas has melded itself into an adult playground of such awesome scale and complexity as to be unrivalled by anything on Earth.

Entertainment has topped the list, and Vegas has invested billions of dollars in bringing the finest to its venues. The visually stunning productions of the Canadian troupe Cirque du Soleil® reign supreme as people literally fight to acquire tickets to the habitually sold-out shows. A new Elvis production promises to be a massive hit. But there are also stunning shows by Cher, Donny and Marie Osmond, Blue Man Group, Penn & Teller and a legion of others to beguile you. Then there is a constant stream of special concerts, championship boxing matches, Miss Universe pageants and more to draw in the crowds.

Steve Wynn started the Vegas tradition of bringing in greater cultural aspects to Vegas and his Wynn Las Vegas joins Bellagio, Caesars Palace, Venetian and Tropicana with impressive art and museum displays. During a visit to Las Vegas in June 2007, I was able to see gorgeous collections of Matisse at the Venetian, Picasso at Wynn Las Vegas, two impressive museum collections of 'Titanic Artefacts' and 'The Human Body' at the Tropicana and a lovely

The iconic Las Vegas sign

collection of French Impressionists at Bellagio.

The active crowd also has the attention of the resort moguls. A score of world-class golf courses has turned Las Vegas into a top golfing destination. Meanwhile a host of tour operators now offers rock climbing, horse riding, desert walking, parasailing, boating, rollercoastering and nearly any other activity one could imagine – all with style and flair.

But the refined end of Las Vegas aside, Sin City has a reputation, well deserved, of sex and titillation. Has Vegas helped engineer the world's embrace of things once considered naughty, or has Sin City simply welcomed the shift in morality? Whichever is true, the number of 'skin' bars has tripled in recent years.

The arrival of the new millennium has ushered in a new age of ever-more-raunchy nightclubs where beds not settees, sofas not chairs give rise to a greater degree of intimacy. A venue's success in the last few years has gone hand in hand with its ability to offer both exclusive facilities for VIPs and saucy settings for a live-hard, work-hard and play-hard clientele.

The hottest Las Vegas *tour de force* is resorts with 'European-style sunbathing' – Las Vegas code for adult-only poolsides where topless lounging is decadently embraced. Many of these areas are tied to some of Las Vegas's hottest nightspots, such as Venetian's Tao Beach and Hard Rock Café's Sunday Pool Party. Here beautiful people dance and swill unbridled either by children or bikini tops.

Where the shopping is easy

If you want it, Vegas has it all – from designer splurges to bargain deals. Everything from colourful souvenir shops to haute couture boutiques can be found, but there has been a definite trend towards high-class shopping outlets. Forum Shops at Caesars Palace led the way with its 3-storey complex of shops and restaurants. The Fashion Show Mall offers 7 fashion department stores in a one-stop destination and the Bellagio, Wynn Las Vegas and the Venetian have whole promenades of designer shopping. Meanwhile, Chelsea Premium Outlets, which specialises in Bicester Village-style designer outlet stores, is now firmly established with 2 large locations in the city. Miracle Mile Shops has over 170 mid-to-high-priced shops. New in Vegas is The Esplanade at Encore, a selection of 11 boutiques from Rock & Republic to Chanel; The Shoppes at The Palazzo with its flagship Barneys New York and the Town Square Las

Vegas on the south end of Las Vegas Boulevard with more than 150 shops to spend your dollar, not to mention CityCenter's new shopping precinct right on the Strip.

Big is beautiful

None of this has happened by accident. The city has one of the most well co-ordinated and determined marketing strategies of any city in America (if not the world). Galvanised into action in the 1980s and '90s by the growth of Atlantic City, the Las Vegas Convention and Visitors Authority (LVCVA) has overseen marketing strategies that have helped the city reach a figure of 37.4 million visitors in 2008. The worldwide recession has meant that the 5-year plan to attract a phenomenal 43 million visitors per annum by 2009 looks unlikely, yet this is a city that will never rest on its laurels.

Las Vegas opened 7,600 new rooms in 2008 and projects 16,000 new rooms to open over the next 3 years. As of April 2009, there were 140,559 rooms – and the city's management aims to ensure those rooms are filled. The developers only plan new resorts because the LVCVA works tirelessly to attract new visitors and to increase repeat customers.

One of the most significant sources of visitors is the ever-expanding convention industry that ensures those all-important bums are plopped on hotel beds during the week. As the party capital of America, the city has no problem reaching near 100% occupancy at the weekend, but to be truly successful (and provide the expected levels of return on the billion-dollar investments made in resort hotels) the hotels need to reach 80% occupancy all week long, all year round. And they are dazzlingly successful, as in 2008 room occupancy was 86%, a full 25% above the national average.

Downtown is also becoming a must-see for visitors. Third Street's popularity is quickly growing as a top-notch entertainment district with an impressive list of bars and restaurants including Hogs & Heifers and Celebrity, a live music venue. Classic properties such as the Golden Nugget and The Plaza are investing millions in renovations to keep guests coming back.

So the appeal of Las Vegas remains strong and the city continues to grow and grow. A forest of construction cranes reach into the Strip's skyline as the newest creations take shape to shock, inspire and lure us back again and again. And here's where to start planning your trip.

1 | ENTERTAINMENT CITY

What the city is all about, when to go and other useful information

Las Vegas is a mere 150 years young, built in the middle of the desert, and lives like some old American West frontier town. In many ways it is the modern equivalent of an 1880s gold rush town, where thousands of hopeful miners elbowed space on to gaming tables next to Chinese coolies and ranching cowboys. Piano players played loudly, dance hall girls swished their dresses provocatively and the drunken crowds whooped and fired their guns in the air.

Today's Las Vegas is just a bit more modernised, with her casinos, shows, nightclubs and showgirls. Sin City has it all, yet it's not until you see the staggering line-up of monster-sized hotels for yourself that the enormity of it sinks in. In fact, the city never fails to impress. From the revolving restaurants and bars, to the chichi lounges, spectacular thrill rides and state-of-the-art nightclubs, it is such an incredible experience from beginning to end that you'll need to remind yourself to close your mouth on a regular basis!

⚓ BRITTIP

Luke, a seasoned high-roller, suggested to me that a first visit to Vegas can be so overwhelming that when booking, you should choose the number of days you'd like to stay and halve it!

As you drive up Las Vegas Boulevard South – the Strip, as it is known – from the airport, you'll encounter the triple-pronged Mandalay Bay resort, then the amazing

Fremont Street – the original strip

pyramid of the Luxor on your left and the gigantic golden lion of the MGM Grand to your right. Other wondrous sights appear, including the beautiful drawbridge castle of the Excalibur and a complete replica of New York's skyline at the New York-New York resort. And that is before you even reach what used to be the most famous part of the Strip – the old Four Corners that include the Greco-Roman empire of Caesars Palace and the Flamingo Hilton. Then it all comes in a rush, with the massive resorts of CityCenter, Planet Hollywood (the old new Aladdin), Paris, Mirage, Treasure Island, Venetian, the Wynn and many more.

Towering over it all is the Stratosphere, the world's tallest free-standing observation tower (1,148ft/350m high) at the top end of the Strip on the way to Downtown Las Vegas. Head farther down Las Vegas Boulevard and you'll run across the Old Las Vegas. Here you'll find the last vestiges of Las Vegas's former neon culture known as Glitter Gulch in the Fremont Street Experience that totally encloses Fremont Street. Then on your right is the new East Fremont Entertainment District, a 3-block cluster of cool nightclubs, jazz venues and chic eateries, all within walking distance of each other.

What it's all about

Las Vegas is a great source of employment. Up to 6,000 people move into the area every month from southern California, Utah and beyond. In 2008 the US Census Bureau estimated the population of Las Vegas to be 603,093, making it the 28th most populous city in the US. The predictions are that the current population of 1.8 million in Clark County, which

The lion outside the MGM Grand

encompasses Las Vegas, will have increased by over 50% to 2.7 million by the year 2018, after expanding from just 350,000 in 1992. The people come because the jobs are here. The Las Vegas area created 47,000 new jobs in 2006, with employment up 5.7% to 875,000. The unemployment rate held steady at a mere 4%. There have been no figures released since the worldwide recession, but building continues apace.

Not all the jobs are in the gambling industry. Many other businesses, especially those in the high-tech industry, are attracted by the low property tax and the lack of income or corporate income taxes. Aggressive advertising campaigns in trade publications such as the *Hollywood Reporter* have played a key part in the expansion of Nevada's film industry, leading to an income state wide of $100m from this source alone.

The golfing industry, too, has had a massive impact, creating 4,500 jobs and bringing $891m to the southern Nevada area, with Las Vegas at its epicentre. All these growth areas have been supported by a $91m expansion of the city's airport, McCarran International, and the opening in the summer of 2005 of the $650m Las Vegas Monorail.

Developers have been quick to spot the influx of smart, young professionals – lured by wages that vastly outstrip other American cities – and have rushed to

Painted Desert Golf Club

provide a wealth of sparkling condos in the heart of the city's most exciting corridor: the Strip. It is these professionals – along with cooler, smarter types of visitor – who have contributed to the explosion of trendy bars, ultra-lounges (see page 149), sophisticated nightclubs and an array of celebrity-chef restaurants. They also played a part in the growth of thrill rides, such as the heartline-twister Manhattan Express™ around New York-New York and Speed at the Sahara Hotel.

A holiday here can also encompass the fabulous natural sights of the Red Rock Canyon, Valley of Fire, Grand Canyon (by helicopter or plane in a day) and Mount Charleston, not so far away. You can find a venue for nearly every activity you fancy and there are plenty of opportunities to experience the real West. You can go horse riding at any of the national parks, go on a cowboy trail, meet the Native American tribes north and south of the city, go swimming, water-skiing and fishing at Lake Mead and even go skiing in Lee Canyon in winter. If that's not enough action for you, then try skydiving from Boulder City airport near the Hoover Dam.

The power of plastic comes into its own in the myriad shopping centres that have sprung up since Caesars Palace's Forum Shops gave a whole new meaning to the word 'mall'. Now locals and tourists spend even more money flexing their credit-card muscle shopping than they do on gambling, making Las Vegas the most successful place for the retail industry in all of America.

History in brief

It's a long way from the days of mobster Bugsy Siegel and, before him, the railroad settlers and Mormons. In fact, the history of southern Nevada reaches back into prehistoric times when it was a marsh full of water and lush vegetation that was home to dinosaurs.

Eventually, as millions of years went by, the marsh receded, rivers disappeared beneath the surface and the wetlands evolved into a parched, arid landscape that can now only support the hardiest of plants and animals. Water trapped underground in the geological formations of the Las Vegas Valley sporadically surfaced to nourish plants and create an oasis in the desert, while life-giving water flowed to the Colorado River.

Hidden for centuries from all but Native Americans, the Las Vegas Valley oasis was protected from discovery by the surrounding harsh and unforgiving Mojave Desert until around 1829 when Mexican trader Antonio Armigo, leading a 60-man party along the Spanish Trail to Los Angeles, veered away from the route and discovered Las Vegas Springs.

On the gold rush trail

The discovery of this oasis shortened the Spanish Trail to Los Angeles and hastened the rush west for the California gold. Between 1830 and 1848, the name Vegas was changed to Las Vegas, which means 'the meadows' in Spanish. In 1844, John C. Fremont camped at the springs while

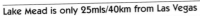
Lake Mead is only 25mls/40km from Las Vegas

leading an overland expedition west, and his name is immortalised in the downtown Fremont Hotel and Fremont Street.

In 1855, Mormon settlers from Salt Lake City started to build a fort of sun-dried adobe bricks in Las Vegas to protect pioneers travelling between Utah and Los Angeles. They planted fruit trees and vegetables and made bullets from lead mined at Potosi Mountain, 30mls/48km from the fort. With Mormon influence, Las Vegas could have become a conservative, religious oasis in the desert. But it wasn't to be. The Mormons abandoned the settlement in 1858, largely because of Indian raids. The remains of their occupation is the oldest non-Indian structure in Las Vegas and has been designated a historic monument. Las Vegas had a different future ahead of her.

Working on the railroad

By 1890, railroad developers had chosen the water-rich valley as a prime location for a stop facility and town. When work on the first railroad into Las Vegas began in 1904, a tent-town sprouted, with saloons, stores and boarding houses, and the San Pedro, Los Angeles and Salt Lake Railroad (later absorbed by Union Pacific) made its first run east from California. The advent of the railroad led to the founding of Las Vegas on 15 May 1905. The Union Pacific auctioned off 1,200 lots in a single day in an area that is now known as the Fremont Street Experience.

Gambling got off to a shaky start in the state, which introduced anti-gambling laws in 1910. They were so strict that even the western custom of flipping a coin for a drink was banned. But the locals set up underground gambling dens for their roulette wheels, dice and card games. They stayed illegal but were largely accepted, and flourished until 1931 when the Nevada Legislature, cash starved by the horrific economic depression sweeping America, approved a legalised gambling bill that was designed to generate tax revenue to support local schools. Now more than 41% of Nevada's income comes from gambling tax revenue and more than 31% of its fund is used to provide state education.

In the same year, construction work began on the Hoover Dam project, which at its peak employed more than 5,000 people. During these economically disastrous years, employment was scarce and money was hard to come by. Yet here were legions of men from the project seeking a break from their 12-hour-a-day, six-days-a-week work regimen. They descended on the town with ample coin in their pocket and normally only 12 to 24 hours to enjoy their riches. After a tour of gambling, drink and women, the men would tumble into the back of a truck and blearily head back to work. Las Vegas traditions of 24-hour fast times and midnight breakfast specials became iconic fixtures. The young town of Las Vegas thrived even during the harsh realities of America's Great Depression.

The Second World War delayed major resort growth, but the seeds for development were sown when Tommy Hull opened the El Rancho Vegas Casino in

Northern Nevada Railroad near Ely

The plume of lights at the Flamingo

1941 on land opposite what is now the Sahara Hotel. During the Second World War, the nearby Nellis Air Force Base was a key military installation and later became a training ground for American fighter pilots and provided more gamblers to swell the city's halls.

Mob rules

The success of El Rancho Vegas triggered a small building boom in the late 1940s. Capitalising on the expanding traffic from Los Angeles, several hotel-casinos were launched on the two-lane highway leading into Las Vegas from Los Angeles and these evolved into today's Strip. Early hotels included the Last Frontier, Thunderbird and Club Bingo.

By far the most famous was the Flamingo Hotel, built by mobster Benjamin 'Bugsy' Siegel, a member of the Meyer Lanksy crime family. Complete with a giant pink neon sign, replicas of pink flamingos on the lawn and a bullet-proof, high-security apartment for Bugsy, the hotel opened on New Year's Eve in 1946. Nevertheless, Bugsy was gunned down six months later as he sat in the living room of his girlfriend's home in Beverly Hills. After numerous owners, the Flamingo now belongs to the Hilton Hotel Group. Today, only the name remains as the last of the original motel-like buildings were replaced by a $104m tower in 1995.

The early building boom continued and Wilbur Clark, a former hotel bellman,

opened the Desert Inn in 1950. Two years later, Milton Prell opened the Sahara Hotel on the site of the old Club Bingo. Despite many changes of ownership, the Sahara has survived. So, too, has the Desert Inn, which underwent a $200m remodelling and construction programme in 1997 and remains a part of Steve Wynn's new Wynn Las Vegas resort, which opened in March 2005.

The Sands Hotel, a showroom and once the playground for the 'Rat Pack' of Frank Sinatra and his buddies, high-rollers and Hollywood stars, opened in 1952, but was demolished in 1996 to make way for the fabulous Venetian.

In 1976, Atlantic City in New Jersey legalised gambling and so began a new era in Las Vegas's history, as gamblers from the American East Coast were kept away by Atlantic City's proximity. Las Vegas hotel-casinos saw they would need to create a true resort destination to compete. Caesars Palace had been the first hotel on the Strip to create a specific theme for its resort-hotel when it opened in 1966, and two years later Circus Circus opened its tent-shaped casino with carnival games and rides. But it was not until the late 1980s and early 1990s that the boom in resort-hotels began in earnest.

A new day dawns

In 1989, the $630m upmarket Mirage Hotel opened with a white tiger habitat, dolphin pool, elaborate swimming pool and waterfall and a man-made volcano that belched fire and water. Mirage's owner at the time, Steve Wynn, then built the $430m Treasure Island resort next door, which is now home to the Sirens of TI show. Wynn also went into a joint venture with Circus Circus Enterprises to develop another luxury resort hotel – the Monte

The white tiger habitat at the Mirage

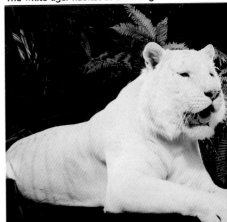

Carlo, which opened in 1996 – and his next venture – the luxurious Bellagio, styled as an Italian lakeside village – opened in 1998 on the site of the former Dunes Hotel. Wynn sold all his holdings in these hotels in June 2000 and snapped up the Desert Inn 10 days later.

The Excalibur medieval castle opened in 1990 with court jesters and King Arthur's jousting knights entertaining visitors in the massive $290m complex. Circus Circus Enterprises then developed the amazing $375m Luxor next door, opening in 1993.

In the same year, Grand Slam Canyon Adventuredome opened at the Circus Circus hotel, as did Treasure Island and the MGM Grand Hotel and Theme Park. Now one of the world's largest resorts, the MGM Grand has three of the largest concert and sports venues in Las Vegas, some of the top restaurants and myriad swimming pools and tennis courts.

In 1997, the £460m resort hotel New York-New York that re-creates the Big Apple's skyline, added 2,000 rooms. Then came a whole raft of luxury resorts aimed specifically at the sophisticated traveller, including the Mandalay Bay, Paris and Venetian in 1999 – themed as a South Seas island, the French capital and Venice respectively. The Aladdin opened in 2000, almost immediately faced a host of economic problems and descended into bankruptcy. Then the Palms opened in 2001. It all went quiet for a few years until the unveiling of Wynn Las Vegas in 2005, which coincided with a new round of building projects. The Aladdin became Planet Hollywood, and in 2008–2009 the massive constructs of the Cosmopolitan, Trump International and the greatest of them all, CityCenter, are due to open their doors. The CityCenter Project, built by MGM/Mirage, is the most massive

privately financed building project. These new hotels break from the Las Vegas of decadent, themed resorts. Instead, all of them, starting with the Wynn Las Vegas, are not just the last word in luxury, or just magnificent creations on a theme, but have also swelled the cultural and dining coffers of the city.

It seems that after going through all its different marketing ploys – the city that never sleeps, a family town, adults only – Las Vegas has finally become the sophisticated mecca of fun that Bugsy Siegel envisaged so many decades ago. Recent market research shows that consumers want some comfort that this is the Vegas they've always known and loved. People come here to exhale and splurge a little. After a year of flirting with tourism pitches that directly addressed the recession, the city in the desert has resurrected its successful marketing theme: 'What happens in Las Vegas stays in Las Vegas' – unless you've put it on the credit card, of course!

Getting around

Las Vegas has been growing at such a phenomenal rate in the last 20 years that her roads, especially around the Strip, are hopelessly clogged, especially in the afternoons. In the evenings, it is much faster to walk than to drive along Las Vegas Boulevard, especially if there is a special event happening.

BRITTIP

Don't hire a car from the airport or you'll be charged exorbitant airport 'surcharges'. Take a cheap shuttle to your hotel and sort it out from there.

The Excalibur

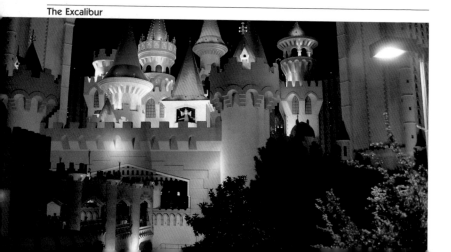

BRITTIP

Many upmarket resorts like the Venetian and Bellagio have counters at the airport where you can check in to your room at the airport. You'll save lots of time doing it there!

If you arrive by plane, a taxi ride to a Strip hotel (where most of the major theme resorts are located) will cost $10–20, and to a downtown hotel $20–30, depending on the route taken and the time of day. Airport shuttle fares cost $8 to Strip hotels. The airport shuttles are excellent value for money and can be found immediately on your right as you exit the baggage reclaim area. The ticket office is on your left. In addition, most major hotels run shuttles to and from the airport. If you're a high-roller, a limo will no doubt be there to whisk you to your mega suite.

Walking

Let's face it, walking is the way most people want to explore the Strip, yet it can be a highly dodgy activity. For one, in the summer months the heat is suffocating, and while you might see your destination, trust me, it is still a very long way off. Resorts seem so near because they are so massive!

Also, the city – like most of those in America – is mostly geared to cars and is not just pedestrian-unfriendly, but downright dangerous. The seemingly never-ending construction and the heavy traffic make drivers frustrated and hasty: dangerous conditions for pedestrians. In some parts of the Strip, where many of the never-ending construction sites are located, there are no pavements at all. In other parts, where there are pavements and even pedestrian crossings, there is not enough time to get across the road before the lights change. What's worse is that most of the road-users seem to see pedestrians as targets. When the light changes they have the right of way and you'd better dash across.

BRITTIP

Websites are all preceded by 'www.' unless they are indicated as 'http://'.

However, the hotels and city councillors have been taking action – footbridges have been built at many of the junctions and I strongly advise you to use them.

The monorail

Web: lvmonorail.com
Prices: Single ride ticket $5; 1-day pass $12, valid for unlimited travel for any 24-hour period; 3-day pass $28, valid for 72 hours from first use. Automated ticket machines can be found at all the stops and some of the resorts
Hours: 7am–2am Mon–Thurs, 7am–3am Fri–Sun

The $650m monorail opened in 2004 and is a happy, if somewhat flawed, way to get around. In fact, most times it is by far the fastest way to travel from one part of the Strip to another. The monorail grew from an original transit venture between the MGM Grand and Bally's Hotel in 1993. The Las Vegas Monorail Company, which owns the new transit service, was created in 2000 as a non-profit corporation and now owns the original monorail system.

Monorails come every 4–12 minutes and whisk you along to your destination, avoiding the horrid traffic of the Strip. There are two niggles about the monorail service. First, when it opened in 2004 a single fare was only $3, but this was raised in 2007 to $5, which makes it far less of a bargain than originally. Second, all the stops are poorly marked, often difficult to find, and they are also in the very back of each property. This means you must do a lot of walking through these massive resorts to get there, then you face another long walk to get to where you want. It can be much faster simply to walk to your destination if it is only one or two stops down the line.

Las Vegas monorail

The monorail runs on the east side of the Strip, and there are 6 stops, starting here with the southernmost stop:

- MGM Grand main hotel entrance services the Tropicana, Mandalay Bay, Luxor, Excalibur, New York-New York and Monte Carlo
- Bally's and Paris Las Vegas services the Paris, Planet Hollywood, Bellagio, City Center and Bally
- Flamingo/Caesars Palace
- Harrah's/Imperial Palace services the Mirage, Treasure Island and Venetian
- Las Vegas Convention Center and Las Vegas Hilton
- Sahara services Circus Circus and Stratosphere.

Three other monorails run on the western side of the Strip between Treasure Island and the Mirage; the Bellagio and the Monte Carlo; and the Excalibur, Luxor and Mandalay Bay resorts. These monorails are free. In the meantime, an extension has already been approved to connect the Sahara to Fremont Street in the downtown area, but it has run into a series of delays and there is no current completion date. There are also plans to connect to McCarran International Airport.

Buses and taxis

If you're sticking to the main drag, the monorail will be the fastest bet. However, the bus service – Citizens Area Transit (CAT) – has a 24-hour service on the Strip and downtown, plus 40 other routes that operate 5.30am–1.30am daily.

Mandalay Bay Convention Center

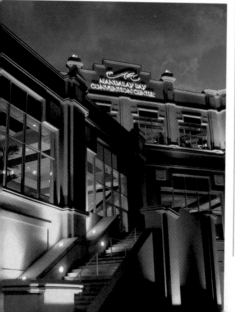

'The Deuce' is the route for Las Vegas Boulevard, sporting double-decker buses that come approximately every 5–10 minutes. Exact change is required, but you can get all-day passes as you board the bus, that are reasonably priced at $4. In the afternoons and evenings the buses can be terribly crowded, with long queues at the (fortunately) shaded bus stops. For information about routes and schedules, call 702 228 7433 or visit rtcsouthernnevada.com.

More than 1,100 taxis service the city but costs will mount if you use them all the time. My caveat would be to avoid using taxis where possible and try to use the monorail. A full list of 16 cab companies can be found at taxi.state.nv.us/taxicabinfo.htm. They include Ace Cab Co: 702 736 8383; Checker Cab Co: 702 873 8012; Desert Cab Co: 702 386 4828; Lucky Cab Co: 702 477 7555; Union Cab Co: 702 736 8444; Whittlesea Blue Cab Co: 702 384 6111.

The Nevada Taxicab Authority (taxi.state.nv.us) has good taxi information including a chart of simple fares.

BRITTIP

Not only is taking a taxi pricey, but also it is almost impossible to flag one down on the street. You must either pick one up from a hotel (where there's often a queue) or from designated stops.

The trolley

The Las Vegas Strip Trolley runs 8am–midnight every day at roughly 20-minute intervals. Northbound from the Mandalay Bay to the Stratosphere, it stops at the Tropicana, MGM, Bally's, Imperial Palace, Harrah's, Riviera, Hilton and Sahara. Southbound from the Stratosphere, it stops at Circus Circus, Slots of Fun, Stardust, Fashion Show Mall, Caesars, Jockey Club, New York-New York, Excalibur and Mandalay Bay. The newest addition to the route is Bass Pro Shop/Silverton Hotel, the Hard Rock Hotel and Café, and the Terribles Hotel and Casino. Single journeys cost $2.50 and exact change is required. A day pass costs $4.25 (8.30am–5pm) as does a night pass (5pm–midnight). This is a very cheap way of seeing the Strip, but also the slowest – it takes about 50 minutes to travel the entire length in one direction. See lasvegas-how-to.com/trolley.php.

BRITTIP

Some trolley stops are harder to find than others – especially at Caesars Palace where there are no signs at all and the bellboys are the rudest on the Strip if you don't brandish a tip. The first stop is on the right-hand side of the road just by the entrance to the Forum Shops. The second stop is at the end of the entrance to Caesars Palace, just by the bus stop.

Car rental

For travelling about the Strip or downtown, you are best off without a car. However, if you want to explore the outlying areas like the Grand Canyon, Hoover Dam and elsewhere a car is a necessity.

Before hiring a car, read Chapter 14 (see page 257) first so you know exactly what you'll have to pay for. Most cars can be hired locally to travel throughout California, Nevada and Arizona. However, if you are travelling outside that area, check with the car hire firm for limitations.

BRITTIP

The one bonus to riding the trolley is the close-up views you'll get of the Strip and the major resorts – without pounding the streets or getting run over!

If you do plan to arrange car rental on arrival in Las Vegas, look out for special deals advertised in the local press. You might find excellent prices and extras such as free long-distance phone cards. You should also look at the offers with our *Brit Guide* partner, Alamo.

Car rental companies in Las Vegas include:
Airport Rent-A-Car: 702 678 6666; Alamo: 702 263 8411; Allstate: 702 792 5984; Avis: 702 735 0349; Budget: 702 736 1212; Dollar: 702 731 1898; Enterprise: 702 795 8842; Hertz: 702 648 8834; National: 702 261 5391; Rent A Vette Sports Cars/Exotics/Motorcycle Rentals: toll-free 866 871 1893; Thrifty: 702 896 7600.

BRITTIP

Keep an eye on the total cost of your car hire. Many car hire firms advertise an extremely low rate from the airport, but then you are charged exorbitant airport 'surcharges' that often make the total cost much higher than if you'd rented at your hotel. On the other hand, at relatively quiet times in Vegas, the specials offered at the airport are much cheaper than those in town. Make a few phone calls, asking for the total price 'including all taxes and fees'.

Some companies have rental sites at many of the major resort hotels. If booking on site in Las Vegas at a quiet time, you may be offered very cheap upgrades, but beware of hard-sell tactics and if you're certain you don't want or need a bigger car, don't be persuaded.

Limos

It won't cost you an arm and a leg to travel in style in Las Vegas – think tuxedo-ed chauffeurs and neon lighting. You can hire a limo for the ride into town from the airport for as little as $6.50 per person if there are several of you. Check out the deals available on arrival. If you're having

Hire a limo for that special night out

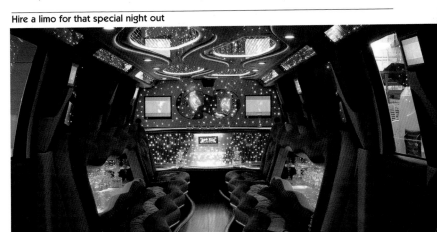

a big night out on the town and want to have a drink, hiring a limo for the night often works out at about the same price as a taxi.

Limo companies include: Ambassador Limousines: 702 362 6200;
Bell Trans/Limousines and Buses: 702 739 7990 or toll-free 1 800 274 7433;
Las Vegas Limousines and Party Bus Charters: 702 480 2231;
On Demand Sedan-Black Car Service: 702 876 2222;
Presidential Limousine: 702 731 5577.

BRITTIP

Some of the smaller rental companies may be cheaper, but always ensure that your rental agreement will allow you to drive outside the state of Nevada.

The best times to go

As of April 2009, Las Vegas had a staggering 140,559 rooms, but at many times of the year it still gets absolutely packed. A staggering 7,600 new rooms opened in 2008 with 16,000 due to open over the following 3 years. The average room price skyrocketed from 'only' $104 in 2005 to a hefty $120 in 2006. Now is as good a time to go as any as rates have fallen to an average $97.31 as of April 2009.

The busiest times are Christmas, June, July, August, Easter and the American bank holidays: President's Day (George Washington's birthday) – the third Monday in February; Memorial Day – the last Monday in May and the official start of the summer season; Independence Day – 4 July (slap bang in the middle of the high season anyway); Labor Day – the first Monday in September and last holiday of summer; and Thanksgiving – always the fourth Thursday in November.

The best times to visit – providing there are no major conferences or boxing matches going on – are from January to the end of April (excluding the bank holidays) and Easter, and October to November. August and September are busier, but are still good times to go, though stiflingly hot.

The weather

One thing you can be sure of – you're not going to freeze! Having said that, in December 2008, Las Vegas experienced as much as 8in/20cm of snow, the most in 30 years.

Generally, Las Vegas has about 300 days of sunshine a year, with an average rainfall of 4.2in/10.2cm throughout the year, making it an arid climate. June to September tends to be the hottest period, with daytime temperatures above 100°F /38°C in July and August. So if you're going out for the day, always make sure

The Conservatory at the Bellagio

Month	Temperature °C/°F min	max	Humidity % am/pm	Rainfall in/mm	Sunshine %
January	1/34	13/55	41/30	.5/13	77
February	3/37	19/66	36/26	.46/12	80
March	5/41	20/68	30/22	.41/10	83
April	9/48	25/77	22/15	.22/6	87
May	15/59	30/86	19/13	.22/6	88
June	20/68	36/97	15/10	.09/2	92
July	24/75	40/104	19/15	.45/11	87
August	22/72	38/100	14/18	.54/14	88
September	18/64	34/93	23/17	.32/8	91
October	11/52	27/81	25/19	.25/6	87
November	5/41	19/66	33/27	.43/11	80
December	1/34	14/57	41/33	.32/8	77

you put a good sunblock on before you leave your hotel, cover up when necessary and carry water with you.

What to wear

Fortunately, given the climate, the dress code is pretty relaxed in Las Vegas with casual clothes permitted around the clock. But wearing swimming costumes inside a casino or restaurant is not acceptable and it is normal to dress up for a big evening out. In fact you can be as flamboyant as you like and not feel out of place. If you're visiting in early spring or late autumn, take a sweater or light jacket for the evening and something a bit warmer for winter.

BRITTIP

When buying US dollars before your trip, always ask for plenty of $1 bills – known as singles – so you can tip porters and taxi drivers on arrival. Also, at many American airports it will cost you $1 to use a baggage trolley.

Tips on tipping

Tipping is not just a way of life in America but a genuine source of income for most employees in the hotel and casino industries – they are even taxed on an expectation of tips received. Sadly, tipping is something that we Brits tend to overlook.

There are some fairly loose customs in Las Vegas, but here is a guide to how much we should tip.

- Bartenders and cocktail waitresses: $1 a round of drinks for parties of 1–4 people, more for larger groups.
- Bellboys: $1–2 per piece of luggage.
- Concierge service: $5.
- Food servers and room service: 15–20%.
- Hotel maids: $2 a day at the end of a visit.
- Slot machine change girls/men and casino dealers: $1–2 for the service and at least a small percentage of any win. Some gamblers who play for long periods tip even if they've lost!
- Maître d': Many showrooms sell assigned seating tickets, which may include the tip. In resort showrooms that have restaurant-style reservations and seating, you can tip the maître d' (Americans don't have head waiters, they have maître d's like the French!) $5–20 to improve your seats.

The Grand Wok and Sushi Bar

The new CityCenter development

- Pool attendants: 50 cents–$1 for towels, pads, loungers, etc.
- Showroom servers: $5–10 for a party of 2–4 people at a cocktails-only show, or $10–20 for a dinner show, depending on the service and food quality.

BRITTIP

Be generous with taxi drivers. Unlike most other cities, it is rare for drivers in Las Vegas to be their own bosses and wages are low, so a decent tip would be appreciated!

- Taxi drivers: $1–2 per person at the end of the trip, or follow the 15–20% rule, whichever is greater.
- Valet parkers: $2, depending on how quick the service has been.

BRITTIP

Most casinos provide free drinks for genuine gamblers, but at busy times the service can become quite slow. One way to receive fast attention is ask everybody in your party or at your gambling table to offer an additional dollar tip when you first sit down. Give it to the server when you make your first order. Guaranteed, she'll always check your table first and most often!

You can often get great room upgrades for a $20 tip to the desk clerk when you book in. Take a look at the Brit tip on page 27.

Medical emergencies

The number for the emergency services is 911.

Medical help: If you need medical help in Las Vegas that does not require an ambulance, there are 3 main options, all of which are open 24 hours a day, 7 days a week: Harmon Medical Center, 150 East Harmon Avenue (702 796 116); Fremont Medical Center, 4880 South Wynn Road (on the corner of Tropicana and Wynn, 702 671 6819); and UMC Hospital, 1800 W Charleston Boulevard (702 383 2000).

Many prescription and over-the-counter drugs are produced under different generic names in America. If you take any kind of regular medication, e.g. for a heart condition or epilepsy, it's a good idea to ask your doctor or pharmacy to find out the American name for your particular prescription drug. Keep this written down with your prescription or put both English and American drug names inside a clear plastic case that is easily accessible for medical crews, in case you are involved in an accident. The American term for paracetamol is acetaminophen.

'Vegas Vickie' at Glitter Gulch

Useful websites

visitlasvegas.co.uk: The official Las Vegas Tourism website by the Las Vegas Convention and Visitors Authority.

visitlasvegas.com: Run by the city's Convention and Visitors Authority, this website not only supplies information but also carries a preview of good deals.

BRITTIP

The city's Information Center can be found at 3150 Paradise Road. Call 1 877 VISIT LV (847 4858) or 702 892 0711. Lines are open 6am–9pm.

ilovevegas.com: Provides current information, supplied by the magazine *What's On, The Las Vegas Guide*, about hotels, casinos, dining, entertainment and recreation. Useful for booking shows and tours online.

lasvegasadvisor.com: Run by Huntington Press and Anthony Curtis, a Las Vegas icon for good deals and bargain hunting. Here are rankings of the best deals for gambling, meals, drinks and shows. It also has one of the best web portals for finding cheap Las Vegas hotel rooms.

lasvegas.com: Excellent source of information, discounts and booking for hotels, restaurants and clubs.

lasvegasgolf.com: First-rate guide for golfers with great deals on packages.

reviewjournal.com: One of the most useful websites with links to entertainment, local news and maps, run by *The Las Vegas Review Journal*.

lasvegasnevada.gov: Government-run site offering a more wholesome view of the city including free family events and the city's green policies. A special 'visitor' section gives useful information on how to get married plus great interactive maps.

BRITTIP

If you run out of cash, you'll find many ATMs (cash machines) in virtually every hotel.

Useful numbers

Airport information:	702 261 5743
Airport parking:	702 261 5121
Citizens Area Transit:	702 228 7433
Convention information:	702 892 0711
Directory assistance:	702 555 1212
Emergency Service Dispatch:	911
Highway Patrol:	702 486 4100
Las Vegas Fire Department:	702 383 2888
Las Vegas Transit System:	702 384 3540
Marriage License Bureau:	702 671 0600
Metro Police:	702 828 4348
Road conditions:	702 263 9744
Show Hot Line:	702 258 5188
Tourist information:	702 892 7575
Weather:	702 736 3854

Paris Las Vegas

Language in Las Vegas

It has often been said that Brits and Americans are divided by a common language and when you make an unexpected *faux pas* you'll certainly learn how true this is. For instance, never ask for a packet of fags as this is the American slang word for gays and a sense of humour is not their strong point! There are plenty of other differences, so this list should help to avoid confusion. Remember, too, that spellings sometimes vary.

Travelling around

English	American
Aerial	Antenna
Articulated truck	Semi
Bonnet	Hood
Boot	Trunk
Caravan	House trailer
Car park	Parking lot
Car silencer	Muffler
Crossroads/junction	Intersection
Demister	Defogger
Dipswitch	Dimmer
Dual carriageway	Four-lane or divided highway
Flyover	Overpass
Give way	Yield
Jump leads	Jumper cables
Lay-by	Turn-out
Lorry	Truck
Manual transmission	Stick shift
Motorway	Superhighway, freeway, expressway

Luxury suite at the Venetian

No parking or stopping	No standing
Pavement	Sidewalk
Petrol station	Gas station
Request stop	Flag stop
Ring road	Beltway
Slip road	Ramp
Subway	Pedestrian underpass
Transport	Transportation
Turning	Turnoff
Tyre	Tire
Underground	Subway
Walk	Hike
Wheel clamp	Car boot
Windscreen	Windshield
Wing	Fender

🇬🇧 BRITTIP

If you arrive at a hotel by car or taxi, one bellhop will take your luggage out of the boot (trunk) – for which you have to tip him – then another takes it up to your room – and, yes, he needs a tip, too.

Food and drink

There are plenty of differences in US and UK food terms. For instance, Americans don't flick oil over the top of an egg when frying it, but turn it over to cook on both sides. So, for eggs the way I like them, cooked on both sides but soft, I don't order 'sunny-side up' but 'over easy'. If you like yours well done, then ask for eggs 'over hard'. Many standard American dishes come with a biscuit – which is a scone to us! They also have something called grits, which is a porridge-like breakfast dish made out of ground, boiled corn, plus hash browns – grated, fried potatoes.

English	American
Aubergine	Eggplant
Bill	Check or tab
Biscuit (savoury)	Cracker
Biscuit (sweet)	Cookie
Chickpea	Garbanzo bean
Chips	French fries or fried potatoes
Choux bun	Cream puff
Cling film	Plastic wrap
Coriander	Cilantro
Corn	Wheat
Cornflour	Cornstarch
Courgette	Zucchini
Crayfish	Crawfish
Crisps	Chips
Crystallised	Candied
Cutlery	Silverware or place setting

Superb food is on the menu at Café Bellagio

Minced meat	Ground meat
Off-licence	Liquor store
Pastry case	Pie shell
Pips	Seeds (in fruit)
Plain/dark chocolate	Semi-sweet or unsweetened chocolate
Pumpkin	Squash
Scone	Biscuit
Shortcrust pastry	Pie dough
Single cream	Light cream
Soda water	Seltzer
Sorbet	Sherbet
Soya	Soy
Spirits	Liquor
Sponge finger biscuits	Ladyfingers
Spring onion	Scallion
Starter	Appetizer
Stoned (cherries, etc.)	Pitted
Sultana	Golden raisin
Sweet shop	Candy store
Take-away	To go
Tomato purée	Tomato paste
Water biscuit	Cracker

Demerara sugar	Light-brown sugar
Desiccated coconut	Shredded coconut
Digestive biscuit	Graham cracker
Double cream	Heavy cream
Essence (e.g. vanilla)	Extract
Golden syrup	Corn syrup
Grated, fried potatoes	Hash browns
Grilled	Broiled
Icing sugar	Confectioner's sugar
Jam	Jelly
Ketchup	Catsup
King prawn	Shrimp
Main course	Entree
Measure	Shot

Shopping

English	American
Bumbag	Fanny pack
Chemist	Drug store
Ground floor	First floor
Handbag	Purse
High Street	Main Street
In (Fifth Avenue, etc.)	On
Jumper	Sweater
Muslin	Cheesecloth
Suspenders	Garters
Tights	Pantyhose
Till	Check-out

L'Atelier de Joël Robuchon

Tights	Pantyhose	Anti-clockwise	Counter-clockwise
Till	Check-out	At weekends	On weekends
Trainers	Sneakers	Autumn	Fall
Trousers	Pants	Behind	In back of
Underpants	Shorts	Camp bed	Cot
Vest	Undershirt	Cinema	Movie theater
Waistcoat	Vest	City/town centre	Downtown
Zip	Zipper	(not the rundown	
		bit!)	
		Coach	Bus

Money

English	American
Banknote	Bill
Bill	Check
Cheque	Check
1 cent	Penny
5 cents	Nickel
10 cents	Dime
25 cents	Quarter
Dollar	Greenback

General

English	American
Air steward(ess)	Flight attendant

Cot	Crib
Diary (appointments)	Calendar
Diary (records)	Journal
Doctor	Physician
From … to …	Through
Lift	Elevator
Long-distance call	Trunk call
Nappy	Diaper
Ordinary	Regular, normal
Paddling pool	Wading pool
Post, postbox	Mail, mailbox
Pram, pushchair	Stroller
Queue	Line, line up

The Strip at night

The biggest and the best hotels and how to choose the right one for you

Bugsy Siegel started it all and Howard Hughes, the famously reclusive billionaire, lent an air of respectability to the city, but modern Vegas is really a reflection of the dream of one man: Steve Wynn.

Steve Wynn, Las Vegas's modern-day casino mogul, provided the bridge between Mob City and Sin City when he opened the dazzling Mirage Hotel in 1989. The first major hotel to be built on the Strip in 16 years and with a $630m price tag, dolphin pool, white tiger habitat, man-made volcano and elaborate swimming pool, it set a new standard and sparked off a building rush. Wynn went on to build the pirate-themed Treasure Island and upmarket Italianate Bellagio before selling out and starting a new project at the Desert Inn. Between 1989 and 2004 a host of resorts, inspired by Wynn's success, erupted along the Strip and turned Las Vegas into an adult fantasyland.

Wynn's first solo project – Wynn Las Vegas – opened in 2005 to a fanfare of publicity after one of the most tightly guarded developments the city has ever seen. Unlike the über-fantasy of Luxor, Excalibur and Circus Circus, or destination fantasies of Mandalay Bay, Paris or Venetian, the Wynn Las Vegas was simple luxury. Its opening also coincided with another hotel 'gold rush' of building. Just when the whole world is feeling the bite of recession, Las Vegas declares the show must go on with the opening of MGM/Mirage's massive CityCenter development housing 4 resorts: Aria Resort & Casino, Vdara Hotel, Mandarin Oriental hotel and The Harmon. In addition there's the transformation of the old Aladdin into Planet Hollywood and the opening of Encore, M Resort and Trump International Hotel & Tower.

BRITTIP

The biggest problem the major resort-hotels have is registering guests – a 30-minute wait is not unusual at busy times! Depending on the room type, you can have access to VIP check-in which will be quicker than standard check-in. Most hotels also offer an express check-out. You register your credit-card details at check-in and then just drop off on check-out.

Recent years have also seen a sharp increase in lodging costs. The Las Vegas Convention and Visitors Authority says the average lodging expenditures per night in 2003 were $81.43, but in 2006 they had bounced to $107.12. By 2008 the figure had risen to $119.19. It remains to be seen whether Las Vegas can fill its many new rooms, and as hotels fight it out to win customers, rates may drop.

The magic line-up

To really appreciate the sight of the glittering spectacles that are both resorts and attractions in their own right, it's best to fly into Las Vegas so you can get a bird's eye view as you land at McCarran International airport – either that, or take a fun helicopter flight. However, it's just as fascinating from the seat of a car.

As you come out of the airport you turn right on Las Vegas Boulevard and soon you'll pass the South Seas paradise of Mandalay Bay on your left, before spotting the daunting pyramid of the Luxor and the castle-like vistas of Camelot at Excalibur. At the new Four Corners of Las Vegas on the Strip, you will see the Tropicana to your right. Before you've had time to let out a gasp of amazement, you'll be passing the lion of MGM Grand, opposite the towers of New York-New York and its famous Big Apple landmarks. The Monte Carlo is next on the left, a fine re-creation of the ritzy Place du Monaco, then there is the edifice of CityCenter rising to the skies. Planet Hollywood (originally the Aladdin) is on the right, followed by the Eiffel Tower in Paris – but don't forget to glance left for a swift look at the Italian village setting of the Bellagio.

BRITTIP

Internet access through the TV is now available pretty much as standard in the major resort-hotels. Think around $6 for 2 hours or around $10 for 24 hours (plus tax!).

Now you've reached the old Four Corners, the original section of the Strip that was home to Bugsy Siegel's Flamingo, and here you'll see the majestic Caesars Palace with its Greco-Roman ramparts on the left. Opposite the Forum Shops at Caesars is the modern Flamingo Hilton. Then, further north on the right, is the Japanese-inspired Imperial Palace opposite the posh Polynesian resort of The Mirage and its erupting volcano. If arriving any time after 4pm, Treasure Island's *Sirens of TI* could well be in action, but don't forget to look right to see the spectacular Venetian with its re-creation of St Mark's Square and the Doge's Palace.

The new CityCenter at night

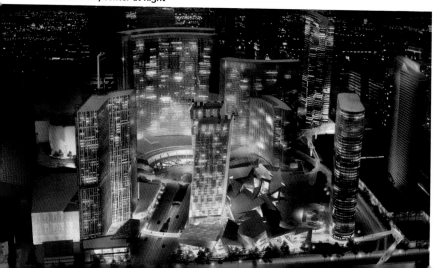

BRITTIP

For a complete list of all dining options – both fine dining and casual – available in each of the resort-hotels see page 128.

Soon, on the left is the circus-dome shape of the Grand Slam Canyon and Circus Circus, a family resort on the theme of a travelling circus. The rose citadel of the Wynn Las Vegas is tantilisingly screened by a large man-made hill and ranks of cool evergreen trees. After that is the spire of the Stratosphere Hotel, the tallest free-standing tower in America.

BRITTIP

The term 'the Strip' was coined by a former Los Angeles police captain in 1938. Guy McAfee said the stretch of road with its brightly lit hotels and casinos reminded him of Hollywood's Sunset Strip, another mecca for night owls!

Choices, choices! It's an amazing line-up – and it's all thanks to money and the making of it. But where do you choose to stay? There are 3 schools of thought, depending on your budget and your interests.

Resort-hotels

Undoubtedly, for the best time ever, stay in one of the main resort-hotels – all of which are featured in this chapter. The good part is if you stay and play at the same place you will get the most in convenience (no time-eating drives in Las Vegas traffic), attractions and night-time thrills. However, these places are pricey. For instance, rooms can often be had at the Venetian for $129 midweek, but on a busy convention

BRITTIP

Staying at a resort-hotel may be more pricey but you might get better value for money as rates often include gaming, entertainment and dining credits and airport limousine transportation, which are sometimes worth more than the room price itself. If the hotel is part of a group – for example MGM Mirage includes the Bellagio, the MGM Grand and The Mirage – you will get preferred seating across all their entertainment venues and restaurants.

day the minimum room price often soars to $750/night! Then the gambling minimums and odds are also more expensive in these posh surroundings. Still, for many, being able to have the ultimate experience makes the budget less important, especially since the resorts do have a number of different price ranges.

On a budget on the Strip

For the budget conscious, a great option is to stay at one of the many budget establishments on the Strip, downtown or on the locals' Boulder Highway Strip area where budget casinos offer clean and cheap rooms with great gambling odds. Then make the trip into the Strip area to enjoy the attractions and shows along the expensive real estate. While cheaper, the hotels are definitely not memorable and you spend a lot of time travelling back and forth.

Strip resorts

A third option is to stay in Strip resorts for delightful accommodation and for the attractions. Then for those intent gamblers, take a trip down to Fremont Street where the loose slots and advantageous gambling odds give you much longer play on your gambling budget.

Making your choices

To try to make your life easier – for both choosing a hotel and for seeing them as the attractions they are – I've given a full run-down of their facilities and roughly how much it costs for a room with 2 people sharing.

BRITTIP

One tradition left over from the old mob-run casino days is the '$20 room upgrade'. When you check in, you'll need to show the desk clerk your passport and a credit card. When you do, add a $20 bill (as a tip) and say 'Am I eligible for any complimentary room upgrades?' If there are any better rooms available, be they larger or perhaps with a lovely view of the Strip, the desk clerk will book you into one at the cost of your original reservation. If they can't, because the hotel is booked full or for some other reason, the desk clerk will apologise and return the $20 to you. It usually works, and I've often been able to stay in rooms costing several hundred dollars more than I paid for!

I have not given the major resorts a rating for the simple reason that they are aimed at different types of people, so a comparison would not really be appropriate. Also, do remember that in Las Vegas, as in no other city on Earth, supply and demand vary greatly and the differences are reflected in hugely fluctuating room prices. My notes on booking your hotel room in Chapter 13 (page 254) give a more detailed picture of how to find a room not only at the inn of your choice, but also at the right price.

Major resorts on the Strip

Aria Resort & Casino

If you want to be part of the in-crowd, book into this flagship CityCenter gem.
Location: Part of the CityCenter development on the Strip between Bellagio and Monte Carlo resorts
Grand opening: 16 December 2009
Theme: Breathless avant garde
Cost: Part of the $8.5b CityCenter development
Web: arialasvegas.com
Reservations: 866 359 7757
Rooms: 4,004
Room rates: From $179 for guestrooms and from $500 for suites
Restaurants: 13 restaurants of incredible diversity. Making his Las Vegas debut, Chef Masayoshi Takayama's Bar Masa has a ceiling that soars 35ft/10.6m above diners' heads as he serves up modern Japanese food. In Sage, chef Shawn McClain named Best Chef Midwest offers farm-to-table produce, artisan meats and sustainable seafood. American Fish draws inspiration from America's lakes, rivers and

Aria Resort & Casino

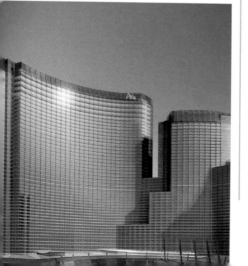

coasts. Then there's a whole array of steakhouses, Italian, patisseries, Chinese, Thai and cafés. Put it this way, you won't be going hungry here.
Nightlife: 9 bars and lounges and a spectacular nightclub
Show: Resident Cirque du Soleil®'s *Viva ELVIS* is staged in a custom-built theatre and celebrates the musical legacy of Elvis Presley
Attractions: At reception, guests are wowed by artist Maya Lin's 84-ft/26-m silver cast of the Colorado River, which is made from reclaimed silver and represents Nevada's standing as the 'Silver State'.
Gambling: More than 160,000ft2/15,000m² of gaming
Chilling out: 3 swimming pools and 1 European pool, 50 cabanas and a huge tropical oasis pool deck
Shopping: Just outside Aria is Cystals, CityCenter's retail and entertainment district with more than 500,000ft²/46,450m² of shopping including Louis Vuitton, Hermes, Prada, Dior, Tiffany & Co. And new to Vegas are Tom Ford, Miu Miu and Marni amongst others.
Other amenities: 2-storey spa and salon with 62 treatment rooms and 3 spa suites for couples or hen parties; championship golf nearby

BRITTIP

'European', when applied to swimming pools, means topless.

Aria is a spectacular new gaming resort and part of CityCenter, the dazzling new vertical city on the Las Vegas Strip. Designed by the world-renowned firm Pelli Clarke Pelli, it's high tech meets arty with an exterior of elegantly sweeping ripples of steel and glass with lavish natural elements indoors including plants, wood and stone. Guestrooms are bursting with technology. When guests enter they are greeted by lights filling the room, curtains parting to show the view and a TV asking for your preferences. Every time you return to your room, your preferences are remembered. Guests can wake up gradually through controlled temperature, lighting, curtain opening and choice of music. If you're feeling a bit green, you can opt for low lighting. There are some of the most innovative restaurants in town, the most exciting show to hit the Strip for years and properly cool places to hang out. Definitely on the hip list.

Bellagio

Based on an entire village in northern Italy, this truly is a treat for romantics!

Location: The Strip at the corner of West Flamingo

Theme: Upmarket, romantic Italian lakeside village

Cost: $1.6b, plus $375m in 2005 for the new Spa Tower

Web: bellagio.com

Reservations: 888 987 6667

Fax: 702 693 8546

Rooms: 3,933

Room rates: From $159

Restaurants: 7 fine dining options including the award-winning Picasso, Le Cirque and Michael Mina Bellagio and 12 casual eateries including FIX for Classic American food and Jean Philippe Patisserie for fabulous cakes

Nightlife: The Bank nightclub plus 7 bars and lounges

Show: Cirque du Soleil® theatrical circus spectacular, O

✚ BRITTIP

Room rates are a rough guide only as they can vary wildly. If there's a large convention booked to stay at the hotel of your choice, rates can easily rise by $200 or more. Do your homework before booking your flights – see page 21 for details of good websites to check.

Attractions: The Fountains of Bellagio, the Conservatory and Botanical Gardens and the Bellagio Gallery of Fine Art

Gambling: Blackjack, Craps, Mini-Baccarat, Roulette, European Roulette, Baccarat, Pai Gow Poker, Pai Gow, Big 6, Caribbean Stud Poker, Let it Ride, War, Three Card Poker, Sic Bo, Poker Room, 2,400 slot machines, video poker and The Race & Sports Book

Chilling out: 5 outdoor pools; 4 whirlpools; 52 private cabanas in a Mediterranean courtyard setting

Shopping: Via Bellagio filled with designer shops including Prada, Chanel, Giorgio Armani, Tiffany & Co., Hermes and Fendi; Via Fiore with Giardini Garden Store and many other outlets

Other amenities: 2 wedding chapels and Terrace of Dreams; a salon for facials, manicures and pedicures; barber room; Zen-influenced Spa Bellagio has 56 treatment rooms including 4 couples' rooms, meditation room and men's spa areas for 'shy guys'; Shadow Creek Golf Course

One of Las Vegas's largest luxury mega-resorts, its 'signature' show is the free Fountains of Bellagio – a $30m aquatic spectacle created by colourful, soaring fountains in a synchronised water ballet accompanied by lights and soaring music by Copland and Strauss, and famous renditions by Celine Dion and Elton John. Another enjoyable freebie is the Conservatory and Botanical Gardens. The Conservatory is a 55ft/17m high, glass-ceilinged edifice with floral displays that reflect the seasons and major American holidays. Each display is planned a year in advance to ensure the necessary flowers, plants and trees are available. The Bellagio is also home to its own art gallery, which houses travelling exhibitions of exceptional art.

The real crowd-puller of the hotel is O, the show by the world-famous Cirque du Soleil®. A special $70m theatre, modelled on the Paris Opera House, was built as a permanent home for the theatrical acrobatics and breathtaking stunts that make Cirque shows so amazing. The Bank nightclub is sought after and has a glass encased dance floor and elegant VIP booths. For daytime lounging, the Pool Bar serves great Bellagio Mojitos with fresh blueberries.

✚ BRITTIP

If you want to experience the vibes of the Bellagio without paying to stay, check out the sophisticated new Caramel Lounge. Have a drink, take the weight off your slingbacks and just watch the beautiful people while the band plays in the background. You may even spot a celeb or two!

Queen suite at the Bellagio

From each of the many rooms are panoramic views of the 8.5acre/3.4ha lake, classical gardens, elegant pools and landscaped grounds filled with fountains, waterfalls and pools. There 512 suites and a new Executive Suite Lounge opened in January 2009.

The restaurants range from casual bistros to the gourmet restaurants Le Cirque and Picasso, which are among the most successful and popular in Las Vegas. When you have a spare moment (and a spare million), try browsing round the esplanade lined with Chanel, Armani, Prada and Tiffany boutiques, before taking afternoon tea – one of the more affordable pleasures at the Bellagio!

Caesars Palace

Originally designed for high-rollers, it's still posh but is now accessible to all and should at least be on your must-see list.
Location: On the Strip at the famous Four Corners with Flamingo
Theme: Greco-Roman empire
Web: caesarspalace.com
Reservations: 702 731 7110
Fax: 702 946 4925
Rooms: 3,300 in 5 towers: Augustus, Centurian, Forum, Roman and Palace
Room rates: From $200 Mon–Thurs; from $260 Fri–Sun
Restaurants: 26 in total from contemporary French dining to a casual 24-hour café. Top of the list are the fine-dining establishments of Guy Savoy (with his new Krug Champagne Room), Bradley Ogden and Rao's. Across from Rao's is Payard Patisserie & Bistro, one of the most luxurious pastry shops in the country. Serendipity 3, one of New York's most beloved eateries has opened. One of the

The lobby at Caesars Palace

greatest budget eateries you'll find on the Strip is the Cypress Street Marketplace, just outside the Colosseum's ticket office
Nightlife: Cleopatra's Barge and Pure, which has become hot with the young Hollywood crowd, and Shadow Bar live music lounge

🇬🇧 BRITTIP

If you want to smoke in your hotel room, you must specify you want a smoking room, both when you book and when you check in. Even if you do get a smoking room, the ashtray may be hidden away in a drawer.

Shows: Its 4,100-seat Colosseum spotlights world-class entertainers like Bette Midler, Cher and Jerry Seinfeld. It also hosts outdoor events in the Roman Forum
Gambling: Blackjack, craps, roulette, baccarat, pai gow poker, pai gow tiles, slots, poker, race and sports book and keno
Chilling out: Garden of the Gods pools and gardens featuring the Venus Pool Club
Shopping: Appian Way in the hotel, plus the fabulous Forum Shops
Other amenities: Spanish Steps, 4 wedding chapels, 3 late-night lounges with live music, plus an outdoor amphitheatre, Qua Baths & Spa, salon and golf through Cascata Golf Course

The first Las Vegas hotel to be entirely based on a theme, Caesars Palace opened in 1966, specifically aiming at big-money gamblers. Although it allows more ordinary mortals to enter its palatial doors these days, the emphasis is still very much on luxury and opulence. The Palace underwent a $600m expansion at the turn of this century, which included building the 17-storey Palace Tower, a Garden of the Gods outdoor area, with pools and landscaped gardens, and a wedding chapel.

🇬🇧 BRITTIP

Be warned – there are no mini bars in your rooms – the hotels want you drinking downstairs where you can gamble, too! Nor are there any tea- or coffee-making facilities, so remember to buy water or orange juice for yourself in the morning.

Throughout the 85-acre/34-ha resort are spectacular fountains, majestic cypress trees, gleaming marble statues and beautiful

An executive suite at Circus Circus

landscaping. The Garden of the Gods area has 3 outdoor swimming pools inlaid with marble and granite, adjoined by 2 whirlpool spas and rimmed by lush gardens. There are also 3 floodlit tennis courts and an intimate outdoor amphitheatre.

The massive Colosseum quickly became a Strip landmark when it opened. Specifically built to house Celine Dion's *A New Day* one-woman show, the 4,100-seat, state-of-the-art venue can also be adapted to accommodate headliners and host major boxing events. Celine Dion has been replaced by an extravaganza headlined by singer/actress/comedienne Bette Midler and her *The Showgirl Must Go On* show.

The hotel has joined the ranks of other major Strip properties in providing more adult-orientated entertainment and its Shadow Bar – right in the centre of the casino – is one of the places to visit during a stay in Vegas. A relaxed, comfy lounge by day, by night it is home to topless dancers who perform sexy routines behind backlit screens. There is also a secluded adult area for 'European sunbathing' for those who wish to go topless.

All of the rooms have Jacuzzi tubs and wireless internet, while the fabulous Forum Shops are also known as the Shopping Wonder of the World (see page 85). If you want to see how the other half lives, take a wiggle on down to the posh baccarat and VIP high-roller areas. You never know, you may just get a proposal of sorts!

Circus Circus

A great-value, family-fun destination with some surprisingly good restaurants.
Location: The Strip between West Sahara and the Convention Center

Theme: Circus carnival featuring the world's largest permanent circus
Web: circuscircus.com
Reservations: 702 734 0410
Fax: 702 734 5897
Rooms: 3,767 plus KOA Circusland Recreational Vehicle Park with 399 spaces
Room rates: From $31.95 weekdays and from $69.95 weekends
Restaurants: Despite its emphasis on good prices, Circus Circus has 8 good eating outlets and The Steak House consistently wins awards for great food. For more casual dining there's Mexitalia Xpress, The Garden Grill and West Side Deli
Attractions: Free circus acts, carnival games, IMAX® theatre and Adventuredome indoor theme park
Gambling: Blackjack, craps, roulette, big six, pai gow poker, let it ride, Caribbean stud, casino war, poker, over 2,250 slots, video poker, video keno machines and the race and sports book. Complimentary gaming lessons
Chilling out: 2 pools and one at the RV park
Shopping: 40,000ft^2/3,720m^2 promenade with fun shops like Criss Angel – MINDFREAK Superstore
Other amenities: The surprisingly stunning Chapel of the Fountain wedding chapel; Année of Paris Beauty Salon (702 731 3201 for appointments)

The owners of Circus Circus were the second operators to build a theme casino on the Strip. It originally opened in 1968 as the world's largest permanent circus tent plus casino but without any hotel rooms. Now it has 3 towers housing nearly 3,800 rooms and an RV park, 3 major gambling areas, a whole raft of shops and some major family attractions. Inspired by the turn-of-the-century circuses that used to visit towns throughout America, it aims its services directly at the cost-conscious family market.

During the 1990s, Circus Circus had started to become seriously worn from

The bright lights of Circus Circus

years of gamblers and herds of kids. However, recently MGM Mirage has dumped untold millions into the property and today it is a comfortable place. Part Circus tent and part renaissance fair, it can also be a quirky place.

BRITTIP

Circus Circus is so popular with families that it can seem that you're surrounded by wall-to-wall kids!

The Circus Arena appears in the *Guinness Book of Records* as the world's largest permanent circus and covers 120,000ft²/11,160m² with a 90ft/27m high tent-shaped roof. The Carnival Midway is a circus-themed amusement arcade and its centre stage is where free half-hourly shows are presented 11am–11pm (Sun–Thurs) and 11am–midnight (Fri–Sat) by top circus acts, from high-wire daredevils to flying trapeze artists, acrobats, magicians and jugglers.

BRITTIP

Circus Circus provides rooms with roll-in showers that have been designed for the disabled. It also has its own phone line for the hearing impaired: 1-800 638 8595.

The Circus Circus theme park – the Adventuredome – is a fully enclosed 5acre/2ha elevated theme park, which is climate-controlled to provide temperatures of 72°F/21°C all the year round. This first-ever Las Vegas amusement park has been improved over the years and now has thrilling rides in a canyon-like setting (see Chapter 10).

If you're a novice and fancy a flutter on the Strip, this is the place to try out your luck on the roulette wheels as it has 4 areas (Main Casino, West Casino, Skyrise Casino and Slots of Fun) offering 100,000ft²/9.3m² of gaming. You can then move on to a high-stakes poker game elsewhere (we can dream, can't we?).

BRITTIP

Las Vegas hotels are not known for their fantastic rooms. Unless you're paying top dollar for rooms at the Venetian, Wynn, Four Seasons or Bellagio or a suite at one of the new hotels at CityCenter, they are fairly plain affairs with few facilities.

Encore

More of the Wynn-ing formula is rolled out in this upscale hotel.
Location: Next door to the flagship Wynn Las Vegas property on the Strip
Grand opening: December 2008
Theme: Tasteful extravagance with European touches
Cost: $2.3b
Web: encorelasvegas.com
Reservations: 702 770 8000
Rooms: 2,034
Room rates: From $169
Restaurants: In keeping with the culinary standards set by Wynn Las Vegas, Encore introduces a new all-star team of chefs, all of whom are in their kitchens cooking dinner every night. Sinatra is a salute to Ol' Blue Eyes. Chef Theo Schoenegger's modern Italian cuisine riffs with Sinatra tunes. At Switch, chef Marc Poidevin's French-inspired seafood and steakhouse is a surprise. Diners can appreciate the art collection by Columbian artist Fernando Botero at Botero Steak while sampling chef Mark LoRusso's modern cuisine. Society Café Encore was designed with the whimsical era of Oscar Wilde in mind, to match the imaginative cooking of chef Kim Canteenwalla. Turn a corner in the casino and come face to face with a 27ft/8m crystal dragon, mounted at Wazuzu, where rising star chef Jet Tila serves up pan-Asian cuisine.
Nightlife: XS nightclub
Show: Attracts the likes of Beyonce. *Le Rêve* at Wynn Las Vegas
Gambling: A new softer, intimate approach to casino life with columned pavilions and draped private chambers with garden or pool views
Shopping: The Esplanade at Encore has 11 boutiques including the edgy Rock & Republic, Hermes, Chanel and an array of clothing, shoe, jewellery, home décor and accessory stores
Other amenities: Spa and salon
Steve Wynn is back for more with Encore, sister resort to Wynn Las Vegas, offering the same high levels of service and style. Central to Encore's fanciful and intimate feel are sunlit corridors with flowering atria and sprawling pools visible from throughout the property. Natural light floods the resort to reveal gardens, vibrant butterflies and signature mosaics.

Encore has 2,034 spacious suites that offer casual elegance in a comfortable, residential setting. The Resort Suites span up to 700ft²/65m² and Tower Suites measure up to 5,800ft²/540m². Two

CityCenter

Located between the Bellagio and Monte Carlo resorts, CityCenter (citycenter.com) features Aria Resort & Casino, Vdara Hotel, Mandarin Oriental hotel, the residential Veers Towers, a fine art collection and Crystals retail and entertainment district where Eva Longoria Parker is opening Beso restaurant. The Harmon, a luxury 400-room boutique hotel is due to open late 2010. For more information on each hotel, see them listed alphabetically in this chapter.

CityCenter is the new address to have on the Strip and the place to be seen. We're talking not millions, but billions – $8.5b to be exact. MGM Mirage is making what's being billed as the single largest private investment in US history. Opening at the end of 2009, CityCenter signals the move away from themes and into dreams of sophisticated living with fine art and sustainability at its still hedonistic heart. It brings a new level of environmental consciousness to the world famous Strip as 8 renowned architects including Studio Daniel Libeskind and Foster + Partners, have created the largest sustainable development in the world. The project is designed to achieve more than 30% improvement in energy efficiency.

separate arrival and check-in areas pamper guests and showcase the textured details of Roger Thomas's interior design.

Todd-Avery Lenahan designed The Spa and The Salon at Encore. Upon arrival in the grand Spa Court, guests are welcomed into a vaulted, softly lit and glass-enclosed courtyard. The Salon is full-service and The Spa contains 37 treatment rooms, 14 naturally lit garden rooms and 4 oversized couples' suites for massage, body treatments and facials.

A top attraction is XS, the new nightclub. After-dark impresario Victor Drai combines an outdoor pool environment with a sizzling club atmosphere. The club's design is inspired by the sexy curves of the human body, while the dance floor has 10-ft/3-m rotating chandeliers!

Excalibur

Great for family fun at reasonable prices, it should also be on your must-visit list.
Location: The Strip at West Tropicana
Theme: King Arthur and the Knights of the Round Table
Cost: $290m
Web: excalibur.com
Reservations: 702 597 7777
Fax: 702 597 7040
Rooms: 4,000
Room rates: From $36

✸ BRITTIP

Beat the queues! You can fast track your check-in by filling out the King's Express form in advance or by going to one of the self check-in kiosks on arrival to get your keys instantly.

Restaurants: 7 restaurants including an all-you-can-eat Roundtable Buffet, the Steakhouse at Camelot, Sherwood Forest Café and the lively Dick's Last Resort
Nightlife: Octane – a Vegas take on a classic biker bar
Attractions: *Tournament of Kings* dinner show; comedy from Louie Anderson – *Larger than Life; Defending the Caveman;* live music in Minstrel's Lounge; free fire-breathing dragon show; strolling entertainers; 2 magic-motion cinemas; Australia's *Thunder from Down Under*, one of the hottest male strip shows in town and a Spongebob Squarepants 4D ride
Gambling: Slot and table games, poker room, full-service race and sports book and live keno round the clock
Chilling out: New pool area with cabanas, a fire pit, sundecks and a water slide, a 25-seat spa, snack bar and cocktail bar, open 9am–7pm daily (subject to seasonal change)
Shopping: Castle Walk Shops
Other amenities: The Royal Treatment Spa and Fitness Center; links to 6 challenging golf courses including Bali Hai, Resort Pines, Royal Links and Stallion Mountain Golf Club; Kristina's Salon is open 7 days a week and also specialises in bridal

Excalibur

Splash down

Cool down from Las Vegas's dry heat with a dip in one of its ultra hip pools.

Fashionistas head to **Bare** at The Mirage (mirage.com), whose pool lounge offers the ultimate pampering with private daybeds and cabanas, two saltwater dipping pools and DJ to get the party started. The adventurous may prefer **The Tank** at the Golden Nugget (goldennugget.com), where a 3-storey chute takes you straight through some of the sea's deadliest creatures, including sharks and rays. If that's too scary, try the 3-acre/1.2-ha adult playground with 2 waterfalls, 3 pools and 4 bars at **The Palms** (thepalmslas vegas.com), Vegas' most lavish, lush and stylish watering hole, whose pool deck can hold 3,000 people. **Sapphire**, the gorgeous adults-only Brazilian lagoon at The Rio (riolasvegas.com) comes complete with a sand beach, waterfalls, 3 pools, 4 Jacuzzi-style spas – and eye candy. Recover with Rockstar Lemonades and dance to world-famous DJs at **Rehab** at the Hard Rock Hotel and Casino (hardrockhotel.com). Other top pool parties in town include Wet Republic at MGM Grand (mgmgrand.com), Beach Casino at Mandalay Bay (mandalaybay.com), The Venus Pool, Caesars Palace (caesarspalace.com) and TAO Beach at The Venetian (venetian.com).

parties (702 597 7255); 2 wedding chapels on a light and airy medieval theme (truly not an oxymoron in this case!)

BRITTIP

Don't miss the medieval-costumed staff at the Excalibur, where entertainers wander around playing medieval trumpets!

The beautiful spires of the Camelot-style entrance building are set between 2 huge castle-like towers that house the 4,000-odd rooms at this family-orientated resort. Make no mistake, though, the free Dragon Battle that takes place every hour on the hour 10am–10pm to draw the crowds has the sole purpose of inviting you in to part with your cash in the casino. But there are plenty of other free entertainments to keep you amused as you wander round the Castle Walk shops and restaurants, from the strolling entertainers to the free variety acts on the Court Jester's Stage from 10am every day.

The lobby at the Four Seasons

You can eat dinner and see the Tournament of Kings at either 6pm or 8.30pm any day of the week, or dance to live music at the Minstrel's Lounge. The house of fun also has 6 restaurants and parking is free and relatively accessible by Las Vegas standards.

Four Seasons Hotel Las Vegas

Provides an oasis of elegance – predominantly for business people – as the original non-gambling hotel-cum-retreat on the Strip.

Location: The Strip, just south of the Mandalay Bay
Theme: Understated luxury
Web: fourseasons.com/lasvegas
Reservations: 702 632 5000
Rooms: 424 including 86 suites
Room rates: From $270
Restaurants: 3 restaurants and lounges including the Verandah Bar and Lounge, Charlie Palmer Steak Lounge and Pool Bar
Gambling: None, it's a non-gambling hotel
Chilling out: Pool and health and fitness club (and the *only* hotel in Las Vegas to provide those facilities free and exclusively to guests)
Other amenities: The opportunity to wed in 3 of the most amazing suites in Las Vegas

Although the guestrooms of the hotel are located on floors 35 to 39 of the Mandalay Bay, the Four Seasons is a separately functioning hotel. The first hotel in recent history to open on the Strip without massive theming, it is also the only one without a casino and one of only 5 with a 5-diamond rating in Las Vegas.

The real beauty of the hotel comes in its divine suites, where spaciousness, supreme elegance and to-die-for views reign supreme. The Four Seasons is most famous for its Specialty Suites with 180-degree views of the glistening Strip and glistening desert. With the added bonus of separate lounge and dining areas filled with sumptuous furnishings, these suites were designed to provide the ultimate safe haven from the never-ending ker-chink, ker-chink of Las Vegas's casinos!

Ostensibly geared up to business people – it is the only hotel in Las Vegas to have a corporate rate – it still attracts tourists, many of whom are dedicated followers of the Four Seasons brand. While guests have access to all the facilities of the Mandalay Bay, they have their own exclusive facilities, too, starting with the private drive and entrance, and the casino-free, super-cool, gleaming lobby plus the lavishly landscaped private pool (where attentive staff are on hand to give you a cooling Evian spritz!), 2 whirlpools and an exclusive health and fitness club.

⚜ BRITTIP

You've got more chance of getting a room – and cheaply – at the resort-hotels if you go between Monday and Thursday.

The restaurants – including celebrity chef Charlie Palmer's Steak Lounge – have been building up a regular band of loyal locals as well as guests of the hotel. Nor are they overpriced. At the Four Seasons it's all about understated elegance, darlink!

The Spa at Four Seasons is open 8am–7pm and features result-orientated treatments conceived to hydrate the skin, promote anti-ageing and elevate the art of relaxation. There are 16 elegant treatment rooms and a large steam room. Its signature Four Seasons Desert Oasis Treatment begins with a brisk, full-body, salt exfoliation followed by a massage with the essential oil of your choice. A warm blanket wrap during a relaxing scalp, shoulder and facial massage completes the treatment. Can you think of any reason why you would ever want to leave this paradise?

⚜ BRITTIP

The Four Seasons has been ranked the Best Business Hotel in Las Vegas by America's *Travel & Leisure* magazine. Its spa was also ranked 13th out of all the top hotel spas in North America and Canada.

Luxor

Ancient Egyptian theme resort at good-value prices.
Location: The Strip between Tropicana and Reno
Theme: Ancient Egypt
Cost: $375m, plus a $240m expansion
Web: luxor.com
Reservations: 702 262 4444
Rooms: 4,887
Room rates: From $50
Restaurants: 10 dining options include Fusia Luxor, a Pan Pacific, Asian-inspired restaurant; CatHouse by celebrity chef Kerry Simon combining dining with a DJ and lingerie-clad performers; Tender steak & seafood; Pyramid Café and Burger Bar.
Nightlife: LAX Nightclub and a range of bars
Shows: *Criss Angel Believe* with Cirque du Soleil®, Comedian Carrot Top, the adult revue *Fantasy* (formerly *Midnight Fantasy*) and *Menopause the Musical*
Attractions: Bodies … The Exhibition and Titanic: The Artifact Exhibition
Gambling: Slots, tables, poker room, high limit area, race and sports book
Chilling out: 4 swimming pools and relaxing Jacuzzis in a luxurious oasis setting; the Oasis Spa; access to golf at 4 different courses
Shopping: Luxor Galleria Stores
Other amenities: Nurture, the Spa at Luxor; wedding chapel

⚜ BRITTIP

One company now owns the Mandalay Bay, Luxor and Excalibur and has built a monorail linking all 3. There are also well-signposted walkways between them. The walkway from the Excalibur to its neighbouring rival, New York-New York, is NOT signposted but can be found just outside the main entrance.

The lobby at the Luxor

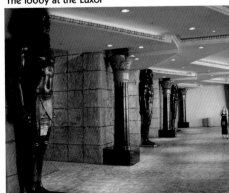

For us Brits this is the hotel that is synonymous with Las Vegas extravagance, and staying in the fabulous replica of a pyramid is up there on many people's must-do list. With its trademark beacon of light that can now be seen from outer space (along with the Great Wall of China), the hotel is one of the most tastefully executed theme resorts in the middle-market sector. You enter the beautiful structure through a life-size replica of the great Temple of Rameses II, which takes you directly into the casino (funny that!) and 120,000ft^2/ 11,150m^2 of gambling space.

On the show front, Carrot Top, a wacky entertainer who delights crowds with his idiosyncratic gadgets and sometimes coarse humour, draws great crowds, while the adult topless revue *Fantasy* keeps people out late.

To get to your room, you'll travel on the elevator at a bizarre 39-degree angle, while there are shops selling Egyptian antiquities, gemstones, charms and limited-edition art.

BRITTIP

Make sure you have lip balm with you all the time as the constant air conditioning in the hotels really dries out your lips.

Chill out in one of the attractive swimming pool areas or pay $20 ($25 to non-hotel guests) for a day Spa Pass, which includes use of the hot and cold whirlpools, steam bath, dry sauna, fitness centre and a complimentary fruit juice or mineral water.

Mandalay Bay

A luxury resort filled with must-see shows, must-eat-at restaurants and some of the coolest nightlife venues in town.
Location: The Strip, just south of West Tropicana Avenue (entrance off Hacienda Drive)

Standard suite at the Mandalay Bay

Theme: South Sea Islands
Cost: $950m
Web: mandalaybay.com
Reservations: 702 632 7777
Rooms: 3,724
Room rates: From $89

BRITTIP

The Mandalay's wave pool is generally closed for maintenance from around the end of October to March.

Restaurants: 10 signature restaurants including Aureole with its very own Wine Angel stewards who gracefully ascend the tower to retrieve wine, 9 casual restaurants and 4 quick eats
Nightlife: 8 full-on bars and nightclubs including the House of Blues and Rumjungle
Shows: Disney's *The Lion King*, ongoing calendar of concerts and shows
Attractions: Shark Reef Aquarium
Gambling: Slots, tables, blackjack and poker in lush surroundings

BRITTIP

Never use the phone in your hotel room – you'll be charged a small fortune. Get an international phone card before you go instead.

Chilling out: Sand-and-surf beach and the lazy river ride
Shopping: Selection of shops on the South Seas theme, selling everything from cigars to Bali treasures
Other amenities: Spa Mandalay, 2 wedding chapels

Aimed at a slightly more sophisticated traveller than its sister property, the Luxor, Mandalay Bay is still excellent value for money and well worth forking out that bit extra for.

For starters, it's one of the few hotels on the Strip where you don't have to walk through the casino to get to your room and, secondly, many of the rooms have massive soaking/Jacuzzi tubs plus a separate shower. A large number also have fabulous views down the entire Strip and, despite being the nearest hotel to the airport, you don't hear a peep out of those planes thanks to some pretty nifty double glazing.

Dan Aykroyd's House of Blues, the first of which opened on Sunset Strip in Los Angeles, has a home here. The live music venue is drawing such crowds that you need to book at least four weeks in advance. And if you just can't get enough of the blues, then ask for a room on the 34th floor of the hotel – it's filled with House of Blues-themed guestrooms.

Among the numerous upmarket restaurants are 2 celebrity-chef hot spots: Charlie Palmer's Aureole, and Trattoria del Lupo, owned by Wolfgang Puck, one of the most influential chefs in the US. The Mix offers amazing views of the Strip from its lofty spot, while it also has a wonderful chill-out lounge. In addition, there's Red Square, the Russian-inspired homage to vodka and caviar. Celebrities have their own vodka lockers, but the less well-to-do can try the frozen ice bar where there are more than 100 frozen vodkas and infusions, Martinis and Russian-inspired cocktails. You can also dine on an extensive selection of caviars or Russian classics.

Try Rumjungle for some dinner and dancing. Here the food and drinks are turned into works of art from a flaming wall to cascading waterfalls, while volcanic mountains of rum and spirits rise before you at the illuminated bar. Many of the sizzling meals are cooked over a giant open fire pit for that authentic South Seas flavour, while dancing is to Latin, Caribbean and African beats until the small hours.

It's not all fast-paced at the Mandalay, though, as there are plenty of ways to unwind in the 11acre/4.5ha tropical water environment. Try out the city's first sand-and-surf beach, take a dip in one of the many swimming pools or just go for a lazy river ride. You can now also get a day pass to the spa or opt for one of the many excellent massages, body treatments or facials. For something more thrilling, try diving with sharks at the Shark Reef Aquarium.

On the site of the Mandalay Bay is its cousin property, THEhotel, which has an additional 1,117 suites in 43 storeys of upscale and secluded sanctuaries.

Mandarin Oriental Las Vegas

Location: At the entrance to CityCenter on the Strip between Bellagio and Monte Carlo
Grand opening: December 2009
Theme: Holistic Eastern luxury
Cost: Part of the $8.5b CityCenter development
Web: mandarinoriental.com/lasvegas/
Reservations: 800 2828 3838
Rooms: 392

Room rates: Not yet available
Restaurants: An all-day dining establishment called MOzen Bistro serves Asian and multi-national cuisine; Mandarin Bar; Tea Lounge; Poolside Café and Amore Patisserie on Las Vegas Boulevard – an adaptation of the Mandarin Cake Shop at the Hong Kong Mandarin Oriental – offers gourmet foods, homemade breads and pastries
Attractions: Some of the finest inroom entertainment and technology systems. Top concierge. On its exterior, *Typewriter Eraser, Scale X, 1998–1999*, a legendary sculpture by Claes Oldenburg and Coosie van Bruggen – basically a 4-tonne, 19-ft/5.8-m stainless steel and fibreglass typewriter eraser
Chilling out: 2 outdoor swimming pools, Jacuzzi, deck and 20 cabanas
Shopping: Close to Crystals, CityCenter's retail and entertainment district
Other amenities: Mandarin Spa including 17 treatment rooms, 3 VIP suites, 3 couples' suites, rasul and hamam. Fitness centre, Pilates, spinning and yoga studios

BRITTIP

While most fine dining establishments close around 10pm or 10.30pm, all the major resort-hotels have at least one café that's open round the clock (24/7) and many others that stay open late.

Mandarin Oriental

The arrival of the prestigious Manadarin Oriental chain is another indication that Vegas courts sophistication. With its 47-storey glass facade, this 5-star resort that brings Eastern chic to the Strip is connected to the rest of CityCenter by glass-enclosed sky bridges. Unlike most hotels, guests will check in on the 23rd floor at the Sky Lobby with dramatic views of the Las Vegas skyline through a wall of glass. This hotel is all about luxury and service and doesn't pander to any of the gaudy excesses of the town it's in, though it will help you to access them!

BRITTIP

If you're staying at the MGM Grand or New York-New York, then head to the south baggage area at McCarran airport to check in while waiting for your luggage to come off the plane. For an extra fee you can even take the direct shuttle to your hotel.

MGM Grand

Massive resort-hotel that is good fun for the whole family, yet provides plenty of adult entertainment.
Location: The Strip at Four Corners with East Tropicana
Theme: The City of Entertainment
Cost: Originally $1b, plus a $950m expansion and theme transformation
Web: mgmgrand.com
Reservations: 702 891 1111
Rooms: 5,780
Room rates: From $79
Restaurants: Michelin-starred chef Joël Robuchon has created Joël Robuchon at the

The stunning MGM Grand

Mansion, while other fine dining highlights (6 in all) include the Japanese Shibuya. Other stalwarts remain, including Nobhill Tavern and Craftsteak; and 10 casual outlets including the Rainforest Café
Nightlife: Studio 54 nightclub, Tabu Ultra Lounge, Centrifuge and Zuri bars
Shows: *Kà* by Cirque du Soleil®; sporting events and major concerts in the Grand Garden Arena (seats 16,325); smaller gigs in the 650-seat Hollywood Theatre; plus the *Crazy Horse Paris* adult show
Attractions: CSI: The Experience interactive exhibit; Arcade centre with high-tech virtual reality games; the free Lion Habitat; the Youth Activity Center
Gambling: Poker, blackjack, slot machines and VIP lounge
Chilling out: Wet Republic Ultra Pool and Grand Pool Complex
Other amenities: 2 wedding chapels; MGM Grand Spa & Health Club; access to golf at Shadow Creek

BRITTIP

Speed up your check-out times by taking advantage of the check-out systems available on many of the hotel's TVs. DO check the bill thoroughly, though, before paying, as mistakes can occur, and always resolve any queries before leaving the hotel.

The MGM Grand is so huge it can be all things to all people. It is easy to get lost in the array of opportunities to eat, drink and generally be merry. In recent years, there has been a shift away from the old-style family-orientated entertainments to a more adult-based scene.

The hotel is famous for staging headliner shows and big fights in its Grand Garden Arena and Hollywood Theatre.

In an effort to cater to the adult market, the hotel opened Tabu Ultra Lounge, while the Studio 54 nightclub has a more raunchy twist, and Zuri supplies a 24-hour drinking spot.

Many rate MGM Grand's pool offerings as the best in Vegas and the South Beach ambience of Wet Republic Ultra Pool is certainly lively. Meanwhile you can check out your cardiovascular rating in the state-of-the-art fitness centre at the spa. Afterwards, there are seemingly no end of eating choices available and if you wish you can even pop out to the neighbouring United Artists Showcase cinema.

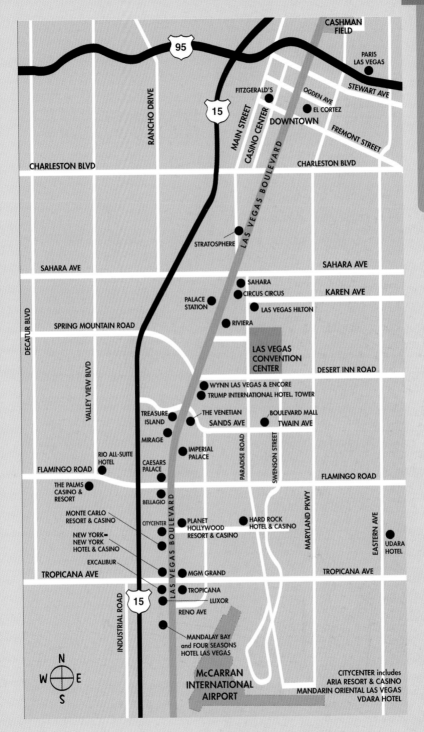

CASHMAN FIELD

PARIS LAS VEGAS

STEWART AVE

FITZGERALD'S

OGDEN AVE

EL CORTEZ

DOWNTOWN

FREMONT STREET

95

15

RANCHO DRIVE

MAIN STREET

CASINO CENTER

LAS VEGAS BOULEVARD

CHARLESTON BLVD

CHARLESTON BLVD

SAHARA AVE

SAHARA AVE

KAREN AVE

STRATOSPHERE

SAHARA

CIRCUS CIRCUS

PALACE STATION

LAS VEGAS HILTON

RIVIERA

DECATUR BLVD

SPRING MOUNTAIN ROAD

VALLEY VIEW BLVD

LAS VEGAS CONVENTION CENTER

DESERT INN ROAD

WYNN LAS VEGAS & ENCORE

TRUMP INTERNATIONAL HOTEL. TOWER

TREASURE ISLAND

THE VENETIAN

SANDS AVE

BOULEVARD MALL

TWAIN AVE

MIRAGE

IMPERIAL PALACE

PARADISE ROAD

SWENSON STREET

RIO ALL-SUITE HOTEL

FLAMINGO ROAD

CAESARS PALACE

FLAMINGO ROAD

THE PALMS CASINO & RESORT

BELLAGIO

MONTE CARLO RESORT & CASINO

CITYCENTER

PLANET HOLLYWOOD RESORT & CASINO

HARD ROCK HOTEL & CASINO

MARYLAND PKWY

EASTERN AVE

UDARA HOTEL

NEW YORK- NEW YORK HOTEL & CASINO

EXCALIBUR

TROPICANA AVE

MGM GRAND

TROPICANA AVE

15

TROPICANA

LUXOR

RENO AVE

INDUSTRIAL ROAD

MANDALAY BAY and FOUR SEASONS HOTEL LAS VEGAS

N
W E
S

McCARRAN INTERNATIONAL AIRPORT

CITYCENTER includes
ARIA RESORT & CASINO
MANDARIN ORIENTAL LAS VEGAS
VDARA HOTEL

The rooms, especially the suites, are very good for the price, with each one having artwork of Hollywood movies and celebrities of the past. A great game is to walk down your hallway trying to put names to the famous faces mounted on the walls.

The 'cousin' towers – the Signature at MGM Grand and Skylofts – offer another 1,441 luxury suites for those looking for the most pampered of settings.

The Mirage

An elegant taste of paradise, yet within reach of most budgets.

Location: The Strip, between Flamingo and Spring Mountain

Theme: Polynesian, South Seas oasis

Cost: $730m

Web: mirage.com

Reservations: 702 791 7111

Rooms: 3,044

Room rates: From $99

Restaurants: 6 fine dining experiences including the award-winning Onda and Fin restaurants, plus 6 casual options

Nightlife: The hopping JET nightclub, plus a superb lounge scene for live music at the Japonaisa Lounge, the Onda lounge and the Beatles Revolution lounge

Shows: Cirque du Soleil's® Beatles tribute, LOVE™; America's Got Talent winner Terry Fator with his amazing impressions and ventriloquism; plus a roster of visiting acts

Attractions: Siegfreid & Roy's Secret Garden & Dolphin Habitat, Volcano show and aquarium

Gambling: Extensive casino

Chilling out: 2 pools and cabanas in a lush, tropical setting; the Bare pool area allows 'European-style' sunbathing

Shopping: The Street of Shops promenade. Don't miss the couture lollipops from the

Sugar Factory – a hit with celebrities including Britney Spears and the Pussycat Dolls

Other amenities: Mirage Spa and Kim Vo Salon – spa access is free when you book a treatment, otherwise $20; the hotel has a link with Shadow Creek Golf Course

BRITTIP

One of the most unusual experiences Las Vegas has to offer is available at the Dolphin Habitat, where you can learn the art of being a trainer.

The entrance garden surrounds you with a mass of foliage and waterfalls that cascade over 50ft/15m rocks to the lagoon below before you reach the Mirage signature volcano. This erupts every 15 minutes from dawn till dusk, spewing smoke and fire 100ft/30m above the water. The Mirage has just joined forces with legendary Grateful Dead drummer Mickey Hart, Indian music sensation Zakir Hussein, and the Fountains of Bellagio design firm WET to create an all-new audio-visual spectacle for its famous volcano attraction with massive fireballs that shoot more than 12ft/3.7m into the air. The reception area is a tropical rainforest, filled with 60ft/18m high palm trees, more waterfalls, banana trees and tropical orchids, kept in perfect condition with natural sunlight and a computerised misting system. Behind the check-in desk is a massive coral reef aquarium that is home to sharks, puffer fish and angel fish, swimming among the buildings of a sunken city. The forest provides the delightfully exotic setting for Kokomo's, one of the Mirage's top-notch restaurants, serving steaks and seafood.

The Mirage joined the rank of Las Vegas resorts which host a Cirque du Soleil® fantasy, when in 2007 it opened LOVE™. The Beatles' old studios, Abbey Road, provided the digital recording masters to make the music as real as possible.

When it opened in 1989, the Mirage's theme of a Polynesian island oasis was a taste of the big things to come in Las Vegas, and it has stood the test of time. Once host to the famous Siegfried & Roy magical show of illusions featuring tigers, lions, leopards and other animals, the habitat for the dolphins remains. It has become an educational and research facility and it is possible to spend a day with a trainer. The Secret Garden, where you can see white lions, and the vast Dolphin Habitat were built to create public

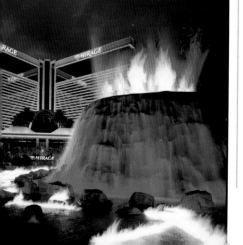

The volcano at the Mirage

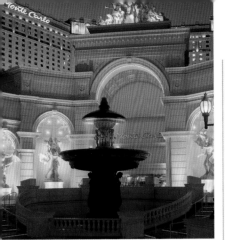

The Monte Carlo at dusk

⚡ BRITTIP

Skip the expensive buffet at the Monte Carlo and go for one of the gourmet restaurants instead.

awareness of the plight of endangered animals.

Accommodation ranges from luxurious standard rooms to opulent bungalows with their own private garden and pools, and eight 2- and 3-bedroom private residences. Admission to the luxurious day spa and fitness centre costs $25, but is free if you book any one of the pampering treatments.

Monte Carlo Resort & Casino

Posh-but-worth-it hotel with great chilling-out facilities.
Location: The Strip just north of West Tropicana
Theme: Re-creation of the Place du Casino in Monte Carlo
Cost: $344m
Web: montecarlo.com
Reservations: 702 730 7777
Rooms: 2,900
Room rates: From $59.95 at Monte Carlo and from $250 at HOTEL32 Monte Carlo
Restaurants: 9 places to dine including the famous André's and the sinfully seductive Diablo's Cantina on The Strip. There's also a Brand Steakhouse, Buffet and Monte Carlo Brew Pub. Dragon Noodle and d.vino Italian restaurant are on the cards for 2010
Nightlife: Monte Carlo Brew Pub nightclub
Shows: Lance Burton, Master Magician
Gambling: Table games, slots, poker room, race and sports book and players club
Chilling out: 21,000ft^2/1,950m^2 pool area with waterfalls, spa, children's pool, wave pool and rafting down the Easy River
Shopping: Street of Dreams promenade
Other amenities: A wedding chapel; spa and exercise room

This elegant, upmarket resort-hotel is so popular that it is hard for British travel agents to find you a room here. Modelled on the famous Place du Casino in Monaco, the emphasis is definitely on providing an elegant and refined atmosphere in which to part with wads of cash in the casino. Massive chandeliers, marble flooring, ornate fountains and gas-lit promenades all go towards setting the elegant tone. After a hard day seeing the sights, make sure you get back in time to make full use of the water facilities, which include a heated spa, children's pool and wave pool that re-creates both the sound and feel of ocean surf waves.

Resident entertainer Lance Burton is one of the top magicians in America and produces some of the most spectacular illusions in the world.

The Monte Carlo Brew Pub not only offers an excellent selection of beers, but also a DJ and live music from a band kicking off around 9pm most nights.

If you're feeling particularly flush, book into HOTEL32 at Monte Carlo which opened August 2009. Located on the top floor of the Monte Carlo, things go up a notch in this exclusive boutique hotel with flash interiors, limousine transfer to and from the airport, a dedicated 'suite assistant', 12 pillow types, a private Lounge 32 for cocktails and preferred reservations at MGM Mirage restaurants and shows.

New York-New York Hotel & Casino

The most electrifying club scene in Vegas!
Location: The Strip at West Tropicana
Theme: The Big Apple – doh!
Cost: $460m
Web: nynyhotelcasino.com
Reservations: 702 740 6969
Rooms: 3,490
Room rates: From $69
Restaurants: 9 choices from fine dining to casual including Gonzalez Y Gonzalez and Gallagher's Steakhouse, Chin Chin Cafe and the ESPN Zone
Nightlife: Rok Vegas nightclub. Dulce Latin Night at Gonzalez Y Gongalez. Great range of bars including Coyote Ugly, Nine Fine Irishmen, the Bar at Times Square and the Big Apple Bar

Shows: *Zumanity*, the adult-themed Cirque du Soleil® extravaganza
Attractions: Manhattan Express™ roller-coaster ride; ESPN Zone
Gambling: Slots, table games, race and sports book
Chilling out: Outdoor pool with 3 relaxing whirlpools
Shopping: Numerous gift shops in the Central Park area
Other amenities: Wedding chapel; spa and fitness centre

BRITTIP

It's a good 10-minute walk through shops and casinos to get to the New York-New York's roller-coaster ride, but it's well worth the trek!

Dubbed the 'greatest city in Las Vegas', the resort's façade re-creates the Manhattan skyline with 12 of its most famous skyscrapers from the Empire State Building to the Statue of Liberty, along with a 300ft/90m long replica of Brooklyn Bridge and a Coney Island-style roller-coaster called Manhattan Express™. From the food and the architecture, to the sights and sounds of America's capital city, this Las Vegas resort re-creates the energy and vibrancy of New York – then adds the Central Park casino!

Just like the Big Apple – New York-New York

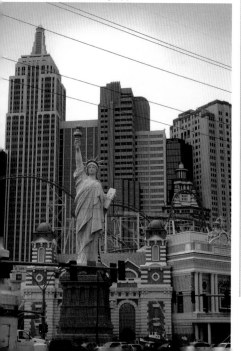

The resort is part of the MGM Mirage – whose empire includes the MGM Grand, Mirage, Bellagio and Treasure Island – and entertainment is an important facet of the experience. Cirque du Soleil's® *Zumanity* has turned into a long-running success.

The ESPN Zone, a sports-themed dining and entertainment complex with more than 165 TV screens so you don't miss a moment's action, also continues to be very popular. The Studio Grill offers classic casual American grub in a sports-themed environment, The Screening Room provides multi-game viewing, direct audio control for all televised games around two 14ft/4m screens and a dozen 36in/90cm video monitors with tiered seating, while the Sports Arena has more than 10,000ft^2/930m^2 of interactive games.

However, it is the bar scene with its fun entertainment and live music that puts the 'party, party, party' atmosphere into New York-New York. Top of the pile is Coyote Ugly, which is based on a Southern-style bar, complete with gyrating female bartenders atop the bar. No fancy drinks here, just shots and beer. Anyone who asks for a water or soda is given a shower of water that is sprayed over the entire crowd! Then there is the Big Apple Bar, a hot live-music joint with speciality drinks, and the Bar at Times Square, where you can sing along to tunes played by two pianists. The party-style ambiance is continued into the dining area Gonzalez Y Gonzalez, a New York Mexican-style café famous for its tequilas. The addition of the Rok Vegas nightclub provides a sexy late-night edge to proceedings.

Chilling-out facilities include a pool area with patio chairs for the cool cabanas. The new restaurant sets a lively vibe, while other fun elements include volleyball, poolside chair massages and a sound system. The spa is open daily 6.30am–7pm, and golf is provided through Primm Valley Golf Course.

Paris Las Vegas

A tribute to the French capital, from the undersized Eiffel Tower to the Arc de Triomphe.
Location: The Strip, south of East Flamingo
Theme: Capital of France!
Cost: $785m
Web: parislasvegas.com
Reservations: 702 946 7000
Rooms: 2,900
Room rates: From $80
Restaurants: 11 dining establishments include the popular Eiffel Tower Restaurant,

Paris Las Vegas

the wonderful Mon Ami Gabi, with outside dining right on the Strip, and the poolside Le Café du Parc

Nightlife: Fabulous ultra-lounge Risqué, plus Napoleon's and the Eiffel Tower lounges

Attractions: Observation deck on the Eiffel Tower; the Le Rendez-Vous Lounge on the 31st floor offers drinks with a fab view of the Strip. Paris has developed itself into one of the finest adult entertainment stops in Las Vegas: Anthony Cool's stunning hypnotism and some cool lounges like Risqué

Gambling: The usual rundown of gaming in an extraordinary setting in the base of the Eiffel Tower!

Chilling out: Roof-top swimming pool in a manicured French garden setting; tennis courts

BRITTIP

For a complete low-down on getting married in Las Vegas, see Chapter 8, Going to the Chapel.

Shopping: French shops in the resort's Rue de la Paix district

Amenities: 2 wedding chapels; Paris Spa by Mandara; golf is offered at the Cascata Golf Club

Bringing to life the ambience and spirit of the French capital, this theme resort opened in the autumn of 1999 with replicas of the Eiffel Tower, Arc de Triomphe, Paris Opera House and the Louvre. The 34-storey hotel tower is fashioned after the famous Hôtel de Ville. Like the Mandalay Bay and Venetian, the Paris is aimed at the more sophisticated traveller, with prices – by Las Vegas

standards, at least – to match.

The hotel is home to one of the city's chicest ultra-lounges – Risqué – plus Napoleon's, a gorgeous champagne and jazz bar, while the new Le Rendez-Vous Lounge provides some of the best views in the city at a nominal fee.

All the restaurants – in true French fashion – provide wonderful food, while Ah Sin quickly became a popular spot for both its delicious Asian cuisine and outdoor patio dining overlooking the Strip.

There is a caveat, though. While so many aspects of this resort are wonderful, the service can be poor and prices are on the expensive side. It can feel as though you really are in Paris! Well, maybe not. Look out for signs such as L'Hôtel Elevators and Le Service Captain. On top of this, all the staff have been trained to say 'bonjour' and 'merci' but can't actually understand a word of French. Of all the resorts, this is the one that comes off with the thinnest veneer.

Planet Hollywood Resort & Casino

A well-priced mega resort now home to some of the most adult-orientated entertainments on the Strip.

Location: The Strip on the corner of Harmon Avenue, south of the Paris resort and almost directly opposite the Bellagio

Theme: The outrageously popular Planet Hollywood formula of film styling and memorabilia

Cost: $1.4b in 2000, plus $100m in 2006–2007

Web: planethollywoodresort.com

Reservations: 702 785 5555

Rooms: 2,500

Room rates: From $79

Restaurants: 9, headlined by the Japanese offerings of Koi and the popular Chinese-fusion food of PF Chang's. The lone

Paris Las Vegas

Heart Bar at Planet Hollywood

holdover from the Aladdin days is the Spice Market Buffet, one of the best value buffets in Vegas. Plus the Miracle Mile shopping area has more great dining with Trader Vic's. Pink's Hot Dogs opened its first location in Vegas here in August 2009
Nightclubs: South Beach style clubbing at Privé, a favourite with celebs, The Living Room, The Playing Field Lounge, Extra Lounge, the Heart Bar and Koi Lounge
Shows: Peepshow with dancers and performers from the world of pop music, film, television and broadway and *Tony 'n' Tina's Wedding*, the second longest running show in Off-Broadway history
Gambling: Nearly 3 acres/1.2 ha of casino including the Pleasure Pit which features blackjack and roulette dealt by scantily clad women as go-go dancers do their thing
Chilling out: 26th-floor outdoor terrace and

swimming pool areas overlooking the Strip
Shopping: The Miracle Mile – once The Desert Passage at the Aladdin – is a massive shopping area with more than 170 shops including H&M and Urban Outfitters and 6 fine-dining restaurants including hot city favourites the Commander's Palace from New Orleans, Sevilla, Bice and Anasazi, plus 6 casual eating outlets
Other amenities: Spa by Mandara; 2 wedding chapels

BRITTIP

If you don't want to walk miles to your hotel room, request one near to the lifts. These hotels are massive and rooms can be a considerable distance from the lifts!

Seemingly born under an unlucky star, Planet Hollywood is hoping that her original (and unlucky) life as the Aladdin is behind her and she can look forward to a profitable future by mixing Hollywood Glamour with Vegas Sin.

Having opened in 2000, the Aladdin had one of the bumpiest rides of any of the major resort-hotels in recent time. Of course, it didn't help that the project went massively over budget, nor that the opening was postponed for 5 months, nor that when it did finally open there weren't enough hotel rooms ready for all the reservations taken. So much for a 'grand' opening!

The Aladdin was bought by Planet Hollywood, Starwood Hotels and Bay Harbor in the bankruptcy courts for $637m in 2004. A further $100m was spent on renovations that changed the facade, improved the casino and added

The lobby at Planet Hollywood

The *Pulp Fiction* suite at Planet Hollywood

restaurants, a 1,300-seat showroom and a 500-seat TV studio.

Planet Hollywood has also worked on her contacts in the entertainment industry to attract crowds of celebrities on a daily basis. *Extra* is a popular television show of big-name interviews and gossip mongering, and it has set up its headquarters in the Extra Lounge. They bring in a daily influx of beautiful people who willingly glad hand and pose for photos with their adoring fans.

A programme to improve guest facilities means that rooms now come with marble bathrooms with oversized bathtubs, and in-room personal computers.

Stratosphere

Extremely good-value hotel with some of the best gambling odds on the Strip.
Location: At the northern end of the Strip
Theme: Tallest building west of the Mississippi
Cost: $550m
Web: stratospherehotel.com
Reservations: 702 380 7777
Rooms: 2,577
Room rates: From $40.99
Restaurants: 2 fine-dining experiences including the revolving Top of the World restaurant on the 106th floor and Fellini's Ristorante, plus 3 casual dining outlets
Nightlife: Romance at The Top of the World, Back Alley Bar, C Bar, Images Lounge and Big Shot Bar
Shows: *American Superstars* and *Bite*
Attractions: Highest observation tower in America, world's highest roller-coaster and world's highest thrill ride, Big Shot!
Gambling: Bikini-clad blackjack dealers poolside each Friday, Saturday and Sunday in the summer
Chilling out: Beach Club 25 and pool and recreation deck; Roni Josef Salon Spa
Shopping: The Tower Shops
Other amenities: Wedding chapel; state-of-the-art video arcade

Stratosphere has paid the price for being located at the most northern point of the Strip – just that little bit too far from the rest of the action and in a little seedier part of town. Having faced bankruptcy, then received an injection of capital to provide a raft of new amenities, the Stratosphere finds itself offering party-time products in an environment that always looks as if it needs a lick of paint.

In its favour, though, are some real crowd-pleasers. XScream, Big Shot! and the High Roller attract the roller-coaster thrill seekers. Those with a less robust constitution can enjoy the observation deck in the tallest building in the city and enjoy a drink as the bar gently circles so you can see every dramatic view.

The restaurant scene is one of the hotel's biggest hits. Its Top of the World restaurant provides great food and an incomparable view of the Strip.

Beach Club 25 was the first of the 'European-style' sunbathing facilities in Las Vegas. It is a popular, secluded adult environment with table tennis, fitness equipment, water volleyball and fun parties, with fantastic views of the Strip from its 25th-floor location. It is also incredibly popular with cast members of the topless *Bite* show who frequent the facilities to perfect their tans and allow the males to drool.

Another chill-out zone is provided on the eighth floor of the tower block. The 67,000ft^2/6,224m^2 pool and recreation deck offers a huge pool, oversize spa, waterfall and private cabanas.

The Stratosphere

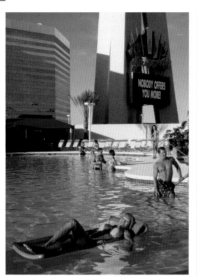

The pool at the Stratosphere

The competitively priced rooms are among the cheapest on the Strip, although they aren't quite as good value as at first blush. The otherwise budget-priced hotel charges a sometimes pricey 'resort fee' on top of your hotel bill, which makes the value go from amazingly cheap to merely very good. But the odds available in the casino make it the best place to try out your newfound skills on the tables (see Chapter 7)!

Treasure Island

It's kept the family-style brand, but is now offering a more adult package of entertainments.
Location: The Strip at Spring Mountain Road
Theme: Robert Louis Stevenson's novel *Treasure Island*, as only Vegas can do
Web: treasureisland.com
Reservations: 702 894 7111
Rooms: 2,885
Room rates: From $88
Restaurants: 3 fine-dining including Khotan, The Steak House and Isla Mexican Kitchen plus 6 casual eateries
Nightlife: Christian Audigier The Nightclub, Mist Bar, Isla Tequila Bar, Breeze Bar and Kahunaville Party Bar with live entertainment
Shows: Cirque du Soleil's® *Mystère* and the *Sirens of TI* sea show
Gambling: All the usual suspects
Chilling out: Tropical paradise pool with private cabanas and a 25-person hot tub
Shopping: The Pirate's Walk shopping promenade
Other amenities: 2 wedding chapels; spa and beauty salon

Built by Steve Wynn, who was also responsible for the Mirage and the Bellagio (before selling up to create Wynn Las Vegas and Encore), the hotel now has new owners, MGM Mirage, who have steered the resort towards being a more adult-orientated destination.

The unmistakable Treasure Island

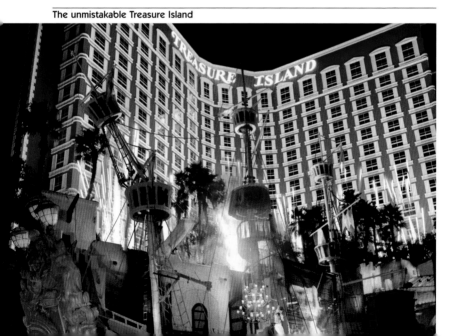

BRITTIP

If you plan to see the *Sirens of TI* show at Treasure Island, arrive early to grab a prime spot as crowds build quickly.

The free *Sirens of TI* show is a steamy affair, with wanton sirens tempting buccaneers in a wild, outdoor sea battle 4 times nightly every 90 minutes starting at 7.30pm. While you can see it from Las Vegas Boulevard, it is best viewed from the Christian Audigier The Nightclub – a space formerly occupied by Tangerine and now a nightclub resplendent with roses, skulls, gleaming crystals and black glass chandeliers. And while Cirque's *Mystère* show continues to wow audiences twice nightly, there is a much more adult selection of bars. The Kahunaville Party Bar is a tropical hotspot with eclectic music and flair bartenders that turn the venue from restaurant to party central until 3am every morning.

Trump International Hotel & Tower

Aside from its flashy exterior, this is one of Vegas's more reserved hotels.
Location: Where the Strip meets Fashion Show Drive near Wynn Las Vegas
Grand opening: 31 March 2008
Theme: Luxury
Cost: $2.1 billion
Web: trumplasvegashotel.com
Reservations: 877 878 6711
Rooms: 1,282
Room rates: From $89
Restaurants: DJT
Chilling out: The Spa at Trump, heated outdoor pool and fitness center and salon
Shopping: Across the street from the Fashion Show Mall

True to Donald J. Trump's ostentatious style, Trump International Hotel Las Vegas resembles a shot of gold bullion, its 64-storey tower encased in 24-carat gold glass. There's nothing so humble as a guestroom here, rather studio suites rising to ten 3-bedroom penthouse suites. There are white-gloved doormen and the signature services of a Trump Attaché to help your stay run smoothly and noting all your preferences. The Spa at Trump has some great treatments to ease yourself through a hectic stay including the Sun-Worshipper Body Wrap, the Royal Flush Facial and the Morning-After Eye Cure.

Vdara Hotel

One of a new line of tasteful non-gaming hotels.
Location: Part of the CityCenter development on the Strip attached to the Bellagio
Grand opening: Accepting reservations from 1 October 2009
Theme: Sophisticated non-gaming retreat
Cost: Part of the $8.5b CityCenter development
Web: vdara.com
Reservations: 866 745 7767
Rooms: 1,495 suites
Room rates: From $159
Restaurants: Martin Heierling, innovator behind Bellagio's AAA Four Diamond restaurant Sensi, is executive chef for all food including the Silk Road, a modern trans-ethnic restaurant which transforms as the day evolves from fresh at daybreak to sexy at nightfall. Bar Vdara is an eclectic lobby lounge that works for morning espressos or late-night cocktails
Nightlife: Bar Vdara connects to an intimate outdoor space with a garden-oasis feel where guests can lounge on spacious swings
Attractions: Nancy Rubins' immense installation, Big Pleasure Point, made up of numerous row boats, kayaks, canoes, small sailboats and so on – in gravity defying form
Chilling out: The Sky Pool & Lounge has spa cabanas, semi-secluded plunge pools, a high-energy bar and lounge open day and evening
Shopping: Crystals is CityCenter's retail and entertainment district with more than 500,000ft^2/46,450m^2 of shopping including Louis Vuitton, Hermes, Prada,

Vdara Hotel

Dior, Tiffany & Co. And new to Vegas are Tom Ford, Miu Miu and Marni among others
Other amenities: Vdara Health & Beauty is a 2-level spa, salon and advanced fitness area focusing on holistic health

Soaring 57 storeys above the Strip, Vdara Hotel is an all-suite and spa hotel with exclusivity at its heart. There are all the vices of Vegas out there waiting to be discovered, but here you have a non-gaming, smoke-free and sustainable retreat to take a breath from the madness. Vdara's distinctive crescent shape and skin of patterned glass is one of the biggest design statements in the city. Corner view suites are sought after with expansive views of the city and mountains beyond. Each has a gourmet kitchen. The spa is a focus of the hotel's holistic approach with a champagne and smoothie bar.

The Venetian

Luxurious recreation of the romantic city of Venice, and a favourite with celebrities and CEOs alike.
Location: The Strip at East Spring Mountain Road
Theme: Renaissance Venice
Cost: $1.2b, plus $275m Venezia Tower
Web: venetian.com
Reservations: 702 414 4100
Rooms: 4,000 suites, plus another 3,025 in the familial Palazzo next door
Room rates: From $199

The pool at The Venetian

A stunning view of The Venetian

Restaurants: 11 fine-dining establishments throughout the hotel and Grand Canal Shoppes, including AquaKnox, Bouchon and Tao, plus 9 casual dining outlets
Nightlife: TAO nightclub, Tao Beach, V Bar and La Scena Lounge
Shows: Joan Rivers at The Venetian Showroom, Chazz Palminteri's *A Bronx Tale*, Andrew Lloyd Webber's *Phantom of the Opera*, Blue Man Group, comedians Wayne Brady and David Spade
Attractions: Madame Tussauds and gondola rides
Chilling out: Pool deck with private cabanas, Tao Beach for 'European-style' sunbathing
Gambling: The Venetian House Casino has state of the art video poker and slot games under hand-painted frescoed ceilings. Surreal and totally Vegas
Shopping: Grand Canal Shoppes and the new Shoppes at The Palazzo
Other amenities: A massive wedding chapel, which can be divided up into 3; and Canyon Ranch SpaClub – one of the most luxurious on the Strip

BRITTIP

For a truly romantic wedding, you can get married on the Ponte al di Piazza bridge overlooking The Venetian's St Mark's Square.

Here you will find replicas of everything that Venice stands for, from the Doge's Palace to St Mark's Square, the Grand Canal and Rialto Bridge, all re-created in the finest detail by sculptors with the help of two Italian historians to 'ensure the integrity of the design and architecture'. In fact, its beauty and style is only matched by its service, which has established The Venetian as one of the most successful resorts on the Strip.

For many years the one thing missing at The Venetian was first-rate entertainment, but no more. The Venetian spent a raft of money to develop a dazzling theatre for a lavish production of Andrew Lloyd Webber's *Phantom of the Opera*. Then they wooed the staggeringly popular Blue Man Group from the Luxor and now have popular comedians Wayne Brady and David Spade with separate shows.

The Venetian has a host of bars, lounges and restaurants that will help make your nights memorable. The flagship is Tao, both a fabulous Asian restaurant and a nightclub, with a 40-ft/12-m long outside terrace, giving spectacular views of the Strip, and go-go dancers. The swanky V Bar, based on LA's sophisticated Sunset Room, continues to be popular, as does La Scena Lounge. The Venetian is the king of upscale Las Vegas dining with no less than 11 top restaurants, starting with Emeril Legasse's Delmonico's Steakhouse.

The pool deck is based on a Venetian garden and includes a swimming pool, 3 spa pools and ornate gazebos. It is highly prized as a remarkable location for wedding receptions.

If you need refreshing, try the Canyon Ranch SpaClub, next to the 5acre/2ha pool deck, which has private cabanas and is modelled on a Venetian-style garden. The state-of-the-art spa, beyond a shadow of a doubt the best in Las Vegas, features massage and treatments, a 40ft/12m rock-climbing wall, Pilates studio, spinning gym, therapeutic Watsu pools and Canyon Ranch Café.

The centrepiece of the main shopping mall, known as the Grand Canal Shoppes, is the reproduction of Venice's majestic Grand Canal and St Mark's Square and for a price you can even take a romantic gondola ride. There are actually two places you can take a gondola ride – along the Grand Canal but also outside the main entrance by the massive edifice of the Doge's Palace. The ride in front is special, as all the gondoliers are accomplished singers who sing romantic Italian songs while they take you through the tunnels of the front waterways. Our boatman confided he was from Italy, studied at Juilliard and was working until he could find a job at one of Las Vegas's shows. There is nothing like an Italian song to fire the flames of romance! Also, there are a number of eateries along St Mark's, making it a great place to have a coffee or lunch, and watch Las Vegas-Venice pass by.

Another in the line of 'cousin' properties, the Palazzo, opened in 2007 next door to The Venetian to add another 3,025 luxury suites spread over 50 floors to the mix.

Wynn Las Vegas

The last word in luxury, glamour and elegance.
Location: The Strip at Spring Mountain Road
Theme: Understated glamour
Cost: $2.7b
Web: wynnlasvegas.com
Reservations: 702 770 7000
Rooms: 2,359 rooms, 270 parlour and salon suites, 45 executive suites, 36 one- and two-bedroom fairway villas, 6 private-entry villas
Room rates: From $159
Restaurants: 12 including Okado and Daniel Boulud's Brasserie, plus The Buffet
Nightlife: Blush and Tryst
Shows: The $13m *Le Rêve*
Gambling: Extensive casino
Shopping: High-scale promenade with designers such as Chanel, Manolo Blahnik,

Wynn Las Vegas

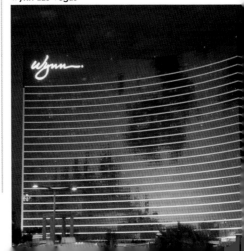

Dior, Louis Vuitton, Cartier, Gaultier, Oscar de al Renta, Jo Malone and Graff
Other amenities: 3 wedding chapels; spa and salon
Golf: The only hotel on the Strip with its own golf course; the 18-hole course has been designed by Tom Fazio

Steve Wynn decided on a complete change of tack with his new resort. He snapped up the elegant but failing Desert Inn and its 215acre/87ha site for a mere $275m. He then went back to the drawing board for 18 months before announcing plans for the Le Rêve (the dream) in 2002. Eventually, it evolved into Wynn Las Vegas, hands-down the provider of the finest, most elegant, most luxurious service in a hotel casino. And the proof is that the Wynn Las Vegas is the only hotel-casino in the world to have been awarded both Mobil 5-star and Diamond AAA 5-star ratings.

⚡ BRITTIP

Steve Wynn has brought another first to the city: the hotel's Oscar de la Renta store is the only Oscar boutique in the world.

A budget of $13m alone was given for the fantastic new *Le Rêve* production (all that remains of the original name for the hotel), which was created by Franco Dragone, the man behind so many Cirque du Soleil® spectaculars. *Le Rêve* is now unquestionably the swankiest show in Sin City.

And golfers will be delighted by the 18-hole golf course designed by Tom Fazio, in conjunction with Wynn himself, that requires no trip out of town, only a greens fee of $500 per round.

While there is no theme to this resort, it is inspired by Steve Wynn's love of the Impressionist painters. The original name, Le Rêve, comes from a well-loved Picasso painting, while much of the decoration of the hotel lobby and casino are based on Matisse colours and themes. None of the resort's facilities can be seen from the Strip and only those who journey up the long driveway will get to see the 50-storey, curved tower covered in bronze glass that is this new hotel.

Guestrooms provide a jaw-dropping spectacle in themselves. Executive suites come with floor-to-ceiling glass that spans the entire room from wall to wall, over 26ft/8m, to give breathtaking views of the Strip and the mountains surrounding the desert floor of the city. These vast suites include separate bathrooms for him and her – his with glass-enclosed shower, hers with soaking tub, and both equipped with LCD TVs and over-sized Turkish towels. The living area is home to a sofa, console, coffee table, plus dining room table and chairs. And as you jump into the king-size bed you can snuggle into 320-count European linens before picking up the controls for the curtains and TV. In-room services include massage, manicure, pedicure and hair styling.

If you ever wish to leave your suite, then the resort's buffet is one of the best in town – with 17 live-action exhibition cooking stations and a sumptuous array of dishes, redefining the notion of buffet dining. As you would guess, food is toe-curlingly excellent with places like Corso Cocina, Daniel Boulud's Brasserie and Okada.

You can party the night away at Blush Boutique Nightclub with its onyx lit dancefloor or head to Tryst where the dancefloor extends into a breathtaking 90-ft/27-m waterfall that cascades into a secluded lagoon.

The following morning allow your body a chance to recover in the spa, which offers 45 treatment rooms for massage, body treatments, facials and hydrotherapy. There are also separate his and hers facilities with showers, steam room, sauna and whirlpool for ultra comfort and privacy.

Resort-hotels off the Strip

Hard Rock Hotel & Casino

A big hit with models and celebrities, plus trendy young things.
Location: 4455 Paradise Road
Theme: Rock 'n' roll
Web: hardrockhotel.com
Reservations: 702 693 5000
Rooms: 670
Room rates: From $89
Restaurants: 3 fine-dining experiences, including the famous Nobu, and 3 casual establishments, including the Mexican Pink Taco, which is great for outdoor seating
Nightlife: Wasted Space rock lounge, The Joint live gig venue, Body English the Nightclub, Center Bar, Rehab pool party,

⚡ BRITTIP

Right next to the Hard Rock Hotel is the amazing Ice nightclub, with state-of-the-art special effects and 4,000ft²/372m² of dance space.

Poolside shows and Pink Taco Bar
Gambling: Poker Lounge Hell's Belles where blackjack meets go-go dancers, table games, slots and race and sports book
Shopping: Hard Rock Store, Rocks jewellery and Love Jones lingerie
Chilling out: Beach Club and Rock Spa
Other amenities: Golf is offered through Walters Golf. Hart & Huntington Tattoo Company

A truly trendy hangout and an instant hit when it opened at the end of the 1990s, it has remained a mecca for celebs and the beautiful people despite new competition in the guise of The Palms. It's all set for a $750 million expansion project that will include another 950 guest rooms, more casino space, more food outlets, a larger pool, new shops and spa. A new rock lounge, Wasted Space, has already opened and exalts the decadent rock 'n' roll lifestyle, also known as 'anti-club'. Signature drinks include Hart Attack (after co-owner and action sports star Carey Hart) and Sunday bloody Sunday. A new Paradise Tower is an 18-floor tower with 490 guest rooms designed with the Hard Rock's signature party attitude in mind but with a jolt of luxury and sophistication. There's a mega penthouse and 10 pool suites, 2 of which have their own cabana or pool deck and glass balconies.

Existing restaurants are some of the best in town and in 2005 three of them won a total of 4 Epicurean Awards, including Best Japanese Restaurant for Nobu, Best New Restaurant off the Strip for Simon Kitchen & Bar, and Best Mexican Restaurant for Pink Taco.

Definitely not for the faint-hearted, there is a strong adult vibe at this resort. In addition to the very raunchy nightlife scene, the Beach Club (open to hotel guests only) has become a haven for 'some of the most

beautiful bodies in Las Vegas'. With palm-shaded sandy beaches and blue water lagoons, the grass-shack cabanas (with phone, fridge and misting system!) are highly sought after. Every Sunday is a hard-partying, adults-only pool party which has become a Las Vegas tradition. After a hard day by the pool, if you need a little more R&R, try the Rock Spa to prepare you for a night of partying. You can even get your gaming and pool lounging at the same time, with Hard Rock Café's Poolside Blackjack.

M Resort Spa Casino

Modern and fresh with fabulous city views, you can't go wrong here.
Location: Approximately 10mls/16km to the south of the Strip on Las Vegas Boulevard South, just minutes from the airport
Theme: Modern with warm touches
Grand opening: 1 March 2009
Cost: $1 billion
Web: themresort.com
Reservations: 702 797 1000
Rooms: 390
Room rates: From $79
Restaurants: 9 restaurants including Studio B, the resort's show kitchen buffet with a live-action cooking studio. At Marinelli's guests can enjoy authentic Italian dishes. Terzetto combines great charcoal-grilled steak and seafood with a buzzy social scene. Gracing the summit of the M Resort, Veloce Cibo has an extensive menu of appetizers, entrées, sushi, sashimi and nigiri. Red Cup Café is a 1920s art-deco inspired 24-hour gathering spot and the place for hand-prepared American classics
Nightlife: Ravello entertainment lounge for live bands
Gambling: Casino floor with tables games, poker room and slots
Chilling out: Phenomenal pool with infinity feature in the piazza area and 20 VIP

The Hard Rock Hotel is off the Strip but still popular

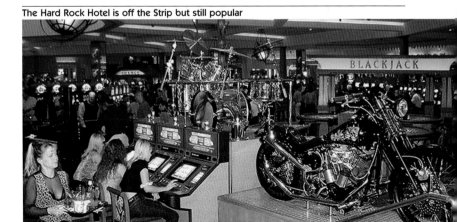

cabanas. A more private pool, Daydream, is a bit hipper and more locals oriented
Shopping: Vice shop and convenience store. Up to 1 million ft²/92,900m² of retail in the planning
Amenities: Spa Mio has 16 treatment rooms, Jacuzzi and sauna

Set at an elevation of 400ft/122m higher than most other properties around, M Resort has fantastic views of the city and the mountains from its lobby, restaurant and most guestrooms. This classy modern hangout was built by Anthony Marnell, III, son of casino-building pioneer Tony Marnell, who has built much of Las Vegas including the Mirage, Caesars Palace, Wynn and much more – a family hotel so to speak. And it shows. The Marnell family, for example, owns and operates all the restaurants so nothing is leased out. The concepts are all their own and everything is made fresh daily. Dining selections at the M Resort include recipes from the Marnell family recipe book and a reserve list of American-raised Wagyu Kobe Beef from the Marnell family ranch. Guests can also taste wines from the Marnell family private label. Each room offers a living space that includes high-technology amenities such as a Bose® Wave sound system, iPod® docking station and 42" HD LCD flat screen television. The spa-like bathrooms offer guests a marble vanity with double sinks, inlaid mirror television and separate bathtub and shower. All resort rooms and suites feature automatic lighting controls for energy efficiency and floor-to-ceiling windows with unrivalled views of the Las Vegas Strip or mountains. Uniquely

designed, the M Resort does not feature reflective glass and includes skylights on the casino floor allowing natural light in – a rare feature in the casino industry.

Las Vegas Hilton

Filled with conventioners, it now has a lively night scene.
Location: Paradise Road and Karen Avenue (behind the Strip)
Web: lvhilton.com
Reservations: 702 732 5111
Rooms: 3,174
Room rates: From $69.95
Restaurants: 6 fine-dining restaurants including the delightfully Mediterranean Casa Nicola and the Japanese Benihana, plus 8 casual eateries including classic Vegas Buffet
Nightlife: 7 popular bars from Tempo lounge bar to SpaceQuest Bar set in the 24th century
Gambling: One of the largest off-strip casinos with everything from state of the art slots to classic table games
Shows: Barry Manilow, *Voices* starring Earl Turner and Lani Misalucha and *Sin City Bad Girls*
Chilling out: Pool, spa, tennis courts
Shopping: 2 promenades

BRITTIP

When Elvis first appeared in Las Vegas at the Last Frontier Hotel on the Strip in 1956 he was a flop. He didn't return until 1969 when he mostly appeared – to great acclaim, of course – at the Las Vegas Hilton.

Las Vegas Hilton

Salon suite at The Palms

An understated elegance pervades what is ostensibly an upmarket hotel resort for business people attending one of the over 20,000 annual conventions held in Las Vegas. For them, its location near the Convention Center is perfect, but it's about a 12-minute walk to the Strip, so it's a little off the beaten track for real tourists. Fortunately, the tram has a stop right outside the Convention Center to whisk you away to the wilder parts of Sin City.

The Palms Casino Resort

A sultry boutique resort, which has rapidly established itself as the city's top place to party, attracting both the hip and the famous.
Location: Flamingo Road, west of the Strip, close to the Rio All-Suite Hotel
Theme: Sophisticated adult playground
Cost: $265m, plus $600m
Web: thepalmslasvegas.com
Reservations: 702 942 7777
Room rates: From $79
Rooms: 455 deluxe rooms
Restaurants: Include N9NE from Chicago, Little Buddha Café from Paris, the upmarket Alizé, Garduños Mexican restaurant and the Blue Agave Oyster and Chile Bar
Nightlife: This is club city, a long list of popular hotspots including the Playboy Club, Rain in the Desert Nightclub, Moon Nightclub and Ghost Bar, an indoor-outdoor lounge

Attractions: The Brenden Theater Complex, a state-of-the-art 14-screen cinema complex; a drive-in betting shop; and 2 Bachelor Suites for stag parties and hen nights
Gambling: No casino. But gamers fear not. Just a short stroll through a SkyTube is the adjacent Palms Casino Resort
Chilling out: Skin Pool Lounge
Other amenities: $20,000ft^2/1,860m^2$, 3-storey spa featuring candlelit yoga classes and fun and fruity body treatments

The hotel opened to a fanfare of glory in 2001, and from the outset the Texas-based Malouf family targeted celebrities, making this the home of the Cine Vegas Film Festival and thus ensuring its status as one of the most star-laden hotels in Las Vegas.

The original 455 rooms – a mere drop in the ocean for this city – has been added to with a whopping $600m expansion programme that includes a 347-room Fantasy Tower, 2,200-seat showroom, 50-storey condo hotel and spa and a new pool. The Hardwood Suite is clearly targeted at the money-is-no-object end of the market with its own indoor basketball court (the new must-have!), scoreboard, pool table, poker table and dance floor, among many other facilities. As it is, revellers can choose between bungalows, Playpen Suites or 'Hugh Hefner's Skyloft for ultimate party hospitality where the likes of Kanye West hold court.

The Palms quickly became one of the most coveted private party spots in Las Vegas and its Real World Suite has already been used to host events for Leonardo DiCaprio, Avril Lavigne and Mark

Superior room at The Palms

The pool at The Palms

Wahlberg. Ordinary mortals need not miss out on the fun as the hotel also has 2 Bachelor Suites, fitted out with dance poles (think Jamie Lee Curtis in *True Lies!*), a wooden dance floor and sophisticated sound system. The ultimate playrooms, perfect for both stag parties and hen nights, they're decked out in 1960s retro colour patterns, a mirror wall made up of fragmented squares of glass to create the effect of a disco ball, the same type of mirror above the bed, an LED lighting system and plasma TV screens.

BRITTIP

Just to give you an insight into VIP prices: a private room at The Palm's Rain Nightclub goes from $300 to $1,000 a night!

In the meantime, punters flock to what is still just a bijou gem due to its huge array of entertainment amenities.

The award-winning Rain nightclub, located on the casino level, is a multi-storey, multi-environment nightclub and concert. It combines performances by international headliners, with an ultra-cool dance club (see page 154) and private event facility, and comes with some amazing special effects including fog,

haze, 16ft/5m fire plumes and 3ft/1m fireballs, while the bamboo dance floor is surrounded by a computer-programmed river of water with dancing jets and fountains. Ghostbar is a vibrant open-hour lounge on top of the 42-storey hotel tower, which has already won plaudits as a hot nightspot.

BRITTIP

If good service is important, then The Palms could be the place for you as the Malouf family is famous for excellent hospitality.

This resort-hotel also has a fantastic line-up of restaurants that cover upmarket, steaks, casual and bistro-style dining. Top of the pile is the Alizé, the latest and probably swankiest offering from Las Vegan gourmet masterchef and restaurateur André Rochat. Named after the gentle wind that runs along the Mediterranean, it offers a French Riviera-style dining experience in an amazing glass atrium with aquamarine glass walls that provide spectacular views of the city. VIP tables are in front of the windows and secluded from the rest of the dining room by a curved glass partition. Rochat has won a clutch of awards for his distinctive restaurants.

The Skin Pool Lounge set a new trend in exotic oasis indulgence with relaxation pools, chaise longues, 4 bars, billiard tables, outdoor swings, poolside blackjack and trampolines. You can even hire one of the private cabanas that come with TVs, fridges, telephones and VIP amenities, while DJs spin tunes day and night and food can be ordered from the Nine Steakhouse. The whole area is only open to hotel guests during the day, but is turned into a voyeuristic club at night (see page 158).

Rio All-Suite Hotel

Proving there is life beyond the Strip, the Rio is an entertainment city in its own right.
Location: 3700 West Flamingo
Theme: Tropical paradise
Cost: $200m expansion
Web: riolasvegas.com
Reservations: 702 252 7777
Rooms: 2,563 suites
Room rates: From $49
Restaurants: 16 in all including fine-dining, city favourite Buzios Seafood Restaurant plus the Gaylord India Restaurant. More casual places include the funky VooDoo Steak Lounge
Nightlife: Great spots include the Flirt

lounge, Voodoo Lounge and I-Bar ultra-lounge

BRITTIP

The Rio may be off the beaten track of the Strip, but if you're near Harrah's, take the free shuttle bus between the 2 hotels – you don't have to be a guest of either to get a ride.

Shows: The amazing Penn & Teller and Chippendales
Attractions: *Masquerade Show in the Sky* (free); Lucky Strike Bowling Alley
Gambling: State of the art slots, video poker, 80 gaming tables, Keno Lounge and race and sports book
Chilling out: Sand beach and outdoor recreational area, plus Rio Spa and Salon
Shopping: Masquerade Village
Other amenities: 3 wedding chapels; golf is available at the Rio Secco Golf Course

The Rio is consistently voted the best-value hotel in America and has some of the finest restaurants in Las Vegas including Gaylord India Restaurant. Its buffet is second to

Rio All-Suite Hotel

Poolside waterfalls at the Rio

none. It is also home to the city's first Wine Cellar Tasting Room, which has the world's largest collection of fine and rare wines, along with an array of tasting accessories.

The *Masquerade Show in the Sky*, one of Vegas's best free shows, allows guests to ride aboard fantasy floats that glide above the crowds in a Mardi Gras-style fiesta of music and dance. This is an adult-orientated show with topless girls for the evening performances, while the hotel has generally shifted in a more raunchy direction with two chi-chi lounges for grown-ups: Flirt and the ever-popular VooDoo Lounge.

During June and July it is impossible to get a room here, as it hosts the annual World Series of Poker (see page 167) and poker pros and addicts descend on it in droves.

Outside, the Ipanema Beach comes with real sand beaches at the edge of a tropical lagoon, complete with waterfalls, plus 4 nautical-shaped swimming pools and 5 Jacuzzi-style spas. Here you can bask in the sun or order a variety of services including personal massages, poolside cocktails and food.

Imperial Palace casino

When it comes to weddings, the Rio does it in style. An entire floor of the Masquerade Tower has been given over to wedding facilities including 1 chapel and 1 themed, 1,200ft^2/111m^2 honeymoon suites and reception areas.

Other resort-hotels

The following hotels still have their place in the city's hall of fame, but cannot compete with the big shots!

Imperial Palace

Friendly, reasonably priced hotel in prime location.
Location: The Strip at West Flamingo
Theme: Japanese
Web: imperialpalace.com
Reservations: 702 731 3311
Rooms: 2,700
Room rates: From $20
Restaurants: 7 including the Emperor's Buffet
Show: The athletic Matsuri Japanese Musical, Smokey Robinson's *Human Nature*
Attractions: A collection of over 250 antique and collectible cars
Gambling: Straightforward casino with Champagne Pit
Chilling out: Olympic-size swimming pool with waterfall and heated spa
Other facilities: A wedding chapel; the only 24-hour medical facility on the Strip (phone direct on 702 735 3600)

When the reviews of Las Vegas accommodation are given, the Imperial Palace hardly takes centre stage, yet it has reasonable prices and good gambling odds. The resort is home to a collection of vintage and special-interest cars and has a good-value full-service spa. It holds a Hawaiian-style Imperial Luau complete with Polynesian fire dancers, roast pig and unlimited piña coladas and mai tais!

Tropicana

Exotic chilling-out environment for grown-ups.
Location: The Strip at Tropicana
Theme: Tropical paradise island
Web: tropicanalv.com
Reservations: 702 739 2222
Rooms: 1,875
Room rates: From $35
Restaurants: 5, including Legends Steak & Seafood and the Garden Café
Nightlife: The Celebration Lounge and Tropics Lounge
Shows: *The Soprano's Last Supper,*

Garden room at the Tropicana

Hypnosis Unleashed, comedian Bobby Slayton, *Xtreme Magic* with Dirk Arthur
Attractions: Live poolside entertainment
Gambling: Some of the loosest slots and video poker on the Strip
Chilling out: Pool Coconut Grove Bar and Swim-up Blackjack. Indoor heated pool
Other amenities: A wedding chapel; barbers shop and salon
Shopping: Trop Shops – 35 speciality shops

The Tropicana has a colourful Caribbean Village facade, while its 'signature' is a spectacular laser light show on its Outer Island.

The $12,000\text{ft}^2/1,115\text{m}^2$ main pool is the centre of the summer action with its bar and swim-up blackjack games. There's also a swim-up bar, next to which sliding glass doors partition off a $1,500\text{ft}^2/139\text{m}^2$ heated indoor pool, one of the only indoor pools in Vegas, surrounded by lush tropical garden views. There is also an adults-only lagoon pool and a garden pool, where over 60 varieties of trees, ground cover, foliage and flowers create explosions of colour.

Staying in Henderson

Just a 17ml/27km drive from the Strip, Henderson is a small but important location overlooking the brilliant blue waters of the 320-acre/130-ha manmade Lake Las Vegas. Ultra-romantic settings with wonderful water-based amenities, they're a great place to base yourself if you want to escape the maddening kerchink, kerchink

of slot machines yet be within easy reach of the city's fun-filled attractions.

Ritz-Carlton, Lake Las Vegas

An ultra-romantic, deluxe desert retreat-style resort that is still conveniently close to the hustle and bustle of Las Vegas.
Location: MonteLago Village, 1610 Lake Las Vegas Parkway, Lake Las Vegas Resort, Henderson
Theme: Classic, Tuscan-inspired elegance.
Web: ritzcarlton.com/en/Properties/LakeLasVegas/Default.htm
Reservations: 702 567 4700
Rooms: 348
Room rates: From $129

Ritz-Carlton Lake

Restaurants: Medici Café and Terrace, Firenze Lobby Lounge, Poolside Café and Grill
Nightlife: Firenze Lobby Lounge with live music
Chilling out: Pool and gardens, beach and water activities
Other amenities: The Ritz-Carlton Spa; access to 2 golf courses; fly fishing; gondola rides; 3 wedding chapels; Ritz Kids day sessions; family activities such as nature hikes and sandcastle building on the resort's White Sand Beach

The upper-crust Ritz-Carlton group knows a thing or two about location and the sandy shores of the beautiful Lake Las Vegas don't disappoint, especially if you're looking for an oasis of calm that's just a short ride from the Las Vegas Strip and the delights of Sin City.

Guests can stroll from their rooms over a quaint stone bridge, fashioned after Florence's Ponte Vecchio, to find themselves in an olde worlde area filled with shops, restaurants and the neighbouring Casino Monte Lago. The landscaped grounds provide a series of scenic walkways and cycling trails around the lake's shoreline, or guests can take to the waters in canopied water taxis, sailing boats or kayaks.

BRITTIP

The Ritz Carlton now offers the best of both worlds: a gambling-free environment but with adjoining casino. The separately run Casino Monte Lago sits next to the hotel, adjacent to The Village at Monte Lago, an upscale shopping complex.

A relaxed but elegant Mediterranean ambience is reflected in the arched doorways, clay tile roofs, interior courtyards and the palette of sun-washed colours that are reflective of European waterside towns and lakeside villas. The rooms live up to the high Ritz-Carlton standards and come with top-notch Frette bed linen, oversized marble bathrooms and a casual yet classy decor. Many of the rooms also have private balconies that look over the vine-covered trellises, shaded loggias, water features, white sand beach and heated swimming pool. There are also 35 suites and 2 whopping 2,400ft^2/223m^2 suites.

The fabulous Medici Café and Terrace is set in an incredibly romantic courtyard with pretty Florentine gardens for outdoor dining

El Cortez

and views over the lake. Elegant yet relaxed, you can have breakfast and lunch here, while it turns into a fine-dining experience for dinner.

The luxurious, 30,000ft^2/2,790m^2 Ritz-Carlton Spa is the first spa in America to offer desert- and Tuscan-inspired treatments. It's particularly good for couples, with Massage Mentoring which teaches couples how to massage one another.

Henderson and nearby Boulder City, Nevada are home to several world-class golf clubs and courses, all within just a few minutes of Lake Las Vegas. Highlights include the renowned Cascata, Revere at Anthem and Rio Secco.

Top budget hotels

There are also a host of inexpensive hotels that follow the Las Vegas tradition of cheap hotels, food and drinks to draw the budget-conscious gambler. You will never gush about the rooms, but many have an engaging character sometimes missed in the massive resorts. If you want to experience Las Vegas and want to spend less money on your hotel room and more on the sights and fun, then here are some good places to consider.

El Cortez

Mobbed-up hotel getting a new life.
Location: Fremont Street and North Sixth, one block from Las Vegas Boulevard
Web: elcortezhotelcasino.com
Reservations: 702 385-5200
Rooms: 250
Room rates: From $30

Restaurants: 5 including 2 awesome value options, The Flame Steakhouse and Café Cortez

Many experienced Las Vegas travellers might raise their eyebrows at the inclusion of El Cortez. This was one of Bugsy Siegel's first properties and was long known for its great promotions, cheap lodging and fantastic gambling odds as well as mouldy carpets, smoky and dilapidated rooms and a clientele of wheelchair-bound octogenarians spending their pension cheques. That time is history. A $12m renovation in 2007 to go along with the development of the East Fremont Street Entertainment District has made the old girl into a freshly scrubbed belle of the ball.

The room rates are still wonderfully low, but the rooms are astonishingly comfortable. The Flame Steakhouse and Café Cortez also put out the best cheap food you will ever find anywhere.

The best part is getting rooms in the oldest part of El Cortez. There are no lifts to these rooms, only narrow stairs, but here Bugsy Siegel lorded over his early Las Vegas empire, and it has been said that more than one card shark had his hands broken, or some mob swindler met a bloody end here.

Fitzgerald's

Friendly, reasonably priced hotel in downtown Las Vegas.
Location: Fremont Street
Web: fitzgeraldslasvegas.com
Reservations: 702 388 2400

Rooms: 638
Room rates: From $29
Show: Kevin Burke – *Fitz of Laughter*
Restaurants: 4 including Krispy Kreme Doughnuts

In the centre of the Fremont Street Experience, 'the Fitz' is the tallest building downtown, and if you get the right room you can have a dazzling view of the best of Las Vegas. Try the '$20 upgrade' (see page 27) to get a south-facing corner room on an upper floor.

It has its own 40,000ft²/3,716m² casino, is easy walking to all the downtown activities, is just 2 blocks from 'the Deuce' bus to the Strip, and 3 blocks to the East Fremont Street Entertainment District. Rooms are clean and comfortable, if nothing special. This is also a place very popular with Brit and Aussie tour groups, and after a few days listening to the Yanks mangle the language, you'll be happy to hear a familiar accent.

Palace Station

One of the best-value hotels in Las Vegas.
Location: 115 at West Sahara
Web: palacestation.com
Reservations: 702 367 2411
Rooms: 1,000
Room rates: From $24
Attractions: Live Las Vegas Music at Jack's Irish Pub and Bonkerz Comedy Club
Restaurants: 8 including a raw Oyster Bar
Chilling out: 2 pools and a Jacuzzi
Other facilities: Free shuttle to the airport and the Strip for guests with room keys

Fitzgerald's

Station Casinos own 8 'locals' casinos in the Las Vegas area. They don't particularly cater to tourists, but to local gamblers. This means they offer great deals, and you can get a room at an unbelievable price, plus the brand offers an aggressive marketing campaign of special freebies for customers. I've often stayed for free here; in fact, the most I've ever paid is $12 a night for 2 people. Again, the rooms are nothing to write home about, but the free shuttle to the Strip is a huge boon.

Sahara

Traditional Las Vegas.
Location: The Strip at West Sahara
Theme: African desert oasis
Web: saharavegas.com
Reservations: 702 737 2111
Rooms: 1,700
Room rates: From $25
Restaurants: 6 including the House of Lords Steakhouse and NASCAR Café
Shows: The Platters/Drifters/ Coasters, Magic of Rich Thomas and Comedy Stop
Attractions: NASCAR which includes Cyber Speedway, Pit Pass Arcade, Speed the Ride, MTV's Rocketman
Chilling out: Beautiful pool with cabanas

Sahara is one of the oldest properties on the Strip and it is steeped in history. The likes of Elvis Presley, Dean Martin and Frank Sinatra played here, and it shows on the photos along the walls of Las Vegas in the good old 'mobbed-up days'. The Sahara is a bit tired and run down, with constant rumours of it being sold and either torn down or renovated into a new spectacular. Now it is a smoky, inexpensive place to stay on the Strip.

Coming soon

As the CityCenter development makes its presence felt, it awaits the arrival of the Harmon Hotel in late 2010. Las Vegas's first environmentally friendly boutique hotel, this 400-room contemporary tower is being

The Vdara at CityCenter

Room at the Sahara

hailed as one of the most exclusive boutique hotels in the world. Designed by Foster + Partners, led by the UK's very own Lord Norman Foster, it promises to cause a stir, not least for Isa Genzken's *Rose II* – a stainless steel, aluminium and lacquer single-stem rose frozen in full bloom on its exterior. Highlights also include private butlers, KeSARI spaHair salon by the world-renowned hair stylist Frederic Fekkai and Las Vegas's first MR CHOW restaurant.

The Grand Hyatt Corporation is due to make its Las Vegas debut late 2010 or into 2011, with the opening of the Cosmopolitan, one of the few independently owned, operated and privately financed developments on the Strip.

⚡ BRITTIP

You cannot register at any hotel with a casino if you are under the age of 21 – nor can you gamble if you are under 21.

Owners of the Cosmopolitan, which will be superbly located in the mid-Strip, have taken more than a leaf or two out of the very successful Palm's book and are clearly focusing on attracting a youthful, celeb-driven clientele. Plans include 2 high-rise hotel and condo-hotel towers, providing around 3,000 luxury rooms, suites and condo-hotel residences, a shopping mall, fine-dining restaurants, 1,800-seat theatre, 500-seat cabaret, 50,000ft^2/4,650m^2 spa, salon and fitness centre, and multiple nightclub venues. The Cosmo Beach Club, with its 5acre/2ha pool deck, will not only overlook the Strip, but will offer activities from dawn until dusk.

The urban myth that Vegas is the 'brightest place on earth' is certainly continuing with its many new resorts. The home of safe excess marches on.

|3| SHOWTIME

All the best shows from major productions to adults only

It has long been a Las Vegas basic that if you keep the customers entertained they will happily slap money on to the gaming tables. As the years have passed, the entertainment offerings have grown from scantily clad show girls to headliners like Elvis Presley and Frank Sinatra, and to a modern entertainment scene that rivals, and often surpasses, anything you might find in London, New York or even Los Angeles.

The top shows here are the incredible, mind-boggling, gravity-defying multi-million-dollar Cirque du Soleil® extravaganzas for which auditoriums have been purpose built up and down the Strip. Adding to the already hugely successful *Mystère, O, Zumanity, Kà, Le Rêve* and *Love*, the opening of CityCenter heralds the arrival of *Viva ELVIS*, a new show based on the life and music of Elvis Presley at Aria Resort & Casino, featuring state-of-the-art technology and captivating visuals. What, after all, could be more Vegas than the King?

Stage plays are also the rage in Las Vegas these days. Many resorts have spent lavish amounts on Broadway hits like Andrew Lloyd Webber's *Phantom of the*

Opera, Jersey Boys, The Producers and *Mamma Mia!* and others that play to packed houses. The latest to appear is *The Lion King* at the Mandalay Bay. This is Vegas, though, so there are changes. Most of the plays offered are a shorter version than the originals, in fact *Phantom – The Las Vegas Spectacular* is only 95 minutes long and full of jaw-dropping special effects. Keep them happy but out there gambling, right?

There is a glut of high-profile magicians – think Penn & Teller, Lance Burton and Steve Wyrick. Cirque du Soleil® has teamed up with master illusionist Criss Angel to present *Believe* at the Luxor, which reinvents the traditional magic show. There are more intellectually challenging stand-up acts such as the irrepressible Rita Rudner and a raft of rip-roaringly funny

Classic Las Vegas showgirls

BRITTIP

If you don't mind waiting until the last minute, you can save a lot on show tickets. There are many half-price ticket stands along the Strip and Fremont Street. You can often get tickets for shows at 50% off by buying a ticket on the day from one of these shops. But sorry, this won't do for hard-to-find tickets, so Cirque extravaganzas are rarely available this way.

impersonators like Danny Gans who does everyone from Al Pacino to Kermit the Frog. Terry Fator, winner of NBC's *America's Got Talent* signed a 5-year deal with The Mirage to perform his ventriloquism and impressions of everyone from James Blunt to Marvin Gaye.

Of course, where Las Vegas sets itself apart from the rest with its entertainment blockbusters. Cher and Bette Midler's *The Showgirl Must Go On* packs them in at The Colosseum, Caesars Palace.

If there is a downside to the spectacles and headliners, it is undoubtedly the ticket prices, which have skyrocketed during the last decade. A single ticket will quickly hit the $100 mark and rise steeply to more than $200. So, for something a little kinder on the pocket, make the most of the lounge music scene. Nowhere does it better than Las Vegas. And when you've done all that there is, there are those adult revues. As the city's motto goes: 'What happens in Las Vegas stays in Las Vegas' – unless, of

The new Elvis Theater

course, you take the video camera!

In previous years, some prices included sales tax. Alas, now almost all ticket prices require you to add 7%.

There are other acts that are booked on a 1- or 2-night basis and you can check these out before you go at: visitlasvegas. com (the city's official website with details of all current shows), lasvegas.com (a comprehensive section on shows, comedians, regular local acts and live music venues) and vegas.com (a great place for show tickets). You can visit ticketmaster.com to book more mainstream events.

BRITTIP

Want to know why you pay so much to see some of these Las Vegas shows? It's reported that Cher, the 61-year old singer who claimed she would never perform live again, has signed a deal worth more than £100 million for a 3-year residency at Caesars Palace hotel.

Guide to ratings: ***** **pure brilliance;** **** **fantastic;** *** **a great show;** ** **poor value for money**

Major productions

Viva ELVIS

Aria Resort at CityCenter, 702 590 7757
Open December 2009, this Cirque du Soleil® production pays tribute to Elvis's music and life, fusing dance and acrobatics, live music and iconic tracks, nostalgia and modernity, high technology and raw emotion. In short, the show is in Elvis's image: powerful, sexy, whimsical and truly unique. The creative combination of live musicians and singers, projections, dance and the latest multimedia sound and lighting technology stimulate the senses. If you're a die-hard Elvis fan, you might have to hold back the tears of emotion.
Rating: Unrated, but we expect you won't be disappointed. Blue suede shoes at the ready!
Shows: Not yet available but check out cirquedusoleil.com/en/shows/elvis/show. aspx
Tickets: Currently only released to Cirque members (sign up is free on their website). Range from $89.68–$149.38 for preview performances; regular performances will be $99–$175. There's no news yet on when these will be released for general sale.

Kà

Kà Theater, MGM Grand, 702 891 777, ka.com

The circus-based Canadian performance company Cirque du Soleil® is noted for making visually stunning productions. Las Vegas is its playground and the magnificent *Kà* is the standard bearer for the MGM Grand. Each show has a theme, *Kà* has fire. The main subplot revolves around fire's dual powers both to destroy and create.

Essentially a tale of duality, *Kà* tells the epic story of separated twins who set out on a perilous journey through challenging landscapes, such as a mysterious sea shore, menacing mountains and foreboding forests, to fulfil their shared destinies. What makes it different from all the astonishing acrobatic performances available in other Cirque shows is that this production (a mere snip at $165m!) also incorporates the thrills and action of different martial arts forms from all over the world, plus amazing innovations in puppetry, multimedia and pyrotechnics.

Female archers in *Kà*

Something for nothing

Don't miss the amazing – and free – **Fremont Street Experience** in downtown Las Vegas. In addition to the multi-million dollar electronic light and sound show, which takes place in the enclosed, traffic-free pedestrian mall, the city also provides 5 blocks of street performers and live music. Street performers abound. Live bands usually perform at stages on First Street and Third Street Tues–Sat and the Fremont Street Experience takes place every hour on the hour 7pm–midnight. Call 702 678 5777 for information, visit vegasexperience.com or just head downtown in the evening.

Most spectacular new entrant in the category of free shows is **Azure** at the Mermaid Restaurant & Lounge at the Silverton Hotel & Casino, 702 914 8557, silvertoncasino.com. An underwater fantasy show, all the action takes place inside a 120,000gall/545,530l saltwater aquarium as mermen and mermaids execute innovative choreography among the 4,000 fish and stunning coral. Shows run hourly on the hour Mon–Sun 5–11pm. You will of course have to pay for dinner or at least have drinks at the bar!

You can get into the carnival spirit at the Rio All-Suite Hotel by either watching or taking part in the newly reinvented **Masquerade Show in the Sky** which features dancers in costumes on floats suspended above the crowd. Three different performances include sexy and seductive scenes co-ordinated to popular hits. Free shows hourly 7pm–midnight, Thurs–Sun or you can pay $12.95 to don an exotic costume and ride on one of the main floats. You have to buy the costumes in person at least 1 hour before the show and they do sell out! Call the Rio for more information on 702 252 7776.

Treasure Island's free show is also worth a mention. The **Sirens of TI** re-creates the age-old battle of the sexes between mermaids and pirates nightly at 7, 8.30, 10 and 11.30pm. Viewing is on a first-come, first-served basis, but guests at the hotel get exclusive VIP viewing access.

Other free shows include fiery illusion stunts in **Lumineria** at Caesars Magical Empire, daily 11am–4.30pm, and free **circus acts** in the Main Arena of Circus Circus 11am–midnight every day. At Planet Hollywood's Miracle Mile shops don't miss the free **laser and fountain shows**, and there's even a **rainstorm** outside the Merchants Harbor Coffee House. Then there's the famous **volcano** at The Mirage which erupts every 15 minutes from dusk to midnight, the Bellagio **fountain shows** plus its conservatory and botanical gardens and finally, the **lion habitat** at the MGM Grand.

Rating: ***** Breathtaking stunts that dazzle to the max
Shows: Tues–Sat, 7pm and 9.30pm
Tickets: $69, $99, $125 and $150, all plus tax

LOVE

The Beatles LOVE Theater, Mirage, 702 792 7777, mirage.com
Unveiled in 2007, The Beatles' LOVE™ grew out of a mutual admiration between the late George Harrison and Cirque founder Guy Laliberté. This is a different Cirque show compared to the others in Vegas. Here they have taken the original master recordings from the Abbey Road Studios and, instead of the traditional Cirque acrobatic wonders, have melded a celebration of modern marvels as rollerbladers and skateboarders fly and twist in youthful energy. There are still the dazzling sound and visual effects you would expect of a Cirque display, but mixed with a rawer emotion.
Rating: **** A Beatles Love-fest only Cirque du Soleil® and X-Games could produce
Shows: Thurs–Mon 7pm and 9.30pm
Tickets: $93.50, $99, $125 and $150 plus tax

Mystère

Treasure Island, 702 894 7722, treasureisland.com
The first of the Cirque du Soleil's® Las Vegas marvels, *Mystère* takes you on a journey through time that allows the supreme athletes to show off their strength and extraordinary flexibility with a mesmerising aerial bungee ballet, a precision performance based around Chinese poles and an awe-inspiring trapeze act. This is the most acrobatic of all the Cirque shows,

Africa from *O*

BRITTIP

At all of the Cirque shows, including Dragone's *Le Rêve*, try to be in your seats by 20 minutes before curtain up. There is always a comedic pre-show show as cast members go out into the audience and do humorous bits with unsuspecting victims. Maybe you!

and the most circus-like. It is also truly state-of-the-art theatre. The show originally cost $20m to stage and should definitely be on your must-see list.
Rating: ***** You'll want to go back again and again
Shows: Sat–Wed 7pm and 9.30pm
Tickets: $69, $79, $95, $99, $109 plus tax

O

Bellagio, 702 693 7722, bellagio.com
If you've ever been lucky enough to see the Cirque du Soleil® troupe in action, you'll know what makes these artists so special. The 70-odd cast of dancers, acrobats, actors, clowns, comedians and musicians may represent age-old talents of an old-style circus (without the animals), but that is where any similarities with the past come to an end. *O*, like all the shows performed by the troupe, is a surrealist celebration of trapeze, dance, high-flying acrobatics and humour. In this case though, every act is performed in, on and above water in a $70m theatre that was developed specifically for the Bellagio resort and Cirque du Soleil®.

BRITTIP

If you're trying to decide between *Mystère* and *O*, most people find *Mystère* more accessible. *O*, although brilliant, is more ethereal.

O takes its title from the phonetic spelling of the French word for water – *eau*. The story takes you on a 90-minute voyage through the history of theatre in the trademark Cirque style with daring displays of aerial gymnastics, high-flying trapeze numbers, synchronised swimming, fire-eating, mind-boggling contortions, clowns and high-diving stunts.
Rating: ***** Breathtaking
Shows: Wed–Sun 7.30pm and 10.30pm
Tickets: $93.50, $99, $125 and $150 all plus tax

Provocative and erotic *Zumanity*

Le Rêve

Wynn Theater, Wynn Las Vegas, 702 770 9966, wynnlasvegas.com

Franco Dragone, former creative collaborator with Cirque du Soleil® – responsible for top-selling shows such as *Saltimbaco*, *Mystère* and *La Nouba* – set up his own production company Dragone in 2000.

Now he has returned to Las Vegas to create a world of dreams for another epic at Steve Wynn's Wynn Resort. What sets this work apart is not only the visually stunning performances themselves, but also the design of the theatre, which means that no one sits more than 42ft/13m from the main stage.

BRITTIP

Most big shows have a dinner and show package on offer. For example, *Le Rêve* Taste of Wynn Package offers a saving of $25 on show tickets to *Le Rêve* and a 3-course meal at a choice of 9 restaurants from £29 per person (https://boxoffice.wynnlasvegas.com/packages.html). Check details at the time of booking.

The main aim was to allow people to forget the world as they entered the dream-like realm of the theatre and this is achieved through a set that seems to owe more to the form of a temple than a stage. The dream-like quality is enhanced by a bank of digital windows that change displays from statues to clouds to birds as

effortlessly as the performers execute feats of impossibility (to the ordinary mortal) in front of you. This is, without doubt, the most visually stunning show in Las Vegas.
Rating: ★★★★★ Thrilling perfection
Shows: Thurs–Mon 7pm and 9.30pm
Tickets: $99, $119 and $159 for true luxury of seating in overstuffed chairs with chocolate-dipped strawberries and a bottle of champagne for two, plus tax of course

Zumanity

New York New York, 866 606 7111, nynyhotelcasino.com

Billed as the provocative, erotic, adult side of the Cirque du Soleil®, this show combines the usual amazing Cirque stunts, acrobatics and high-flying – only this time with a sensual, passionate and sometimes raunchy twist. There is also a feel of an old Parisian cabaret here. The cast of 50 performers and musicians blend erotic rhythm with dance with ribald comedy to create a world in which inhibitions are discarded.
Rating: ★★★★★ Sensual and stunning
Shows: Tues, Wed and Fri–Sun 7.30pm and 10.30pm
Tickets: $69, $79, $99 and $135 (per person on a duo sofa) plus tax

BRITTIP

Love birds wanting a romantic night out will adore the love seats and duo sofas that have been specially created in New York-New York's new theatre – custom-built for Cirque's over-18s-only *Zumanity*.

Cher at Caesars Palace

Bette Midler

Colosseum at Caesars Palace, 702 731
7208, caesarspalace.com
Starting in February 2008, the Divine Miss
M has cast her spell over Vegas with her
The Showgirl Must Go On show. Created
exclusively for The Colosseum at Caesars
Palace, the show has plenty of girls, gags
and guffaws and some of Midler's favourite
colourful characters, a 13-piece band and
20 female dancers.
Rating: **** No one belts out the songs
and gags better than Bette
Shows: Every day except Mon and Thurs,
7.30pm
Tickets: $95–250 plus tax

Bette Midler at Caesars Palace

Cher

Colosseum at Caesars Palace, 702 731
7208, caesarspalace.com
Whatever you think about Cher, she
certainly has staying power and has been
a world-famous superstar for over 40 years
selling over 100 million records. Looking
ludicrously young, she delivers her many
hit songs with panache in her trademark
outrageous costumes designed by Bob
Mackie.
Rating: **** Age-defying entertainment
Shows: Every Sat, Sun, Tues and Wed,
with extra days thrown in
Tickets: $95–250 plus tax

Donny & Marie

Flamingo Showroom, Flamingo Las Vegas,
702 733 3333, flamingolasvegas.com
The Osmond family flame still burns bright
with this brother and sister act. This
energetic 90-minute variety show includes
singing (hits such as 'Paper Roses' and
'Puppy Love'), dancing, comedy and the
stars' signature sibling banter.
Rating: *** A must for anyone who grew
up with The Osmonds
Shows: Daily except Sun, 7.30pm
Tickets: $90, $104, $120, $255 plus tax

BRITTIP

To get a better deal on the
major shows, pick up as many of
the visitor magazines as you can and
look through for discount coupons
and two-for-one specials.

Toni Braxton Revealed

Flamingo, 702 733 3333, harrahs.com
International singing sensation and 8-time
Grammy winner Toni Braxton exploded on
to the Vegas scene with her steamy
extravaganza. The music is hot, the dance
and choreography sizzling, the wardrobe
steaming and her unique voice dazzling in
a superb production.
Rating: ***** Hot, hot, hot!
Shows: Every day except Mon and Sun,
7.30pm
Tickets: $69, $89, $109 plus tax

V – The Ultimate Variety Show

V Theater at Miracle Mile at Planet
Hollywood Hotel & Casino, 702 932 1818
This is traditional old Las Vegas
entertainment, like when Dean Martin
would be performing and suddenly Sammy
Davis Jr would show up and perform a few

numbers. There is a core of show entertainers plus a plethora of talented acts who perform elsewhere on the Strip through the week, so no two shows are ever the same. When it first started, the acts were sometimes a hodgepodge, and you could get some real rotten tomatoes in the mix, but over the years the booking has improved so every show includes a breathtaking combination of magic, special effects, death-defying stunts and wild comedy. *V* has become a Las Vegas icon.
Rating: ***** Top-notch entertainment
Shows: Nightly at 7.30 and 8.30pm
Tickets: $66, $77, $97 plus tax

V – The Ultimate Variety Show

Donny and Marie Osmond

this isn't. Throughout the black stage the three 'blue men' explore the world with both child-like innocence and social incompetence. Here, plastic pipes and breakfast cereal are musical instruments and toilet paper is a signal for a riotous party. Children delight in it, even though it is not a 'children's show'. As an adult, you either love this show or hate it; there is no in between.
Rating: **** Delightfully kooky
Shows: 7pm and 10pm nightly
Tickets: $71.50, $93.50 and $121 plus tax

Charo

Riviera Hotel & Casino, 702 794 9433, rivierahotel.com
Larger than life Latino singer Charo returns to the Las Vegas Strip in her new show, *Charo in Concert: A Music Sensation*, debuting at the Riviera Hotel & Casino. The musical variety show features Charo's virtuoso flamenco guitar accompanied by a

The Blue Man Group

Other productions

Blue Man Group

Blue Man Group Theater, Venetian, 702 414 9000, blueman.com
The off-the-wall, off-off-Broadway production, which has been surprising, terrifying and entertaining theatre-goers in New York, Boston and Chicago, has become a Las Vegas staple. Mainstream

full orchestra performing her biggest hits and a cast of world-famous Spanish flamenco dancers.
Rating: *** Loud and very Vegas!
Shows: Wed–Mon 7.30pm
Tickets: $49.95, $59.95, $69.95 plus tax

Human Nature

Imperial Theater, Imperial Palace, 702 794 3261, imperialpalace.com
Smokey Robinson presents Australian quartet Human Nature who offer *The Ultimate Celebration* of Motown with their distinctive harmonies.
Rating: **** If you love Motown, you'll be in heaven
Shows: Daily except Fri, 8pm
Tickets: $49.95, $59.95 plus tax

ICE: Direct from Russia

Versailles Theater, Riviera, 702 794 9433, rivierahotel.com
This is cool entertainment based on the works of the famous Moscow Ice Circus and it brings 42 of Russia's most disciplined and athletic performers to an ice rink in the desert to entertain. Skating on thin blades are clowns, acrobats, animal acts and mimes interspersed with gloriously beautiful and romantic on-ice performances and breathtaking aerial acrobatic displays.
Rating: **** A cool difference to the Las Vegas entertainment scene
Shows: Sat–Thurs 8pm
Tickets: $76.77, $85.86 plus tax

Matsuri

Imperial Theater, Imperial Palace, 702 794 3261, imperialpalace.com
Not quite a Cirque du Soleil® standard production, or a simple musical, *Matsuri* is

ICE

Human Nature is on at the Imperial Palace

Japan's famed 'Muscle Musical' with highly skilled athletic performers that let their muscles do the talking with stunts like the Human Jump Rope, Lion Dance and Foot Drums.
Rating: *** A good high-energy afternoon show
Shows: Daily except Tues, 4pm
Tickets: $49.99, $59.99 plus tax

Master magicians

Criss Angel Believe & Cirque du Soleil®

Luxor 702 352 0197, luxor.com
Hearthrob Angel re-invents the traditional magic show and adds a big helping of gothic fantasy in this partnership with Cirque du Soleil®. Fusing together

BRITTIP

Shows generally last 90 minutes and there are no intervals. You can take drinks into shows in plastic containers.

Great nightlife at the Sahara

revolutionary illusions and mystical artistry with acrobatics, dance, puppetry, music and poetry, there's plenty to keep you riveted.
Rating: **** Something for the rebels out there
Shows: Tues–Sat 7pm and 9.30pm
Tickets: $59, $79, $99, $125, $160

The Magic & Tigers of Rick Thomas

The Sahara, 702 737 2515, saharavegas.com
Along with Dirk Arthur (see page 70), Rick Thomas keeps the spirit of Siegfried & Roy's big cat show alive. Weaving magic, music, dance and exotic animals such as Bengal tigers, it's riveting but not one for animal rights activists.
Rating: *** A cool show if you like big cats on stage
Shows: Tues–Sun 7pm, Sat and Sun 4pm
Tickets: $39.95, $49.95 and $19.95 for 12s and under

Lance Burton, Master Magician

Lance Burton Theater, Monte Carlo, 702 730 7160, monte-carlo.com
Lance Burton has been running for years at the Monte Carlo, where they built a $27million theatre in his honour, and he just keeps going on. Dubbed a World Champion Magician by his fellows, he is the finest magician-entertainer in town. Burton's show involves classic feats of levitation, Houdini-style escapes and mysterious disappearing acts, all done with the flair and pazzazz expected of modern-day magicians. It all starts with the illusion that won him the Grand Prix at the Federation International Society of Magique.

Rating: **** Two hours of awe-inspiring, rib-tickling entertainment
Shows: Tues–Sat 7pm
Tickets: $71.50, $77.55 including tax

Penn & Teller

Calypso Showroom, Rio All-Suite Hotel, 702 777 7776, riolasvegas.com
The famous duo have one of the funniest and most tantalising shows around. They are defiantly proud as they take many traditional magic tricks and expose their secrets to the audience. Then they stun you with a dazzling magical extravaganza, all the while making you hold your sides in pain from the laughter.
Rating: ***** Both riveting and funny
Shows: Sat–Wed 9pm
Tickets: $75, $85 plus tax

Penn & Teller

Scarlett

Mardi Gras Plaza on the third floor of the Riviera, 702 794 9433, rivierahotel.com
Scarlett, accompanied by her Seductive Ladies of Magic, has carved a niche for herself in the male-dominated business of magic. She has mastered some of the most difficult feats performed by Harry Houdini.
Rating: *** Good to see her breaking through the glass ceiling of magic
Shows: Nightly 10pm
Tickets: $44.55, $53.64 plus tax

Steve Wyrick Real Magic

Steve Wyrick Theater, Miracle Mile Shops at Planet Hollywood, 702 777 9974, stevewyricktheatre.com
This no-holds-barred style of magic is certainly a spectacle and will pep up any evening shopping trip to the Miracle Mile! Think Lear Jet 35s and AS 350 helicopters appearing out of thin air.
Rating: **** A fresh addition to the glut of magic in town. Breathtaking
Shows: Sat–Thurs 7pm and 9pm
Tickets: $69.95, $91.95 plus tax

Xtreme Magic starring Dirk Arthur

Tiffany Theater, Tropicana Resort, 702 739 2411, tropicanalv.com
With the departure of Siegfried & Roy, it was only a matter of time before someone

Steve Wyrick

else mixed big cats with magical illusion. In this mesmerising show, beautiful blue-eyed Bengals, African black leopards and a pure white snow tiger appear out of nowhere.
Rating: **** Truly entertaining
Shows: Wed–Mon, 4.10pm and 7pm
Tickets: $31.90, $37.40 plus tax and surcharge

New York-New York after dark

Magical comedy

The Amazing Jonathan

The Harmon Theatre inside Miracle Mile Shops at Planet Hollywood Hotel & Casino, 702 836 0836, harmontheater.com
Two-time winner of the Best Comic Magician of the Year by the World Magic Awards, Jonathan may not be well known to British audiences, but he is famous in America for his razor-sharp wit and bizarre illusions. Dubbed the Freddy Krueger of Comedy, he has his own TV show and has a long string of TV appearances.
Rating: ***** Crazy, wild, hilarious – don't miss it!
Shows: Tues–Sat 9pm
Tickets: $65.95, $76.95, $98.95 plus tax

The Mac King Comedy Magic Show

Comedy Cabaret, Clint Holmes' Theatre, Harrah's Las Vegas, 702 369 5222, harrahs.com
Mac King spent his summer holidays doing a 2-person magic act with fellow college student, the now legendary Lance Burton, before taking his show on the road. Along the way he has made a name for himself as a talented magician with an off-beat, witty twist, and has appeared on shows such as *The World's Wildest Magic, An Evening at the Improv, Penn & Teller's Sin City Spectacular* and *Comic Strip Live.* Surprisingly, discounted tickets are regularly available for his show, and he is a fixture on the *Las Vegas Adviser's* list of Top Ten Las Vegas Values.
Rating: ***** Great fun and excellent-value entertainment
Shows: Tues–Sat 1pm and 3pm
Tickets: $24.95 plus tax

Stand-up comedy

Carrot Top

Luxor, 702 822 6262, luxor.com
Standing up for redheads everywhere, Carrot Top (Scott Thompson) offers a young and energised comedy set using very, very silly visual props.
Rating: **** Loveable!
Shows: Mon, Wed and Sat 8.30pm
Tickets: $49.95 plus tax

David Spade Live

The Venetian Showroom, The Venetian, 702 414 9000, venetian.com
With success on tough shows like *Saturday Night Live,* Spade is best known for his sarcastic sense of humour and cutting one-liners. Spade's stand-up performance runs 75 minutes and features real-life situations that only he can turn into laughs.
Rating: **** A regular guy who'll make you laugh out loud – a lot
Shows: 9pm. Check scheduled dates
Tickets: $65.75, $85.75, $105.75 including tax. A limited number of VIP tickets cost $175.75 with front row seats and an opportunity to meet Spade after the show

Rita Rudner

Harrah's Las Vegas, 702 369 5222, ritafunny.com
It's rare that a woman makes it to the top in Las Vegas without taking her clothes off, yet the multi-talented Rita has done just that. She stands on the stage in a long, classically leggy dress making wry, quirky comments on everything from relationships to family and cleaning women. She was named Las Vegas Comedian of the Year 5 years running. She moved her show from New York-New York to Harrah's Las Vegas, and the shows keep selling out.
Rating: ***** Comedic genius
Shows: Sat, Mon and Wed 8.30pm
Tickets: $54 plus tax

Rita Rudner

George Wallace

Flamingo Showroom, Flamingo Las Vegas, 702 733 3333, flamingolasvegas.com
Wallace began his career as a comedy writer for *The Redd Foxx Show* and made a big splash on *The Big Laugh Off*, one of America's top stand-up competitions. His humour is based on making observations about everyday life – a type of comedy that had been selling out venues all over North America before he arrived in Las Vegas.
Rating: *** Great fun
Shows: Tues–Sat 10pm
Tickets: $39.95 plus tax and fees

Wayne Brady

The Venetian Showroom, The Venetian, 702 414 9000, venetian.com
This all-round performer has modelled himself on the likes of Sammy Davis Jr. He can do improv, imitations (don't miss his version of Prince) and generally hilarious stuff along the way.
Rating: **** An improv master!
Shows: Mon–Thurs 9pm
Tickets: $54, $76, $98 plus tax. VIP tickets cost $164 with front row seats and a chance to meet Wayne after the show

Impressionists

American Superstars

Broadway Showroom, Stratosphere, 702 380 7711, stratospherehotel.com
A celebrity-tribute extravaganza. Here you can see stars such as *Men in Black*'s Will

George Wallace at the Flamingo

Smith strut his stuff Big Willie Style and a full line-up of the Spice Girls, alongside impressionist favourites Madonna and Britney Spears. A Michael Jackson *Tribute To The Legend* is currently running.
Rating: *** Fun, but not as good as Legends, this is for real fans of *Stars in their Eyes*!
Shows: Wed, Fri and Sat 6.30pm and 8.30pm; Sun–Tues 7pm
Tickets: $39.99 plus tax

Terry Fator

Terry Fator Theater, The Mirage, 702 792 7777, mirage.com
Terry Fator, winner of NBC's *America's Got Talent* and The Mirage signed a 5-year deal from March 2009, with an option for an additional 5 years. Talk about rags to riches! The comic impersonator, along with his cast of 7 puppets, combines the art of ventriloquism with celebrity impressions. Fator and his puppets, Cowboy Walter, Emma Taylor and Winston the Impersonating Turtle, effortlessly perform the singing styles of an eclectic group of stars including Elvis, Maroon Five, Nat King Cole, James Blunt and Marvin Gaye.
Rating: ***** So bizarre, it has to be seen to be believed
Shows: Tues–Sat, 7.30pm
Tickets: $59, $79, $99, $129

Check out the Comedy Stop website

Headliner showrooms

Celebrity Room: Bally's, 702 739 4567 for information, times and reservations. Headliners include Liza Minnelli and Penn & Teller.

Circus Maximus: Caesars Palace, 702 731 7333, caesarspalace.com. Recent acts include Huey Lewis and the News; Earth, Wind and Fire and Tony Bennett.

Circus Maximus Showroom: Caesars Palace, 702 731 7333, caesarspalace.com. Judy Garland, Frank Sinatra, Diana Ross and Liberace have all headlined here since the gala opening in 1966. More recent stars include David Copperfield, Liza Minnelli, Julio Iglesias and Celine Dion.

The Colosseum at Caesars Palace: Caesars Palace, 1 888 702 3544, caesarspalace.com. When Celine is not in action, the massive auditorium is used for major headliner shows.

Congo Room: Sahara on the Strip, 702 737 2515, saharavegas.com. The Drifters, the Platters and the Coasters have headlined here.

Grand Garden Arena: MGM Grand on the Strip, 702 891 1111, ticketmaster.com. The biggest venue in Las Vegas regularly hosts major concerts and sporting events. This is where Holyfield met Tyson for their heavyweight champion title clash and where top-notch performers like Sting, Elton John, Bette Midler, Gloria Estefan and Phil Collins play when they're in town. The 16,325-seat venue has also hosted the Professional Bull Riders Championships and national league hockey. Tickets are likely to cost anything from $100.

Hilton Theater: Las Vegas Hilton, 702 732 5755, lvhilton.com. Headliners include Johnny Mathis and Barry Manilow.

Hollywood Theater: MGM Grand, 702 891 7777, mgmgrand.com. The MGM's more intimate venue (a mere 740 seats) is still big enough to attract such names as Tom Jones, David Copperfield and Howie Mandel.

Mandalay Bay Events Center: Mandalay Bay, 702 632 7580, mandalaybay.com. A 12,000-seater which has seen the likes of Beyonce, Bob Dylan and B.B. King perform.

Orleans Showroom: The Orleans, 702 365 7075, orleanscasino.com. Recent headliners include KC and The Sunshine Band and Alice Cooper.

Comedy clubs

Comedy Stop

Congo Room, Sahara Hotel Casino, 702 737 2111, comedystop.com
After 19 years at the Tropicana, Comedy Stop moved to the Sahara in 2009. Featuring 3 of the best comedians on the circuit every week, there's a good chance

Bill Robbins at the Riviera Comedy Club

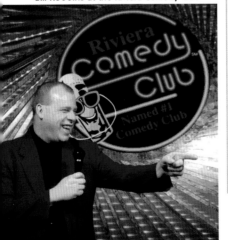

you'll find something that tickles your fancy. Plus, there are always loads of coupons floating around Sin City for a $5 discount off the entrance, which is one reason Comedy Stop is a fixture on the *Las Vegas Advisor*'s Top Ten Value list.
Shows: Nightly at 9pm
Tickets: $24.95 plus tax

Improv Comedy Club

The Improv, Harrah's Las Vegas, 702 369 5223, harrahs.com
Recently voted Best Comedy Club in the *Las Vegas Review Journal* by readers and critics for its stand-up routines by up-and-coming stars of comedy.
Shows: Tues–Sun 8.30pm and 10.30pm
Tickets: $29.05, $44.95 plus tax

Riviera Comedy Club

Mardi Gras Plaza on the first floor of the Riviera , 702 794 9433, rivierahotel.com
A nightly line-up of top stand-up comedians and comedy acts, many of whom have appeared on American TV, in an intimate nightclub setting.
Shows: Nightly at 8.30pm and 10.30pm
Tickets: $24.99 plus tax

Dinner shows

Tony 'n' Tina's Wedding

Planet Hollywood Resort & Casino, 702 949 6450, tonyandtinavegas.com
Having moved from the Rio to Planet Hollywood, a new lease of life has been given to this comedy dinner show which takes you on a romp through a classic American-Italian wedding as Anthony Nunzio Jr marries Valentina Lynne Vitale. The satire begins with the announcement of the wedding, then members of the audience join in the entire event from wedding ceremony to rowdy reception complete with Italian buffet dinner – allowing for plenty of improvisation along the way!
Rating: **** Great fun
Shows: Nightly except Sun, 7pm
Tickets: $54.90, $84.99, $89.99, $140.80 including tax and an Italian buffet dinner

Tournament of Kings

King Arthur's Arena at the Excalibur, 702 597 7600, excalibur.com
Central to this re-creation of a knights' battle are the laser lights, fireworks and clouds of billowing water vapour that give the production an air of mystery and magic. The musical begins when Merlin grants a young boy's wish to be a knight by transporting him back to the Middle Ages and transforming him into the White Knight of Kent. Along the way he meets King Arthur and Queen Guinevere and battles with the treacherous Dark Knight to win a princess's hand in marriage. The trick to seeing this show is to finish off your dinner before you become engulfed in water vapour!
Rating: **** One of the top shows – good for horses, feasts and magic!
Shows: Nightly except Tues, 6pm and 8.30pm
Price: $61.21 plus tax

Dragon Knight at the Tournament of Kings

Afternoon shows

The Mac King Comedy Magic Show. See review and details on page 71.
Matsuri: Japan's famed Muscle Musical. See review and details on page 68.
Xtreme Magic starring Dick Arthur. See review and details on page 70.

Adults only on the Strip

Watch out if you go down to the big theme resorts today, for you're more and more likely to find topless shows in what were once considered family-friendly hotels. Of course, adult shows have always been a facet of Las Vegas entertainment, but never quite so blatantly on the Strip. Is it a reflection of waning interest in traditional shows – unlikely – or just another cleverly disguised attempt to get punters into gambling dens? Your guess is as good as mine, but either way, here they are.

Bite

Theater of the Stars, Stratosphere, 702 380 7711, stratospherehotel.com
A topless revue loosely based around a vampire 'story' of sin, sex and seduction.

BRITTIP

You must be over 21 to see any of these adult shows, with the exception of *Jubilee!* for which you must be over 18. For *Thunder From Down Under* 18–20-year-olds must be accompanied by an adult.

The Lord Vampire, aided by a coven of sultry dancers, goes on a search for the perfect female specimen to make the queen of the night. The story is told through the classic rock songs of the '70s, '80s and '90s. Best shock/surprise of all: members of the audience are chosen to become part of the erotic adventure.
Rating: **** Once bitten, you'll be going back for more!
Shows: Daily except Thurs, 10.30pm
Tickets: $45.45 including tax and tip

Jubilee!

Jubilee Theater, Bally's, 702 967 4567, ballyslv.com
A lavish, 7-act tribute to American music, with topless showgirls and scantily clad guys. From the roaring twenties to the rock 'n' roll era of Elvis, it also features a seductive Samson and Delilah sequence, a

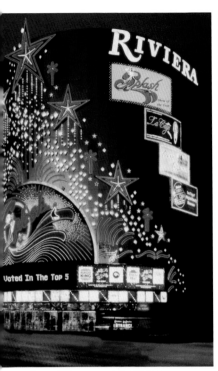

Crazy Girls are on at the Riviera

Rating: **** Lavish, wonderful over-the-top production numbers
Shows: Sat–Sun and Tues–Thurs 7.30pm and 10.30pm; Mon and Wed 7.30pm
Tickets: $52.50, $72.50, $92.50, $112.50

Peepshow

CHI Showroom at Planet Hollywood Las Vegas, 1 800 745 3000, lasvegaspeepshow.com
Peepshow is one of the hottest adult shows in Vegas. A full-throttle production, there are 25 sizzling dancers and performers from the world of pop music, film, television and Broadway. Holly Madison from *E!'s The Girls Next Door* stars, while former Spice Girl Mel B, has been replaced by Broadway actress, Shoshana Bean.
Rating: **** A sexy modern take on showgirls
Shows: Fri–Sat 8pm and 10.30pm; Sun, Mon, Tues and Thurs 9pm
Tickets: $65, $75, $165 plus tax

Showgirls

Crazy Girls Sexiest Topless Revue

The Mardi Gras Pavilion, Riviera Hotel, 702 794 9433, rivierahotel.com
Updated version of the classic topless revue with music, dance, song and comedian Stuart May.

master magician who makes a 26-ft/8-m long helicopter appear, and a spectacular sinking of the *Titanic* in which 2,000galls/9,000l of water flood on to the stage. Just to give you some idea of the scale of its lavishness, more than 1,000 costumes are worn by the cast of 100 dancers and singers, while 70 different sets and backdrops and about 100,000 light bulbs are required to create the enchanting spectacles.

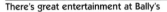

There's great entertainment at Bally's

SHOWTIME

Rating: *** Enjoyable
Shows: Nightly 9.30pm
Tickets: $44.95, $72.50 plus tax

Fantasy

Pharaoh's Theater, Luxor, 702 262 4400,
luxor.com
Featuring singing, dancing and a lot more
besides in an outrageous and provocative
topless revue.
Rating: **** Filled with sexy ladies
Shows: Nightly 10.30pm
Tickets: $45 plus tax

MGM Grand's Crazy Horse Paris

Crazy Horse Paris Theater, MGM Grand,
702 891 7777, mgmgrand.com
Billing itself as a show that 'celebrates
beautiful women and the art of the nude',
all the 12 dancers are members of the
original Crazy Horse dance troupe from
one of the hottest popular nightspots in
Paris. This is the same show that used to be
called La Femme. It has just reverted to the
same name used in Paris.
Rating: *** Classy nudes!
Shows: Wed–Mon 8pm and 10.30pm
Tickets: $50.50, $60.50 including tax and
programme

Girls' night out

American Storm

Variety Theater, Planet Hollywood Hotel &
Casino, 702 932 1818, varietytheater.com
A lot of muscle is on show at this sexy male
revue, voted 'Best Male Strip Show of
2008' by the Las Vegas Review Journal.
Many of the cast members are winners of
VH1's Strip Search reality show and
several have appeared on the cover of
Playgirl.
Rating: *** Good unclean fun
Shows: Fri 10pm and Sat 11.30pm
Tickets: $55 plus tax

Crazy Horse Paris finale

The Chippendales is a great girls' night out

Chippendales – The Show

Club Rio, Rio All-Suite Hotel, 702 777
7776, riolasvegas.com
One of the loudest of the all-male revue
shows, which leaves very little – a floss-thin
G-string – to the imagination. Think
motorcycles, beds and a giant computer
monitor and imagine über-fit men writhing
all over them and you'll build up a good
picture of what's in store. Prepare to get
your best screaming voice ready!
Rating: ***** Polished perfection
Shows: Thurs–Sat 8pm and 10.30pm; Sun–
Wed 8pm
Tickets: $39.95, $49.95 plus tax

BRITTIP

Most shows offers special rates
for group bookings.

Thunder from Down Under

Merlin Theater, Excalibur, 702 597 7600,
excalibur.com
Once a trio of Aussie beefcakes, this
troupe has expanded to a cast of 8
breathtaking hard bodies. However, the
troupe remains one of the best all-male
entertainers in town – largely because they
don't take themselves seriously and
because they like to include members of
the audience in the show. Watch out if you
get pulled on stage, you could find yourself
murmuring 'Oh baby' into a microphone in
your best Meg Ryan-faking-it voice!
Rating: ***** Just ... WOW!
Shows: Sun–Thurs 9pm; Fri–Sat 9pm and
11pm
Tickets: $39.95 or $49.95 plus tax

Booking tickets in advance

By and large you should have no problem getting tickets to see most of the shows, and you can usually buy them in advance by phone or in person at the hotel's theatre box office. Just bear in mind that getting show tickets in Las Vegas depends on the time of year, the day of the week and whether there is a huge convention in town. For details of the best times to visit see The best times to go (page 18). In all cases, phone ahead to confirm show times, dates and prices as these are subject to change without notice. You can find out exactly who will be performing – including the big top-billing stars – during your visit to Las Vegas by visiting the Las Vegas Convention and Visitors' Authority's official website at vegas.com. Many of the major tour operators will also be able to book tickets in advance for the major shows or you can try attraction specialists Keith Prowse (0844 209 0381, keithprowse.com). Most shows are now available through Ticketmaster – just visit ticketmaster.com.

Cinemas

Brenden Theaters

The Palms, 4321 West Flamingo Road, 702 507 4849, brendentheaters.com
A state-of-the-art, 14-theatre cinema complex at this ultra-hip resort-hotel. The brainchild of Johnny Brenden, grandson of the legendary Mann's Chinese Theater developer in Hollywood, LA, it has wall-to-wall curved screens, THX digital sound and stadium seating with comfortable, high-backed rocking chairs, plus love seats.

BRITTIP

The CineVegas Film Festival takes place each June (in 2009 it was held at the Palms Casino Resort and Brenden Theatres). CineVegas combines the excitement of red carpet premieres (such as *Ocean's Thirteen* in 2007 and *The Rocker* and *Get Smart* in 2008) with the glitz and glamour of Vegas. The festival annually presents the best new independent films, documentaries and shorts, as well as parties up and down the famed Las Vegas strip. Great for celeb spotting!

Brenden Theaters has fast become the hottest Cineplex in town and now hosts many film premières with post-première parties at The Palms' Little Buddha restaurant.

Rave Motion Pictures

Town Square 18 Las Vegas, 6587 Las Vegas Boulevard South, 702 362 RAVE, townsquarelasvegas.com
A great choice of popular movies if you need a respite from shopping. Typically over-the-top choice of screens, popcorn and comfort!

United Artists Showcase

Showcase Mall, 3785 Las Vegas Boulevard South, 702 740 4911
Still the only cinema on the Strip, you may have a hard time finding it as it's tucked down the side of the MGM Grand complex next to the parking garage. Parking is free if you keep your cinema ticket for validation.

Bonanza of musicals and plays

There's a growing trend for Broadway shows to be staged at some of the classier theatres. Of course, we get them all in London as well now, but there's a big difference between something being available on our own doorstep – and actually seeing it. Here is a selection of the venues and their offerings at the time of going to press.

A Bronx Tale

Venetian Showroom, 702 414 9000, venetian.com
Academy award nominated actor Chazz Palminteri brings *A Bronx Tale* fresh from Broadway to the Venetian Showroom. This intense (for Vegas) play depicts a young boy's rough childhood in the 1960s-era Bronx and the unforgettable people he encountered. A classic coming-of-age story.

Vegas showgirls

Hot venues

Here are some other venues worth checking out for their edgier vibe.

House of Blues: Mandalay Bay Resort, 702 632 7600, ticketmaster.com
A massive array of acts such as Norah Jones covering everything from gospel to blues, jazz and even country.

The Joint: Hard Rock Hotel, 702 693 5066, hardrockhotel.com
Attracts the likes of Aerosmith, Blondie, Lenny Kravitz and No Doubt and has signed legendary guitarist Carlos Santana as its first rock and roll resident artist.

Mandalay Bay Beach: Mandalay Bay Resort, 702 632 7580, ticketmaster.com
A great location for enjoying acts such as the Doobie Brothers.

The Pearl: The Palms, 866 942 7777, palmspearl.com
The Palms new concert hall seats 2,400 and has state-of-the-art technology for recording live albums. Depeche Mode, Mariah Carey and Kylie Minogue have all played.

Jersey Boys

The Palazzo, The Venetian, 702414 9000, jerseyboysvegas.com
This blockbuster musical takes you inside the lives and music of Frankie Valli and The Four Seasons from the streets of Newark to the Rock and Roll Hall of Fame. Hits include 'Big Girls Don't Cry' and 'Can't Take My Eyes Off You'.

The Lion King

Mandalay Bay Theater, Mandalay Bay, 702 632 4766,
mandalaybay.com/entertainment
It was only a matter of time before *The Lion King* made its way to Vegas. This worldwide phenomenon with spectacular sets, music and costumes takes pride of place at the Mandalay. A great family show.

Menopause the Musical (MTM)

Luxor, 702 262 4400, luxor.com
An international sensation that has landed in Las Vegas. A musical comedy inspired by 'a hot flush and a bottle of wine', it is a celebration of all women over 40 who have survived life.

Phantom – The Las Vegas Spectacular

Paris Opera House, Venetian, 702 414 9000, venetian.com
A lavish production of Andrew Lloyd Webber's classic *Phantom of the Opera* in a dazzling recreation of the Paris Opera House.

Coming soon

The Smith Center for the Performing Arts

702 614 0109, lvapacfoundation.org
Boosting Las Vegas's bid for sophistication, came the groundbreaking Smith Center for the Performing Arts on 26 May 2009. Scheduled to open in 2012, this 4.75-acre/2-ha complex in the Union Park in downtown Vegas, will house the Nevada Ballet Theater and the Las Vegas Philharmonic and become the city's cultural hub. It will foster local talent and feature music, theatre and dance companies from all over the world.

The Lion King

4 SHOPPING

Everything from top designer malls to discount shopping outlets

The wild success of the opening of the Forum Shops gave the business community an epiphany. People come to Las Vegas to spend money – and not just on gambling! Since then, Sin City merchants have outdone themselves in piling on one new shopping experience after another, each new mall and store more wildly successful than the last! In fact, Las Vegas is now an international mecca for high-end merchandise. In past eras, a hot producer would first think about opening a new store in London, or Paris, New York or Los Angeles. No more – it's on to Vegas!

So shopping addicts beware: Las Vegas can do serious damage to your credit cards! According to a Las Vegas Visitor Profile Study, Las Vegas shoppers spent an average of $114.50 per trip, more than twice as much as on sightseeing and show tickets combined. But then the Las Vegas malls do it in such style and with so much 'free entertainment' attached, it's hardly surprising we can't resist. The trend for providing more and more shopping continues and over the last few years so

many major American department stores have opened in the city that it now rivals, and perhaps surpasses, New York and San Francisco for upscale shops.

The explosion of more sophisticated hotels has brought with it even more high end shopping choice – think Chloe, Dolce & Gabbana and Prada with the opening of the Esplanade at Encore, The Shoppes at The Palazzo, Town Square Las Vegas and the incredible array of shopping at CityCenter's Crystals which opened in December 2009.

Major shopping malls: At the top of the pile is the **Fashion Show Mall**, which spent $1b to turn itself into the largest shopping destination on the Strip attracting more than 10 million visitors every year. In keeping with its name, Fashion Show includes an elevated runway for staging events such as fashion shows and special promotions. The title of biggest and best used to belong to the **Forum Shops at Caesars**, which set new standards for shopping malls when it opened in 1992. It's still an excellent shopping destination and remains an attraction in its own right

There are endless retail therapy opportunities

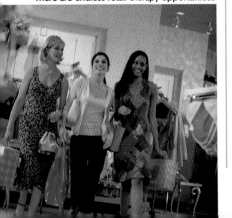

with its Roman décor and wide range of restaurants including Wolfgang Puck's Spago. Other high-end shopping malls can be found at the **Grand Canal Shoppes** at The Venetian. Apart from the Fashion Show Mall, best by far for a rounded shopping experience, with more mid-range shopping, is the **Miracle Mile Shops** at Planet Hollywood. There's also the **Hawaiian Marketplace**.

Discount shopping: Designer junkies got a great shot in the arm with the opening in August 2003 of the **Las Vegas Premium Outlets** right in the heart of downtown. There are many other discount outlet shopping malls, too, including the **factory outlet district**, so it really is possible to leave Las Vegas with your overdraft intact!

Hotel shopping: Each of the major resort-hotels has its own range of shopping opportunities, topped by **Le Boulevard** at Paris Las Vegas, **Mandalay Place** at Mandalay Bay and **Via Bellagio** at the Bellagio.

Off-Strip shopping: If you want to shop like the locals you can find plenty of shops off the Strip too at **The Boulevard Mall**, **The District at Green Valley Ranch**, **The Fashion Outlets of Las Vegas**, **Galleria Mall**, **Las Vegas Outlet Center** and **Meadows Mall**.

BRITTIP

The Las Vegas Convention and Visitors Authority offers visitors a Shop Las Vegas Passport, a collection of vouchers and discounts at major shopping centres and outlets around the city. Download from visitlasvegas.com or call 020 7367 0979.

Crystals at CityCenter

Location: CityCenter lies between Excalibur and the Bellagio on Las Vegas Boulevard
Web: citycenter.com/retail_district/
The story so far: Opening 3 December 2009, CityCenter resort will bring an architectural edge to shopping in Las Vegas. Crystals, a high-end shopping precinct designed by Studio Daniel Libeskind, will offer luxury brands under a crystalline canopy. Opening hours and a full store list hadn't been finalised at the time of going to press but Crystals will cover 500,000ft^2/46,450m^2 and feature Prada, Christian Dior, Louis Vuitton, Tiffany, de Grisogono jewellery and watches, Ermenegildo Zegna menswear, H. Stern jewellery, Marni, Mikimoto pearls, Tom

An artist's impression of the new Crystals

Ford, Mui Mui, Bally, Emilio Pucci, Ilori, Dale Chihuly, Paul Smith and Boutique Tourbillon with an exclusive range of Swatch watches. On the eating and drinking side, there will be a groundbreaking pub by Todd English and 2 new dining concepts by Las Vegas old hand, Wolfgang Puck. The first is a contemporary interpretation of a traditional French brasserie and the second, known as the Wolfgang Puck 'Pods', will be centrally located on the iconic Crystals staircase with dramatic views and serving high quality, light American and Mediterranean cuisine. Actress Eva Longoria Parker is also opening her Beso and Mastro's Ocean Club. It all looks set to be the place to hang out.

Fashion Show Mall

Location: 3200 Las Vegas Boulevard South, at Spring Mountain Road, just north of Treasure Island and opposite the site of the Wynn Resort
Tel: 702 784 7000 (information) or 702 369 8382 (concierge desk)
Web: thefashionshow.com
Open: Mon–Sat 10am–9pm and Sun 11am–7pm
Parking: Underground car park is accessible via Spring Mountain Road and Fashion Show Drive North, then take the escalators to the shopping level, or use the North and South parking decks accessible from Industrial Road West, then follow the signs; there is also complimentary valet parking available at 3 points around the mall

Fashion Show Mall Major Stores

(S) = ATM
(♿) = Disabled Access
(☑) = Escalator
(?) = Information
(□) = Lift
(P) = Parking
(♿) = Restrooms
(☎) = Telephone

Attractions: The only mall in America with 7 major US department stores under one roof: Neiman Marcus, Saks Fifth Avenue, Macy's, Dillard's, Robinsons-May, Bloomingdale's Home and Nordstrum, plus a further 240 shops; plus a live fashion show runway

Cafés and restaurants: The main restaurants include the Spanish Café Ba Ba Reeba!, the Capital Grille Steakhouse, Maggiano's Little Italy and RA Sushi Bar Restaurant; plus a raft of casual dining options include California Pizza Kitchen, Mariposa at Neiman Marcus and Bloomingdale's B-Café

Services: Cashpoints (ATMs) and phone booths, where you can use a pre-paid phone card, are dotted around the mall and there's a foreign currency exchange centre; the Concierge Desk can supply directions, concert tickets and show reservations, multilingual brochures, golf tee times and special event information. Wheelchairs are also available

For those who are serious about shopping, this is the place to come. Following a massive renovation and expansion programme, the Fashion Show Mall doubled in size within a few short years of opening and in the process turned itself into an entertainment experience as well.

Hard to miss is the Cloud structure, which rises 20 storeys above the Strip, and is nearly 500ft/152m long, providing a much-needed shaded area during the day and a giant image projection surface at night. Below it is the 330ft/100m long Media Bank with 4 extraordinarily sized LED screens that are used to broadcast videos and events inside the mall and around the city.

The Great Hall, a 72,000ft²/6,689m²

🇬🇧 BRITTIP

Maggiano's Little Italy restaurant is a dazzling dining room on the second floor of the Fashion Show Mall, with great views of Wynn Las Vegas across the Strip. It also has a pianist in its lounge during dinner.

pedestrian plaza, is home to both the elevated Food Court overlooking the plaza and the Strip, and the $28ft^2/2.6m^2$ stage and $80ft/24m$ retractable runway, which is now used for fashion shows and other events.

Save as you go

Before you start to browse around the shops, join the Premier Shopper Club by going to the Customer Service Center and filling out the form or using the Smart Shopper Pavilion touch screen. Once you have been accepted, you can browse through the website and pick up a startling array of money-saving coupons from the stores. You can also find out about all the latest promotions and activities going on at each of the stores. As a club member, you will automatically be entered into free prize draws simply by swiping your card at the Smart Shopper Pavilion! There are many other bonuses, but most are really aimed at people living in America.

BRITTIP

While Fashion Show Mall closes at 9pm, the main restaurants stay open until around 11pm or midnight, and Café Ba Ba Reeba!'s bar stays open until 2am on Sat and Sun nights.

The show must go on!

There are now 6 major anchors to the mall – the most in any American mall – and it is the only one to have all the main department store brands in one location: Macy's, Dillard's, Nieman Marcus, Nordstrum, Bloomingdale's Home and Saks Fifth Avenue. There are over 240 other shops, too. Here is a rundown of the main beauty boutiques, women's stores, men's stores, shoe shops and electronic outlets.

BRITTIP

Always take a bottle of water with you on a shopping trip – the air con will have you dropping before you finish shopping!

Accessories

Bally of Switzerland: 702 737 1968, wbally.com
Banana Republic: 702 697 2011, bananarepublic.com
BCBG Max Azria: 702 737 0681, bcbg.com
Claire's Boutique: 702 650 9006, claires.com
Cole Haan: 702 731 3522, colehaan.com
Swarovski: 702 732 8161, swarovski.com

The superb Fashion Show Mall

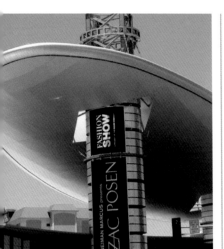

The Cloud at the Fashion Show Mall

Clothes for women

A Pea in the Pod: 702 893 8484, apeainthepod.com
Abercrombie & Fitch: 702 696 6509, abercrombie.com
Abercrombie Kids: 702 3690653
Ann Taylor: 702 734 8614, anntaylor.com
Ann Taylor Loft: 702 731 0351, anntaylorloft.com
Arden B: 702 735 0090, ardenb.com
Banana Republic: 702 697 2011, bananarepublic.com
BCBG Max Azria: 702 737 0681, bcbg.com
Beachworks: 702 737 6930, beachworksshops.com
bebe: 702 892 8083, bebe.com
Betsey Johnson: 702 735 3338, betseyjohnson.com
Caché: 702 731 5548, cache.com
Chico's: 702 791 3661, chicos.com
The Coach Store: 702 759 3451, thecoachstore.com
Diesel: 702 696 1055, diesel.com

BRITTIP
One of the things the Americans do brilliantly is smart-yet-casual outfits at great prices for career women.

Everything But Water: 702 734 7946, everythingbutwater.com
Express: 702 737 8999, expressfashion.com
Fossil: 702 369 3986, fossil.com
Fredericks of Hollywood: 702 893 9001, fredericks.com

French Connection: 702 369 0852, frenchconnection.com
GAP: 702 796 0010, gap.com
Guess: 702 691 2541, guess.com
Hot Cats: 702 796 1870, hotcats.com
J Crew: 702 731 2060, jcrew.com (favoured by Michelle Obama)
Jessica McClintock: 702 733 4003, jessicamcclintock.com
Kate Spade: 702 691 9968, katespade.com.
LaCoste: 702 796 6676, lacoste.com
Lucky Brand: 702 369 4116, luckybrandjeans.com
Paul Frank: 702 369 2010, paulfrank.com
SoHo Collections: 702 732 0430
Talulah G: 702 433 1145, talulahg.com
Tommy Bahama's: 702 731 6868, tommybahama.com
Victoria's Secret: 702 737 1313, victoriassecret.com
Wet Seal: 702 796 0344, wetseal.com
White House: 702 697 0247, whitehouse.com
Zara: 702 733 1113, zara.com

Clothes for men

Abercrombie & Fitch: 702 650 6509, abercrombie.com
Bally of Switzerland: 702 737 1968, bally.com
Banana Republic: 702 697 2011, bananarepublic.com
The Coach Store: 702 759 3451, thecoachstore.com
Cole Haan: 702 731 3522, colehaan.com
Express Men: 702 737 8999, expressfashion.com
French Connection: 702 369 0852, frenchconnection.com
GAP: 702 796 0010, gap.com
Guess: 702 691 2541, guess.com
Harris & Frank: 702 737 7545
Hollister: 702 696 0480 hollisterco.com
Hot Cats: 702 796 1870, hotcats.com

Fossil at the Fashion Show Mall

J Crew: 702 731 2060, jcrew.com
LaCoste: 702 796 6676, lacoste.com
Lucky Brand: 702 369 4116,
luckybrandjeans.com
No Fear: 702 792 3327, nofear.com
Paul Frank: 702 369 2010, paulfrank.com
St Croix Knit: 702 794 4333,
stcroixshop.com
Tommy Bahama's: 702 731 6868,
tommybahama.com
Zara: 702 733 1113, zara.com

Health and beauty

Aveda: 702 733 6660, aveda.com
Bath & Body Works: 702 693 5944,
bathandbodyworks.com
The Body Shop: 702 737 1198,
thebodyshop.com
GNC Live Well: 702 651 9090
H2O Plus: 702 893 1332, h2oplus.com
L'Occitane En Provence: 702 369 1286,
loccitaine.com
Omni Chemists Pharmacy & Drug Store:
702 731 1162
Regis Hair Stylists: 702 733 1400,
regishairstylists.com One of the largest and
most experienced hair salons in the world.
Victoria's Secret Beauty: 702 796 0110,
www2.victoriassecret.com/beauty

BRITTIP

The Fashion Show Mall's Café Ba
Ba Reeba! and the Capital Grille
restaurants became an instant hit
when they opened in 2005. See
Chapter 5 for full reviews.

Evening at the Fashion Show Mall

Even the decorations are amazing

Music and electronics

Brookstone: 702 650 2048,
brookstone.com
EB Games: 702 731 1733, ebgames.com
Futuretronics: 702 387 1818,
futuretronics.com

BRITTIP

Just remember that American
videos are not compatible with
the VHS system used in the UK. DVDs
are only compatible if you have a
multi-region DVD player.

Shoes

Aerosoles: 702 796 4144, aerosoles.com
Aldo: 702 735 5590, aldoshoes.com
Ann Taylor: 702 734 8614, anntaylor.com
Ann Taylor Loft: 702 731 0351,
anntaylorloft.com
Bakers: 702 737 0108, bakersshoes.com
Bally of Switzerland: 702 737 1968,
bally.com
Banana Republic: 702 697 2011,
bananarepublic.com
BCBG Max Azria: 702 737 0681,
bcbg.com
Boot Star: 702 682-0848, boot-star.com
Champs Sports: 702 893 7745,
champssports.com
Clarks England/Bostonian: 702 732 1801
Cole Haan: 702 731 3522, colehaan.com
Easy Spirit: 702 693 4732, easyspirit.com
Footlocker: 702 369 0401, footlocker.com

Guess: 702 691 2541, guess.com
Johnston & Murphy: 702 737 0114, johnstonandmurphy.com
Journeys: 702 732 0130, journeys.com
Lady Foot Locker: 702 735 7030, ladyfootlocker.com
Nine West: 702 693 4128, ninewest.com
Nurielle: 702 733 0693, nurielle.com (J Lo, Carmen Electra and Lil Kim are among many enthusiasts)
Payless Shoe Source: 702 697 0280, payless.com
Puma: 702 892 9988, puma.com
Shiekh Shoes: 702 369 5881, shiekhshoes.com
Skechers: 702 696 9905, skechers.com
Steve Madden: 702 733 2904, stevemadden.com
Wet Seal: 702 796 0344, wetseal.com

Cafés

NM Café: 702 697 7340 Contemporary-style lunch and dinner cuisine in a fashionable yet casual setting. Located on the second level of Neiman Marcus. Open Mon–Sat 11am–6pm and Sun 12pm–5pm.

BRITTIP

The NM Café has a brilliant Happy Hour for Martinis and food, served nightly on the outdoor terrace overlooking the Strip.

Nordstrum Marketplace Café: 702 862 2525 Salads, sandwiches, pastas, pizzas and an assortment of daily specials, plus a wide variety of drinks. On the third level of Nordstrum, you can even order food and drinks to take away.

Restaurants

Cafe Ba Ba Reeba!: 702 258 1211, cafebabareeba.com Serving great Spanish tapas with favourites like paella and sangria on the menu.
California Pizza Kitchen: 702 893 1370, cpk.com Part of one of America's leading casual dining chains, it features a wide variety of pizzas, pastas, salads, soups, sarnies, starters and desserts. Located on the lower level of the West Expansion next to Bloomies.
Maggiano's Little Italy: 702 732 2550, maggianos.com Lavish portions of southern Italian cuisine are served in a vibrant dining environment. Dishes range from homemade pastas to salads, prime steaks, fish and chicken.
Mariposa at Neiman Marcus: 702 731

3636, neimanmarcus.com A fine-dining establishment on the first floor of the upper crust department store. Serving Mediterranean cuisine with French, Italian and Asian infusions, it even has entrances on the Strip and at Spring Mountain Road. Open for lunch Mon–Sat 11am–3pm and for dinner nightly 5.30–10pm (11pm on Fri and Sat).
RA Sushi: 702 696 0008, rasushi.com An upbeat, lively restaurant where the music and the food are as hot as a dollop of wasabi. Japanese fusion cuisine is served here in a sleek and contemporary environment. Additions include a sushi bar, cocktail bar and lounge and upbeat music, with a weekend DJ spinning hot tunes and fresh mixes.

Forum Shops at Caesars

Location: Right next to Caesars Palace
Tel: 702 893 4800
Web: simon.com/mall/directory
Open: Sun–Thurs 10am–11pm, Fri and Sat 10am–midnight; most of the restaurants are open throughout
Parking: Either in the Caesars Palace free covered car park or make use of the valet parking in the underground traffic tunnel at Caesars Boulevard
Attractions: Festival Fountain, Atlantis and the Great Hall shows, plus the aquarium
Cafés and restaurants: Fine-dining outlets include the Palm and Spago, plus BOA Prime Grill and Joe's Seafood, Prime Rib & Stone Crab; casual outlets include the Cheesecake Factory, La Salsa, Planet Hollywood and Sushi Roku
Services: Contact the hotel's concierge desk for wheelchair and buggy rentals and lost and found

The Forum Shops

The malls offer catwalk shows

BRITTIP

All cafés and food outlets are open at the same time as the mall unless otherwise stated.

More than 22 million people – including 6.9 million non-Americans – visited the Forum Shops in 2006. Annual sales average more than $1,600 per ft^2 of retail space, far exceeding America's national average of $300–400.

Heralded as the 'Shopping Wonder of the World', the Forum Shops are so amazing they should be on your must-visit list, even in the unlikely event you don't plan to do any shopping (yeah, right!). It was deliberately built as an entertainment mall and transports people back in time to the great Roman Empire era with architecture, materials and street lighting to match. Even the piazzas and streets are laid out in the traditional format of a Roman town. The entire mall is enclosed, temperature-controlled and covered with a 'sky' that changes throughout the day from a rosy-mauve dawn to high noon, the fading gold of the afternoon, twilight and finally night-time with twinkling stars.

The original $110m complex, which opened in 1992, proved so successful that it was expanded and a further 35 stores

Macy's Las Vegas store

and entertainment outlets opened in 1997. A second extension opened in the summer of 2000, adding another 240,000ft^2/ 22,297m^2 to the existing 533,000ft^2/ 49,517m^2. There are now more than 160 stores.

Fabulous features include a sweeping plaza with replicas of the fountains of Treviano Triton, a massive reflecting pool, dazzling skylight and amazing spiral escalator.

The Festival Fountain undertakes a 7-minute Tale of the Roman Gods show using music, sound effects, animatronics and special scenic projections every 90 minutes from 10am.

At the Great Roman Hall, Atlantis comes to life in a spectacle that has the gods unleashing their wrath on the ancient city. Fire, water, smoke and special effects are used to create a show in which the animatronic characters of Atlas, Gadrius and Alia struggle to rule Atlantis.

Surrounded by a massive saltwater aquarium, the mythical sunken continent rises and falls before your eyes. The Great Hall is surrounded by giant projection screens which, together with lasers and other special effects, help create the illusion that you are genuinely part of the action.

Another free show is the dive into the aquarium for maintenance and feeding, which takes place several times a day. Inside are sharks and schools of coral-reef fish.

Visit the website for all the latest details of the stores.

Accessories

Anthropologie: 702 650 0466, anthropologie.com
Balenciaga: 702 732 1660, balenciaga.com
BCBGMAXAZRIA: 702 699 5498, bcbg.com
Brighton Collectibles: 702 933 1330, brighton.com
Calvin Klein: 702 732 7860, calvinkleininc.com
Christian Lacroix: 702 731 0990, christian-lacroix.com
Coach: 702 651 0363, coach.com
Davante: 702 737 8585, davante.com
Intermix: 702 731 1922, intermixonline.com
Judith Leiber: 702 792 0661, judithleiber.com
Louis Vuitton: 702 732 1227, vuitton.com
Marciano: 702 369 0322, marciano.com
Miss Sixty: 702 732 3548, misssixty.com
Montblanc: 702 732 0569, montblanc.com

The galleries at the Forum Shops

Swatch: 702 734 1904, swatch.com
Tumi: 0800 783 6570, tumi.com
Vilebrequin: 702 894 9460, vilebrequin.com

Clothes for men

7 For All Mankind: 7forallmankind.com
Abercrombie & Fitch: 702 731 0712, abercrombie.com
AIX Armani Exchange: 702 733 1666, armaniexchange.com
American Apparel: 702 369 9192, americanapparelstore.com
Banana Republic: 702 650 5623, banarepublic.com
Bernini: 702 893 7786, bernini.com
BOSS Hugo Boss: 702 696 9444, hugoboss.com
Brooks Brothers: 702 380 3081, brooksbrothers.com
Calvin Klein: 702 732 7860, calvinkleininc.com
Christian Lacroix: 702 731 0990, christianlacroix.com
D & G: 702 732 9292, dolcegabbana.com
Diesel: 702 791 5927, diesel.com
DKNY: 702 650 9670, dkny.com
Dolce & Gabbana: 702 892 0880
Elie Tahari: 702 732 2454, elietahari.com

BRITTIP
Most restaurants have long wait times to be seated, so make a reservation. Or better still, place your name with the maitre'd, and go shopping for an hour!

Emporio Armani: 702 650 5200, emporioarmani.com
Ermengildo Zegna: 702 650 2312, zegna.com
Etro: 702 792 3876, etro.com
GAP: 702 737 1550, gap.com
Gianni Versace: 702 796 7222, versace.com
Guess: 702 727 1816, guess.com
Just Cavalli: 702 893 0389, robertocavalli.net

BRITTIP
Arrive early for the Atlantis shows as the crowds build up early and you'll want a good view of the sunken city.

Lacoste: 702 791 7616, lacoste.com
Lucky Brand Jeans: 702 369 2536, luckybrandjeans.com
Marc Jacobs: 702 369 2007, marcjacobs.com

The entrance to the Forum Shops

The Forum Shops at Caesars
Major Stores

$ = ATM
□ = Lift
P = Parking
⊕ = Restrooms
☎ = Telephone

Michael Kors: 702 869 0010, michaelkors.com
Roberto Cavalli: 702 893 0369, robertocavalli.com
Ted Baker: 702 369 4755, tedbaker.com
Thomas Pink: 702 696 1713, thomaspink.com
Tommy Bahama's: 702 731 6868, tommybahama.com
Versace Jeans Couture: 702 796 7332, versace.com
Vilebrequin: 702 894 9460, vilebrequin.com

Clothes for women

7 For All Mankind: 7forallmankind.com
Abercrombie & Fitch: 702 731 0712, abercrombie.com
Agent Provocateur: 702 696 7174, agentprovocateur.com

Fountain at the Forum Shops

American Apparel: 702 369 9192, americanapparelstore.com
AIX Armani Exchange: 702 733 1666, armaniexchange.com
Ann Taylor: 702 794 0494, ann taylor.com
Anne Fontaine: 702 733 6205, annefontaine.com
Anthropologie: 702 650 0466, anthropologie.com
Banana Republic: 702 650 5623, banarepublic.com
bebe: 702 735 8885, bebe.com
BOSS Hugo Boss: 702 696 9444, hugoboss.com
Calvin Klein: 702 732 7860, calvinklein.com
CH Carolina Herrera: 702 894 5242, carolinaherrera.com
Christian Dior: 702 737 9777, dior.com
D & G: 702 732 9292, dolcegabbana.com
Diesel: 702 791 5927, diesel.com
DKNY: 702 650 9670, dkny.com
Emporio Armani: 702 650 5200, emporioarmani.com
Ermengildo Zegna: 702 369 5458, zegna.com
Escada: 702 791 2300, escada.com
GAP: 702 737 1550, gap.com
Gianni Versace: 702 796 7222, versace.com
Intermix: 702 731 1922, intermixonline.com
Juicy Couture: 702 365 5600, juicycouture.com
Just Cavalli: 702 893 0389, robertocavalli.net
Lacoste: 702 791 7616, lacoste.com

Lucky Brand Jeans: 702 369 2536,
luckybrandjeans.com
Marc Jacobs: 702 369 2007,
marcjacobs.com
Marciano: 702 369 0322, marciano.com
Miss Sixty: 702 732 3548, misssixty.com
Nanette Lepore: 702 893 9704,
nanettelepore.com
Shanghai Tang: 702 255 9090,
shanghaitang.com
St John: 702 893 0044, stjohnknits.com
Tadashi: 702 733 6071,
tadashicollection.com
Ted Baker: 702 369 4755,
tedbakercollection.com
Thomas Pink: 702 696 1713,
thomaspink.com
Tommy Bahama's: 702 731 6868,
tommybahama.com
Valentino: 702 737 7603, valentino.com
Versace Jeans Couture: 702 796 7332,
versace.com
Victoria's Secret: 702 765 5425,
victoriassecret.com

Health and beauty

Anthropologie: 702 650 0466,
anthropologie.com
Bath & Body Works: 702 796 4902,
bathandbodyworks.com
Estee Lauder: 702 737 9011,
esteelauder.com
Fresh: 702 631 5000, fresh.com
Kiehl's: 702 784 0025, kiehls.com
MAC Cosmetics: maccosmetics.com
Oro Gold: 702 369 0752,
orogoldcosmetics.com
Perfumes Christian Dior: 702 369 6072,
dior.com
Victoria's Secret: 702 765 5435,
victoriassecret.com

Jewellery

Bvlgari: 702 734 2001, bulgari.com
Cartier: 702 418 3904, cartier.com
Chopard: 702 862 4440, chopard.com
David Yurman: 702 862 4440,
davidyurman.com
De Beers: 702 650 9559, debeers.com
Fred Paris: 702 650 0090, fred.com
Harry Winston: 702 933 7370,
harrywinston.com
Hyde Park: 702 794 3541,
hydeparkjewelers.com
Intermix: 702 731 1922,
intermixonline.com
Judith Ripka: 702 792 5900,
judithripka.com
Michal Negrin: 702 737 1735,
michalnegrin.com

Montblanc: 702 732 0569,
montblanc.com
Swarovski Crystal: swarovski.com
Swatch: 702 734 1093, swatch.com
Tiffany & Co: 702 644 3065, tiffany.com
Tourneau: 702 732 8463, tourneau.com
Vicci: 702 734 3008, vicci.com

Music and electronics

Apple Computer: 702 684 8800,
store.apple.com
Sony Style: 702 697 5420, sonystyle.com

Shoes

a. testoni: 702 735 7732, testoniusa.com
Bally: 702 893 7718, bally.com
BCBGMAXAZRIA: 702 699 5498,
bcbg.com
Donald J. Pliner: 702 796 0900,
donaldjpliner.com
Giuseppe Zanotti: 702 866 0055,
giuseppezanotti.com
Jimmy Choo: 702 691 2097,
jimmychoo.com
Louis Vuitton: 702 732 1227, vuitton.com
Moda Scapa: 702 696 9786,
salvatory.com
Shoooz at the Forum: 702 734 7600,
shoooz.com
Stuart Weitzman: 702 369 9222,
stuartweitzman.com
Taryn Rose: tarynrose.com
The Walking Company: 702 792 8400,
thewalkingcompany.com

Boulevard entrance at Caesars Palace

Speciality shops

Antiquities: 702 792 2274, antiquities.com
The Art of Peter Max: 702 644 7070, petermax.com
Burberry: 702 731 0650, burberry.com
Caesars: 702 731 7851
Christian Dior: 702 737 9777, dior.com
Chrome Hearts: 702 893 9959, chromehearts.com
Coach: 702 651 0363, coach.com
Custo Barcelona: 702 893 0015, custo-barcelona.com
Davante: 702 737 8585, davante.com
Elie Tahari: 702 732 2454, elietahari.com
Emilio Pucci: 702 735 7731, emiliopucci.com
Fabergé: faberge.com
Fendi: 702 893 2616, eluxury.com
Field of Dreams: 702 792 8233, fieldofdreams.com
Galleria di Sorrento: 702 369 2085, gdsorrento.com
Georg Jensen: 702 369 2424, georgjensen.com
Gucci: 702 369 7333, gucci.com
Houdini's Magic Shop: 702 866 0010, houdini.com
Ice Accessories: 702 696 9700, iceaccessories.com
Jay Strongwater: 702 732 4448, jaystrongwater.com
Judith Leiber: 702 792 0661, judithleiber.com
La Perla: 702 732 9820, laperla.com
Longchamp: longchamp.com
Louis Vuitton: 702 732 1227, vuitton.com
Michael Kors: 702 869 0010, michaelkors.com
Montblanc: 702 732 0569, montblanc.com
Niketown: 702 650 8888, nike.com
Planet Hollywood Superstore: 702 369 6001, planethollywood.com
Playboy: 702 851 7470, playboy.com
Roman Times: 702 733 8687
Saint Andrews Golf Shop: 702 837 1234, saintandrewsgolfshop.com

Scoop NYC: 702 734 0026, scoopnyc.com
Tod's: 702 792 1422, tods.com
Tumi: 0800 783 6570, tumi.com
West of Santa Fe: 702 737 1993, westofsantafe.com

Stationery, cards, books and gifts

Anthropologie: 702 650 0466, anthropologie.com
Essentials at The Forum: 702 866 1207
Forum Gifts & Sundries: 702 734 0678
Magnet Maximus: 702 369 0195
Montblanc: 702 732 0569, montblanc.com

Toys and games

FAO Schwarz: 702 796 6500, faoschwarz.com

Cafés

Cafe Della Spiga: 702 731 7110
Café Expresso: 702 893 4045

Restaurants

BOA Prime Grill: 702 733 7373, boasteak.com
Cheesecake Factory: 702 792 6888, cheesecake-factory.net
Il Mulino New York: 702 492 6000, ilmulinonewyork.com
Joe's Seafood, Prime Steak & Stone Crab: 702 792 9222, joes.net
La Salsa: 702 735 8226, lasalsa.com
The Palm Las Vegas: 702 732 7256, thepalm.com
Planet Hollywood: 702 791 7827, planethollywood.com
Spago: 702 369 6300, wolfgangpuck.com
Sushi Roku: 702 733 7373, sushiroku.com
Trevi Italian Restaurant: 702 735 4663, trevi-italian.com

Miracle Mile Shops

Location: Wrapped around Planet Hollywood Resort & Casino with entrances on the Strip and Harmon Avenue
Tel: 702 866 0703
Web: miraclemileshopslv.com
Open: Sun–Thurs 10am–11pm; Fri and Sat 10am–midnight
Parking: Free parking available at Planet Hollywood
Attractions: Rainstorm in Merchant's Harbor every hour on the hour Mon–Thurs and every half hour on Fri and Sat; plus live entertainment from musicians in the courtyards

Fountains at Caesars Palace

Miracle Mile shops

terrifying 'Death Drop' escape performed by Daredevil Magician Steve Wyrick. Just your average shop launch in Sin City!

Clothes and accessories for women

Alpaca Imports: 702 862 8297, alpacapetes.com
American Apparel: 702 691 2506, americanapparel.net
Ann Taylor Loft: 702 732 3348, anntaylorloft.com
BCBG Max Azria: 702 735 2947, bcbg.com
bebe: 702 892 0406, bebe.com
Bebe Sport: 702 733 8999, bebe.com
Ben Sherman: 702 688 4227, bensherman.com
Betsey Johnson: 702 731 0286, betseyjohnson.com
Bettie Page: 702 636 1100, bettiepage.com
Bikini Bay: 702 699 5597
Caché: 702 699 5448, cache.com
Carlo Ferre Leather Collection: 702 450 9777
Champs Sports: 702 693 6996, champssports.com
Chico's: 702 732 2816, chicos.com
Club Tatto: 702 363 2582, clubtattoo.com Tattoo and body piercing.
Crazy Shirts: 702 893 7780, crazyshirts.com
DC Shoes: 702 369 2730, dcshoes.com
Foot Locker: 702 733 4942, footlocker.com
Frederick's of Hollywood: 702 731 9360, fredericks.com
French Connection: 702 733 6420, frenchconnection.com
Front Row Sports: 702 369 8158, fronrtrowsports.com

Cafés and restaurants: Fine-dining outlets include Lombardi's Romagna Mia and Pampas Churrascaria Brazilian Grill; the casual options are Aroma D'Italia, Blondies Sports Bar & Grill, La Salsa Cantina, Merchant's and Todai Sushi Bar. Trader Vics has now been replaced by the rockin' Cabo Wabo Cantina restaurant and nightclub, owned by rock legend Sammy Hagar – all very in keeping with the Planet Hollywood ethos. Think tacos, tequila and tunes

Miracle Mile invites you to 'shop the planet'. And with an incredible array of shops, you do feel like you're on some incredible shopping planet. You'd never know this was once the Desert Passage under the old Aladdin. What was once a façade of a Moroccan shopping fantasy has been completely ripped away as part of a $100m make-over to the new Miracle Mile Shops. The exterior 1001 Arabian Nights theme was taken down in 2007, replaced by the new Rodeo Drive hipness of the Miracle Mile Shops. Now it's all tall windows and floor-to-ceiling heavy glass doors with brushed steel accents, and flat-screen monitors offering directions and advertisements. Don't miss the free laser show and fountain show at the heart of Miracle Mile shops with its water effects, colour-changing fog and dramatic soundtrack. There's even a rainstorm outside Merchant's Harbor Coffee House!

This is the place that's seen shop after trendy shop opening in true Vegas style. Chester Bennington, co-owner of the new Club Tatoo and Linkin Park band member, held an autograph-signing session plus an acoustic performance with his new side project Dead by Sunrise, and hosted a

Miracle Mile shops

Swarovski at the Miracle Mile

GAP: 702 862 4042, gap.com
GapBody: 702 862 4042, gap.com
Guess by Marciano: 702 650 9928,
marciano.com
H&M: 702 369 1195, hm.com
Herve Leger: 702 732 4529,
herveleger.com
Lucky Brand Jeans: 702 733 6613,
luckybrandjeans.com
Marshall Rousso: 702 733 0611,
marshallretailgroup.com
Max Studio: 702 732 2592,
maxstudio.com
Metropark: 702 650 7200,
metroparkusa.com
Mimi Mango: 702 650 2295, bikini-
bay.com/mimimango
Napoleon: 702 733 6005,
napoleonfashions.com
Parallel: 702 732 4489, bdbg.com
Rock & Roll Religion: 702 836 9990
Roxy: 702 731 1521, roxy.com
Scat: 702 734 7228
Sisley: 702 733 3083, sisley.com
Stash Womens: 702 794 0003,
stashclothing.com
Tommy Bahama: 702 731 3988,
tommybahama.com
True Religion Brand Jeans: 702 893 2340,
truereligionbrandjeans.com
United Colors of Benetton: 702 731
2317, benetton.com
Urban Outfitters: 702 735 0058,
urbanoutfitters.com
Vegas Royalty: 702 731 1956
Victoria's Secret: 702 735 3174,
victoriassecret.com
Volcom: 702 369 2340, volcom.com

West Coast Wraps: 702 731 1805
White House/Black Market: 702 732
2562, whiteandblack.com

Clothes and accessories for men

Alpaca Imports: 702 862 8297
alpacapetes .com
American Apparel: 702 691 2506,
americanapparel.net
Ben Sherman: 702 688 4227
bensherman.com
Carlo Ferre Leather Collection: 702 450
9777
Champs Sports: 702 693 6996,
champssports.com
Club Tatto: 702 363 2582, clubtattoo.com
Tattoo and body piercing
Crazy Shirts: 702 893 7780,
crazyshirts.com
DC Shoes: 702 369 2730, dcshoes.com
Foot Locker: 702 733 4942,
footlocker.com
French Connection: 702 733 6420,
frenchconnection.com
Front Row Sports: 702 369 8158,
frontrowsports.com
GAP: 702 862 4042, gap.com
GapBody: 702 862 4042, gap.com
H&M: 702 369 1195, hm.com
Lucky Brand Jeans: 702 733 6613,
luckybrandjeans.com
Metropark: 702 650 7200,
metroparkusa.com
Napoleon: 702 733-6005,
napoleonfashions .com
Quiksilver: 702 731 1521, quiksilver.com
Rock & Roll Religion: 702 836 9990
Scat: 702 734 7228
Shaunz: 702 792 5255, shaunz.com
Sisley: 702 733 3083, sisley.com
Stash Men's: 702 893 0010,
stashclothing.com
Tommy Bahama: 702 731 3988.
tommybahama.com

Shoppers at the Miracle Mile

True Religion Brand Jeans: 702 893 2340, truereligionbrandjeans.com
United Colors of Benetton: 702 731 2317, benetton.com
Urban Outfitters: 702 735 0058, urbanoutfitters.com
Vegas Royalty: 702 731 1956
Vercini: 702 369 5951
Volcom: 702 369 2340, volcom.com

Besides shopping, Miracle Mile is host to the Variety Theater, which means it is one of Las Vegas's entertainment hot spots. The performance line-up is tantalising, including *After the Show*, where artists try out their material from comedy to acrobatic, *Amazed* magic show, *American Storm* strip show, *Fab Four Live* Beatles act, Marc Savard's *Mesmerized*, *Popovich Comedy Pet Theater*, *Sin City Comedy*, *Stripper 101*, *The Mentalist* and *V – The Ultimate Variety Show*.

Just a few steps away are the entertainment options of Planet Hollywood, which includes *Amazing Jonathan*, *Hitzville* and *Tickled Pink*. This makes Miracle Mile a great way to spend a day shopping, eating, taking in a show followed by some late-night dancing or gambling.

The Shoppes at The Palazzo

Location: 3327 Las Vegas Boulevard, South
Tel: 702 414 4525
Web: theshoppesatthepalazzo.com
Open: Sun–Thurs 10am–11pm; Fri–Sat 10am–midnight
Parking: An underground self-parking site is available under the Palazzo with elevators and escalators that arrive at the centre of the casino. Alternatively, you can use the 24-hour complimentary valet parking available at the front of the Palazzo Hotel Casino
Cafés and restaurants: Restaurants are headed up by some of the world's most famous celebrity chefs and include Wolfgang Puck's Cut and Emeril Lagasse's Table 10

Anchored by a flagship, 85,000ft²/ 7,897m² Barneys New York, The Shoppes at The Palazzo offers more than 60 luxury boutiques. In addition to Barneys New York, 20 stores and luxury brands have made their Las Vegas debuts at The Palazzo. They include Chloe, Tory Burch, Christian Louboutin, Diane Von Furstenberg, Van Cleef & Arpels, Catherine Malandrino, Anya Hindmarch, Michael Kors, Ralph Lauren, Jimmy Choo, Piaget,

Burberry, Salvatore Ferragamo, Fendi, Bottega Veneta and Montblanc. Elton's men's store was named 2008 Best Retailer of the Year for Best Contemporary Store in the United States by *MR Magazine*, the industry's leading publication for men's retail. Worth checking out!

Accessories for men and women

7 For All Mankind: 702 369 0570, 7forallmankind.com
Anya Hindmarch: 702 566 8900, anyahindmarch.com
Bellusso: 702 650 2988, rolexreferencepage.com/travel/25_files/vegas1.html
Bottega Veneta: 702 369 0747, bottegaveneta.com
Burberry: 702 382 1911, burberry.com
Canali: 702 862 4447, canali.it
Canturi Jewels: 702 851 1555, canturi.com
Catherine Malandrino: 702 369 7300, catherinemalandrino.com
Charriol: 702 699 7155, charriolusa.com
Chloé: 702 266 8122, chloe.com
Christian Louboutin: 702 818 1650, christianlouboutin.com
Coach: 702 547 1772, coach.com
Cole Haan: 702 369 2381, colehaan.com
Diane von Furstenberg: 702 818 2294, dvf.com
Fendi: 702 369 0587, fendi.com
Links of London: 702 733 4065, linksoflondon.com
Mezlan: 702 893 6116, mezlanshoes.com
Michael Kors: 702 731 2510, michaelkors.com
Montblanc: 702 696 0185, montblanc.com
Optica: 702 699 9678, optica.co.nz

The Shoppes at The Palazzo

Piaget: 702 418 3033, piaget.com
Piazza Sempione: 702 650 3137,
piazzasempione.com
Poleci: 702 835 1246, poleci.com
Prosecco: 702 607 3956,
lvtsg.com/news/publish/Fashion/article_2
4195.shtml
Ralph Lauren: 702 650 5656,
ralphlauren.com
Salvatore Ferragamo: 702 369 0251,
salvatoreferragamo.com
Scene: 702 696 9528
Tory Burch: 702 369 0541, toryburch.com
Van Cleef & Arpels: 702 696 7139,
vancleefarpels.com
Victoria's Secret: 702 696 0110,
victoriassecret.com

Clothes for women

7 For All Mankind: 702 369 0570,
7forallmankind.com
Annie Creamcheese Designer Vintage: 702
452 9600, anniecreamcheese.com
Bottega Veneta: 702 369 0747,
bottegaveneta.com
Burberry: 702 382 1911, burberry.com
Catherine Malandrino: 702 369 7300,
catherinemalandrino.com
Chloé: 702 266 8122, chloe.com
Claudio Milano: 702 733 8837,
claudiomilano.com
Cole Haan: 702 369 2381, colehaan.com
Diane von Furstenberg: 702 818 2294,
dvf.com
Fendi: 702 369 0587, fendi.com
MaxMara: 702 948 8400,
maxmarafashiongroup.com
Michael Kors: 702 731 2510,
michaelkors.com
Piazza Sempione: 702 650 3137,
piazzasempione.com
Poleci: 702 835 1246, poleci.com

Jimmy Choo at the Palazzo

Ralph Lauren: 702 650 5656,
ralphlauren.com
Salvatore Ferragamo: 702 369 0251,
salvatoreferragamo.com
Thomas Pink: 702 369 2469,
thomaspink.com
Tory Burch: 702 369 0541, toryburch.com
Victoria's Secret: 702 696 0110,
victoriassecret.com

Clothes for men

7 For All Mankind: 702 369 0570,
7forallmankind.com
Andrew's Ties: 702 242 4506,
andrewstiesusa.com
Billionaire Italian Couture: 702 765 5551,
billionairecouture.com
Bottega Veneta: 702 369 0747,
bottegaveneta.com
Burberry: 702 382 1911, burberry.com
Canali: 702 862 4447, canali.it
Catherine Malandrino: 702 369 7300,
catherinemalandrino.com
Cole Haan: 702 369 2381, colehaan.com
Fendi: 702 369 0587, fendi.com
Mezlan: 702 893 6116, mezlanshoes.com
Ralph Lauren: 702 650 5656,
ralphlauren.com
Salvatore Ferragamo: 702 369 0251,
salvatoreferragamo.com
Thomas Pink: 702 369 2469,
thomaspink.com

Clothes for kids

7 For All Mankind: 702 369 0570,
7forallmankind.com
Burberry: 702 382 1911, burberry.com
Cole Haan: 702 369 2381, colehaan.com
Ralph Lauren: 702 650 5656,
ralphlauren.com

Shoes

Bottega Veneta: 702 369 0747,
bottegaveneta.com
Burberry: 702 382 1911, burberry.com
Catherine Malandrino: 702 369 7300,
catherinemalandrino.com
Christian Louboutin: 702 818 1650,
christianlouboutin.com
Coach: 702 547 1772, coach.com
Cole Haan: 702 369 2381, colehaan.com
Jimmy Choo: 702 733 1802,
jimmychoo.com
Mezlan: 702 893 6116, mezlanshoes.com
Michael Kors: 702 731 2510,
michaelkors.com

Department

Barneys New York: 702 629 4200,
barneys.com

Homewares and home

Catherine Malandrino: 702 369 7300, catherinemalandrino.com

Cafés and restaurants

Café Presse: 702 607 0730
Double Helix Bar: 702 735 9463, doublehelixwine.com
FIRST Food Bar: 702 607 3478, www.palazzolasvegas.com/first.aspx
SUSHI SAMBA by chef Jose Mendin: 702 607 0700, sushisamba.com
Table 10 by Emeril Lagasse: 702 607 6363, emerils.com
Woo By Ming See Woo and Peter Woo: 702 607 0740, woorestaurant.com

Town Square Las Vegas

Location: 6605 Las Vegas Boulevard, South
Tel: 702 269 5000
Web: townsquarelasvegas.com
Open: Mon–Thurs 10am–9.30pm; Fri and Sat 10am–10pm; Sun 11am–8pm
Parking: Town Square has 5,800 parking spaces available in 3 different parking garages or sidewalk parking. It also offers valet parking
Attractions: Rave Motion Pictures Cinema, Children's Park at Town Square, Town Square Park
Cafés and restaurants: 13 great places to drink, snack or dine

This is definitely a place where you'll rub shoulders with Las Vegans and their kids! Town Square Las Vegas is an open-air centre featuring 22 buildings detailing a collage of Old World and contemporary architectural styles, along with pedestrian-friendly streets and lushly landscaped walkways. As well as having a great range of shops, unusually it has a fabulous Children's Park with superb attractions like a 42-ft/13-m tree house in a live oak tree that features a rock wall and a fort. There's a Princess Tower, a Bakery Café Playhouse, Hedge Maze, merry go round and even a children's theatre. A rare find, in a city now geared mostly for adults. Next door, is the equally family friendly Town Square Park with a picnic area, bridge and water fountain and pavilion for concerts and fashion shows. As for the shopping, there are more than 150 retail stores including H&M, Abercrombie & Fitch, Juicy Couture, Lucky Brand Jeans, bebe, Robb & Stucky and more, plus a great range of kids' clothes shops.

Clothes and accessories for women

Abercrombie & Fitch: 702 270 2889, abercrombie.com
Aeropostale: 702 914 9311, aeropostale.com
American Eagle Outfitters: 702 260 0486, ae.com
Ann Taylor: 702 270 0692, anntaylor.com
AX Armani Exchange: 702 2633393, armaniexchange.com
Banana Republic: 702 260 0551, bananarepublic.com
BCBGMAXAZRIA: 702 616 2249, bcbg.com
Beachworks: 702 270 8612, beachworksshops.com
bebe: 702 260 6274, bebe.com
bebe sport: 702 260 4283, bebe.com
Cache: 702 256 0100, cache.com
Chico's: 702 361 4904, chicos.com
Concrete Jungle: 702 492 0100, concretejungleclothing.com
English Laundry: 702 794 3070, englishlaundry.com
Express: 702 270 6479, expressfashion.com
Finish Line: 702 263 6023, finishline.com
GAP: 702 361 2447, gap.com
GUESS by Marciano: 702 617 3489, guess.com
H&M: 702 260 1481, hm.com
Hollister Co.: 702 260 4591, hollisterco.com
J. Crew: 702 263 8950, jcrew.com
Juicy Couture: 702 269 3199, juicycouture.com
LeSportsac: 702 260 9106, lesportsac.com
Lucky Brand Jeans: 702 614 5260, luckybrandjeans.com
Lucy: 702 260 0574, lucy.com
Marciano: 702 269 8601, marciano.com
Martin + Osa: 702 260 4775, martinandosa.com
New York & Company: 702 260 0532, nyandcompany.com
Next: 702 256 6398, next.co.uk

Town Square

Old Navy: 702 361 7479, oldnavy.gap.com
Pacsun: 702 260 8237, shop.pacsun.com
Puma: 702 759 0435, puma.com
Roxy: 702 260 1741, roxy.com
Soma Intimates: 702 270 0168, soma.com
Tommy Bahama's Emporium: 702 948 6828, tommybahama.com
Victoria's Secret: 702 270 0088, victoriassecret.com
White House/Black Market: 702 269 3043, whitehouseblackmarket.com
Zumiez: 702 260 1887, zumiez.com

Clothes for men

Abercrombie & Fitch: 702 270 2889, abercrombie.com
Aeropostale: 702 914 9311, aeropostale.com
American Eagle Outfitters: 702 260 0486, ae.com
AX Armani Exchange: 702 2633393, armaniexchange.com
Banana Republic: 702 260 0551, bananarepublic.com
Beachworks: 702 270 8612, beachworksshops.com
Concrete Jungle: 702 492 0100, concretejungleclothing.com
Eddie Bauer: 702 492 4791, eddiebauer.com
English Laundry: 702 794 3070, englishlaundry.com
Express: 702 270 6479, expressfashion.com
Finish Line: 702 263 6023, finishline.com
GAP: 702 361 2447, gap.com
GUESS by Marciano: 702 617 3489, guess.com
H&M: 702 260 1481, hm.com
Hollister Co.: 702 260 4591, hollisterco.com
J. Crew: 702 263 8950, jcrew.com
Lucky Brand Jeans: 702 614 5260, luckybrandjeans.com

Town Square at night

Martin + Osa: 702 260 4775, martinandosa.com
Next: 702 256 6398, next.co.uk
Old Navy: 702 361 7479, oldnavy.gap.com
Pacsun: 702 260 8237, shop.pacsun.com
Puma: 702 759 0435, puma.com
Quiksilver: 702 260 8773, quiksilver.com
Tommy Bahama's Emporium: 702 948 6828, tommybahama.com
Zumiez: 702 260 1887, zumiez.com

Clothes for kids

abercrombie: 702 260 7693, abercrombiekids.com
Finish Line: 702 263 6023, finishline.com
Gymboree: 702 740 7000, gymboree.com
H&M: 702 260 1481, hm.com
Juicy Couture: 702 269 3199, juicycouture.com
Justice: 702 263 3860, justiceclothing.com
Lucky Brand Jeans: 702 614 5260, luckybrandjeans.com
Old Navy: 702 361 7479, oldnavy.gap.com
Quiksilver: 702 260 8773, quiksilver.com
Tommy Hilfiger Childrenswear: 702 361 3773, tommyhilfiger.com

Shoes

ALDO: 702 269 6173, aldoshoes.com
Clarks: 702 617 4674, clarksoriginals.com
Finish Line: 702 263 6023, finishline.com
Journeys: 702 269 7236, journeys.com
Puma: 702 759 0435, puma.com
Quiksilver: 702 260 8773, quiksilver.com
Skechers: 702 361 8958, skechers.com
Steve Madden: 702 361 2871, stevemadden.com
The Walking Company: 702 240 9255, thewalkingcompany.com

Health and beauty

Bath & Body Works: 702 734 2929, bathandbodyworks.com
The Body Shop: 702 269 0273, thebodyshop.co.uk
ElevenSpa Vegas: 702 967 1100, elevenspavegas.com
Fruits & Passion: 702 405 8888, fruits-passion.com
Luxury Perfumes: 702 893 4003, luxuryperfume.com
MAC: 702 492 1173, MACcosmetics.com
Origins: 702 407 8955, origins.com
Perfumania: 702 269 9208, perfumania.com
Sephora: 702 361 3727, sephora.com

Music and electronics

Apple: 702 221 8826, apple.com
Cells Planet: 702 896 0050,
cellsplanet.com
Fry's Electronics: 702 932 1400, frys.com
Guitar Center: 702 450 2260,
guitarcenter.com

Cafés and restaurants

Anthony's Coal Fired Pizza: 702 361
7500, anthonyscoalfiredpizza.com
Blue Martini bar and tapas: 702 949
2583, bluemartinilounge.com
Brio Tuscan Grille: 702 914 9145,
brioitalian.com
Cadillac Ranch: 702 294 7300,
cadillacranchgroup.com
California Pizza Kitchen: 702 896 5154,
cpk.com
Cana Tapas Kitchen & Bar: coming soon
Claim Jumper classic American cuisine:
702 270 2509, claimjumper.com
The Grape: 702 220 4727,
thegraperestaurant.com
Johnny McGuire's: 702 982 0002,
johnnymcguires.com
Kabuki Japanese Restaurant: 702 896
7440, kabukirestaurants.com
Nu Sanctuary Lodge: coming soon
Texas de Brazil: 702 614 0080,
texasdebrazil.com
Tommy Bahama's Restaurant & Bar: 702
948 8006, tommybahama.com
Whole Foods Market: 702 734 9273,
wholefoodsmarket.com
Yard House: 702 734 9273,
yardhouse.com

Grand Canal Shoppes

Location: The Venetian, 3377 Las Vegas
Boulevard South Suite 2600
Tel: 702 414 4500
Web: thegrandcanalshoppes.com
Open: Sun–Thurs 10am–11pm; Fri and Sat
10am–midnight
Parking: Parking at the Venetian; valet
parking available
Cafés and restaurants: Fine dining is
unparalleled here with one fantastic place
after another. There's the Delmonico
Steakhouse, Lutece and Pinot Brasserie to
name just a few, while you can listen to
live music at Tao

This is another luxurious shopping
environment that has been specifically
created to provide entertainment as well as
retail outlets. As you enter from the Strip,
you are greeted by extravagant vaulted
ceilings adorned with images reminiscent

of Italy's great pointed palazzos.
　Along the streets of this recreated 15th-
century Venice are high-fashion luxury
boutiques, national branded stores of
America and entertainment retailers. After
wandering past some of these shops you
arrive at the huge space called St Mark's
Square from where you can take a
gondola ride – just like those on Venice's
fabled canals – and enjoy the illusion
created by decorated second-storey
balconies.
　Posh stores include Burberry, Jimmy
Choo, Mikimoto, which is famous for its
pearls, and Oliver & Company, the latter
filled with men's fashions by Ralph Lauren,
Donna Karan, Giorgio Armani and Borrelli.
Other retailers include Ann Taylor, Banana
Republic and bébé. Interesting one-off
shops include Il Prato, which sells authentic
Venetian masks, Ripa di Monti for Venetian
glass and collectibles, and Sephora beauty
emporium.
　The whole process of browsing or
parting with your cash is made sweeter by
the entertainments, with jugglers
showcasing their talents along the
cobblestone walkways and the glass
blowers demonstrating their craft in St
Mark's Square.

Hawaiian Marketplace

Location: 3743 South Las Vegas
Boulevard, just south of Harmon Avenue
and in front of the Polo Towers
Tel: 702 795 2247
Web: vegas.com/shopping/hawaiian.html
Open: Hours vary, but generally 10am–
10pm daily
Parking: A small car park is available next

Luxury shops at the Grand Canal Shoppes

to the market or you can try the Polo Towers public car park

Attractions: Animatronic bird show in the Enchanted Forest on Fri, Sat and Sun; and Thurs–Sat Team Aloha puts on extended shows that include singing, dancing, fire-knife dancers and live bird shows

Cafés and restaurants: Indian Tamba, Zinger's hamburger joint and Chinese Star Buffet

BRITTIP

If you are having trouble finding a parking spot, try the valet parking at the side entrance of Polo Towers and you'll be just steps away from the Hawaiian Marketplace.

While the outdoor market is still popular, with several dozen thatched huts and carts from which you can buy a wide range of shirts, mobile phone accessories and tourist memorabilia, the interior of this $175m centre is dead, including most of the restaurants. The story goes that one group of investors bought out almost all of the interior stores, then promptly went bankrupt. A shame, as this was a pleasant shopping experience. It still is, but on a much smaller scale. Until the owners get the problems sorted out, there is little reason for a special trip, but if you are near the MGM Grand/Planet Hollywood area, it is worth stopping by.

Las Vegas Premium Outlets

Las Vegas Premium Outlets

Location: 875 South Grand Central Parkway, downtown Las Vegas, just off Interstate 15
Tel: 702 474 7500
Web: premiumoutlets.com
Open: Mon–Sat 10am–9pm; Sun 10am–8pm
Parking: Free and immediately outside the village
Cafés and restaurants: Auntie Anne's Soft Pretzels, China Pantry, Dairy Queen/Orange Julius, The Great Steak & Potato Co., Italia Express, Japan Café Grill, Makino's, Starbucks Coffee and Subway
Services: Go to the management office to collect a map to see the full layout; there you can also rent a pushchair, wheelchair, get a trolley, arrange for international shipping and buy international phone cards; three sets of WCs; three cashpoints (ATMs), foreign currency exchange; telephones
Additional services: Attraction tickets, dinner and show reservations and sightseeing tours available through the Allstate Ticketing (Showtickets.com) located in the kiosk in front of Timberland at suite 1901

Discount shopping in Las Vegas took a turn for the better with the arrival of Chelsea Premium Outlets' latest village – the $95m Las Vegas Premium Outlets. Run by the same people who run Woodbury Common in New York, this is one of the best discount outfits in America. Each of their village-style settings is picturesque, well laid out and fully serviced by food and drink outlets and plenty of toilets.

On top of that, it provides high-end designer gear at 25–65% of the original price on a year-round basis, while also running fabulous sales with even cheaper prices – generally held on the major American holidays and over Christmas.

However, with its open design, and paucity of shade, it can be an uncomfortable experience trudging around on very hot or very windy days.

To get to Premium Outlets by car, take Interstate 15 northbound, then take Exit 41B Charleston Boulevard, southbound, and exit at Charleston Boulevard. This will take you on to Martin Luther King Boulevard. Turn left into Charleston Boulevard and left again into Grand Central Parkway. If you are going by taxi, there's a pick up behind Ann Taylor at Suite 1201 and a drop off between Adidas and Brooks Brothers, suite 1701.

Factory outlet district

Just a short trip south of the MGM Grand along the Strip is the district of factory shops where many famous brand names are sold at 20–70% discounts. First stop is the Belz Factory Outlet World at the corner of Las Vegas Boulevard South and Warm Springs Road. Here, the 625,000ft²/58,064m² mall is home to a permanent laser show plus 140 outlet stores that include Nike, OshKosh, Off 5th, Saks Fifth Avenue and Levis.

A mile/1.6km further south is the open-air Las Vegas Factory Outlet Stores of America that has a huge range of shops from men's and women's clothing to bookstores and shoe shops. Both are open Mon–Sat 10am–8pm and Sun 10am–6pm.

Hotel shopping

In addition to the major shopping parades featured at different hotels, earlier in this chapter, here is a full guide to the shops available in each of the major resort-hotels. Some offer high-end items – such as the Paris Resort – while many provide shopping that fits in with the theme of the hotel.

Bally's Hotel

Bally's Avenue Shops, 702 736 4111, ballyslasvegas.com
More than 20 stores from jewellery to fashion, plus men's and women's hair salons and an ice-cream parlour.

Open 7 days a week. Most shops open at 9am; closing times vary.

The Bellagio

Via Bellagio, 702 693 7111, bellagio.com
The tenants of the Bellagio's shopping 'mall' – a street which winds its way from the hotel down to the Strip – fit in perfectly with the elegant surroundings. Prada, Georgio Armani and Chanel cater to the Bellagio's well-heeled clientele, as does Tiffany & Co, the epitome of subdued shopping style.

Open 7 days a week. Most stores open 10am–midnight.

Caesars Appian Way Shops

Appian Way, 702 731 7110, caesarspalace.com
Despite its proximity to the Forum Shops at Caesars, Appian Way is a fair-sized corridor winding through the hotel and connecting the Roman, Palace and Centurion Towers, which is filled with some of the most exclusive shops and finest salons in the world.

Shops include Ancient Creations, filled with high-quality jewellery and rare coins and artefacts; Cartier; Le Paradis jewellery store; Venus Salon for hair, nail, make-up and skin services; Cottura for hand-painted ceramics; Galerie Michelangelo filled with fine art; Emperors Essentials for Caesars logo merchandise; Piazzas Del Mercato for sportswear, perfumes, golf collections and spa products; Godiva Chocolatier; Colosseum Cigars, Bernini Couture; Cuzzens for men's clothing; Paul and Shark for men's sportswear; Carina for women's designer clothes, shoes and accessories; and Paradiso for swimwear.

Open 7 days a week from 10am; closing times vary.

Circus Circus

Circus Circus Shops, 702 734 0410, circuscircus.com
Want a break from high-falutin', designer-by-the-dozen, serious shop-till-you-drop malls? Then, head to the hotel's 40,000ft²/3,716m² shopping promenade. You won't find Dior's latest must-have sunglasses, but you will find a whole lot of laughs in shops such as Criss Angel Mindfreak, Nothing But Clowns (yup – they come in all shapes and sizes!), Houdini's Magic Shop, Circus Kids and LYSONSPL8 for fun licence plates. Also pretty handy are the off-licence, newsagent and gift shop. Circus Circus is also a frequent host of liquidation sales, where overstock jeans and other merchandise from national chains are heaped in massive boxes and sold at pennies on the retail dollar.

Open 7 days a week from 10am; closing times vary.

Giorgio Armani at the Bellagio

Encore

The Esplanade at Encore, 702 770 8000, encorelasvegas.com
Definitely one for fashionistas! All 11 shops are delicious and a little bit edgy. There's Rock & Republic, the distinguished Hermes and the eternally classic Chanel, along with Ensemble, Homestore, In Step, Nite Life Shop, Shades, Swim and Wynn & Company. An additional store featuring cooking products designed by and used by the Wynn Las Vegas and Encore Las Vegas chefs is due to open. The Spa Shop is located upstairs inside the Encore Spa. The Esplanade has the Botero Restaurant and is adjacent to the XS nightclub if you're late night shopping and fancy a boogie!
Open daily 10am–11pm.

Excalibur Hotel

Excalibur Shoppes at Castle Walk, 702 597 7850, excalibur.com
Fantasy shops on the medieval theme include the Excalibur Shoppe, Castle Souvenirs, Gifts of the Kingdom, Spirit Shoppe, Dragon's Lair and Desert Shoppe, which sell everything from swords and suits of armour to Excalibur merchandise.
Open 7 days a week from 10am; closing times vary.

Las Vegas Hilton

Hilton Shops, 702 732 5111, lvhilton.com
Don't forget to pick up your *Star Trek* souvenir merchandise and other goodies at the Hilton shops.
Open 7 days a week from 10am; closing times vary.

The Luxor

Giza Galleria, 702 262 4444, luxor.com
The Galleria contains 18 shops selling everything from King Tut's souvenirs to ice cream and sweets. Other shops include the

Via Bellagio

Pyramid Shop for hieroglyphic T-shirts and sweatshirts, Innerspace for limited-edition Egyptian collections, and the Logo Shop selling everything from Luxor key chains to stuffed animals and glassware. Exclusive is the exciting women's clothing store that has everything from business outfits to cutting-edge designer gear.
Open 7 days a week from 10am; closing times vary.

Mandalay Bay

Mandalay Bay Shops, 702 632 7777, mandalaybay.com
A selection of tropically themed shops to match the hotel, Mandalay Place is 100,000ft^2/9,290m^2 and connects Mandalay Bay and the Luxor via a 310-ft/95-m retail sky bridge. The 41 retailers include Urban Outfitters, 55 Degrees Wine + Design, The Art of Shaving, Elton's men's store, GF Ferre and the world's first Nike Golf store.
Open 7 days a week from 10am; closing times vary.

MGM Grand

MGM Grand Avenue, 702 891 3300, mgmgrand.com
The City of Entertainment has fun and exclusive shops that provide something for everyone from fine jewellery to men's, women's and children's fashions. You can browse through the luxurious shops along Studio Walk, visit Star Lane Shops on the lower level of the main lobby, or explore the shopping outlets located throughout MGM Grand. Studio Walk is a magnificent 115,000ft^2/10,684m^2 shopping promenade located between the casino and the gardens and is designed to look like a Hollywood sound stage, while the shops and restaurants have been inspired by Hollywood's legendary buildings and landmarks. Star Lane Shops has a variety of outlets in a fun and colourful shopping arcade.
Open 7 days a week from 10am; closing times vary.

The Mirage

The Street of Shops, 702 791 7111, mirage.com
An exclusive collection of designer boutiques offering everything from unique gifts to beautiful jewellery and designer clothes in a sophisticated Parisian/Italian boulevard setting. Designers include DKNY, Moschino and La Perla, while there are also souvenir shops for Siegfried and Roya and Cirque du Soleil®.

Shopping hints and tips

Duty free: Buy your booze from US liquor stores – they're better value than airports, but remember your allowance is 1 litre of spirits and 2 bottles of wine. And take ID. The USA is much more stringent on age checks.

Measurements: The Americans still work in feet and inches, which is great for anyone over the age of 40!

Sizes: Clothes sizes are one size smaller in America, so a dress size 10 in the US is a size 12 in the UK. It means you can travel out in a size 12 and come back in a size 10! It is the same for men: a jacket size 42 is the English size 44. But it's the opposite with shoes: an American size 10 is our size 9.

Taxes: In all cases you will have to add local taxes on to the cost of your goods. In Nevada this adds 7.5% on to the final price.

UK shopping allowances: Revenue and Customs set the rules for duty free and currently state that from outside the EU you can bring in goods up to £340 without paying tax or duty. If you arrive by private plane or boat, there's a limit of £240. It is worth noting that if one item is worth more than the total (for example, you bring in a £400 item), you have to pay tax on the full item value, not just the value above £340. It is always advisable to check with Revenue and Customs as the limits do change. More info including limits on alcohol and cigarettes can be found at: hmrc.gov.uk/customs/arriving/arrivingnoneu.htm

Open 7 days a week; Sun–Thurs 10am–11pm; Fri and Sat until midnight.

Monte Carlo

Monte Carlo Shops, Street of Dreams, 702 730 7777, montecarlo.com
Boutiques include a small convenience store, sweet shop, flower shop and the Lance Burton Magic Shop with demonstrator shows.
Open 7 days a week from 10am; closing times vary.

M Resort

M Resort shopping, 702 797 1000
Within this new hotel is the Vice Shop and convenience store but a 1 million ft²/92,903m² area of retail and shops is planned.

New York-New York

Soho Village, 702 414 4500, themresort.com
Provides a limited number of stores but still a fun experience. The village is set against a background of New York landmarks and includes both Greenwich Village and Times Square.
Open 7 days. Most Stores open at 10am; closing times vary.

Paris Resort

Le Boulevard, 702 946 7000, parislasvegas.com
Paris Las Vegas features upscale French retail shopping, located within the resort's quaint Le Boulevard District. The interior

buildings are covered with facades representative of real Parisian districts. Picturesque cobblestone streets and winding alleyways take guests on a European shopping spree. Le Boulevard features a wide array of authentic French boutiques, such as Le Cave, where you can sample premier French wines and private labels; Les Enfants, a purveyor of French children's toys and games; Lunettes designer eyewear; Le Paradis fine jewellery and crystal; and La Boutique by Yokohama de Paris.
Open 7 days a week 10am–10pm.

Rio All-Suite Hotel

Masquerade Village Shops, 702 252 7777, riolasvegas.com
The $200m Masquerade Village is actually a combination of shopping, dining, entertainment and gaming woven together

Elton's Men's Store

Off-Strip shopping

If you want to shop like the locals, you can find plenty of shopping excitement off the Strip, too. **The Boulevard Mall** (boulevardmall.com), one of Nevada's largest shopping centres with more than 1 million ft²/92,903m² of retail space, features anchor department stores J.C. Penney, Sears, Dillard's and Macy's. The Boulevard Mall also offers specialty shops such as American Eagle Outfitters, The Gap, Yankee Candle Co., Charlotte Russe and a Footlocker Triplex.

The District at Green Valley Ranch (thedistrictatgvr.com) is one of the more unique shopping experiences in Las Vegas, with more than 40 shops and restaurants situated along a tree-lined street adjacent to Green Valley Ranch Resort & Spa. The anchors at The District include Williams-Sonoma, Pottery Barn and Sharper Image, with other stores being firsts to Las Vegas, such as REI, Coldwater Creek and Anthropologie. The District features cobblestone sidewalks, park benches and even pet-friendly areas.

The Fashion Outlets of Las Vegas (fashionoutletlasvegas.com) shopping mall in Primm, Nevada, features more than 100 brand names such as DKNY, Calvin Klein, Kenneth Cole, Banana Republic, Williams-Sonoma, Harley Davidson®, Alpaca Imports, Bath & Body Works and Wilson's Leather. It is located at the Southern Nevada–California border, 35mls/56km south of Las Vegas off Interstate 15. A shuttle bus service is available from the Las Vegas Strip as well as from New York-New York Hotel & Casino and MGM Grand.

The Southwestern-themed **Galleria Mall** (galleriaatsunset.com) is located at Sunset Road and Stephanie Street in Henderson, Nev., about 12mls/19km east of Las Vegas. Galleria tenants include J.C. Penney, Macy's, Dillard's, Mervyn's California, Ann Taylor, Cache, Champs Sports, Victoria's Secrets, Eddie Bauer, The Disney Store and a 600-seat food court.

With savings of 25–65%, the 130 stores at **Las Vegas Outlet Center** (premiumoutlets. com) include Liz Claiborne, Calvin Klein, Nautica, Nike, Reebok, Levi's, Danskin, Adidas, Bass, Greg Norman, VF Outlet – Vanity Fair Wrangler Lee. This indoor mall, complete with two food courts and an indoor carousel, is located on the southern end of the Strip. The center is a short cab ride from the Strip and is served by a Citizens Area Transit (CAT) bus.

The Meadows Mall (meadowsmall.com) exemplifies the ease of one-stop, convenient shopping in a multilevel center located near the U.S. 95 Expressway at Valley View Boulevard. The Meadows Mall provides its own downtown trolley that travels to and from the Downtown Transportation Center in less than 8 minutes. The mall has 2 levels of speciality stores and 5 courtyards. Anchor stores include Dillard's, Macy's, J.C. Penney and Sears.

by the ongoing carnival atmosphere of the hotel's Masquerade Show in the Sky (see page xx). Here you can stroll down 200-year-old Tuscan-tiled streets filled with eclectic boutiques selling everything from Harley Davidson® clothing to Field of Dreams sports memorabilia.

Open 7 days a week from 10am; closing times vary.

Stratosphere Hotel

Tower Shops, 702 380 7777, stratospherehotel.com
Visitors pass through a variety of shops on themed street scenes reminiscent of Paris, Hong Kong and New York on their way to the Broadway Showroom and lifts to the Observation Deck.

Open Sun–Thurs 10am–11pm; Fri and Sat until midnight.

Wynn Las Vegas

Wynn Esplanade, 702 770 7100, wynnlasvegas.com
In April 2005, the much-anticipated opening of Wynn Las Vegas brought one of the more high-end shopping experiences to the Las Vegas Strip. Wynn Esplanade features the first Oscar de la Renta boutique fashion store and the first Jean Paul Gaultier designer store in the country. Among the big-name shops in the Wynn Esplanade are Manolo Blahnik, Cartier, Louis Vuitton and Christian Dior. Also among the top brands is the Penske-Wynn showroom, home to the hotel's Ferrari-Maserati dealership.

Open 7 days from 10am; closing times vary.

5 RESTAURANTS

Your choice of the best restaurants and eating places in town

food, glorious food abounds in Las Vegas from the classiest gourmet restaurants to the cheap and cheerful diner and from relaxed lounge-style settings to trendy bistros. Not so long ago, the city was most famous for its 99-cent shrimp (giant prawn) cocktails and the amazing all-you-can-eat buffets and not a lot else in the dining department. But, like every other aspect of Las Vegas, things have changed as a result of the massive influx of bright young professionals from California and a surge in sophisticated visitors looking for something more than a bit of casino action.

The resorts have gone far afield to woo top chefs of every country and discipline to open dazzling eateries. While most resorts or hotels worldwide are happy if they have one, or perhaps two, world-class restaurants, the Las Vegas resorts collect them like some do postage stamps. The Venetian alone has at least 12 four- or five-star eating houses of distinction on their property. Most of the other grand resorts have half a dozen each. The king of Las Vegas food must be the iconic celebrity

Celebrity chef, Emil Lagasse

RESTAURANTS

chef Wolfgang Puck, who has no less than 6 restaurants covering Sin City and 2 more opening in the new Crystals Center at CityCenter, plus a Wolfgang Puck Gourmet Express at McCarran airport!

Vegas has more Master Sommeliers than any other city in the world and more wine sold per capita than any other destination. Las Vegas's credibility as one of the globe's centres for fine dining grew even more when, in 2008, it became the fourth US city to be profiled by the authors of the *Michelin Guide*. In 2009, Alex at Wynn Las Vegas and Joel Robuchon at The Mansion at MGM Grand were honoured with a 5-star rating by the *Mobil Travel Guide*.

But while the classy restaurants have taken over the headlines, with $777 Kobe beef hamburgers and $421 white truffle lobsters, there are still quality cheap eats if you know where to look. You can get a huge presentation of shrimp downtown at Golden Gate Hotel & Casino for a mere $1.99, while the Rio All-Suites Hotel & Casino's Carnival World buffet has more than 300 mains and 70 desserts. If you're a fry up kind of person, a massive steak and eggs breakfast can be had for a snip 24-hours a day on Boulder Highway's Arizona Charlie's. Many places retain the 'Midnight Menu' for late revellers and gamblers where filling breakfasts and sandwiches can be had for a pittance after midnight.

Obviously, space dictates that I cannot list all the restaurants on offer, so I have

provided information on what are considered to be the finest restaurants in each category. They're all popular, though, so book a table in advance. I have also included a good smattering of extremely well-priced cafés – some of which are open 24/7 – and plenty of non-resort restaurants with enduring appeal. As the celebrity chef culture is so strong here, I've begun with a quick rundown of every high profile restaurant with a big name at the helm.

Celebrity chef restaurants

Historically, major hotel-casinos featured 'gourmet rooms' in order to cater to high-rollers' tastes. Each restaurant created an ambience designed to transport diners to a world far away from the action of the casinos. However, by the late '90s, high-end eateries became the rage with their appeal extending beyond just high-rollers. Las Vegas hotels recruited some of the top chefs in the world to open and run restaurants inside their properties. Today, Las Vegas has the most comprehensive collection of the world's top chefs and television icons. If you like to namedrop about your food, these are the eateries for you – just make sure your bank balance is healthy.

- Paul Bartolotta (Bartolotta Ristorante di Mare at Wynn Las Vegas)
- Mario Batali (B & B Ristorante and Enoteca San Marco at The Venetian)
- Daniel Boulud (Daniel Boulud at Wynn Las Vegas)
- David Burke (David Burke at The Venetian)
- Kim Canteenwalla (Society Café at Encore)
- Tom Colicchio (Craftsteak at MGM Grand)
- Alain Ducasse (Mix at Mandalay Bay's THEhotel)
- Todd English (Olives at Bellagio)
- Susan Feniger and Mary Sue Milliken (Border Grill at Mandalay Bay)
- Bobby Flay (Mesa Grill at Caesars Palace)
- Jean-Marie Josselin (8-0-8 at Caesars Palace)
- Hubert Keller (Fleur de Lys at Mandalay Bay)
- Joseph Keller (Bistro Zinc at Montelago Village at Lake Las Vegas)
- Thomas Keller (Bouchon at The Venetian)
- Emeril Lagasse (Emeril's New Orleans Fish House at MGM Grand and Delmonico Steakhouse at The Venetian)
- Mark LoRusso (Botero Steak at Encore)

Aureole at the Mandalay Bay

- Sirio Maccioni (Le Cirque at Bellagio and Sirio at ARIA)
- Steve Martorano (Café Martorano at Rio All-Suite Hotel and Casino)
- Nobu Matsuhisa (Nobu at Hard Rock Hotel & Casino)
- Jean-Philippe Maury (Jean Philippe Patisserie at Bellagio and JP Patisserie at ARIA)
- Maurizio Mazzon (Canaletto at the Venetian and Il Fornaio at the New York-New York and Green Valley Ranch)
- Michael Mina (Nobhill Tavern and Seablue at MGM Grand, Michael Mina at Bellagio and Strip Steak at Mandalay Bay and American Fish at Aria)
- Tom Moloney (AquaKnox at The Venetian)
- Rick Moonen (rm Seafood at Mandalay Bay)
- Bradley Ogden (Bradley Ogden at Caesars Palace)
- Charlie Palmer (Aureole at Mandalay Bay and Charlie Palmer Steak at The Four Seasons)
- Francois Payard (Payard Patisserie at Caesars Palace)
- Marc Poidevin (Switch at Encore)
- Wolfgang Puck (Spago and Chinois at The Forum Shops at Caesars, Postrio at The Venetian, Cut at The Palazzo, Trattoria del Lupo at Mandalay Bay and Wolfgang Puck Bar & Grill at MGM Grand)
- Joël Robuchon (L'Atelier de Joël Robuchon and Joël Robuchon at The Mansion at MGM Grand)
- André Rochat (Alizé at The Palms, Andre's Monte Carlo)
- Guy Savoy (Restaurant Guy Savoy at Caesars Palace)
- Theo Schoenegger (Sinatra at Encore)
- Piero Selvaggio (Valentino at The Venetian and Giorgio and Ristorante at Mandalay Place)
- Julian Serrano (Picasso at Bellagio)
- Kerry Simon (CatHouse at Luxor, Simon at Palms Place)
- Joachim Splichal (Pinot Brasserie at The Venetian)
- Alessandro Stratta (Alex at Wynn Las Vegas)
- Jet Tila (Wazuzu at Encore)
- Jean-Georges Vongerichten (Prime at Bellagio and Jean Georges Steakhouse at ARIA)
- Michael White (Fiamma at MGM Grand)
- Takashi Yagihashi (Okada at Wynn Las Vegas)

BRITTIP

If you're a total foodie, head to Vegas in May when the city hosts its annual epicurean event called Vegas Uncork'd (vegasuncorked.com). Four days of grand chefs and grand tastings!

We have included as many websites as possible. In some cases, you can go direct to the restaurant's web page. In other cases, it is quicker to go to the main resort-hotel page, then select the dining option, rather than key in a long URL.

Price codes

Per head for a 3-course meal and a drink:

$	=	under $40
$$	=	up to $80
$$$	=	$81 and over!

American restaurants

All-American Bar & Grille

Rio All-Suite Hotel & Casino, 702 777 7923, riolasvegas.com
The newish All-American Bar & Grille is the place to come for Brits looking for hearty American meals. Think 'Rio Dry Aged' in-house steaks famous for their taste and sizzle. Tuck into mammoth salads, fresh seafood and burgers prepared in an open mesquite wood grill. Make sure you come with an appetite. Afternoon margaritas here are good. Open daily 11am–6am. **$**

Aureole

Mandalay Bay, 702 632 7401, mandalaybay.com/dining/aureole.aspx
Charlie Palmer, famous for his New York Aureole, opened his second outlet, this time in Las Vegas, which now has a Michelin star. The New York restaurant is consistently voted number one for American cuisine by the Zagat survey and Charlie was awarded Best Chef by the James Beard Foundation. Aureole features seasonal dishes including artisan dry-aged beef and fresh seafood that reflect Palmer's progressive American cuisine. For this restaurant, a 4-storey wine tower has been

BRITTIP

For the ultimate fast fix of American food, head to Pink's Hot Dogs at Planet Hollywood Resort & Casino with 14 varieties of hot dog!

LAS VEGAS
TOWN PLAN

created and wine stewards strap on harnesses to be hoisted up the tower to make their wine selections. Open Tues–Sat 6–10.30pm. $$$

Bar Louie

Town Square Las Vegas, 702 263 0480, townsquarelasvegas.com
This hip neighbourhood restaurant and bar is a new addition at Town Square. The popular Chicago-based chain is known for its signature sandwiches, inventive pizzas and specialty cocktails. Open for lunch, dinner or late-night dining. $

Bradley Ogden

Caesars Palace, 877 346 4642, caesarspalace.com
Putting farm-fresh American cuisine at the top of the agenda has earned famous Bay Area chef Bradley Ogden a clutch of awards. Having started at San Francisco's renowned Campton Place Hotel, Ogden opened his first restaurant outside

California at Caesars and immediately picked up Best New Restaurant 2004 by the James Beard Foundation. An incredible line-up of tastes and textures is included in dishes such as Maytag blue cheese soufflé with candy-stripe beets and chilled asparagus soup and Mascarpone lemon cream for starters. Main courses include: steamed Alaskan halibut with Maine lobster, basil vinaigrette, asparagus and parsley froth; Columbia river wild king salmon with sautéed shrimp, black olive gnocchi, arugula, California morels and oregano croutons; and slow-roasted Muscovy duck with endive leaves, purple artichokes, polenta and rhubarb. Open Wed–Sun 5–11pm. $$$

BRITTIP

For a bird's eye view of the pirate ship action outside Treasure Island, book yourself a window seat at the Buccaneer Bay Club.

Best views in the valley

Alizé at the top of the Palms (page 112)

Eiffel Tower Restaurant: Paris Resort (page 113)

Firenze Lobby Lounge: Ritz-Carlton, Lake Las Vegas (page 127)

Medici Café and Terrace: Ritz-Carlton, Lake Las Vegas

Mix: Mandalay Bay (page 114)

Mon Ami Gabi: Paris Resort (page 113)

PF Chang's China Bistro: Planet Hollywood

Signature Restaurant, Mandarin Oriental, Las Vegas (page 115)

Tao: The Venetian (page 109)

The Top of the World: Stratosphere (page 124)

VooDoo Café: Rio All-Suite Hotel (page 111)

Cheesecake Factory

Forum Shops at Caesars Palace, 702 792 6888, thecheesecakefactory.com
Famous for its extensive menu – there are more than 250 items plus nearly 30 specials – this is more of a place to people-watch than expect gourmet cuisine, yet the food is delicious too. Portions are huge, but please find some room at the end for a serving of their excellent, and imaginative, desserts. Open Mon–Thurs 11.15am–11.30pm; Sat 10.15am–12.30am and Sunday brunch 10.15am–11.30pm. $

FIX

Bellagio, 702 693 7223, bellagio.com/restaurants/fix.aspx
The menu, designed to offer the best in classic American fare, focuses on simply prepared, top-quality fish, meat and poultry, cooked to order on a wood-burning grill. The longer-than-usual opening hours allow for both pre-show and après-show dining, while the bar and lounge offer a full menu of speciality cocktails. Open Sun–Thurs 5pm–midnight; Fri and Sat 5pm–2am. $–$$

The Light Group

Aria Resort & Casino (open December 2009), 866 359 7757, arialasvegas
Chef Brian Massie will introduce an edgy American dim sum style concept at Aria, featuring unique interpretations of American favourites made from the finest quality ingredients. Small, sharable plates will supplement the menu and offer diners a variety of dishes to excite the palate. Opening hours not yet available. $$

Nero's

Caesars Palace, 877 346 4642, caesarspalace.com
Nero's specialises in dry-aged prime beef, tender chops and fresh seafood – all artistically presented. House specials include grilled lamb chops on crispy polenta with baby greens and garlic; grilled swordfish with sweet potato purée, herb-roasted onion, pea shoots and lemon aioli; and halibut pan-roasted in lobster oil with braised baby artichokes, steamed clams and saffron couscous. The menu changes according to the season but favourites include crab cakes; carpaccio of beef with shaved Parmesan; and salad of frisée, fennel and roasted red peppers and truffle aioli. Open daily 5–11pm. $$$

Pegasus

Alexis Park Hotel, 375 East Harmon Ave, 702 796 3300
Pegasus offers gourmet dining in a classy environment. Dishes include freshly made pastas, beef, pork and fresh fish that come with delicious vegetables. Open daily 6am–2pm and 4–11pm. $$

Society Café Encore

Encore Las Vegas, 702 248 3463, encorelasvegas.com
Society Café Encore was designed with the whimsical era of Oscar Wilde in mind, to match Chef Kim Canteenwalla's (yes, that's really his name!) wildly imaginative American cooking. The hip place to come with glorious decor. Go for the pink sofa alone! Open Sun–Thurs 7am–11pm; Fri and Sat 7am–1am. $–$$

Tableau

Wynn Las Vegas, 702 248 3463, wynnlasvegas.com
Open for breakfast, lunch and Sunday brunch, Wynn's signature restaurant, Tableau is to be found in a light, airy

Tableau

RESTAURANTS

atrium setting with poolside views. Rising star chef David Spero showcases American ingredients prepared with French flair. Breakfast 8–10.30am; lunch 11.30am–2.30pm. Brunch on Sat and Sun 8am–2.30pm. $

Tommy Rocker's Mojave Beach Bar & Grill

4275 Dean Martin Drive, 702 261 6688, tommyrocker.com
It's unlikely you'll be visiting Tommy's unless you're coming here for the music, as it's a little off the beaten track. What will surprise you though, will be the half-decent, well-priced, largely American grub that allows you to enjoy the live music and DJ well into the night. $

Asian restaurants

Ah-Sin

Paris Las Vegas, 702 946 4593, parislasvegas.com
A new type of dining experience with Japanese sushi, Chinese noodle specialities and a host of favourite cuisines from the Pacific Rim, all prepared by chefs at stations around the dining room. Service begins with a ritual hand-washing ceremony that includes the pouring of pure water scented with jasmine oil. Open Wed–Sun 5.30–10.30pm. $$

BRITTIP

Ah-Sin is right next door to the Risqué ultra-lounge (see page 150) where you can relax on the plush couches while tucking into dessert.

Bamboo Garden

4850 West Flamingo Road, 702 871 3262
Popular spot for locals who love the delicious range of unusual dishes at the very reasonable prices. It looks modest enough, but the friendly staff provide excellent service and dishes include: cream

Pearl at the MGM Grand

Most romantic spots

Alex: Wynn Las Vegas (page 112)
Alizé: The Palms (page 112)
André's: South 6th Street (page 113)
Daniel Boulud Brasserie: Wynn Las Vegas (page 109)
Eiffel Tower Restaurant: Paris Resort (page 113)
Gaylord India Restaurant: Rio All-Suite Hotel (page 115).
Jasmine: Bellagio (page 112)
Le Cirque: Bellagio (page 113)
Picasso: Bellagio (page 119)
Signature Restaurant: Mandarin Oriental, Las Vegas (page 115)

of seafood soup; Mongolian lamb; firecracker beef; emerald shrimp; and Peking duck with Mandarin pancakes. Open Mon–Sat 11am–10.30pm. $$

Chin Chin

New York-New York Hotel, 702 740 6969, nynyhotelcasino.com/restaurants
In a restoration of New York Chinatown, you'll find everything from the Pacific Rim to Szechuan and Cantonese food. Open Mon–Fri 7.30am–11pm; Sat–Sun 8am–11pm. $$

HoWan

3145 Las Vegas Boulevard South, 702 733 4547
Beautifully decorated with tapestries and antiques, and a fish and seafood tank, and the costumed staff provide an excellent service. Many Asians eat here and enjoy tucking into house specialities such as minced squab and crackling shrimp, steamed fish, lobster and seaweed with cabbage and bean curd soup. Open daily 6–11pm. $$$

Pearl

MGM Grand, freephone 702 891 7380, mgmgrand.com/dining
A stylish, upmarket Chinese-meets-Western restaurant based on Cantonese and Shanghai specialities. The largely seafood dishes include both Maine and Australian lobsters, shark fin and lobster spring rolls and Sian bouillabaisse. An added bonus is the trolley with a range of fine Chinese teas – for a good pick-me-up, try green tea. Open Sun–Thurs 5.30–10pm; Fri and Sat 5.30–10.30pm. $$–$$$

Shanghai Lilly

Mandalay Bay, 702 632 7409,
mandalaybay.com/dining/shanghaililly.aspx
Classic Cantonese and Szechuan dishes
using only the finest ingredients make this
one of the best places to enjoy Eastern
cuisine. Open Thurs–Mon 5.30–10.30pm.
$$$

Tao

Grand Canal Shoppes at the Venetian, 702
388 8338, http://venetian.com/tao.aspx
The amazing $20m complex of nightclub
and restaurant specialises in Hong Kong
Chinese, Japanese and Thai cuisines. Chef
Ralph Scarmadella's creations include
everything from Kobe beef to traditional
Peking duck, all prepared by master chefs
from across Asia. How popular is it? It is
by far the most successful privately owned
restaurant in the USA, having twice the
revenue of the second ranked (Tavern on
the Green in New York City) Open Sun–
Thurs 5pm–12am; Fri and Sat 5pm–1am.
$$–$$$

Thai Spice

4433 West Flamingo Road, 702 362 5308
A friendly restaurant that attracts a lot of
the local Asians and tourists alike. Tuck into
traditional Thai food from fish cakes to
noodles, Thai-spiced beef and pepper-
garlic pork. Open Mon–Thurs 11.30am–
10pm; Fri and Sat until 11pm. $

Todai Seafood & Sushi Buffet

Miracle Mile Shops, 702 892 0021,
todai.com
More than a sushi buffet, Todai offers
Japanese, Chinese and Korean cuisine
alongside salads, rice and noodle dishes
and, of course, a full range of fresh sushi.
Open daily for lunch 11.30am–2.30pm
and for dinner Sun–Thurs 5.30–9.30pm;
Fri and Sat 5.30–10pm. $–$$

Tao

Wazuzu

Encore Las Vegas, 702 248 3463,
encorelasvegas.com
Turn a corner in the Encore casino and
come face to face with a 27-ft/8-m crystal
dragon, mounted at Wazuzu, where rising
star Chef Jet Tila serves up innovative pan
Asian delights. This dramatic café-style
restaurant showcases his deft touch with
Chinese, Japanese, Indian, Singaporean
and Thai cuisines. Open Sun–Thurs
11.30am–10.30pm; Fri and Sat
11.30am–1am. $–$$

Bistros and brasseries

Bouchon

The Venetian, 702 414 6200,
venetian.com/bouchon.aspx
World-renowned chef Thomas Keller,
named America's best chef by Time
magazine, is the sole recipient of
consecutive Best Chef awards from the
prestigious James Beard Foundation.
Bouchon opened in 2004 in the beautiful
Venezia Tower and is one of the finest
restaurants in Las Vegas.

An extensive selection of bistro classics
is added to by raw seafood and seafood
platters, including lobster, oyster, shrimp,
mussels and crab. Fabulous main courses
include: roasted leg of lamb with flageolets
beans in a thyme jus; pan-seared prime
flatiron served with maître d'hôtel butter
and French fries; and roasted chicken with
garlic-braised Swiss chard and pommes
sarladaises. Salivating stuff! Open for
breakfast Mon–Fri 7–10.30am; Sat and
Sun for brunch 8am–2pm; nightly 5–10pm
for dinner. $$–$$$

Daniel Boulud Brasserie

Wynn Las Vegas, 702 248 3463,
wynnlasvegas
World-renowned chef Daniel Boulud, who
for many years was the chef at New York's
Le Cirque before opening his own
restaurant, Daniel, in New York, teamed up
with fellow award-winning chef Philippe
Rispoli to create a classic French brasserie
at Wynn's super resort. The laid-back
environment – where you can choose to
dine indoors or by the lake outside – is the
perfect place to enjoy everything from
typical bistro fare to caviar and
champagne. Signature dishes include:
beefsteak tomato with fromage; blanc tarte
pissaladière with onion, anchovies and
black olives; crispy pork belly with lentils
and frisée; and spicy mustard fricassee of

Dover sole amandine. Open nightly 5.30–10pm. $$

Pinot Brasserie

**Venetian, 702 414 8888,
venetian.com/pinot.aspx**
Famous Los Angeles chef Joachim Splichal brings his Pinot concept to the city. The food is delightful and service is spot on. It looks out over the Venetian gardens and the Venezia Tower's pool area, giving the lunch crowd a lovely view. Open for lunch daily 11.30am–3pm; for dinner Sun–Thurs 5.30–10pm; Fri and Sat 5.30–10.30pm. $$

Postrio

**Venetian, 702 796 1110,
venetian.com/postrio.aspx**
Based on Wolfgang Puck's San Francisco bistro, which serves up American food with Asian and Mediterranean influences, Postrio is looking fresher than ever after a recent change of menu and décor. House specialities include: wood-baked pizzas, handmade pastas, sautéed Maine lobster and crab cake. By the way, Postrio has been named one of the 10 best restaurants in the world by *Hotels* magazine. Café open Sun–Thurs 11.30am–10pm, Fri and Sat 11.30am–11pm. Dining room Sun–Thurs 5.30–10pm, Fri and Sat 5.30–11pm. $$

BRITTIP

If you love people-watching, then make the most of Postrio's patio dining area, which gives a great view of the beautiful people who flock to the Venetian.

Sensi

Bellagio, 702 693 7223, bellagio.com
With carved stone, earthy hues, mirrored chrome and waterfalls, Sensi offers a delightful environment in which to discover delicious dishes based around Italian, Asian, seafood and grilled recipes all using quality fresh ingredients. Open Mon–Thurs 5–9.45pm; Fri–Sun 5–10.15pm. $$

The dining room at Sensi

Brazilian restaurant

Texas de Brazil

**Town Square Las Vegas, 702 263 0480,
townsquarelasvegas.com**
Combining the bold flavours of Southern Brazil with the generous spirit of Texas, Texas de Brazil has opened at Town Square Las Vegas. The Las Vegas location marks the restaurant's 14th worldwide. For the fixed price of $44.99, guests can enjoy tantalising cuts of meats, appetisers, soups, salads, gourmet cheeses and a variety of sides served tableside. Texas de Brazil offers guests a truly unique Brazilian experience, complete with sword carrying gauchos (a.k.a. Brazilian cowboys), who roam the dining area serving various delectable cuts and types of meat. Complementing the meal, Texas de Brazil also offers an extensive wine list, signature cocktails, an assortment of desserts and hand-rolled cigars. Open for lunch and dinner. $

Cajun/Creole restaurants

Big Al's Oyster Bar

**New Orleans Hotel, 702 365 7111,
orleanscasino.com**
Get a flavour of New Orleans-style dining with this Cajun/Creole restaurant with a Bayou oyster bar. Opt for oysters and clams on the half-shell with various oyster shooters from the bar, or choose from a range of southern specials including gumbo, Jambalaya pasta, steamed clams, bouillabaisse and Voodoo mussels. Open Sun–Thurs 11am–10pm; Fri and Sat 11am–midnight. $

Big Mama's Soul Food Kitchen

Utopia Center, opposite Rue de Monte Carlo, 702 597 1616, bigmamas-ribshack.com
Good, honest food at rock-bottom prices. Known for its gumbo, fried catfish and barbecue dishes. For a slice of real New Orleans food, try a piece of pecan pie. Open Mon–Thurs 11am–9pm; Fri and Sat 11am–10pm; Sun 12 noon–8pm. $

Emeril's New Orleans Fish House

**MGM Grand, 702 891 7374,
mgmgrand.com/dining**
A real must-visit restaurant if you want to experience celebrity chef Emeril Lagasse's

New Orleans blend of modern Cajun/Creole cooking. Tuck into seared Atlantic salmon served on a wild mushroom potato hash with herb meat juices and a spicy onion crust or grilled fillet of beef with Creole oyster dressing and homemade hollandaise sauce. Open Sun–Thurs 11.30am–2.30pm; Fri and Sat 11.30am–2pm. Dinner nightly 5.30–10.30pm. Next door is the seafood bar, a walk-up style of eatery featuring fresh shellfish and seafood specials. **$$**

VooDoo Café

Rio All-Suite Hotel, 702 777 7923, riolasvegas.com
Superb Cajun and Creole dishes in an elegant New Orleans setting, and the view of the Strip is one of the best in town. Specials include: blue water seafood platter for starters; the ménage à trois of filet mignon, lobster and prawns for entrée; and bananas foster for dessert. Open 5–11pm. **$$**

Caribbean restaurant

Rumjungle

Mandalay Bay, 702 632 7408, mandalaybay.com/dining/rumjungle.aspx
Here food and drink become the artistic environment with a dancing firewall of food that turns into a soothing wall of water, and volcanic mountains of rum and spirits that rise up behind the illuminated bar. The menu is tropically inspired and many of the dishes are cooked over a giant open fire pit. After your meal you can dance to Latin, Caribbean and African beats. Open Sun–Thurs 2–10pm; Fri and Sat noon–9pm. **$$**

🇬🇧 BRITTIP

Rumjungle is one of the best all-rounders in town. It serves superb food, is famous for its wide selection of rums, has great live music and a fabulous atmosphere that attracts the hip and the celebs alike.

Caviar restaurants

The Petrossian Bar

Bellagio, 702 693 7111, bellagio.com
A lavish bar next to the resort's dramatic entrance with its walkway overhung by beautiful cypress trees. It specialises in everything from afternoon tea to caviar,

Entertainment dining

Dining and entertainment go hand-in-hand at several locations throughout Southern Nevada. Dinner theatre options include the *Tournament of Kings* at **Excalibur** where guests are transported to the feasts of the Renaissance while watching a knightly battle. If you're in the mood for love, how about *Tony 'n' Tina's Wedding* at **Planet Hollywood**? Be a special guest of Anthony Nunzio, Jr. and Valentina Lynne Vitale, an Italian–American couple who come from two slightly dysfunctional families. The wedding is complete with drunken guests, a pregnant maid-of-honour, an impromptu 'YMCA' dance and, of course, family bickering. Guests can either participate in the wedding with actors who never step out of character or they can simply watch the family drama unfold!

champagne and smoked salmon. Open Sun–Thurs midday–midnight; Fri and Sat midday–1am. **$$$**

Red Square

Mandalay Bay, 702 632 7407, mandalaybay.com/dining/redsquare.aspx
Check out the extensive caviar selection or try out the menu of updated Russian classics at the frozen ice bar, where you can choose from a selection of more than 100 frozen vodkas and infusions, Martinis and Russian-inspired cocktails. Open Sun–Thurs 5pm–2am; Fri and Sat 4pm–4am. **$$$**

Chinese restaurants

Beijing Noodle No. 9

Caesars Palace, 877 346 4642, caesarspalaace.com
Beijing Noodle No.9 has a watery theme with a large, salt-water aquarium at the entrance to reflect the waters of its cuisine – from the bustling streets of Shanghai,

A brilliant eating experience at Rumjungle

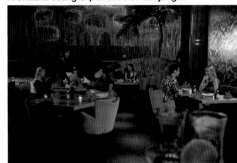

Hong Kong and Beijing. Open Sun–Thurs 11am–11pm; Fri and Sat 11am–midnight. **$$**

Fin

Mirage, 866 339 4566, mirage.com
Sophisticated contemporary Chinese cuisine tempered with an eclectic blend of international dishes. Open Thurs–Mon 5–11pm. **$$**

Jasmine

Bellagio, 702 693 7223, bellagio.com
Chef Philip Lo, an originator of nouvelle Hong Kong cuisine, creates contemporary and classic Cantonese, Szechuan and Hunan dishes in a delightfully romantic setting overlooking the Bellagio lake and gardens. Dishes include: Maine lobster dumplings with ginger sauce; minced squab in lettuce petals; crystal Florida stone crab claws; garlic beef tenderloin; and imperial Peking duck. Open daily 5.30–10pm. **$$**

Lillie's Noodle House

Golden Nugget Hotel, 129 Fremont Street, 702 386 8831
Provides downtown gamblers with delicious and exotic Cantonese dishes in a serene eastern setting with great service. The Great Combination Plate is a favourite starter, before moving on to black pepper steak, stir-fried shrimp or lemon chicken. Open Sun–Thurs 5pm–midnight; Fri and Sat 5pm–1am. **$**

Wing Lei

Wynn Las Vegas, 702 248 3463, wynnlasvegas.com
This Asian delight is an elegantly casual Chinese restaurant with a dramatic yet sumptuous décor that owes much to the colour schemes of French-influenced

Stylish dining at Jasmine

Shanghai. Executive chef Richard Chen oversees the masterful mix of refined Cantonese, Shanghai and Szechuan cooking styles that feature: wok-fried Szechuan Kobe beef; Peking duck for two (served tableside); Mongolian lamb; and beef chow fun and abalone fried rice. Open 5.30–10pm. **$$**

Farm-to-table restaurant

Sage

Aria Resort & Casino (open December 2009), 866 359 7757, arialasvegas
For his first restaurant outside of Chicago, Chef Shawn McClain – named Best Chef Midwest by the James Beard Foundation – will spotlight farm-to-table produce, artisanal meats and sustainable seafood. Designed by Jacques Garcia Decoration, the restaurant will envelop guests in a sophisticated yet comfortable atmosphere. Opening hours not yet available. **$$**

French restaurants

Alex

Wynn Las Vegas, 702 248 3463, wynnlasvegas.com
Chef Alessandro Stratta, winner of the James Beard Foundation's Best American Chef, South-west, brings a taste of the French Riviera to the desert oasis of Las Vegas. And what better setting in which to tuck into roasted monkfish or Tuscan-style pork with stewed tomatoes than in the outdoor seating area? If you find it hard to make a choice, then go for the 'tasting menu' and tuck into tiny courses of carpaccio of red prawns, sea scallops with white asparagus and foie gras ravioli. Open Wed–Sat 6–10pm. **$$$**

Alizé

The Palms, 702 951 7000, andrelv.com/alize
Las Vegas's very own celebrity chef and restaurateur André Rochat, who also owns his own restaurant called André's, has created a gourmet dining experience at the top of the very trendy Palms hotel. Breathtaking views accompany dishes such as sautéed Muscovy duck breast and market-fresh seafood. This is a top-of-the-pile dining experience, which includes the classic French sorbet between courses for cleansing the palate, a cheese trolley and an extensive wine list. Open nightly from 5.30pm. **$$–$$$**

André's

401 South 6th Street, 702 385 5016, andrelv.com/original

André's has been serving up delicious gourmet food to locals and tourists alike for nearly 2 decades. Just one block off the Strip, the restaurant is housed in one of the early homes of Las Vegas – dating all the way back to 1930! The menu changes all the time, but mouth-watering offerings include: chartreuse of Muscovy duck, stewed in Merlot with portabella mushrooms and spring vegetables; sautéed prime fillet of beef with green peppercorn and cognac cream sauce; baked zucchini, gratin dauphinoise and baby carrots anglaise; and Maine lobster. Open nightly from 5.30pm. **$$$**

Les Artistes Steakhouse

Paris, 702 967 7999, parislasvegas.com

A wide choice of gourmet dishes include the signature Scottish pheasant brushed with tarragon mustard sauce and served with red-bliss potatoes; and lime oil-brushed swordfish with basil garlic mashed potatoes. Desserts include classics such as crème brûlée and raspberry clafoutis. Open nightly 5.30–10.30pm. **$$$**

Le Cirque

Bellagio, 702 693 7111, www.bellagio.com

Elizabeth Blau, who has been with the Maccioni family's famous flagship restaurant in New York for more than a decade, re-creates its gourmet French dishes with great aplomb, while the views of the Bellagio's famous fountains lend it more than a touch of elegance. Open 5.30–10pm. **$$$**

Eiffel Tower Restaurant

Paris, 702 948 6937, www.parislasvegas.com

The signature dining experience of this playful resort hotel is set 17 storeys up on the Eiffel Tower replica and has stunning views of Las Vegas's glittering golden mile. The softly lit ambience includes a romantic piano bar where you can enjoy a glass of champagne or an entire meal while absorbing the views, or try the full gourmet experience in the restaurant. Open for lunch daily 11.30am–2.30pm; for dinner Sun–Thurs 5–10.15pm, Fri and Sat 5–10.45pm. **$$$**

Fleur de Lys

Mandalay Bay, 702 632 9400, mandalaybay.com/dining/fleurdelys.aspx

A beautiful offering at the Mandalay Bay gives Hubert Keller the chance to show off his signature French cuisine in Las Vegas. Starters include: ocean baeckeoffe with Maine lobster; crab cake; lobster bisque; leeks and wild mushrooms; and smoked salmon ravioli with guacamole. Mains include: slow-roasted Alaskan king salmon with hazelnut crust, leeks, duck comfit and black Perigord truffle vinaigrette; roasted sea bass with chicken jus flavoured with passion fruit; and filet mignon with braised oxtail tortellini. Open Wed–Sun 5.30–10.30pm. **$$$**

Joël Robuchon at the Mansion

MGM Grand, 702 891 7925, mgmgrand.com/dining

France's Chef of the Century, and the first chef to win 3 consecutive Michelin stars, has been lured to the MGM Grand, providing a counter service setting in which you can watch your dinner being prepared before your eyes. Tapas and entrées include: fresh tomato and king crab; asparagus with Oscetra caviar; fresh scallop with lemon and seaweed butter; pan-fried sea bass with lemongrass foam and stewed baby leeks; and sautéed veal chop with vegetable taglierini flavoured with pesto. Open Sun–Thurs 5.30–10pm; Fri and Sat 5.30–10.30pm. **$$**

Mon Ami Gabi

Paris, 702 944 4224, parislasvegas.com

A Parisian-style café set in the Louvre façade of the Paris hotel. It is on the Strip and you can even opt to sit outside. Open for breakfast 7–11am; for brunch 11.30am–3pm Sat and Sun; for lunch 11.30am–3.45pm Mon–Fri; for dinner 4–11pm Sun–Thurs, 4pm–midnight Fri and Sat. **$$**

Alizé is André Rochat's restaurant

RESTAURANTS

Pamplemousse

400 East Sahara Avenue, 702 733 2066, pamplemousserestaurant.com
Like all the top French restaurants, this small but elegant establishment is pricey – but it's worth it. House specialities include: roast duckling in red wine and banana rum sauce; and veal medallions in cream sauce; plus a huge selection of fresh seafood according to the season from mussels to monkfish and salmon. Open daily 6–11pm. $$$

Restaurant Guy Savoy

Caesars Palace, 877 346 4642, caesarspalace.com
The famous French restaurateur, winner of 3 Michelin stars and Chef of the Year, France in 2002, opened his first restaurant in America in Caesars Palace. Run by his son and protégé Franck Savoy, the new restaurant takes pride of place on the second floor of the hotel's Augustus Tower, offering delightful views of the Roman Plaza. Open Wed–Sun 5.30–10.30pm. $$$

Switch

Encore Las Vegas, 702 248 3463, encorelasvegas.com
A surprise awaits at Switch as Chef René Lenger's French-inspired seafood and steakhouse fare is served in a dramatic space with an ambience that shifts throughout the evening. Go see! Open nightly 5.30–10pm. $$

Mix Lounge at the Mandalay Bay

Fusion restaurants

Fusia

Luxor, 702 262 4000, luxor.com/dining
A delightful blend of tastes and textures is served in a series of generously portioned appetisers, such as: satay beef skewers served in spiced tempura rings, drizzled with sweet cilantro sauce and spiked with a zesty mango papaya salsa; spiced Indonesian crab stack; and Fusia Nigiri-style sushi. Open daily 6–11pm. $

Little Buddha

The Palms, 702 942 7778, littlebuddhalasvegas.com
Based on the award-winning Buddha Bar and restaurant in Paris, this stylish eatery serves up both Pacific Rim and Chinese dishes with a French twist. There are 3 dining areas, all decorated in an opulent East-meets-West style, plus a sushi bar. Open Sun–Thurs 5.30–10.45pm; Fri and Sat until midnight. $$

Mayflower Cuisinier

Sahara Pavilion, 4750 West Sahara at Decatur Boulevard, 702 870 8432, mayflowercuisinier.com
One of the most highly rated restaurants in Las Vegas, Mayflower Cuisinier consistently appears in the Zagat Top 10. Here you will find Mongolian/Chinese cuisine served Californian style in a casual, but elegant environment. Book ahead for a table at weekends. Open for lunch Mon–Fri 11am–3pm; for dinner Mon–Thurs 5–10pm, Fri and Sat 5–11pm. $$

Mix

Mandalay Bay, 702 632 9500, mandalaybay.com/dining/mix.aspx
With its cutting-edge interior and fab views of the Strip, Mix is the perfect place to enjoy wonderful fusion cuisine. Think roasted Maine lobster 'au curry' with coconut basmati rice; bison tenderloin with sauce au poivre; seared rare tuna with prosciutto shavings, and Colorado rack of lamb with Mediterranean condiment. Open 6–11pm. $$

Restaurants with live music

Cabo Wabo Cantina: Miracle Mile Shops at Planet Hollywood Resort & Casino (see page 119)

Drai's: Barbary Coast

Eiffel Tower Restaurant: Paris Resort (see page 113)

House of Blues: Mandalay Bay (see page 124)

Harley-Davidson® Café: Southern end of Strip (see page 126)

Kahunaville: Treasure Island (see page 115)

N9NE Steakhouse: The Palms (see page 122)

Rumjungle: Mandalay Bay (see page 111)

Tommy Rocker's Mojave Beach Bar & Grill: 4275 Dean Martin Drive (see page 108)

VooDoo Café: Rio All-Suite Hotel (see page 111)

Roy's

620 East Flamingo Road, 702 691 2053, roysrestaurant.com
Hawaiian fusion is the name of the game in a restaurant that serves up European-style dishes with an Asian and Pacific flavour. Open Sun–Thurs 5.30–10pm; Fri and Sat 5.30–11pm. **$**

Signature Restaurant

Mandarin Oriental, Las Vegas, 00 800 2828 3838, mandarinoriental.com/lasvegas/
Opening December 2009, the 23rd floor Signature Restaurant is the only restaurant in the US where you can experience the cuisine of 3-star Michelin chef Pierre Gagnaire, who is celebrated as a pioneer of the fusion movement. Here he introduces another entirely new concept combining flavours and textures in the most unexpected way. Each dish will delight the senses with the familiarity of classic French cuisine and the modern twist. The interior is designed by Adam D. Tihany. It is a match for the Las Vegas skyline with 300 illuminated gold globes seeming to float across the ceiling and a dramatic suspended wine loft, reached by a glass staircase. Platforms throughout the restaurant ensure each guest enjoys these rare views of the glittering city heights through 20-ft/6-m high windows. Opening hours not yet available. **$$$**

Hawaiian restaurant

Kahunaville

Treasure Island, 702 894 7111, kahunaville.com
A lively (too much so for some) tropical restaurant setting complete with tiki torches and plants, this features Hawaiian dishes such as teriyaki ginger steak, Hawaiian pork tenderloin and coconut shrimp. It also doubles as a supper club with live entertainment and a 'Rock the Mic' live karaoke every Thurs, Fri and Sat, and there is a great choice of margaritas, coladas, beers and wine. Open daily at 8am; for lunch 11am–4pm; for dinner 4–10pm. The bar is open 11am–3am. **$**

Indian restaurant

Gaylord India Restaurant

Rio All-Suite Hotel, 702 777 7923, riolasvegas.com
A romantic setting with authentic Indian artefacts in which to enjoy tandoori and Mughlai-style dishes from the creators of the award-winning San Francisco restaurant. One of its main features is the Combination Dinners, in which you can choose different starters and entrées for an all-inclusive price. Open daily 5–11pm; Fri–Sun 11.30am–2.30pm. **$$**

Irish restaurant

Nine Fine Irishmen

New York-New York, 702 740 6969, ninefineirishmen.com
In a town where everything is copied, it was only a matter of time before an 'authentic' Irish pub with drink, food, music and entertainment opened its doors. And where better than the New York-New York hotel, which is evocative of the city that is home to so many Irish-Americans. Dishes

Fine Indian food at the Gaylord

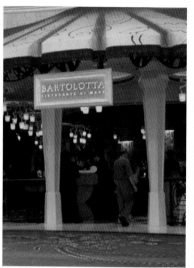

Bartolotta serves great seafood

have been created by 9 of Ireland's top chefs, though the name is based on the lives of nine Irishmen from the 19th century. Open daily 11am–11pm. **$–$$**

Italian restaurants

Al Dente

Bally's Hotel on the Strip, 702 967 7999, ballyslasvegas.com
Contemporary Italian cuisine served in a bright setting with plenty of favourites from bruschetta to gourmet pizzas, antipasti, spinach and chicken dishes. Open Wed–Sun 5.30–10.30pm. **$$**

B&B Ristorante

Grand Canal Shoppes, The Venetian, 702 266 9977, thegrandcanalshoppes.com
Celebrity chef Mario Batali, winner of the 2005 James Beard Foundation Chef of the Year Award and the genius behind several intensely popular New York restaurants brings his genius to The Venetian along with friend and expert wine maker Joseph Bastianich. It is wine and Italian cooking that 'captures the soul of an Italian grandmother dancing the tango with pop rock hipsters'. Open daily 5–11pm. **$$$**

Bartolotta Ristorante di Mare

Wynn Las Vegas, 702 248 3463, wynnlasvegas.com
Paul Bartolotta, winner of the James Beard Foundation's Best American Chef Midwest

award, has fresh seafood flown in daily from fish markets in Europe for his casual yet vibrant restaurant that offers outdoor seating near the lake and gardens. Alongside the signature seafood dishes are classic Italian specialities such as homemade pasta dishes. Open nightly 5.30–10pm. **$$**

Battista's Hole in the Wall

4041 Audrie Lane, 702 732 1424, battistaslasvegas.com
This old Vegas landmark serves Italian fare in a fun and friendly atmosphere that makes it a great eating place for locals and tourists alike. Open for dinner only 6–11pm. **$$**

California Pizza Kitchen

Mirage Hotel 702 791 7111 and Town Square Las Vegas 702 896 5154 cpk.com
Part of a growing national chain that highlights 'California Fusion' food and serves mostly delicious pizzas with mouth-watering selections of fresh ingredients. Think Chocolate Pizza and Thai Chicken Pizza. Open Mon–Thurs and Sun 11am–10pm; Fri and Sat 11am–11pm. **$**

Canaletto

Grand Canal Shoppes, the Venetian, 702 733 0122, thegrandcanalshoppes.com
Based on a concept by Il Fornaio's Larry Mindel, classics include homemade ravioli filled with fresh Maine lobster in a lobster cream sauce topped with shrimp, all overlooking the Grand Canal with gondolas passing by! Open Sun–Thurs 11.30am–11pm; Fri and Sat until midnight. **$$**

Casa Nicola

Las Vegas Hilton, 702 732 5755, lvhilton.com/dining
Specialises in fine northern Italian specialities in a beautiful setting. The exhibition kitchen gives customers the chance to watch chefs preparing the fresh pastas, pastries and sauces. Open 5.30–11pm. **$$**

Chicago Joe's

820 South 4th Street, 702 382 5637, chicagojoesrestaurant.com
Chicago Joe's is an ageless Las Vegas standard and is famous for its Italian sauces. Try the cream garlic dressing with one of the many delicious salads, Mexican Gulf shrimp and Maine lobster. Open Tues–Fri 11am–10pm; Sat 5–10pm. **$**

Francesco's

**Treasure Island, 702 894 7111,
treasureisland.com**
Filled with artwork by celebrities including
crooner Tony Bennett, the menu here
includes fresh pastas, antipasti,
Mediterranean-style seafood and signature
freshly baked breads. Open Sun–Thurs
11am–11pm; Fri and Sat 11am–midnight
(closed daily 4–5pm). **$**

Il Fornaio

**New York-New York, 702 650 6500,
ilfornaio.com**
A superb re-creation of an Italian restaurant
from New York's Little Italy neighbourhood,
here you'll find classic Italian cuisine and
signature breads, rolls and pastries from
the in-house bakery. By the way, most of
the waiters migrated to Las Vegas from
New York when the hotel opened, so the
accents are real! Open Sun–Thurs 7.30am
–midnight; Fri and Sat until 1am. **$$**

Marinelli's

**The M Resort, 702 797 1000,
themresort.com**
You'll discover authentic and regional
Italian cuisine here. Designed with social
spaces in mind, the restaurant lends itself to
intimate conversation. Menu selections
include risottos, handmade pastas, seafood
specialties, steaks, chops and veal dishes,
as well as selections from the Marnell
family (M Resort owners) recipe book and
wines from the Marnell family private label.
With outdoor terraces overlooking the
adjacent steakhouse, Villaggio Del Sole
events piazza and the Las Vegas Strip,
Marinelli's is the place to see and be seen.
Open daily 5–11pm. **$$**

Martorano's

**Rio All-Suite Hotel, 3700 West Flamingo
Road, 702 777 7740, riolasvegas.com**
Like all the Rio restaurants, Martorano's
makes an excellent choice for those in
search of a delicious Italian meal and this
place caters for the cast of *The Sopranos*!
Don't miss the meatballs! Open nightly 6–
10.30pm. **$$–$$$**

Onda

Mirage, 866 339 4566, mirage.com/dining
Regional Italian and new American cuisine
inspired by Todd English and served up in
an elegant setting. All-you-can eat mussels
Sun through Thurs 5–7pm for $20 per
person. Open 5.30–11pm. **$–$$$**

Sergio's Italian Gardens

**1955 East Tropicana Avenue, 702 739
1544, sergiosrestaurant.com**
Consistently rated as one of the best Italian
restaurants in town, Sergio's has a
delightful garden with Roman columns.
Dishes include calamari, Belgium endive
salad, sautéed veal and filet mignon
Rossini. Open Mon–Fri 11.30am–2.30pm,
and nightly 5.30–11pm. **$$**

Sinatra

**Encore Las Vegas, 702 248 3463,
encorelasvegas.com**
Sinatra is a salute to Ol' Blue Eyes. Chef
Theo Schoenegger's modern Italian cuisine
riffs with Sinatra tunes as guests revisit the
entertainer's legendary charisma. A must
for Sinatra buffs. Open nightly 5.30–
10pm. **$$**

Sirio

**Aria Resort & Casino (open December
2009), 866 359 7757, arialasvegas**
Chef Sirio Maccioni will introduce a menu
of Italian favorites such as Veal Milanese,
Osso Buco and authentic pasta dishes.
Guests will enjoy traditional cocktails of
Italy and one of Las Vegas's largest
selections of Italian vintages at a wide
array of price points. Designed by long-
time Maccioni collaborator Adam Tihany,
Sirio will channel old-time Italy with its
fantastical, Fellini-esque décor. Opening
hours not yet available. **$$**

Trattoria del Lupo

**Mandalay Bay, 702 632 7410,
mandalaybay.com/dining/trattoria.aspx**
Another of celebrity chef Wolfgang Puck's
6 eating outlets in Las Vegas, this one is
pure Italian with traditional recipes cooked
in pizza ovens and wood-burning
rotisseries. The interior was designed by
Adam Tihany, who has re-created a typical
small, secluded piazza in Milan with views
of pasta, meats and bakery production
areas. Open Sun–Thurs 5–10pm; Fri and
Sat 5–11pm. **$$**

Onda's Wine Lounge

Japanese restaurants

Bar Masa

Aria Resort & Casino (open December 2009), 866 359 7757, arialasvegas
Making his Las Vegas debut, Chef Masayoshi Takayama's concept will comprise 2 distinct dining experiences. The restaurant's casual dining space will feature an à la carte menu of modern Japanese cuisine. Shaboo, an intimate and exclusive venue within Bar Masa, will have an ever-changing menu based on the best seasonally available ingredients. Each table will feature its own induction cooking element to create the ultimate dining experience. The restaurant, designed in collaboration with Richard Bloch, will be refined and sleek, yet awe-inspiring with ceilings that soar to 35ft/11m. Opening hours not yet available. **$$**

Benihana Village

Las Vegas Hilton, 702 732 5755, lasvegashilton.com
Japanese fantasyland in an enchanting garden setting complete with thunder and lightning storms, lush flowers, flowing ponds and an authentic torii arch. There are 2 restaurants to choose from – the Hibachi where skilled chefs chop, slice and grill your food tableside and the Seafood Grille, where delicious delicacies are the order of the day. You can enjoy drinks and Oriental hors d'oeuvres in the Kabuki Lounge while your table is prepared. Open Sun–Fri 5.30–11pm; Sat 5–11pm. **$$$**

Hamada's Asiana

Rio All-Suite Hotel, 702 777 7923, riolasvegas.com
The waitresses are dressed in kimonos, which gives this restaurant a touch of authenticity. The main dining room features classics such as beef sukiyaki, shabu-shabu and seafood yosenabe. A second dining room, the Teppan Room, is where food is prepared in front of you by knife-wielding chefs. Delicious dishes are made up from shrimp, lobster, steaks and marinated chicken. It also has a sushi bar. Open Sun–Thurs 5–9.20pm. **$$–$$$**

BRITTIP

If you want an early evening appetiser, head for the Hamada's cocktail lounge, where you can get little plates of deep-fried tempura and sushi with your drinks.

Hyakumi Japanese Restaurant and Sushi Bar

Caesars Palace, 877 346 4642, caesarspalace.com
Fresh sushi by masterchefs along with teppanyaki-style cooking and à la carte dishes including noodles – all served at traditional teppan tables. Open for lunch daily 11am–3.30pm; for dinner daily 5–11pm. **$$$**

MOzen

Mandarin Oriental, Las Vegas, 00 800 2828 3838, mandarinoriental.com/lasvegas/
This all-day dining restaurant is a kitchen theatre of Pan-Asian and international cuisine with an exhibition noodle bar, rotisserie and grill. A clean, contemporary feel is complemented by deeply comfortable leather banquettes. Geometry and art introduce some striking creativity, with 3 spectacular circular steel and glass rod chandeliers suspended above round tables. Opening times not yet available. **$$**

Nobu

Hard Rock Hotel, 702 693 5090, hardrockhotel.com
Chef Nobu Matsuhisa's ground-breaking temple of Japanese cuisine with Peruvian influences has already set unmatched standards of excellence in Los Angeles, New York and London. Nobu Las Vegas has been hugely successful for the Hard Rock Hotel. Dishes include squid pasta, miso-infused cod and creamy, spicy, cracked crab. Open daily 6–11pm. **$$$**

Shibuya

MGM Grand, 702 891 3001, mgmgrand.com/dining
An expansive and spectacular environment forms the perfect backdrop to this stylish offering, which takes its name from the Tokyo district of Shibuya. Featuring freshly prepared ingredients and exquisite sushi, the restaurant also boasts one of the widest sake selections available anywhere in America. Open Sun–Thurs 5–10pm; Fri and Sat 5–10.30pm. **$$–$$$**

Teru Sushi

Las Vegas Hilton, 702 732 5111, lvhilton.com/dining
Teru Sushi features more than 40 types of fresh sushi shipped daily from the west coast and prepared by a licensed sushi chef. Reservations are not required. Open Tues–Sat 5.30–10.30pm. **$$**

Yellowtail Japanese Restaurant & Lounge

Bellagio, 702 693 7223, bellagio.com
Adventurous Japanese dining in a stylish contemporary setting with an impressive 25-ft/8-m bronze wall-mounted installation of the dorsal side of the yellowtail fish! Award-winning chef Akira Back's menu includes seasonal fish, sushi, sashimi, tempura and hand rolls. Delicious! Open Mon–Thurs 5–10pm; Fri and Sat 5–11pm. **$$**

Mediterranean restaurants

Olives

Bellagio, 702 693 7223, bellagio.com
Todd and Olivia English bring their famous Boston Olives to Las Vegas with Mediterranean-style dishes in a lively café setting. Open daily 11am–2.45pm and 5–10.30pm. **$$**

Picasso

Bellagio, 702 693 7223, bellagio.com
Julian Serrano, who dazzled diners at San Francisco's Masa, brings his trademark Spanish-tinged French cuisine to one of the world's most opulent settings for a restaurant – dine here and you'll be surrounded by $52m worth of Picasso originals and even some of the artist's ceramics. The menu changes nightly but usually includes Julian's foie gras in Madeira sauce or warm lobster salad with mangoes or potatoes. The views of the Bellagio's dancing fountains finish off a superb dining experience. Open Wed–Mon 6–9.30pm. **$$$**

Mexican restaurants

Blue Agave

The Palms, 702 942 7777, thepalms.com
A fun, casual dining experience at the über-trendy Palms hotel, named after the plant that gives tequilas their flavour. The house specialities are oysters, seafood cocktails and pan roasts, plus a chilli bar with South American favourites. Open Mon

BRITTIP

For a real party atmosphere, head to the Blue Agave, where along with delish Mexican-based cuisine, there is a range of 150 tequilas and a whopping 350 different margaritas to choose from!

11am–9.30pm; Tues–Thurs 11am–10pm; Fri and Sat 11am–11pm; Sunday for brunch 10.30am–3pm and for dinner 4–10pm. **$$$**

Border Grill

Mandalay Bay, 702 632 7403, mandalaybay.com/dining/bordergrill.aspx
Mary Sue Milliken and Susan Feniger, the duo known on American TV as *Too Hot Tamales*, are renowned for their Border Grill in Los Angeles and have now opened an outlet in the new all-jumping hotel, Mandalay Bay. Their bold and tasty Mexican dishes are served in a vibrant beachside setting. Open Mon–Fri 11.30am–10pm; Fri 11.30am–11pm; Sat 11am–11pm; Sun 11am–10pm. **$$**

Cabo Wabo Cantina

Miracle Mile Shops, Planet Hollywood Resort & Casino, miraclemileshopslv.com/dine
In autumn 2009, rock legend Sammy Hagar will open his world-famous Cabo Wabo Cantina. This 2-level, 15,000ft²/1,394m² nightclub and restaurant offers a blend of live music and coastal Mexican food and a cocktail menu with a heavy emphasis on tequila. Get the slammers ready! Opening hours not yet available. **$**

Cozymel's

Hughes Center, 355 Hughes Center Drive, 702 732 4833, cozymels.com
An upscale franchise restaurant serving spectacular seafood specials and delicious fajitas. Open Mon–Thurs 11am–10pm; Fri and Sat 11am–11pm; Sun 1–9pm. **$**

Garduños

The Palms, 702 942 7777, gardunosrestaurants.com
Part of a Mexican cantina chain, this restaurant serves authentic Mexican cuisine and has quickly become a firm favourite in Las Vegas. Margaritas are also available. Open Mon 11am–9.30pm; Tues–Thurs 11am–10pm; Fri and Sat 11am–11pm; Sun 10.30am–3pm and 4–9pm. **$**

Inside Olives at the Bellagio

Gonzalez Y Gonzalez

New York-New York, 702 740 6455,
nynyhotelcasino.com/restaurants
A great spot to soak up the atmosphere of
the hotel's outdoor courtyard with lanterns
and Spanish piñatas, Gonzalez Y
Gonzalez serves authentic Mexican cuisine
at reasonable prices. Open daily 11am–
1am. $

BRITTIP
The real secret of Gonzalez Y
Gonzalez is the long list of
margaritas, which can even be served
by the yard!

Isla Mexican Kitchen & Tequila Bar

Treasure Island, 866 286 3809,
treasureisland.com
Chef Richard Sandoval offers traditional
Mexican cuisine with a modern twist.
Innovations include the roving guacamole
cart armed and ready with freshly made
guacamoles. Dishes include: grilled
Mexican spiced chicken breast with corn
dumplings; crispy red snapper with cactus
salad; and Isla sirloin with mashed
potatoes and chimichurri sauce. Tacos,
enchiladas, tamales and burritos all get a
modern twist, with ingredients such as
battered rock shrimp and wild mushrooms.
The Tequila Bar features an impressive
selection of tequilas plus margaritas,
sangrias and other Mexican cocktail
favourites. Open daily 4–11pm. The bar
and lounge is open daily 11am–2am. $$

Try Mexican at Isla

Pink Taco

Hard Rock Hotel, 702 693 5525,
hardrockhotel.com
A trendy restaurant offering celebrated
Californian chef Tacho Kneeland's fresh
and modern take on Mexican classics.
Choices include tamales nachos,
quesadillas, tacos and a whole range of
tequilas – served the traditional way,
natch! Open Sun–Thurs 11am–10pm; Fri
and Sat 11am–midnight. $$

Viva Mercado's

3553 South Rainbow, 702 655 3663,
vivamercadoslv.com
Regularly wins the local daily paper's poll
for best Mexican restaurant in town due to
its delicious food including chilli relleno,
carnitas and Mexican-style steak at great
prices. Open Sun–Thurs 11am–9.30pm; Fri
and Sat 11am–10.30pm. $

BRITTIP
Be warned: although Las Vegas
is a 24-hour city, most of the top-
notch restaurants close as early as
10pm or 10.30pm.

Moroccan restaurants

Mamounia

4632 South Maryland Parkway, 702 597
0092
Delicious Moroccan dishes are served in a
simulated Middle Eastern desert tent setting
complete with low benches or pillows,
costumed waiters and belly dancers. House
specialities include all the Moroccan
classics such as hummus, kefta, tabbouleh,
briouats, cacik yoghurt dip, shish kebabs
and couscous. Great value. Open daily
5.30–11pm. $$

Marrakech Restaurant

3900 Paradise Road, 702 737 5611,
marrakechvegs.com
The oldest Moroccan restaurant in town
which takes the whole 'eating in the desert'
thing one stage further than Mamounia by
expecting diners to eat with their hands!
The house specialities include Moroccan-
style chicken in a light lemon sauce and
flambéed lamb brochette. Dinner features a
belly-dancing show. Open daily 5.30–
11pm. $$

Seafood and steakhouses

American Fish

Aria Resort & Casino (open December 2009), 866 359 7757, arialasvegas
For his newest concept, James Beard award-winner chef Michael Mina will draw inspiration from the bounty of American lakes, rivers and coasts to create a menu featuring refined American cuisine. Many products will be purchased directly from fishermen, farmers and ranchers, allowing diners to enjoy unique regional dishes. The menu also will feature a wide array of well-sourced meats. Chris Sheffield of SLDesign, LLC, in collaboration with Mina, designed a room that resembles a traditional lodge, with masculine touches such as warm woods and leather accents. Opening hours not yet available. **$$**

AquaKnox

Grand Canal Shoppes, the Venetian, 702 414 3772, grandcanalshoppes.com
Chef Tom Moloney, who honed his skills during 12 years with Wolfgang Puck, won Best New Restaurant in Vegas when his seafood extravaganza opened. Fresh seafood is flown in daily from around the world to provide a superb raw bar alongside wonderful dishes of filet mignon with truffle aioli, and grilled lobster with herb butter. Favourites include the fresh stone crab claws from Florida Keys; sweet shrimp cocktail; Louisiana prawns; jumbo lump crab cocktail; dry-aged prime New York steak; and oven-roasted guinea hen. Open Sun–Thurs 12am–2.30pm and 5.30–11pm; Fri and Sat 11.30am–2.30pm and 5.30–11.30pm. **$$–$$$**

Botero

Encore Las Vegas, 702 248 3463, encorelasvegas.com
Diners can appreciate the art collection by Columbian artist Fernando Botero here while sampling Chef Mark LoRusso's modern cuisine, steaks and chops. Open Sun–Thurs 5.30–10.30pm; Fri and Sat 5.30–11pm. **$$**

Búzio's Seafood Restaurant

Rio All-Suite Hotel, 702 777 7923, riolasvegas.com
Probably one of the best seafood restaurants in town with an extraordinary selection of seafood dishes. This is another fine restaurant based at the Rio All-Suite Hotel and well deserves its appearance in the annual Zagat survey of top restaurants in Las Vegas. Open Wed–Sun 5–11pm. **$$–$$$**

Craftsteak

MGM Grand, 702 891 7318, mgmgrand.com/dining
Craftsteak was created by award-winning chef Tom Colicchio, founder of the critically acclaimed Craft restaurant in New York. The philosophy is simple: use the finest available produce and cook in such a way as to allow the flavours of the ingredients to shine through. Open Sun–Mon 6–10pm; Tues–Thurs 5.30–10pm; Fri and Sat 5.30–10.30pm. **$$–$$$**

Delmonico Steakhouse

Grand Canal Shoppes at the Venetian, 702 4143737, thegrandcanalshoppes.com
Emeril Lagasse's second outlet in Las Vegas features the food surprises that have made him famous. It seems to be on everybody's list of top steakhouses in the USA. Open daily 5.30–10.30pm. **$$$**

House of Lords

The Sahara, 702 737 2111, saharavegas.com/dining/houseorlords
One of the longest-running steak shows in town, the House of Lords keeps putting out good food at a decent price. Favourites – alongside the famous New York strip steak, double lamb chops and roast prime rib of beef – include escargot, lobster bisque, stuffed portobello mushrooms and roasted crab cakes. Open Mon–Thurs 5–10pm; Fri and Sat 5–11pm. **$$**

Hugo's Cellar

Four Queen's, 202 Fremont Street, Downtown, 702 385 4011, hugoscellar.com
Very old school and a popular choice with locals and visitors alike, so book ahead to

House of Lords at the Sahara

RESTAURANTS

Prime's main dining room

get a table. Famous for its excellent wine list. Open daily 5.30–11pm. **$$**

Jean-Georges Steakhouse

Aria Resort & Casino (open December 2009), 866 359 7757, arialasvegas
At Aria, Chef Jean-Georges Vongerichten will eschew tradition by melding beloved steakhouse touches with a decidedly contemporary experience. The menu will highlight the best ingredients and preparations, paying particular attention to an innovative array of side dishes and sauces. Designed by Dupoux Design, the restaurant's high-octane lounge and extensive bar program will focus on classic cocktails. Opening hours not yet available. **$$**

Michael Mina

Bellagio, 702 693 7223, bellagio.com
Celebrity chef Michael Mina has replaced the top-notch Aqua with an even more amazing restaurant that has been drawing ecstatic plaudits for its innovative yet gourmet seafood dishes. Blending fresh ingredients from California, Britain and the Mediterranean, the incredible line-up of tastebud-tickling starters include savoury black mussel soufflé with saffron Chardonnay cream; seared sea scallops and foie gras with a rhubarb-lime compote and Thai coconut soup with Dungeness crab. First courses include the tempura langoustine with young ginger, pickled fennel, saffron aioli, green papaya and mango. Entrées include Angus beef filet mignon, tapioca-crusted black bass with toasted almonds and Chile garlic vinaigrette; Maine lobster pot pie and roasted whole Hudson Valley foie gras. Eat it and weep with sheer joy. Open Sun–Thurs 5.30–10pm; Fri and Sat 5.30–10.30pm. **$$–$$$**

Michael's

Barbary Coast, 3595 The Strip at East Flamingo, 702 737 7111, barbarycoastcasino.com
Despite its unprepossessing setting, this is the choice of Las Vegas high-flyers so tables are hard to get. The food is superb, with reasonable prices. Real foodies will have a ball. Open nightly 6pm–midnight. **$$**

N9NE Steakhouse

The Palms, 702 933 9900, http://n9negroup.com
Another stylish offering from The Palms, the Chicago-style prime-aged steaks and chops are served in a sleek setting. Aside from the restaurant, a champagne caviar bar sits amid comfy suede-covered booths from where you can gaze at the changing colours of the ceiling or try to spot the celebs arriving at the glass-enclosed private dining room. Open Sun–Thurs 5–11pm; Fri and Sat 5–11.30pm. **$$**

Palm Restaurant

Forum Shops at Caesars Palace, 702 732 7256
Following on from the success of the New York restaurant, the Las Vegas version also appears in the Zagat Top 40. Famous for crab cakes, lobster, prime rib and the house speciality, charcoal-burnt steak. Open daily 11.30am–11pm. **$$**

Prime

Bellagio, 702 693 7223, bellagio.com
Award-winning chef Jean-Georges Vongerichten uses only the highest-quality meats, seafood and chops to create a fine dining experience. Open daily 5–10pm. **$$**

rm Seafood

Mandalay Bay, 702 632 9300, mandalaybay.com/dining/restaurantrm.aspx
With two restaurants in one, New York chef Rick Moonen offers the R Bar Café on the ground floor and the gourmet Restaurant rm upstairs. Delicious offerings include abalone in butter with Pacific

Michael Mina at the Bellagio

Lakeside dining

Café Lago: Caesars Palace (see page 128)

Daniel Boulud: Wynn Las Vegas (see page 109)

Jasmine: Bellagio (see page 112)

Le Cirque: Bellagio (see page 113)

Medici Café and Terrace: Ritz-Carlton, Lake Las Vegas

Olives: Bellagio (see page 119)

SW Steakhouse: Wynn Las Vegas (see page 123)

sturgeon caviar, mussel soufflé with green curry sauce, halibut with foie gras and melted leeks in a red wine emulsion, and butter-poached lobster with corn chowder. There is also a 6-course tasting menu that will set you back just over $100. Open downstairs 11am–11pm; upstairs 5–10pm. **$$–$$$**

Ruth's Chris Steakhouse

3900 Paradise Road, 702 791 7011 and 4561 West Flamingo Road, 702 248 7011, ruthschris.com
A chain of franchised steakhouses that started in New Orleans, these places have a reputation for serving prime meat on a sizzling-hot platter with butter. Other offerings include lamb, chicken and fish with delicious vegetables from sautéed mushrooms to creamed spinach. Open daily 4.30–10.30pm. **$$**

Smith & Wollensky

3767 The Strip opposite the Monte Carlo next to the MGM Grand, 702 862 4100, smithandwollensky.com
Alan Stillman's New York steakhouse group's $10m free-standing, 3-storey restaurant seats up to 600 diners in a catacomb-like series of rooms, niches and chambers. Open Sun–Thurs 11.30am–midnight; Fri and Sat 11.30am–1am. **$$**

SW Steakhouse

Wynn Las Vegas, 702 248 3463, wynnlasvegas.com
Star chef David Walzog redefines all the steakhouse classics here. Think charred, prime-aged steaks and chops as well as poultry and seafood specialties. An elegant yet contemporary space, the restaurant offers the chance to dine outside overlooking the hotel's famous lake and mountain. Open 5.30–10pm. **$$**

The Steak House

Circus Circus, 702 794 3767, www.circuscircus.com/dining
An exception to every other rule at the family-friendly Circus Circus, this is definitely adult-friendly (the kids are running around the lobby outside) and serves some of the best steaks and seafood in town, making it one of the finest in its price range. Open for dinner daily from 5pm. **$$**

The Steakhouse at Camelot

Excalibur, 702 597 7777, excalibur.com/restaurants
Gourmet cuisine served in the Excalibur castle overlooking make-believe English countryside creates a truly wonderful eating experience. Epicureans will find everything they are looking for from a fine wine cellar to a cigar room, lounge and private dining chamber, while the casual ambience makes it a friendly place for anyone to enjoy a meal. Dinner specials often available, such as 3 courses for $25. Open nightly 5–10pm. **$–$$**

Terzetto & Terzetto Oyster Bar

The M Resort, 702 797 1000, themresort.com
Exhibition-style kitchen where charcoal-grilled steaks and seafood are expertly prepared such as hand-selected prime cuts of beef, including a reserve list from the Marnell family ranch and fresh-from-the-ocean seafood specialties. Terzetto Oyster Bar offers a casual dining option with made-to-order selections including soups, stews and pan favourites, oysters on the half shell, seafood salads, cocktails, ceviche and pastas. To top it off, guests can enjoy an extensive wine list or hand-crafted cocktails and the fabulous views both inside and outside. Open Sun–Thurs 5–11pm; Fri and Sat 5–midnight. **$$**

The main dining room at rm Seafood

RESTAURANTS

The Tillerman

2245 East Flamingo Road, 702 731 4036, tillerman.com/
One of the best places in town to get a fabulously fresh seafood dinner without breaking the bank. Pacific salmon, Chilean sea bass and Florida snapper are some of the seafood platters on offer, while you'll also find steaks and pasta. Open daily 5–11pm. **$$**

BRITTIP

The Top of the World restaurant is one of the '10 Great Places to Pop the Question' according to America's wedding website, The Knot – theknot.com. Other locations include Paris and New York's Brooklyn Bridge.

The Top of the World

Stratosphere, 702 380 7711, topoftheworldlv.com
The name says it all! More than 800ft/ 240m up the tallest free-standing building in America, the Top of the World revolving restaurant makes a full 360-degree revolution every hour and 20 minutes. Awarded the Best Gourmet Room award by the *Las Vegas Review Journal*, the top-notch food includes sizzling steaks and fresh fish and seafood, tasty salads and flaming desserts. Even if the food wasn't great, the view would be worth it all by itself. Open Sun–Thurs 5–11pm; Fri and Sat until midnight. **$$**

The Tillerman

Private dining

If you want to impress, how about booking a Krug Champagne Room at Caesars Palace? The first of its kind in the US, The Krug Room at Restaurant Guy Savoy (702 731 7731, guysavoy. com) offers private dining rooms for seasonal, 6-course pairing menus of decadent cuisine served with a range of Krug champagnes including vintages. Cheque books at the ready! **$$$**

Yolie's

3900 Paradise Road, 702 794 0700, yolies.qpg.com
A Brazilian steakhouse with large, wood-fired rotisseries that cook the meals in full view of the diners. The selection includes turkey, lamb, brisket, chicken, sausages and steak, plus side dishes of fried brown rice, potatoes and vegetables. Open 11am–11pm weekdays; 5–11pm weekends. **$$**

Southern restaurant

House of Blues

Mandalay Bay, 702 632 7605, mandalaybay.com/dining/houseofblues.aspx
Las Vegas's version of Dan Aykroyd's famous House of Blues on Los Angeles' Strip at the majestic Mandalay Bay is living up to its 'hot' reputation. You'll find every kind of dish from Southern to Creole and Cajun staples as well as wood-fired pizza and burgers. Gospel fans will enjoy the Gospel Brunch, which features live music and an all-you-can-eat Southern-style buffet. At other times of the week expect blues-inspired and other live music. Open Sun–Thurs 7.30am–midnight; Fri and Sat 7.30am–1am. **$$**

South-western restaurants

Chili's Grill and Bar

2011 N Rainbow Blvd, 702 638 1482 and 5 other locations throughout the city, chilis.com
Mexican style with grills, sandwiches, steaks and fajitas at the restaurants in this chain. **$$**

Mesa Grill

Caesars Palace, 877 346 4642, caesarspalace.com
Celebrity chef Bobby Flay turns down the heat on a range of South-western classics

that can usually set your throat on fire. A contemporary approach means: smoked chicken and black bean quesadilla; and lobster and cod griddle cakes, with red cabbage slaw for starters. Main course signatures include: the 16-spices rubbed rotisserie chicken; whole-fried striped bass with five-pepper ginger sauce; and Flay's Cuban burger, sandwiched between slices of roast pork, cheese, ham and pickles. Open for lunch Mon–Fri 11am–2.30pm; for brunch Sat and Sun 10.30am–3pm; for dinner daily 5–11pm. **$$**

Spanish restaurants

Cafe Ba Ba Reeba!
The Fashion Show Mall, 702 258 1211, cafebabareeba.com
The delicious combination of flavours that are the hallmark of Spanish tapas arrives on the Strip in a fun restaurant. Using the freshest seafood, cheeses and vegetables, the speciality is paella, while there is a wonderful variety of sangrias. Open for lunch Sun–Sat 11.30am–3.30pm; dinner Sun–Thurs 3.30pm–1am and Fri and Sat until 2am. **$**

Julian Serrano
Aria Resort & Casino (open December 2009), 866 359 7757, arialasvegas.com
The internationally acclaimed chef's eponymous restaurant will feature a casual atmosphere with menus at different price points. The seafood bar will highlight fresh shellfish and ceviches, while the dining room and lounge will serve tapas and other dishes from Serrano's native Spain. Check website for updates. **$$**

Tavern dining

Nobhill Tavern
MGM Grand, 702 891 7337, mgmgrand.com/restaurants/nobhill-tavern-restaurant.aspx
Nobhill Tavern by Michael Mina brings a new concept all of its own to Vegas – tavern cuisine. Just like the term 'B&B', tavern means something altogether more upmarket in the US. There's an innovative

Outdoor and patio dining
Bartolotta Ristorante di Mare: Wynn Las Vegas (page 116)
BOA Prime Grill: Forum Shops
Bouchon: The Venetian (page 109)
Cafe Ba Ba Reeba!: Fashion Show Mall (page 125)
Daniel Boulud: Wynn Las Vegas (page 109)
Gonzalez Y Gonzalez: New York-New York (page 120)
Mon Ami Gabi: Paris Resort (page 113)
Nine Fine Irishmen: New York-New York (page 115)
Olives: Bellagio (page 119)
Pink Taco: Hard Rock Hotel (page 120)

drink menu that pays homage to classic cocktails, an expansive lounge area and the menu is full of Mina's signature dishes including lobster rolls on buttery toasted brioche and tableside chicken and dumplings. Open Sun–Thurs 5.30–10pm; Fri–Sat 5.30–10.30pm. **$$**

Theme restaurants

ESPN Zone
New York-New York, 702 933 3776, nynyhotelcasino.com/restaurants
With flat-screen TVs throughout showing the latest sport action and a fully stocked bar, this is the place for sports fans to tip up. Food offerings include buffalo wings, burgers, garlic mashed potatoes and grilled steak with salad. Open Sun–Thurs 11am–11pm; Fri and Sat 11am–midnight. **$**

Hard Rock Café
Showcase Mall, next to MGM Grand and adjacent to Monte Carlo, 702 733 1274, hardrock.com/las vegas
Possibly the most rock 'n' roll of all the worldwide Hard Rock Cafes, this 42,000ft^2/3,900m^2 of non-stop action is spread over 3 floors on an all new building that opened September 2009 right on the

Strip. You can't miss it as there's a giant neon guitar on the side! There's an interactive 'Rock Wall', interactive Microsoft surface tables, a contemporary lounge and bar, a patio with Strip views, oh and quite a lot of good food! The café also features a built-in stage with an attached Green Room, so expect lots of celebs dropping by. Open 1–10pm. **$–$$**

Harley-Davidson® Café

The Strip at Harmon Avenue, 702 740 4555, harley-davidsoncafe.com
This is the second outlet that pays homage to the 100-year-old motorbike and is hard to miss with its 28ft/8.5m high, 15,000lb/6,800kg $500,000 Harley Davidson Heritage Softail Classic bike outside! Inside the 20,000ft^2/1,860m^2, 2-storey café is a celebration of the free-spirit lifestyle of Harley Davidsons. And the food and drink lives up to it, too! You can sip on a range of cocktails with names such as Hill Climber, Rockin' Rita and Flat Tracker. Soak up the alcohol with fajitas, hamburgers, barbecue chicken, chillis, pasta or hot dogs. Open Sun–Thurs 11am–midnight; Fri and Sat 11am–2am. **$**

Jimmy Buffett's Margaritaville

The Flamingo, 702 733 3302, margaritavillelasvegas.com
For a themed night out with a difference, head to the great new Caribbean joint at the Flamingo where a 3-storey volcano erupts as it serves up delicious margaritas in the Volcano Bar. Spread over 3 levels, the restaurant has 5 bars and live music, and steaks, seafood, hamburgers and Caribbean cuisine are served up with

toppings such as pineapple-rum sauce. At the top of the restaurant are 2 outdoor patios overlooking the Strip, one of which is home to the 12 Volt Bar, where live music is provided nightly on a theme of island and rock. Even if you don't plan to party the night away, do visit the bar if only to see the giant sails of the life-size Euphoria boat flying high! Open Sun–Thurs 8am–2am; Fri and Sat 8am–3am (dinner served until midnight). **$**

Nascar Café

Sahara, 2535 South Las Vegas Boulevard, 702 734 7223, saharavegas.com/food/nascar-cafe
For lovers of the Las Vegas Motor Speedway or stock racing generally, this is the theme café to visit. A 2-level offering with NASCAR merchandise, giant TV screens showing NASCAR races and authentic stock cars, the centrepiece is a Pontiac Grand Prix car that comes to life every hour, re-creating the excitement of being at the track. Dishes include Talladega tenders, supercharged chilli and dipstick fried cheese. Cocktails include battery acid and caution-flag margaritas. What fun! Open Sun–Thurs 11am–10pm; Fri and Sat 11am–11pm. **$**

Planet Hollywood

Forum Shops at Caesars Palace, 702 791 7827, planethollywood.com
A chain famous more for their décor than the food, the place is overrun with photos and costumes and other Hollywood mementos. It seems every square inch has a Klingon costume or Freddie Kruger mask. The menu includes gourmet pizzas, pastas, fish, burgers and more. Open Sun–Thurs 9am–11pm; Fri and Sat 9am–midnight. **$**

The Rainforest Café

MGM Grand on the Strip, 702 891 8580, mgmgrand.com/dining/rainforest-cafe.aspx
A real-life simulation of a rainforest complete with tropical rainstorms featuring thunder and lightning that boom and spark across the entire restaurant. It's an untamed paradise brimming with exotic tropical birds, animated elephants, leopards and gorillas and tropical trees. You enter the dining area by walking under a massive double archway aquarium filled with marine fish from around the world. The food, quite good by the way, consists of pastas, salads, sandwiches and delectable desserts. Open Sun–Thurs 8am–11pm; Fri and Sat 8am–midnight. **$**

The chain restaurant Hard Rock Café

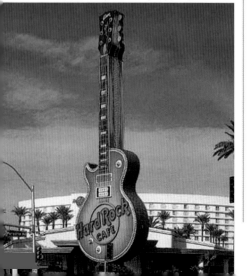

Trans ethnic restaurants

Restaurant Veloce Cibo & Bar Veloce

The M Resort, 702 797 1000, themresort.com

Gracing the summit of the M Resort, Veloce Cibo combines an extensive menu of appetisers, entrées, sushi, sashimi and nigiri with satisfying desserts and a range of hand-crafted cocktails and speciality drinks that take centre stage at Bar Veloce. The newest spot for dining and nightlife, Veloce Cibo offers amazing views of the Las Vegas skyline and one of the most spectacular terraces in the city. Open Sun–Thurs 5–11pm; Fri and Sat 5pm–1am. **$$**

Silk Road

Vdara Resort (opening Oct 2009 as part of the CityCenter development), 866 745 7767, vdara.com

Breaking new ground in Las Vegas, Silk Road is billed as a modern trans-ethnic restaurant, featuring an intimate lounge and bar area, which will transform as the day evolves, from fresh and energetic at daybreak to hip and sexy at nightfall. A must-do dining experience in the new world of Vegas sophistication. Opening hours not yet available. **$$–$$$**

Lounge dining

Lounges are almost unique to Las Vegas. Relaxed yet stylish environments, they all provide live entertainment and in some cases delicious food. Here's a selection.

Firenze Lobby Lounge

Ritz-Carlton, Lake Las Vegas, 702 567 4700, ritzcarlton.com

For a light bite in a relaxing and romantic setting, this is the place to come. With views of the lake and beautiful art around

⚡ BRITTIP

For a moment of refinement, try afternoon Florentine tea at the Firenze Lobby Lounge. Fresh flower arrangements and a live pianist create the perfect setting in which to enjoy scones, sandwiches and savouries while taking in the view of Lake Las Vegas and the mountains.

the walls, you can enjoy hors d'oeuvres, desserts and soufflés before and after your meal. There's live music nightly plus an excellent selection of cocktails, champagne, brandy and liqueurs. Open 11am–midnight. **$$**

Peppermill Café & Lounge

2985 Las Vegas Boulevard South, 702 735 4177

For a taste of old-style Vegas hospitality, the Peppermill should be on your must-visit list. The food is excellent and portions are on the large side. Think burgers, sandwiches, steak, seafood and huge salads. While you're here, have a drink in the romantic lounge, which is famous for its fireplace, candlelit tables and comfy sofas. Open 24/7. **$**

Tea Lounge

Mandarin Oriental, Las Vegas, 00 800 2828 3838, mandarinoriental.com/lasvegas/

A first for Vegas, the Mandarin Oriental's Tea Lounge brings authentic tea ceremonies to Sin City. Whether you fancy English tea and cupcakes or jasmine and some eastern delicacies, it's all here with gracious service and fab views. Opening hours not yet available. **$**

Cafés and diners

America

New York-New York, 702 740 6451, nynyhotelcasino.com/restaurants

A large, open restaurant with a few booths, serves classic casual American food such as roast turkey, meatloaf, pastas, salads and burgers. If all else fails to capture your imagination, try the all-day breakfast. Open 24/7. **$**

Nascar Café for speedway fans

Binion's Coffee Shop

Binion's Horseshoe Hotel, 128 Fremont Street, 702 382 1600
Binion's gets packed with downtown gamblers, so you have to pick your time to avoid long queues. Specialities include Benny Binion's Natural, considered to be one of the best-priced, most delicious breakfasts in town, and Binion's Delight, a hamburger platter with chips. Open 6–10.30pm. **$**

Café Lago

Caesars Palace, 702 731 7845 (groups over 14), caesarspalace.com
Just to prove that the Bellagio isn't the only resort in town with water views, Caesars has opened this large café right by the Garden of the Gods Pool Oasis. Serving international dishes and American favourites throughout the day and night, it also offers live music with pianist David Osborne and other soloists in the evening. The one drawback, of course, is that enjoying the beautiful setting doesn't come cheap. Open 24/7. **$$**

Café Michelle

1350 East Flamingo Road, inside the local mall, 702 735 8686
The place to go for plenty of cheap grub far from the madding crowd. The red-and-white checked tablecloths and Cinzano umbrellas over tables in the plaza create a European ambience, while you tuck into omelettes, crêpes, salads and seafood. **$**

Enigma Garden Café

918 S Fourth Street, 702 386 0999
One of the best cafés downtown, it even has live music outside in the garden at weekends. During the summer it's open 24 hours a day (7am–10pm in winter). **$**

Jazzed Café & Vinoteca

8615 West Sahara Ave, 702 233 2859 and 2055 E Tropicana Ave, 702 798 5995
One of your best bets away from the Strip

Fine dining at Michael Mina

is this fun room on West Sahara Ave that's decorated as a bold piece of living pop art. It seats about 40 for dinner but stays open past the dinner hour as a cosy spot for live music. Open Mon–Thurs 5pm–1am; Fri and Sat 5pm–3am; Sun 10am–2pm and 5pm–1am. **$–$$**

Mariposa

Level Two, Neiman Marcus, 3200 Las Vegas Boulevard South, 702 697 7330
Upscale café for upscale shoppers in need of a pick me up. A favourite of gay and lesbian diners. Open Mon–Sat 11.30am–3pm. **$$–$$$**

Roxy's Diner

Stratosphere on the Strip, 702 380 7711, stratospherehotel.com
A fun place to experience a piece of 1950s America – everything from the decor to the uniforms and music pay homage to the rock 'n' roll era. Food includes chicken, fried steak with homemade gravy and Mom's meat loaf with fresh vegetables and real mashed potatoes. Drinks include thick, cold milkshakes in tall, frosted glasses. Open Sun–Tues 11am–10pm; Fri and Sat 11am–11pm. **$**

Hotel and shopping mall restaurants

Many of the best restaurants that have been reviewed and listed are in the top resort-hotels. To make life easier I have listed all the eating places at the main resort hotels and shopping malls in town. The hotels also have their own buffets!

Aria Resort & Casino (Open December 2009)

866 359 7757, arialasvegas
The restaurants at Aria look all set to raise the bar in Las Vegas dining.
Fine dining:

American Fish	Seafood
Bar Masa	Japanese
Blossom	Chinese
Jean-George Steakhouse	Steak
Julian Serrano	Spanish
Lemongrass	Thai
The Light Group	American dim sum
Sage	Farm to table
Sirio	Italian

Casual:

The Buffet	Buffet
Café Centro	Café
JP Patisserie	Patisserie
Skybox Sports Bar & Grille	Themed

Best gourmet-style dining in a hotel

Alizé: The Palms (see page 112)

Aureole: Mandalay Bay (see page 105)

Búzio's Seafood Restaurant: Rio All-Suite Hotel (see page 121)

Les Artistes Steakhouse: Rio All-Suite Hotel (see page 113)

Michael Mina: Bellagio (see page 122)

Onda: Mirage (see page 117)

Nero's: Caesars Palace (see page 107)

Prime: Bellagio (see page 122)

The Top of the World: Stratosphere (see page 124)

Bellagio

702 693 7111, bellagio.com
From its opening, the Bellagio went out of its way to attract top celebrity chefs, including Elizabeth Blau, Julian Serrano and Todd English. All were a hit from the word go and have remained popular ever since.
Fine dining:

Circo	Tuscany
Le Cirque	French
Jasmine	Chinese
Michael Mina	Seafood
Picasso	Mediterranean
Prime Steakhouse	Steakhouse

Casual:

The Buffet	Buffet
Café Bellagio	24-hour dining
Fix	American
Noodles	Asian
Olives	Mediterranean
The Petrossian Bar	Caviar
Pool Café	Mediterranean
Sensi	Asian
Yellowtail Japanese Restaurant & Lounge	Japanese

Caesars Palace

702 731 7110, caesarspalace.com
The resort is posh and the restaurants reflect that, serving top-notch and largely pricey meals. If you're feeling flush, you can do no wrong by trying any of the following establishments.
Fine dining:

Bradley Ogden	American
Hyakumi	Japanese sushi bar
Nero's	Contemporary American
Rao's	Italian
Restaurant Guy Savoy	French
Sea Harbour	Cantonese seafood

Casual:

Augustus Café	24-hour bistro

Beijing Noodle No.9	Chinese
Café Lago	Buffet
Cypress Street Marketplace	Self-service
Messa Grill	Southwesternn
Payard Patisserie & Bistro	Bistro
Serendipity	Café

Circus Circus

702 734 0410, circuscircus.com
The Steak House is one of the finest of its kind in town and is regularly honoured by local newspaper polls as the best in Vegas.
Fine dining:

Steak House	American

Casual:

Barista Bagels	Bagels and coffee
Blue Iguana	Mexican
Circus Buffet	Buffet
The Garden Grill	American
Mexitalia X-Press	Mexican meets Italian
The Pizzeria	Italian
Westside Deli	Deli

Crystals

citycenter.com/retail_district/
Opening 3 December 2009, Crystals at CityCenter will feature Eva Longoria Parker's BESO and Mastro's Ocean Club. There's an exciting new Pub concept by Todd English and Vegas old hand, Wolfgang Puck, will open 2 innovative new restaurant concepts, including a contemporary interpretation of a traditional French brasserie with tastes of the Mediterranean. Many more luxury dining concepts will be announced at a later date.

Encore

702 770 8000, encorelasvegas.com
Encore introduces a new all-star team of chefs, each of whom is in the kitchen cooking dinner every night.
Fine dining:

Botero Steak	Seafood and steak
Sinatra	Italian
Society Café Encore	American
Switch	French
Wazuzu	Pan Asian

Circo at the Bellagio

Excalibur

702 597 7777, excalibur.com

Themes abound at the eating establishments of this resort that pays tribute to King Arthur's day. Sir Galahad's is a Tudor-style rib house, there's Italian cuisine in an Italian setting at Lance-A-Lotta Pasta and live music and country dancing at Wild Bill's Saloon.

Fine dining:

Sir Galahad's Prime Rib House	English
The Steakhouse at Camelot	Gourmet dining overlooking the English countryside!

Casual:

Baja Fresh	Mexican
Dick's Last Resort	American
Regale	Italian
Roundtable Buffet	Buffet
Sherwood Forest Café	24-hour bistro
Village Food Court	Fast food

Forum Shops at Caesars Palace

caesarspalace.com

The Forum Shops have a huge range of dining options from celebrity chef to other upscale and more casual dining. In some cases you can even dine pavement style and watch the world go by.

Fine dining:

BOA Prime Grill	Steakhouse
Cheesecake Factory	American
Il Mulino New York	Italian
Joe's Seafood	Prime rib and stone crab
The Palm	Steakhouse
Spago	American fusion

Casual:

Cheesecake Factory	American
La Salsa	Mexican
Planet Hollywood	American
Sushi Roku	Sushi bar
Trevi Italian	Italian

24/7 Gems

All the following serve excellent grub at under $10 throughout the day and night. These are perfect locations to get a great breakfast after a big night out or stock up on carbs before you hit the town.

First Food Bar: The Shoppes at the Palazzo, 702 607 3478. From breakfast to late, and they mean really late, this is practically a 24-hour joint. Blending the casualness of a local eatery with the vibe of a late-night spot, chef Sam DeMarco hits the mark. $

Liberty Café: 1700 Las Vegas Boulevard South, 702 383 0196. Just to prove good, old-fashioned grub works, here is an old-fashioned American drugstore with a counter. Famous for its monster breakfasts, it specialises in burgers and chicken-fried steak, while the retro drinks are a speciality. $

Monterey Room: Gold Coast Hotel, 4000 West Flamingo Road, 702 367 7111. Serving classic American grub throughout the day, plus great Chinese cuisine noon–5am, the Monterey is famous for its lunch and dinner specials. Lunch from $6.95 and dinners $5.95–15.95. $

Mr Lucky's 24/7: Hard Rock Hotel, 702 693 5000, hardrockhotel.com. You'll find excellent choices for breakfast, lunch and dinner, while afterwards you can check out the rock 'n' roll memorabilia and a large Jim Morrison mural. Steak and Shrimp (an 8-oz New York sirloin steak, 3 jumbo shrimp, salad and garlic mashed potatoes, all for $7.77. $

Pelican Rock Café: Castaways Hotel & Casino, 702 385 9123. Traditional American breakfasts include omelettes, waffles and pancakes; lunch soups, salads and sandwiches; while dinner offerings include steaks and burgers. This is one of the cheapest joints in town, still famous for its mega-cheap steak and egg deals. $

Red Cup Café: The M Resort, 702 797 1000, themresort.com. Guests can receive their morning jolt or evening 'pick-me-up' while surrounded by the restaurant's 1920s art-deco inspired atmosphere. The Red Cup Café menu offers a wide variety of American classics and Asian cuisine. Dining is available inside or on the outside terrace. $

Ristorante dei Fiore: Hotel San Remo, 115 East Tropicana Avenue, 702 739 9000. Sounds posh, but this is a cheap-as-chips joint serving excellent American and international food. Locals love its prime rib dinner and steak and egg breakfast, both $4.95, which are served 24 hours a day. $

Studio Café: MGM Grand, 1 800 929 1111, mgmgrand.com/dining. Upmarket hearty breakfasts or late-night snacks, this art deco-esque café is the place to head. Think eggs Benedict or filet and lobster. Average bill $18. $

Wine and dine

If you like fine wines, Las Vegas with its 18 Master Sommeliers, is the place to come. Here are just a few highlights of where to find the best cellars in town.

Bellagio has established the record for the most Master Sommeliers at a single property anywhere in the world. The resort currently has 4 Master Sommeliers including Robert Bigelow, the property's director of wine, Robert Smith of Picasso, Jason Smith of Michael Mina Bellagio and Joseph Phillips of Sensi. Additional on-property Master Sommeliers include William Sherer at Aureole (Mandalay Bay), Paolo Barbieri at Alex (Wynn Las Vegas), Luis DeSantos at Spago (Forum Shops at Caesars), Kevin Vogt at Delmonico Steakhouse (The Venetian), Jason Smith at Michael Mina (Bellagio) and Thomas Burke at Red Rock Resort Spa Casino.

Master Sommelier Steven Geddes began his career at **Alizé at The Palms** under the tutelage of the restaurant's owner, André Rochat. Geddes began working for Rochat in 1977 as a busboy. After Geddes expressed his interest in wine, Rochat began mentoring him. He went on to earn the title of Master Sommelier at age 29, the youngest to earn the title at the time. Alizé now boasts a 65-page wine list with more than 1,000 varietals and 5,000 bottles.

In 1999, Chef Charlie Palmer tapped Geddes to serve as wine director for his $11 million restaurant, **Aureole at Mandalay Bay**. There, Geddes built an impressive list of fine wines backed by an inventory of more than 55,000 bottles. Today, many of those bottles are innovatively displayed in a 4-storey, $1.5 million *Mission: Impossible*-inspired wine tower. Guests select their wines from a wine list contained in a tablet PC. Wine angels, who are trained acrobats and gymnasts, scale the tower with the aid of cables to retrieve each bottle from its carefully controlled 55-degree environment. The most expensive bottle in Aureole's collection is a $42,000 bottle of 1900 Petrus.

At **Wynn Las Vegas**, the property's wine director Danielle Price manages the wine lists for 9 fine dining and 6 casual restaurants, in-room dining, banquets, nightclub, and all lounges and bars. The property has an inventory of more than 100,000 bottles, including a $50,000, 6-litre 1990 Cristal Champagne. In addition, she supervises her team of 17 on-property sommeliers.

The Wine Cellar and Tasting Room at The Rio is home to an impressive public wine collection featuring 50,000 bottles valued at more than $10 million. Among the bottles – an 1800 Madeira from the cellar of Thomas Jefferson. The Cellar also has rare 'cult' wines and collectible labels from around the globe.

Napoleon's Champagne Bar at Paris Las Vegas ensures the French are known for more than just fine wine. Napoleon's boasts a selection of more than 100 champagnes and sparkling wines by the bottle and by the glass. Guests can sip everything from Moët to Dom Perignon.

Onda Wine and Cheese Lounge at the Mirage is an Italian-inspired lounge where guests can enjoy a selection of wines by purchasing a tasting flight or individual glasses. A selection of artisan cheeses and meats complements each tasting and all wines are available for purchase.

Le Cirque at the Bellagio

Bargain specials

Las Vegas abounds in great food deals, especially at downtown casinos and those off-Strip casinos that cater to local gamblers. Here are just a few:

Ellis Island Casino (in the Café): $4.99 Steak Dinner includes a sirloin steak, baked potato, salad, vegetable and a drink. Look for 2-for-1 coupons you can use to buy 2 of these dinners for only $4.99. You have to ask for this special, as it is not on the menu (although there are notices at the blackjack tables).

California Casino: $6.99 Prime Rib Dinner includes a trip to a full salad bar, cooked-to-order prime rib, potato, vegetable and a cherries jubilee for dessert. California also has a great Midnight Special of an 8oz New York cut steak with potato and vegetable for $3.99 11pm–9am.

Gold Coast Casino: $10.95 for a massive 16oz T-bone steak cooked to order with 2 sides and a beer!

Golden Gate: 99-cent Shrimp Cocktail gives you a mass of cold-water bay shrimp served in a large tulip glass with a side of homemade cocktail sauce.

Stratosphere: Lucky's Diner has several midnight specials including a New York cut steak and shrimps with vegetables and choice of potato for $9.99 midnight–5am.

Four Seasons

702 632 5000, fourseasons.com/lasvegas
Fine dining:
Charlie Palmer Steak	American
Casual:	
The Verandah	Eclectic

Grand Canal Shoppes at The Venetian

702 414 4500, thegrandcanalshoppes.com
Along with everything else about this resort-hotel, the shops are beautiful and contain some wonderful restaurants.
Fine dining:
AquaKnox	Seafood
B&B Ristorante	Italian
Canaletto	Italian
Canyon Ranch Café	American
David Burke	Modern American
Valentino	Italian

Verandah restaurant at the Four Seasons

Wolfgang Puck's Postrio	American/Italian/ Seafood and steak
Zeffirino	Italian
Casual:	
Delmonico	Steakhouse
Enoteca San Marco	Italian
Grand Lux Café	Café
Pinot Brasserie	French/Californian
Live music:	
Tao	Asian bistro

Hard Rock Hotel

702 693 5000, hardrockhotel.com
The rock 'n' roll memorabilia that adorns the first-ever hotel on this theme makes a visit here a must.
Fine dining:
AGO	Italian
Mr Lucky's	Coffee shop
Nobu	Japanese
Rare 120	Steaks
Casual:	
Pink Taco	Mexican
Starbucks	Coffee shop

Las Vegas Hilton

702 732 5111, lvhilton.com
The elegant resort-hotel has some fine restaurants.
Fine dining:
888 Noodle Bar	Asian
Benihana Village	Japanese
Casa Nicola	Mediterranean
Garden of the Dragon	Chinese
TJ's Steakhouse	Steaks
Teru Sushi	Japanese
Casual:	
The Buffet	Buffet
Fortuna	Wine bar

Luxor

702 262 4000, luxor.com
The Luxor provides a good choice of dining from classic American fare in the Cathouse combined with a nightclub vibe to Mexican favourites at T&T. All offer a lively environment and value for money.

Fine dining:

Cathouse	American
Fusia	Fusion
Tender	Steakhouse

Casual:

Back Stage Deli	Deli
Burger bar	American
Company Kitchen & Pub House	American
Food Court	Self-service
MORE	Buffet
Pyramid Café	American
T&T	Mexican

M Resort

702 797 1000, themresort.com
All 9 restaurants are owned and run by the Marnell family – long-time movers and shakers in Vegas. The concepts are all their own and everything is made fresh daily.

Fine dining:

Marinelli's	Italian
Restaurant Veloce	Trans ethnic
Terzetto	Seafood and steak

Casual:

Baby Cakes	Patisserie
Hostile Grape	Wine
Piazza Grille	American
Red Cup Café	American and Asian classics
Studio B Show Kitchen Buffet	Buffet
The Vig Deli	Deli

BRITTIP

Delis originated in New York and are basically the American version of our sandwich bars, with a heavy Italian feel.

Mandalay Bay

702 632 7777, mandalaybay.com
The hotel is in the top-end bracket and aims directly at the more sophisticated traveller in search of fun. It has 2 cracking live-music venues – House of Blues and Rumjungle – within a selection of celebrity chef restaurants.

Fine dining:

Aureole	American
China Grill	Chinese
Fleur de Lys	French
Mix	Fusion
Red Square	Caviar
rm Seafood	Seafood
Shanghai Lilly	Cantonese
Stripsteak	American
Trattoria del Lupo	Italian

Casual:

Border Grill	Mexican
Burger Bar	American
the café	24-hour dining
Giorgio Ristorante	Italian
Mizuya	Sushi
Noodle Shop	Chinese
Red, White and Blue	French
Verandah	International

Live music:

House of Blues	Southern
Rumjungle	Caribbean

Fusia is just one of many superb restaurants

Craftsteak at the MGM Grand

Mandarin Oriental, Las Vegas

00 800 2828 3838,
mandarinoriental.com/lasvegas/
Drama is definitely on the menu at the new Mandarin Oriental (opens December 2009). Guests arrive at the 23rd floor Sky Lobby with expansive views of Vegas, while dark marble floors lead to all restaurants.

Fine dining:

MOzen Bistro	Japanese
Signature Restaurant	Fusion

Casual:

Poolside Café	Tapas
Tea Lounge	Teas

BRITTIP

Weird but true: at some buffets now you have to queue up to get a table after you've queued to get your food!

MGM Grand

702 891 7777, mgmgrand.com
Celebrity chefs Wolfgang Puck, Joël Robuchon and Emeril Lagassé all have restaurants here.

Fine dining:

Craftsteak	Steakhouse
Fiamma Trattoria	Italian

André's is one of the finest restaurants in Las Vegas

Joël Robuchon at The Mansion	French
L'Atelier du Joel Robinson	French
Nobhill	Californian
Shibuya	Japanese
Casual:	
Cabana Grill	American
Emeril's	New Orleans/Creole
Grand Wok	Asian
MGM Grand Buffet	Buffet
Rainforest Café	Bistro
Stage Deli	New York deli
Starbucks	Coffee shop
Studio Café	24 hours
Studio Wok	Chinese
'wichcraft	Deli

Mirage

702 791 7111, mirage.com
You won't go wrong dining at any of the eateries here, and many offer fine food at mostly reasonable prices.

Fine dining:

Fin	Contemporary Chinese
Japonais	Japanese
Kokomo's	Seafood
Onda	Italian
Samba Brazilian Steakhouse	Steakhouse
Stack	American bistro
Casual:	
BLT Burger	American
California Pizza Kitchen	Californian
Carnegie Deli	NY deli
Coconuts Ice cream Shop	Ice cream
Cravings	Buffet
Dolphin Snack Bar	Café
Paradise Café	Café
Roasted Bean	Coffee shop

Monte Carlo

702 730 7777, montecarlo.com
Here you will find one of the best restaurants in town – André's – and 3 run by top Californian restaurateurs, Salvator Casola, his son Sal, and Chipper Pastron. Their Market City Caffé is an Italian eatery featuring fresh homemade bread and pasta dishes. The Dragon Noodle Company features the Tea Bar with a range of exotic teas and the Golden Bagel is a replica of a classic New York deli.

Fine dining:

André's	Gourmet French
Brand Steakhouse	American
Casual:	
Café	Fusion
d.Vino	Italian
Diablo's Cantina	Mexican
Dragon Noodle Co	Asian
Golden Bagel	Deli
Market City Café	Italian
The Pub	American

New York-New York

702 740 6969, nynyhotelcasino.com
Each of the hotel's restaurants provides a themed dining experience based on the New York areas including Little Italy, Chinatown and Manhattan. The quality is good and the prices are reasonable.

Fine dining:

Chin Chin	Chinese
Gallagher's Steakhouse	Steakhouse
Il Fornaio	Italian

Casual:

America	24-hour bistro
ESPN Zone	American
Gonzalez Y Gonzalez	Mexican
Il Fornaio	Italian
Nathan's Hot Dogs	New York street food
Nine Fine Irishmen	Irish

The Palms

702 942 7777, palms.com
The newest casino hotel on the block is also one of the hippest and has an excellent line-up of restaurants.

Fine dining:

Alizé	French
Garduños	Mexican
Little Buddha Café	French
N9NE Steakhouse	American
Nove Italiano	Italian

Casual:

24 Seven Café	American
Ben & Jerry's	Ice cream
Blue Agave	Oyster bar
Famiglia Pizzeria	Italian

Paris

702 739 4111, parislasvegas.com
The Paris-inspired resort keeps the French theme in all of its dining outlets from gourmet to casual. The restaurants have gone from strength to strength and new ones have even opened.

Nine Fine Irishmen

Fine dining:

Eiffel Tower Restaurant	Gourmet French
Le Provençal	Regional French
Les Artistes Steakhouse	Gourmet French
Mon Ami Gabi	Brasserie

Casual:

Ah Sin	Asian
Café du Parc	Poolside bistro
Café Ile St Louis	French
JJ's Boulangerie	Pastries and salads
La Crêperie	Crêpes
Le Village Buffet	Buffet

Planet Hollywood

702 736 7114, planethollywoodresort.com
PH has an exceptional range of innovative restaurants and retains the Spice Market Buffet from its days as the Aladdin, which continues to be one of Vegas's best value places to eat.

Fine dining:

Alfredo of Rome	Italian
Koi	Japanese
PF Chang's China Bistro	Chinese

Village Street Eateries at New York-New York

RESTAURANTS

Strip House	Steakhouse
Yolo's	Mexican

Casual:

Earl of Sandwich	Deli
Pink's Hot Dogs	American
Planet Dailies	American brasserie
Spice Market	Buffet
Starbucks	Coffee bar

Miracle Mile Shops at Planet Hollywood

702 866 0703, miraclemileshopslv.com
An impressive list of places to dine and watch the world go by.

Fine dining:

Pampas Churrascaria	Brazilian grill

Casual:

Aroma D'Italia	Italian bistro
Blondies Sports Bar & Grill	Sports bar
Cabo Wabo Cantina	Mexican
Cheeseburger Las Vegas	American
Hawaiian Tropic Zone	Hawaiian
La Salsa Cantina	Mexican
Lombardi's Romagna Mia	Italian
Merchant's Harbor	Coffee house
Ocean One Bar & Grill	American
Oyster Bay	Seafood wine bar
Sbarro	Italian
Tacone Flavor Grill & Daquiri Bar	American
Todai	Japanese seafood buffet

Rio All-Suite Hotel

702 252 7777, riolasvegas.com
Many of the Rio's restaurants are consistently highly rated by the Zagat survey. This is one of the most successful off-Strip resort-hotels and has a tremendous range of restaurants and casual dining options to satisfy its ardent fans.

Fine dining:

Búzios	Seafood
Gaylord India Restaurant	Indian
Hamada's Asiana	Asian

Casual:

All-American Bar	American

Carnival World Buffet	Buffet
Janelas	American
Mah Jong	Asian noodle bar
Martorano's	Italian/American
McFaddon's	Bar and grill
RUB BBQ	BBQ
Sao Paulo Café	24-hour diner
Sports Deli	American
Village Seafood Buffet	Buffet
VooDoo Steak & Lounge	Cajun/Creole

Town Square Las Vegas

702 269 5000, townsquarelasvegas.com

Anthony's Coal Fired Pizza	Pizza
Bar Louie	American
Blue Martini	Tapas and martinis
Brio Tuscan Grille	Italian
Cadillac Ranch	American
California Pizza Kitchen	American
Cana Tapas Kitchen & Bar	Tapas
Claim Jumper	American
Kabuki Japanese Restaurant	Japanese
Texas de Brazil	Brazilian-American Steakhouse
Tommy Bahama's Restaurant & Bar	Caribbean
Whole Food Market	Organic
Yard House	American fusion

Treasure Island

702 894 7111, treasureisland.com
The resort tribute to the world of the Caribbean has some great restaurants.

Fine dining:

Isla	Mexican
Khotan	Pan Asian
The Steakhouse	Steakhouse

Casual:

Buffet at TI	Buffet
Canter's Deli	Deli
Delicatessen	Deli
Francesco's	Italian
Kahunaville	Hawaiian
Pho	Vietnamese
Starbucks Coffee	Coffee bar

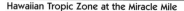

Hawaiian Tropic Zone at the Miracle Mile

The Tropicana

Tropicana

702 739 2222, tropicanalv.com
There is a distinctly tropical theme to many of the restaurants at this resort-hotel – with delicious food to match. After watching the high-roller baccarat players in action you won't go far wrong taking the time out to dine at any of these.

Fine dining:

Mizuno's	Japanese

Casual:

Garden Café	American
Island Buffet	Buffet
Java Java	Coffee bar
Legend's Steak & Seafood	American
Player's Deli	American

Vdara

866 745 7767, vdara.com
Opens October 2009, as part of the new CityCenter development on the Strip. Upmarket dining is assured.

Fine dining:

Silk Road	Trans ethnic

The Venetian

702 414 4100, venetian.com
Aiming at the more sophisticated traveller and diner, this hotel has a host of celebrity-chef restaurants.

Fine dining:

AquaKnox	Seafood
B&B Ristorante	Italian
Bouchon	French bistro
Canaletto	Italian
David Burke	American
Delmonico Steakhouse	Steakhouse
Pinot Brasserie	Gourmet French
Postrio	American
Tao Asian Bistro	Asian
Valentino	Italian
Zeffirino	Italian seafood

Casual:

Canyon Ranch Cafe	Healthy
Enoteca San Marco	Italian
Grand Lux Café	Global
Grill at Valentino	Italian
Noodle Asia	Noodles
Taqueria Cañonita	Mexican
Tintoretto bakery	Italian bakery
Trattoria Reggiano	Italian

⚓ BRITTIP

At some buffets you have to queue up to get a table after you've queued to get your food!

Buffets

These all-you-can-eat-for-little-bucks feasts are what Las Vegas used to be most famous for in the culinary stakes and they are still going strong. The mega-feasts date back to the 1940s when the owner of the El Rancho devised a plan to offer a Midnight Chuck Wagon Buffet – 'all you can eat for a dollar' – and found the crowds rolling in. Other hotels quickly followed suit, introducing breakfast, lunch and dinner spreads, and the buffet boom was born. Now they are known as the gambler's revenge – a way to fill up on food for as little as $3 for breakfast to $15 for dinner – though some of the more

⚓ BRITTIP

If staying at the Rio All-Suite Hotel or playing in the casino, don't forget to use the VIP queue to get a head start on the crowds!

The Rialto Bridge at The Venetian

Getting the most out of buffets

- Generally, avoid breakfast buffets as you won't be able to walk for the rest of the day and the choice is not as good as at other times.
- A lot of buffets change from breakfast to lunch at around 11am. Arrive at 10.45am to pay the breakfast rate and get the lunch spread!
- Never, ever attempt more than one buffet a day or you will explode!
- Try to avoid peak lunch and dinner times or you'll find yourself standing in a queue for an hour and a half. At weekends, even at off-peak times, the queues can take 45 minutes.
- If the queues are long, take a good book or magazine to read – and opt for comfortable shoes!
- Always check out the local magazines for 2-for-1 coupons.

Harrah's

upmarket, speciality buffets run to $30 a head. In fact, there's a whole new wave of gourmet buffets, and knowing Vegas, it could become the in-thing, especially in times of recession.

You'll find buffets at just about every hotel on the Strip and downtown but both the choice and the turnover vary considerably. The Rio All-Suite has the biggest buffet, serving upwards of 12,000 hungry gamblers a day, but the queues are incredibly long!

For a Sunday brunch with a difference, try the Southern cuisine at The House of Blues. Sittings are at 10am and 1pm.

Buffets on (or near) the Strip

Buffet of Champions: Champagne brunch at the Las Vegas Hilton, $17.99, Sat and Sun 8am–2.30pm.
Carnival World Buffet at the Rio All-Suite Hotel: On West Flamingo, this is both the biggest and best. The food is laid out in separate kiosks that have different cuisines from around the globe such as American, Chinese, Japanese and Mexican. It's so

Round Table Buffet at the Excalibur

Sushisamba at the Palazzo

impressive you'll want to go back again and again, but the long queues may put you off as this is a real favourite with locals.

Excalibur: Round Table Buffet includes Buffet All Day for $25 with VIP buffet line passes and unlimited re-entry.

Flavours at Harrah's Las Vegas: One of the newest buffets in town, it has live cooking stations, freshly prepared seafood, prime rib, Churrasco (Brazilian BBQ), hand-rolled sushi and Italian casseroles prepared in a wood-burning oven.

Imperial Buffet: Champagne brunch in the Imperial Palace, Sat and Sun 8am–3pm, $12.99.

Luxor Steakhouse: Champagne brunch, Sun 10am–3.30pm, $17.99.

MGM: The $29.99 Grand Buffet all-day meal pass is available Mon–Thurs and includes 1 breakfast, 1 lunch and 1 dinner.

Mirage: Champagne brunch, 8am–9.30pm, $20.50.

Monte Carlo: Champagne brunch, 7am–3pm, adults $18.95.

Palatium Buffet: Caesars Palace offers a champagne brunch, Sun 10.30am–3.30pm, adults $23.50.

Paris Las Vegas, Le Village Buffet: showcases 5 provinces of France. Breakfast Mon–Sun 7–11am; lunch Mon–Fri 11am–3.30pm; champagne brunch Sat and Sun 11am–3.30pm; dinner Mon–Sun 3.30–10pm.

Seasons Buffet at Silverton Casino Lodge: Brunch Sat and Sun 9am–3pm $16.99; lunch Mon–Fri 11am–3pm $8.99; dinner Mon–Wed 4–8pm. Don't miss the seafood buffet Fri 4–9pm $21.99.

Sterling Brunch: At Bally's Hotel on the Strip, this is truly expensive ($65) but also truly worth it if you want to splash out on a great dining experience, 9.30am–2pm.

Stratosphere: At the northern end of the Strip, this has a wide selection of good quality food at very good prices.

Studio B Show Kitchen Buffet: New-age gourmet buffet at M Resort. The 500-seat Studio B revolutionises the buffet concept, integrating a state-of-the-art restaurant with a live-action cooking studio. Within the show kitchen, chefs prepare delicious appetisers, entrées and out-of-this-world patisserie desserts. Beer and wine can also be enjoyed as part of lunch and dinner meals at no additional cost. Fast-paced, entertaining and ever-changing live

BRITTIP

The buffets are constantly changing hours and prices. To see what the current best deals are check out lasvegasadvisor.com/ buffets.cfm

Cooking classes

If you've ever wanted to learn how to prepare food like a world-class chef, now you can as numerous restaurants offer cooking classes. Renowned restaurateur Piero Selvaggio's Italian eatery, **Giorgio Caffè & Ristorante**, offers custom cooking classes for groups of 15–40 people. Located at Mandalay Place, the classes include a full tasting menu and can be scheduled any day of the week. At **Cafe Ba Ba Reeba!** at Fashion Show, groups can learn how to prepare paella, the classic Spanish dish. This class is offered on Saturdays and includes a 5-course lunch with tapas and 2 wines. **Sushisamba Strip**, located on the retail level of The Shoppes at The Palazzo, has announced an interactive, 2-hour teaching and tasting event called SUSHI+SAKE 101. Participants learn what it takes to become a master sushi chef while sipping sake alongside a 5-course meal. The class introduces students to the art and history of this unique cuisine. In addition to classes on the Strip, there are off-Strip cooking schools as well, such as **Le Cordon Bleu College of Culinary Arts Las Vegas**. Classes cover the culinary gamut, ranging from vegetarian cuisine to Thai to Southwest Thanksgiving. Classes are limited in size and available on a first-come, first-serve basis.

Those in the know

So, where do Las Vegas chefs dine when they aren't in their own restaurants? **Marché Bacchus**, of course! Guests dine on delectable French cuisine expertly prepared by chef Christophe Ithurritze. Patio seating overlooks a lake in the Desert Shores community, on the northwest side of town. Buy a bottle of wine from a cellar, featuring more than 400 wines, and take it with you or enjoy it with your meal. Near the centre of town, discover authentic Italian specialties with a Sicilian accent at **Nora's Cuisine**, a family tradition since 1991, or at the newer **Nora's Wine Bar** inside Boca Park in Summerlin. Head further west to **Vintner Grill**, a lively American Bistro with Mediterranean influences. For dessert, why not venture off the beaten path and try a cupcake from **The Cupcakery in Henderson**? Opened by a former Golden Nugget Casino employee, this bakery caters to a Vegas crowd with a variety of delicious flavours including the Kir Royale, Oh My Gosh Ganache, Tickle Me Pink and the Southern Belle. Or, stop by **Freed's Bakery**, a Las Vegas staple since 1959. Established by Esther and Milton Fried, Freed's Bakery has been serving highest-quality cakes and baked goods for more than 40 years.

BRITTIP

For a Sunday brunch with a difference, try the Southern cuisine at the House of Blues. Sittings are at 10am and 1pm.

cooking and technique demonstrations by culinary experts have guests routinely coming back for more. Studio B is open for breakfast Mon–Fri 7–10am; lunch Mon–Thurs 11am–4pm; lunch Fri 11am–2.30pm; dinner 4–11pm; dinner Sun–Thurs 4–10pm; seafood dinner Fri 3.30–10pm and brunch Sat and Sun 10am–2.30pm and seafood dinner Sat and Sun 2.30–10pm.

Treasure Island: Champagne brunch, 7.30am–3.30pm, $18.

Tropicana: Champagne brunch in the El Gaucho restaurant, 10.30am–2pm, adults $32. The hotel's Island Buffet also has a cheaper champagne brunch, Sat and Sun 10.30am–2.30pm, $16.25.

Village Seafood Buffet: Also at the Rio in the new Masquerade Village, this is more expensive than the norm (around $18) but offers an incredible selection of all the different types of seafood in the world.

Greater Las Vegas

If you really want to get the best out of a Las Vegas buffet then you need to travel downtown to the Garden Court Buffet at Main Street Station. While a bit on the smaller side, compared to the massive resorts, the champagne brunch is a mere $10.99 and the food is rated excellent.

In the opposite direction, the Feast at Boulder Station on the Boulder Highway provides an excellent stop on your way to or from the Hoover Dam. Here you'll find a good choice of quality foods ranging from tacos to pizzas and rotisserie chicken from $7.49.

Christmas at Treasure Island

Bars, lounges, nightclubs, live music venues and strip clubs

The word in Las Vegas nightlife is ultra-lounges! Over the last few years an erotic force of ultra-lounges has taken over Sin City with pounding digitally-enhanced music, dark corners with oversized couches, interactive tables, long queues vying to pass through a velvet rope at the entrance. Paul Oakenfold, new resident DJ at Rain, The Palms has gone so far as to say that Vegas is the new Ibiza (see page 155). Places like XS, iBar, Wasted Space, Gold Diggers, LAX, Blush, eyecandy sound lounge & bar, The Bank, Privé, Living Room, Tryst, Pure and Tao are magnets for the movers, shakers, beautiful people and celebrities with their 'crews' who flock to where skin is flaunted, liquor flows and we little people fight for a glance at the rich and famous. A whole raft of VIP rooms, private booths and sky bars at many of the nightclubs command hundreds of dollars for access. Many of these places actually pay famous party animals fees to come and be seen, and notorious naughty girls Lindsay Lohan and Jessica Simpson reportedly get up to $10,000 for partying at some top clubs.

There is also a druggie side to many of these power party joints. Ecstasy, the popular club drug of choice, is downed like candy in many of these places, along with cocaine. Another open secret, which is pointedly not talked about lest it cut down on the numbers of visiting and near-naked young women, is that these are hunting grounds for those creatures who use 'date rape' drugs like GHB. So make sure that if you go to one of these ultra-lounges, you go with people you trust implicitly.

Even though hotspots abound, you don't have to reveal all or spend a fortune to have a great night out in Sin City. Vegas now has many more nightclubs, lounges and bars where times are good, entertainment is great and prices are reasonable. Even better, most of them are conveniently located along the main drag of the famous Strip.

Enjoy a cocktail on your night out

For those who really need a raunchy fantasy, there are many establishments both on and off Strip where beautiful bodies gyrate in nothing but the briefest of g-strings before panting customers clutching $5 bills. Not just males, either, as a swathe of gin joints cater to the erotic fantasies of bachelorettes on holiday.

Many top nightspots start off as restaurants or bars early in the evening and transform into something altogether hotter around 10 or 11pm. Other venues are dedicated nightclubs, while live music can be found in the plethora of lounge bars – mostly at hotels and usually free, though the drinks are expensive! – and dedicated live music venues, where drinks are cheaper.

Here's a selection of all types of venues that are available to keep you well amused during your time in Vegas. As with the restaurants, it is usually quicker to go to the hotel-resort website, where appropriate, then follow the entertainment or nightlife link, rather than keying in a long URL.

Bars

Bar at Times Square

New York-New York, 702 740 6466, nynyhotelcasino.com/entertainment
The duo of pianists here are famous for trying to outdo each other and have become the best piano show in town. Give them a song and enjoy singing along in a cosy bar based on an old New York City pub. Open nightly. You must arrive by 7.30pm for table reservations. $10 cover.

Bar Vdara

Vdara, vdara.com
Described as a glowing jewel box in the centre of Vdara, one of the first hotels to open in the new CityCenter development,

Bar at Times Square

Bar Vdara

Bar Vdara connects to an intimate outdoor space where guests can lounge on spacious swings. Open for a morning espresso or a late-night cocktail. We like!

Bar Veloce

M Resort, 702 797 1000, themresort.com
High atop the M Tower, Bar Veloce's social and contemporary atmosphere is coupled with spectacular views of the Strip. An open-front bar allows mixologists to interact with guests and prepare cocktails to order. Open Sun–Thurs 5pm–11pm; Fri and Sat 5pm–1am.

C Bar

Stratosphere Hotel, strospherehotel.com/nightlife
The 360 degrees of pulsating beats, banks of plasma screen showing music videos and a bottomless happy hour, make for a good time. Try the C Bar Martini.

BRITTIP

Nevada's legal drinking age is 21. Most places will 'card' you if you appear under 30 so always make sure you've got ID with you – preferably a passport. You can buy alcohol 24 hours a day at both on-premises (bars, etc, assuming they're open) and off-premises (off-licences, etc). It is one of the more relaxed states, with state law rendering public intoxication legal.

Coyote Ugly is popular with celebs

Center Bar

Hard Rock Hotel, 4455 Paradise at Harmon, 702 693 5000, hardrockhotel.com
A flashy circle bar at the heart of the hippest hotel in Vegas, this is filled with the hottest babes in town flashing their cleavage and g-strings. Drinks are pricey but the people-watching is priceless. Celebs spotted here include Gwyneth Paltrow, Ben Affleck and the Backstreet Boys. The only downside, say insiders, are the desperados trying to hit on 'hot chicks' – you know you've been had when you hear the line, 'Are you a model?' Follow the party link on the website. Open 24/7.

Centrifuge

MGM Grand, 702 891 7777, mgmgrand.com/nightlife
The newest bar at the MGM Grand near the Lion Habitat and Poker Room. Remixed top-40 hits pump out of the speakers and drinks are served along the circular black bar. Twice an hour the music pumps up and the bartenders, male and female, ascend the bar for a hip-grinding dance to the delight of the crowd. Open Sun–Thurs 4pm–2am; Fri and Sat from noon.

Coyote Ugly

New York-New York, 702 740 6969, nynyhotelcasino.com/entertainment
This is by far the wildest bar in town. It is like the wild fraternity parties from *Animal House* you've seen on the movies, only like a Southern bar. Based on the New York namesake, this saloon with a dance floor is designed to look like a bar that has seen years of partying. The hot and sassy female bartenders are part of the

Bar and club awards

Best for beautiful people: V-Bar, Venus, Tabu and Risqué

Best for celeb spotting: The Bank, LAX, Tao, Moon, Privé and Pure

Best for cowboys: Gilley's

Best party time: Coyote Ugly

Best for salsa/Latin: Club Rio, Thursday nights, Dulce Latin Night at Gonzalez Y Gonzalez and Vida!

Best Strip views: Curve, Mix Lounge, VooDoo Lounge, Hush, Pure, Moon, Tao and Bar Veloce

Hippest: Shadow, Ghostbar, Christian Audigier The Nightclub and Privé

Hottest club in town: eyecandy sound lounge, Tao, Moon and XS

Swankiest: Tabu, Ghostbar and The Bank

Wildest: Coyote Ugly, BiKiNis and Rumjungle

entertainment – they have not only elevated pouring drinks to an art form, but also get on the bar for an act of sexy dance numbers and amazing stunts from fire-blowing to body shots. Once bartenders have done their thing, female punters are invited to dance on the bar as well and even nail some of their undies on the Bra Wall of Fame. No fancy concoctions served here, only straight shots of liquor and beer. Open Sun–Thurs 6pm–2am; Fri and Sat 6pm–3am. $10 cover after 9pm.

Center Bar at the Hard Rock Hotel

Drai's After Hours

Bill's Gamblin' Hall & Saloon, 3595 South Las Vegas Blvd, 702 737 0555, drais.net
A decadent after-hours joint which resembles some kinky salon decked out in lacquered wood, red sofas and plenty of leopard skin, with fine wines, champagnes and cigars. Don't be put off by its location in the basement of Bill's Gamblin' Hall (previously Barbary Coast Hotel). Open Thurs–Sun 1am–close.

Fontana Bar

Bellagio, bellagio.com/nightlife
The place to take in the dancing waters of Bellagio's 8-acre/3ha lake. Plus live entertainment, dance floor and wide range of drinks. Open Mon–Thurs 5pm–1am; Fri and Sat 5pm–2am.

Gordon Biersch

3987 Paradise Road at Flamingo, 702 312 5247, gordonbiersch.com
Filled with beautiful people, this is one of the city's hottest pick-up parlours. Great brews, good food and live swing music make it a fun place to go. Open Sun–Thurs 11am–midnight; Fri and Sat 11am–1am.

BRITTIP

For a romantic cocktail with a view, head to Romance at The Top of the World at the Stratosphere. www.stratospherehotel.com/nightlife

Harrah's Carnival Court

Harrah's, harrahslasvegas.com
Join the carnival of fun at one of the liveliest of Vegas's outdoor venues. If you're not enamoured with the new sophistication of Vegas, and just want a really good knees up, this is the place for you. Bar staff

The stylish Petrossian Bar

Rouge at the MGM Grand

are well trained to entertain with singing and dancing to juggling bottles on the bar. Open Sun–Thurs noon–2am; Fri and Sat noon–3am.

Kahunaville Party Bar

Treasure Island, treasureisland.com/nightlife
This Hawaiian-inspired bar has a little bit of the frat bars about it, but just manages to keep a lid on it despite the flair bartenders and dancing servers. Live sports on TV, live DJ, oxygen bar and lei girls. Open Sat–Thurs 11am–2am; Fri and Sat 11am–3am.

Petrossian Bar

Bellagio, 702 693 7111, bellagio.com
Those who enjoy the finer things in life should head to the chichi Petrossian. Champagne, smoked salmon, Petrossian caviar, vodka tastings and a choice of cigars are the order of the day here. Afternoon tea 2–5pm, caviar Sun–Thurs noon–midnight; Fri and Sat noon–1am.

BRITTIP

In this city that never sleeps, Pour 24 at New York-New York, does what it says on the label, and is open 24/7. It also celebrates 24 of the best American Craft Beers, which amusingly includes Newcastle Brown Ale! nynyhotelcasino.com/entertainment

There's live entertainment at Zuri

The Pub
Monte Carlo, montecarlo.com/restaurants
A contemporary new 'Pub' is scheduled to open in September 2009.

Rouge
MGM Grand, 702 891 7433, mgmgrand.com/nightlife
Designed by the famed Adam Tihany and featuring a towering wall of liquors, this is a cool cocktail hangout (formerly Teatro). Signature flavoured ice cubes add to the mix! Open Mon–Thurs 3pm–3am; Fri and Sat noon–3am.

Zuri
MGM Grand, 702 891 7433, mgmgrand.com/nightlife
With live nightly entertainment, this 100-seat bar just off the hotel's main lobby specialises in fruit-infused spirits such as frozen Woodford Reserve bourbon infused

Best alfresco hangouts
VooDoo Lounge, Rio All Suite Hotel (page 148)
Ghostbar, The Palms (page 146)
Pure, Caesars Palace (page 153)
Harrah's Carnival Court, Harrah's (page 144)
Tryst, Wynn Las Vegas (page 156)

with peaches, cinnamon-infused vodka and speciality beers from around the globe. Open 24/7.

BRITTIP
If you've had a heavy night, try Zuri's for the Morning after the Night Before menu, which includes a variety of liquid brunch drinks and Bloody Marys!

Hotel lounges

One of the most wonderful things about Las Vegas is the lounge scene, a phenomenon that's unique to the city. Best of all, there is no entrance fee, although there may be a minimum drink order. The lounges all provide live music and just about every hotel has a good one.

The Beatles REVOLUTION Lounge
Mirage, 702 693 8300, thebeatlesrevolutionlounge.com
Along with Cirque du Soleil®'s Beatle's tribute show *LOVE*, the Mirage opened up this 1960s retro lounge inspired by all things Beatles. It has a modern twist on

There's a great lounge at Planet Hollywood

BRITTIP

Fancy a pit stop on your way up and down the Strip, but don't want to sit in a freezing cold, air-conditioned bar? Then head for the outdoor Ava Lounge or the poolside Dolphin Bar at the Mirage, where it's cool, not cold.

'60s psychedelic décor, including viewing holes behind the bar inspired by a yellow submarine. Open Wed–Mon 10pm–4am.

Le Cabaret

Paris Las Vegas, 702 739 4111, parislasvegas.com
Designed to create the feeling of sitting outside in a garden area, this lounge allows you to sit under trees laced with twinkling lights while sipping your drinks and enjoying the live entertainment.

Caramel Lounge

Bellagio, 702 693 7111, bellagio.com
This is an excellent spot to enjoy a pre-show or late-night drink. Opaque marble tables, hand-blown glass sculptures, oversized round ottomans and leather sofas create an elegant and sophisticated setting for a trendy, yet relaxed lounge. It's all done on a theme of caramel – hence the name. Music ranges from the Rolling Stones to

BRITTIP

Drinks take centre stage at many bars and lounges. At Caramel in Bellagio, specialty drinks are served in chocolate and caramel-coated martini glasses. Red Square at Mandalay Bay not only offers more than 100 types of vodka but also keeps drinks cold on their bar made out of ice.

The Caramel Lounge is an excellent nightspot

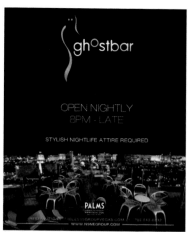

ghostbar

OPEN NIGHTLY
8PM - LATE

STYLISH NIGHTLIFE ATTIRE REQUIRED

PALMS

RESERVATIONS: TABLES.N9EGROUPVEGAS.COM · 702 942 6832
WWW.N9EGROUP.COM

Skydeck at Ghostbar

Frank Sinatra and The Beatles. The food menu includes the classic Las Vegas shrimp cocktail, pâté, smoked salmon and an assorted cheese plate, but the thing to go for here is the signature Martini served in chocolate and caramel-coated chilled glasses. Open Mon–Tues 5pm–3am; Wed–Sun 5pm–4am. DJs on at 10pm.

Fleur de Lys Lounge

Mandalay Bay, 702 632 7777, mandalaybay.com/dining
A cosy and intimate lounge with live music, it opens pre-dinner and provides an excellent spot for a late-night, post-meal nightcap. Open daily 5pm–2am.

Galleria Bar

Caesars Palace, 702 731 7110, caesarspalace.com
An elegantly laid-back lounge in which to relax and enjoy a happy hour cocktail. Open 24 hours a day.

Ghostbar

The Palms, 702 942 6832, http://ghostbar-las-vegas.n9negroup.com
A sultry indoor-outdoor lounge and sky deck on the 55th floor of The Palms, with a 360-degree view of the glittering Las Vegas skyline, that has quickly become one of the hottest places in town. Decked out in silver, white, greens and greys, it has floor-to-ceiling windows, a 30ft/9m ghost-shaped ceiling that changes colour and custom-made ultra-contemporary lounge furniture including plastic egg-shaped chairs that would be perfect in a 1960s sci-fi show. Celebs such as David Schwimmer, Cuba

The Lounge at the Mandalay Bay

Gooding Jr, Samuel Jackson and Mark Wahlberg have all enjoyed the private VIP lounge and the eclectic music and the bar has featured in MTV's *Real World: Las Vegas*. Miss it and miss out. Open nightly 8pm–4am.

Houdini's Lounge

Monte Carlo, 702 730 7423, montecarlo.com/entertainment
An intimate, understated but elegant lounge in which to enjoy a drink while listening to piano music. Live music is offered Thurs–Sun 10pm–1am.

Japonais Lounge

The Mirage, 866 339 4566, mirage.com/nightlife
Overlooking the Mirage casino floor, this lounge is pure Vegas with chandeliers and sushi. Open Sun–Thurs 2pm–midnight; Fri and Sat 2pm–2am.

La Scena Lounge

The Venetian, 702 414 4100, venetian.com
You won't escape the video games here, but you will enjoy the nightly entertainment of high-energy bands performing anything from rock 'n' roll to Motown, disco and top 40 hits.

Living Room

Planet Hollywood, planethollywoodresort.com
The 3,000ft^2/279m^2 Living Room offers a modern twist on the cosy cigar lounges of the 1940s, featuring cushy cognac leather sofas, luxurious burgundy drapery, warm fireplaces and a grand granite bar. Possibly the most seductive cocktail lounge in Vegas and a top pre-club hangout. Open Thurs–Mon 10pm to late.

BRITTIP
Lounges may provide free music, but drinks can start at a pricey $5 and rise to an even more hefty $12 a hit – so sip, don't glug!

The Lounge

Mandalay Bay, 702 632 7777, mandalaybay.com/entertainment
Slink into plush, club chairs, enjoy a match on the TV at the bar or get in a round at the billiards table.

Mist

Treasure Island, 702 693 8300, treasureisland.com
Another stylish yet casual lounge, Mist has state-of-the-art plasma screens, which are used for showing sporting events and music videos, while video poker is also available at the bar. Open Mon–Fri 5pm–4am; Sat and Fri 2pm–4am.

Mix Lounge

Mandalay Bay, 702 632 9500, mandalaybay.com/dining
Atop THEhotel on the 64th floor, the 300-capacity lounge features wall-to-wall black leather décor with red accents. The lounge is located adjacent to Alain Ducasse's restaurant of the same name that features one of the largest chandeliers in Las Vegas. Opens 5pm. Cover $20 weekdays and $25 weekends. THEhotel guests $10 and local ladies free!

Rhumbar

The Mirage, 702 792 7615, mirage.com/nightlife
A relaxing lounge bar serving minty mojitos, Latin Manhattans and other great rum-inspired cocktails. Wth Strip views and a cigar humidor on the patio, this is laid-

Mix at the Mandalay Bay

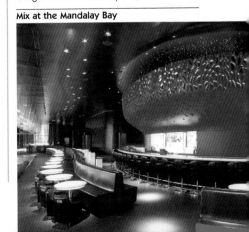

back lounging, Caribbean style.
Open Sun–Wed noon–1am; Thurs–Sat
noon–2am.

Risqué

Paris Las Vegas, parislasvegas.com
This nightclub-style lounge has hot sounds,
VIP bottle service and Strip views from the
second-storey balcony. Watch out for
celebs slipping past the velvet ropes.

Seahorse Lounge

**Caesars Palace, 702 731 7110,
caesarspalace.com**
Inspired by the most captivating elements
of the sea world, a towering 1,700-gall/
7,730-l aquarium filled with seahorses
announces your arrival at one of the most
chilled lounges in town. Tuck into seafood
appetisers and sip on champagne or any
one of the speciality Martinis as you get a
360-degree view of Australian pot-belly
seahorses.

Shadow

**Caesars Palace, 702 731 7110,
caesarspalace.com**
This 'destination' lounge sets itself apart
with its provocative shadow dancers,

whose silhouetted performances dance to
house and hip-hop while punters knock
back high-energy cocktails.

V Bar

The Venetian, 702 414 3200, venetian.com
Known to celebrities and Martini
aficionados, V Bar was created by the
owners of New York's superclub Lotus. This
upscale lounge wrapped in translucent
glass is both relaxing and upbeat. The
focal point is a custom-designed oversized
bed made of pearlised silver leather and
hollowed in the centre to allow space for a
table holding a selection of exotic
cocktails. Open Sun–Wed 5pm–2am;
Thurs–Sat 5pm–3am.

VooDoo Lounge

**Rio All-Suite Hotel, 3700 West Flamingo,
702 777 7800, riovegasnights.com**
The view of the Strip is fantastic and so are
the bottle-juggling bartenders. Sit inside or
outside on the terrace while sipping one of
the many speciality drinks, such as the
Witch Doctor, a mix of 4 rums and tropical
fruit juices. Hot music plays nightly from
9pm. Open 5pm–2.30am.

BRITTIP
Shadow is the perfect place for
a drink after a show and before
hitting your chosen nightclub.

BRITTIP
The lifts to the VooDoo Lounge
and Café are on the second floor
of the Masquerade Tower.

Patio at the VooDoo Lounge

Best lounges for views

Bar Veloce, M Resort (page 142)
Ghostbar, The Palms (page 146)
Moon, The Palms (page 153)
Pure, Caesar's Palace (page 153)
The Top of the World, The Stratosphere
VooDoo Lounge, Rio All-Suite Hotel
(page 148)

Non-hotel lounges

Armadillo Lounge

Texas Station, 2101 Texas Star Lane, 702 631 1000
A real hit with the locals, thanks to the fair prices, this lounge is a happening place most nights of the week. Almost every musical style plays here from rock to blues, jazz, country and reggae. Phone the entertainment hotline for more information on 702 631 1001.

Fireside Lounge

The Peppermill Coffee Shop, 2985 Las Vegas Boulevard South, 702 735 4177, peppermilllasvegas.com/lounge
One of the swankiest and oldest surviving lounges with cosy booths, an intimate atmosphere and the famous fire pit – a circular fireplace surrounded by a pool of bubbling water. Recently named one of America's 10 Best Make-out Bars by *Nerve* magazine, this kitschy spot has attracted the likes of Sharon Stone and Joe Pesci. One of the quirks of the joint is that the waitresses – clothed in long black dresses split to the thigh – sit down at your table to take your order. Try the Scorpion, the giant-sized house special cocktail for 2, a 3.2 pint/1.8l glass with 6 shots of various spirits, ice cream and two 2ft/60cm long straws! Open 24/7.

Ice House Lounge

650 South Main Street, Downtown Las Vegas, 702 315 2570, icehouselounge.com
Not just a lounge, this is a new $5m, 2-storey restaurant and gambling venue with 2 lounges featuring bar tops made of ice to keep drinks cold! The exterior has an art deco look with white stucco and LED lights that shine on the building and turn it different colours. Inside you can play video poker or watch sporting events and concerts and the like on any one of the 13

BRITTIP

Drink-drive penalties are severe and strictly enforced in the city so don't even think about it. Besides most of the best bars, lounges and nightclubs are around the Strip so you can either walk or take a taxi (see page 16).

plasma screen TVs or the 100in/2.5m projection screen. The lounge interior has a retro feel with photos of old downtown Las Vegas and furniture from the 1960s. For a spot of outdoor dining, try the patios available on both levels; even better, the second floor patio has seating around a fireplace. Open 24/7.

Ultra-lounges

Is it a bar? Is it a music venue? Is it a nightclub? Is it a decadent den of iniquity? The new breed of nightlife in Las Vegas is called the ultra-lounge and it combines all of the above. Think luxurious decor, ultra comfy seating, sensuous music and a sense that anything goes and you'll start to build up a picture of the newest kind of scene on the block. Another element that marks an ultra-lounge out from a lounge or a nightclub is the relatively small dance floor – it's all about getting intimate, baby!

eyecandy sound lounge & bar

Mandalay Bay, 702 632 7777, mandalaybay.com/dining
Located at the centre of Mandalay Bay's casino floor, this ultra, ultra-lounge features interactive touch tables, revolutionary iPod® sound stations which, on promotional nights, allow guests the chance to hear their personal music mixes

eyecandy sound lounge

integrated into the lounge's repertoire. Instead of traditional bottle service, eyecandy features tables that can be purchased by the hour, where guests can drink their choice of libations throughout the evening. eyecandy bar is open daily 11am–late and eyecandy sound lounge is open 6pm–late.

Flirt Lounge

Rio Las Vegas, 702 777 6875, riovegasnights.com
One of the breed of ultra-lounges, this bar is pitched at women gathering after seeing the Chippendales show and, as the blurb goes, in the mood to flirt! Whether that's true or not, it's a cool bar. Open to ticket holders Tues–Thurs 6.30pm and to general public Sun–Thurs 8.30pm–late.

I-Bar

Rio All-Suites Hotel, 702 777 6869, riolasvegas.com
The 'I' stands for Ipanema and this is a cool, quiet but erotic place. There are 10 I-Girls – part model, part provocative dancer and part gifted mixologist – who serve up fruity drinks like Tropicana Hypnosis and Peachy Keen. Open from 10pm.

Privé

Planet Hollywood, 702 523 6002, planethollywood.com
Featuring 12,000ft^2/1,115m^2 of luxuriously appointed design elements created by renowned designer Francois Frossard, Privé mixes the ethereal whimsy of South Beach with dramatic elements that are quintessentially Vegas. In addition to a distinct atmosphere, guests can expect surprise performances, celebrity guests and world-class service. Everyone from Pamela Anderson to Eddie Murphy has partied here. Open Fri, Sat and Mon 10pm–late.

Body English at the Hard Rock Hotel

The stylish ultra-lounge of Tabu

Risqué

Paris Las Vegas, 702 946 4589, parislasvegas.com
On the second floor of the chic Paris hotel with dramatic views of the Strip, this ultra-lounge combines classic Parisian architecture with contemporary Asian style and discreet lighting elements in which to lounge or dance until dawn. What makes this place so special, though, are the balconies, plush couches, ottomans, beds, piles of pillows and intimate, lighted dance floor. Open Wed–Sun 10pm–4am.

Tabu

MGM Grand, 702 891 7183, mgmgrand.com/nightlife
The MGM Grand's cutting edge nightclub for the ultra sophisticated beautiful people combines luxury with state-of-the-art technology and excellent service. The funky furniture, marble tops, wooden floors and gorgeous textiles are highlighted by saucy images of body parts that bounce off every surface with reactive imagery. The main room leads to 2 private rooms, one with a bar made of ice and metallic fabrics. Music goes from classic lounge tunes earlier in the night to more progressive vocals later in the evening. Champagne and vodka are the house specials. Open Thurs–Mon from 10pm.

BRITTIP

Ensure yourself a reserved table at the trendy Tabu by ordering a bottle in advance of your visit, through the VIP services manager on 702 891 7129.

The Luxor pyramid looks stunning at night

Tao

Venetian, 702 388 8588, venetian.com

Tao is not only a top restaurant but it also hosts what has become the hottest and sexiest ultra-lounge in Vegas. It is an odd mix of Oriental spirituality – with sensitive rock gardens, candles and waterfalls – and New York Modernism in the clean lines and colours. Just see the modernistic bar surrounded by hundreds of tiny Buddha statues and you will understand. It is also a hands-down favourite with celebrities and home to some of the most raucous parties in Sin City. Think gorgeous go-go dancers and a 40-ft/12-m long outside terrace with stunning views of the Strip. Everyone from Mariah Carey to Janet Jackson have sampled this venue. Open Thurs and Fri 10pm–4am; Sat 9.30pm–4am.

Wasted Space

Hard Rock Hotel & Casino, 702 693 4040, www.hardrockhotel.com/las-vegas/clubs/wasted-spac

The Hard Rock Hotel & Casino has opened the rock lounge Wasted Space as part of its $800 million expansion and renovation. Co-owned and created by action sports superstar Carey Hart and Yankees baseball player Jason Giambi, Wasted Space represents the ultimate depiction of the decadent rock 'n' roll lifestyle, also known as an 'anti-club'. The 5,000-ft²/465-m² space serves 2 signature drinks, the Hart Attack and Sunday Bloody Sunday, and features a unique sound system that can also be used for live performances. Open Wed–Sun 9pm–4am.

Hotel nightclubs

The Bank

Bellagio, 702 693 8300, bellagio.com/nightlife

Previously hot celebrity hangout Light, The Bank is Bellagio's signature nightclub by The Light Group and has helped revolutionise the Vegas club concept with a high energy atmosphere in 6,600 ft²/613m² that includes VIP booths and a glass-encased dance floor. Open Thurs–Sun 10.30pm–4am.

Blush Boutique Nightclub

Wynn Las Vegas, 702 770 3633, wynnlasvegas.com

The newest nightlife venue at Wynn Las Vegas is Blush, a boutique nightclub impeccably decorated and offering a casual-chic atmosphere beginning at 9pm nightly. Blush features a lighted onyx dance floor and evocative coloured lantern ceiling sculpture in an intimate 4,500-ft²/418m² space. Plus there's a fairylit alfresco area. Open Tues–Sat 9pm–late.

Body English

Hard Rock Hotel, 702 693 5555, hardrockhotel.com

The Hard Rock's hot nightclub is firmly aimed at the kind of Hollywood celeb who loves to enjoy the adult environment of Las Vegas at the weekend. With mirrored walls, Baccarat crystal chandeliers and rich leather booths, it screams high class, while a booth on the upper floor overlooking the dance floor will set back 4 people $300 for a bottle. Also upstairs is a VIP area offering an overview of all the action and a bar with standing room for ordinary mortals to mingle and watch the action.

The Bank at the Bellagio

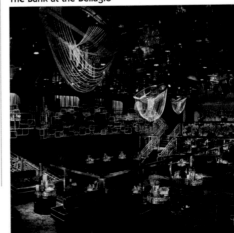

Downstairs is the main dance floor, overhung with a huge crystal chandelier that changes colour throughout the evening. There is also a second bar, more booths and an ultra VIP area that is so discreet the occupants can see out but cannot be seen. The room has its own bar and is soundproof so those inside can choose their own music.

While you may not be able to access all places, women will love the ladies' toilets – the club has one of the largest 'restrooms' in town, an elegant escape with large golden swan faucet fixtures. Open Wed–Sun 10pm–4am.

Christian Audigier The Nightclub

Treasure Island, 702, 466 9723, treasureisland.com/nightlife

Pure Management Group and famed fashion designer Christian Audigier have teamed up to create this hip new nightclub in a space formerly occupied by Tangerine. Audigier's rock 'n' roll, glam-inspired style is evident throughout the club with its roses, skulls, gleaming crystals and black glass chandeliers, not to mention podium poles. Open Thurs–Sun 10pm–4am.

Cleopatra's Barge

Caesars Palace, 702 731 7110, caesarspalace.com

A theme offering from the Greco-Roman resort, this always popular club is housed in an ornate replica of the kind of craft that once transported royalty down the River

Cleopatra's Barge

Jet at the Mirage

Nile. Statues and centurions abound in the beautiful setting where live contemporary dance music is on the menu and drinks are served by luscious hand maidens in diaphanous Cleopatra costumes. Open Tues–Sun 8.30pm–4am.

Gold Diggers

The Golden Nugget, 129 East Fremont Street, 702 385 7111, goldennugget.com

Gold Diggers, the newest nightlife experience at The Golden Nugget, is a state-of-the-art entertainment venue boasting a large dance floor bordered by bartenders serving up enticing libations in a fun-filled atmosphere. Just steps away from the party, the nightspot opens to a 180-degree, oversized balcony providing stunning views of Fremont Street Experience. Open Wed–Sun 9pm–late.

Jet

The Mirage, 702 693 8300, mirage.com/nightlife

Jet is the latest evolution of nightlife artistry developed by the Light Group. Acclaimed designer Jeffrey Beers has transformed the 15,000ft^2/1,394m^2 of space into a modern multi-level nightclub with a laser grid and state-of-the-art cryogenic effects across 3 distinct rooms each with its own dance floor. Open Thurs–Mon 10.30pm–4am.

There are plenty of clubs to enjoy

LAX

**The Luxor, 702 262 4529,
luxor.com/nightlife**
One of LA's hottest nightclubs lights up
Luxor with star power courtesy of celebrity
investors DJ AM and Christina Aguilera.
From the creators of Pure Nightclub, LAX
Las Vegas combines the best of its Los
Angeles namesake with the energy and
excitement that only Pure Management
Group can create. Catering to a
sophisticated Hollywood crowd, LAX is a
'see and be seen' place for club-goers,
A-list celebrities and the social jet
set. Open Wed, Fri and Sat 10pm–late.

Moon

**The Palms, 702 942 6832,
n9negroup.com/#/moon/main/**
With the opening of the Palms' Fantasy
Tower, the hotel added yet another
nightclub, Moon. Located at the top of the
tower and featuring a retractable roof, it
boasts panoramic views of the city below
as well as an outdoor patio, private VIP
room and exclusive table service. Open
Tues, Thurs–Sun 10.30pm–late.

BRITTIP

Las Vegas has no shortage of
bias. Men pay more to get into
nightclubs than women and many
clubs charge out-of-towners double.
Think anywhere from $10 to $30 for
men and up to $20 for women. In
fact, if ladies are prepared to work
their charm, they can often schmooze
their way in for free!

The Nightclub

**Las Vegas Hilton, 702 732 5111,
lvhilton.com**
Showcases up-and-coming singers, while
top resident DJs provide the kind of music
that makes this another of the best
nightspots in town. Dressing up to the nines
is a must! Open Thurs–Sat 11pm–4am.

Poetry

**Forum Shops at Caesars, 702 369 4998,
poetrynightclub.com/index2.html**
Poetry replaces OPM inside the Forum
Shops at Caesars, upstairs from Wolfgang
Puck's Chinois restaurant. The club features
urban pop art, black chandeliers and a
playlist leaning toward hip-hop and R&B.

Pure

**Caesars Palace, 702 731 7873,
caesarspalace.com**
This insanely popular ultra-club was
actually launched by a group of Hollywood
personalities and local tennis hero, Andre
Agassi. It offers 4 distinct areas over 2
storeys. The cream, white and silver decor
of the main room contrasts sharply with the
VIP-only Red Room with its plush fabrics,
chandeliers and upholstered walls. A glass
lift will then take you up to the terrace with

BRITTIP

Want to experience the VIP
treatment? Well, money talks in
Vegas. You don't need to be a celeb –
you just need to hand over the dosh.
You may have to part with at least
$150–200 for a booth – could be
worth it for the special treatment if
you're with a crowd. Call in advance
to check out the prices.

Pure nightclub at Caesars Palace

BRITTIP

Avoid queuing to get into the hippest nightclubs in town. Buy front-of-line tickets in advance from vegas.com.

its dance floor, private cabanas and tables that offer spectacular views of the Strip. The club also provides access to the new burlesque Pussycat Dolls Lounge (see page 160) Open Fri–Sun 10pm–4am.

Rain

The Palms, 702 942 6832, palms.com
The massive multi-level Rain doubles as a nightclub and concert venue and is famous for its special effects, which include water, fire and fog. The back of the stage is flanked by a 16ft/5m, colour-changing water wall and the front by a rain curtain. You enter through a gold-mirrored mosaic tunnel and can either head straight for the elevated bamboo dance floor surrounded by a computer-programmed river of water or find a private booth with water sofas (there are only 8, so it's best to book one!). VIPs and the very wealthy can opt for one of the cabanas with mini-bars or a sky box with a private balcony on the third floor.

Food is available and appetisers include shrimp cocktail, smoked salmon canapés, crab cakes, tenderloin skewers with dipping sauce and full oyster and caviar

Paul Oakenfold's *Perfecto*

menus. Drink specialities include a sake selection, premium tequilas, champagnes and Martinis. Serious clubbers should note that Paul Oakenfold, one of the world's leading DJs has chosen Rain as his first resident DJ position and predicts that Las Vegas is the new Ibiza. Watch out for Paul Oakenfold Presents: Perfecto Las Vegas. Open Fri and Sat 10pm–5am.

Rok Vegas

**New York New York,
nynyhotelcasino.com/entertainment**
Expect rock-inspired imagery, outdoor VIP lounge and high energy music from Rok's resident DJ followed by resident VJ (video jockey) who mixes lighting effects with vivid images displayed through the club. Open Wed–Sun 10.30pm–5am.

Rok Vegas

Why Vegas is the new Ibiza

What Vegas means to new resident DJ at Rain, The Palms, the legendary Paul Oakenfold:

'For me, I think Vegas is the future. I think Vegas is the new Ibiza. I love it; that it's a 24-hour city. It is what New York should be, but isn't. I think it's the future, not just domestically, but internationally. So I had a few offers of various residencies and I felt The Palms was right, because it's youth-oriented and that's what it's all about for me. I think what we're doing is bringing something different to Vegas – certainly in terms of music, because all the clubs tend to play top 40 and we're focussing on underground music, so it's a big difference.

'At Perfecto at Rain nightclub we're playing international, a lot of European music. We're bringing the flavour of Ibiza to here. We've got a produced show. We've got visuals. It's a production. We know what we're doing on the hour, every hour. It's not just a DJ turning up and playing music. You'll see a flying opera singer. You're gonna see some things. We've been working with some of the trapeze artists so they know when to come on. There will probably be a few things we have to iron out, but it's really important for the locals to support it. I really want to emphasise that the locals are an important part of it and I want them to feel proud of it. I'm travelling the world promoting The Palms and Las Vegas now and when I'm on CNN, MTV, I'm talking about, "Listen, you should come to Vegas". I've suddenly become this spokesman for Vegas ... I was in London doing a show and found myself saying, "Come to Vegas".

'I'm in talks with David Guetta, Pete Tong, Tiesto, people like this, so when I'm not around, these guys will fill in. We've got a DJ called Sandra Collins, who in my opinion is the best skilled DJ out there. She's great at what she does. So we wanna support her, and we also support the locals, so if there is any good local DJ, they would be the opener. Also, because Vegas is sexy, we want to bring a celebrity element. So maybe one week have a celebrity "kinda DJing". So we wanna mix it up, but first and foremost is the new music, and everyone kinda realises they can come here and express themselves in those terms. Whether you're a dancer, whether you're a DJ, whatever you are – the idea is not to hear top 40 and not to hear the music you hear everywhere else.

'This is the new Ibiza. I've gone on record saying this a few times, even being in Ibiza last month. What I like about Vegas is that it's 24 hours but what I also like – in Ibiza, no music during the day. Here there is. Also, in Ibiza, the clubs close at 6 o'clock. Here, you can go after hours and do what you want. I like the idea that you could come here, relax, hang out by the pool, go back to your room when the sun sets, take a shower, get dressed, go for dinner, maybe hit a bar, and then come to a nightclub at 1am in the morning. I like that idea, it's very European, actually, especially in what they do in the summer, lounge by the pool or the beaches. You haven't got the beaches, but ... who knows?

'We want you to feel as if when you come into this place, it's called Planet Perfecto, you've come to a completely different planet and a completely different experience. That's the approach of it, it's like a show. That's why you could only really do it in Vegas.'

Rumjungle

Mandalay Bay, 702 632 7777,
mandalaybay.com/entertainment
Still one of the hottest clubs in town. A massive cocktail lounge featuring flaming walls and waterfalls, rum cocktails (natch!), flaming meat skewers and go-go dancers, it is home to the world's largest rum bar (85ft/26m long and 19ft/6m high). Celebs spotted here include Brad Pitt, Pete Sampras, Jimmy Smits and 'N Sync. The queues get long, so arrive early. And don't forget a trip to the restrooms, which are very similar to the unisex version in *Ally*

The Strip at night

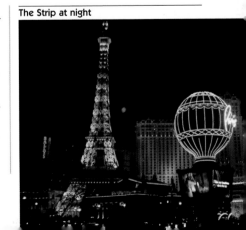

McBeal. Open Mon, Wed, Fri and Sat 11pm–4am; Tues, Thurs and Sun 11pm–2am.

Studio 54

MGM Grand, 702 891 7254, mgmgrand.com/nightlife
The namesake of the '70s and '80s New York nightclub that defined an era, Studio 54 was recently named 'Best Place to Dance' by the *Las Vegas Weekly*'s Readers' Poll. A high-energy nightclub, it has state-of-the-art sound, video and lighting along with a troupe of live dancers. There are 4 separate dance floors and bars, an exclusive area for invited guests, plus the Rainforest Café, a giant show bar with video screens and music. Tuesday evening is Eden – Erotically Delicious Entertainer's Night – and Thursday is Dollhouse night when guests can dress up beautiful life-size 'dolls' in outfits from the club's reach-in closets. The dolls then serve as hosts in place of cocktail waitresses. Tues–Sat 10pm–5am.

Studio 54 at the MGM Grand

Tryst

Wynn Las Vegas, 702 770 3375, wynnlasvegas.com
This could be the cause of the ultimate romantic moment and could only be found at the lavish Wynn Las Vegas. This fiendishly luxurious nightspot has intimate seating under an open-air main room and a sizeable dance floor that ends at a 90ft/27m waterfall that falls under cunning mood lighting. Service and drinks are decadently wonderful – and costly. Cover charge sometimes applies. Open Thurs–Sat 10pm–4am.

XS

Encore, 702 770 0097, encorelasvegas.com
At XS, the new nightclub at Encore, after-dark impressario Victor Drai combines an outdoor pool environment with the sizzling club atmosphere. Destined to be the gold standard in Vegas nightlife, the club's design is inspired by the sexy curves of the human body and embraces the European pool and island bar it envelopes. The

The bright lights of Vegas

Tryst

dance floor at XS is highlighted by a 10-ft/ 3-m rotating chandelier. If you're a high-roller, or just plain stupid, order the Ono Signature cocktail priced at $10,000. Open Fri–Mon 10pm–4am.

Hotel beach clubs

BiKiNis Beach & Dance Club

Rio All-Suite Hotel, 702 252 7777, riolasvegas.com
A year-round indoor beach party with a South Beach-inspired design, the 11,000ft²/1,020m² dance club has a bar and even a shopping area. The real attraction is the sexy bikini- and swimming-trunk-clad cocktail servers, bartenders, dancers and lifeguards, who use the beach showers to cool off after entertaining guests from the top of the lifeguard stands. A lava lounge offers old school and disco music from the 1970s and 1980s and there are 4 bars, but if you get desperate, just flag down one of the shot-toting cocktail servers. Sunday night fever with Boogie Knights. Open Thurs–Sun 9pm–4am.

Rehab

Hard Rock Hotel, 702 693 5555, hardrockhotel.com
Home to some of the naughtiest night scenes in town (and that's saying something), the Hard Rock's poolside paradise comes complete with swim-up blackjack, waterfalls and private cabanas in an Indonesian-style setting. There are Sunday Pool Parties that only just stop short of being called orgies (and sometimes cross the line).

Downtown on the up

Downtown Las Vegas's 3rd Street is quickly gaining popularity as one of the newest hotspots in Las Vegas as a dining and entertainment district featuring some of the best known nightlife hotspots. New York's famous **Hogs & Heifers** (hogsandheifers.com) opened with its unique brand of entertainment where bartenders wear halter tops and leather pants and are armed with megaphones to keep the mood as raucous as possible. Next door, **Triple George Grill** (triplegeorgegrill.com) features not only great food, but also a classic lounge where patrons can relax in oversized leather armchairs, smoke cigars and banter with the pianist. Next to Triple George is **Celebrity Nightclub** (lasvegas.citysearch.com), which features live music regularly, and **Sidebar** (sidebarlv.com), an intimate bar specialising in classic cocktails. Nearby, on Fremont Street East, **Beauty Bar** (beautybar.com) offers patrons a nail polish with their cocktail amidst décor taken straight out of an old New Jersey beauty parlour. Next door is **The Griffin** (thegriffinlounge.com), a new tavern with a movie-set feel, vaulted ceilings and 2 fire pits. Just around the corner, locals discover a cosy, sophisticated lounge called the **Downtown Cocktail Room** (downtownlv.net), serving signature Martinis in a classy atmosphere. And finally, downtown's Main Street Station houses the popular **Triple 7 Restaurant & Brewery**, recently named by the *Las Vegas Review Journal* as 'one of Vegas's hidden gems'.

Rehab at the Hard Rock Hotel

Skin

Skin Pool Lounge, The Palms, 702 942 7777, palms.com

By day, a luxurious outdoor lounge with 2 pools, a lavender-shaded swimming pool and the Mermaid Cove – an elevated pool with portholes where mermaids swim after dark – plus private cabanas and fibre-optically lit water salons, 4 bars, billiard tables, outdoor swings, poolside blackjack, trampolines, massages and other spa services.

Come night-time in the summer, the lounge is transformed into one of the most spectacular outdoor nightclubs and concert venues in Vegas. It has a concert stage, 2 dance floors, including Plexiglass dance platforms where aqua go-go girls emerge from the depths of the lavender pool. An elevated pool-top dance floor allows you literally to dance on water. Atmosphere is added with amazing lighting and fog effects.

Along with the rest of The Palms' venues, this has become a fast hit with locals and visitors alike – a true haven of voyeurism for adults. And if you're hungry, poolside dining is provided by N9NE Steakhouse and includes specialities such as sashimi and ceviche.

During the day, Skin is only open to hotel residents, but in the evening it is open to the public. Cover charges vary depending on the entertainment, while the beach party element is only on during the summer.

At night on Fremont Street

Sky Pool & Lounge

Vdara, vdara.com

Merging the boundaries between pool club and lounge, the Sky Pool & Lounge at the soon to be opened Vdara (part of the CityCenter development) has world class DJs, private retreat and spa cabanas with semi-secluded plunge pools. Rising above Harmon Circle, on the rooftop, there will be made-to-order cocktails and gourmet tapas.

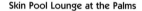

Skin Pool Lounge at the Palms

Fremont Street offers 5 blocks of fun

Live music venues

Back Alley Bar

Stratosphere Hotel,
stratospherehotel.com/nightlife
One of the newst bars on the Vegas scene,
there's live music Thurs–Mon 10pm–3am.
There are daily drink specials, plus 12
different beers on tap.

House of Blues

Mandalay Bay, 702 632 7600,
mandalaybay.com/dining
The legendary chain of restaurants-cum-live
music venues and nightclubs provides an
eclectic mix of music to serve all tastes. The
venue, which can hold 1,900 people,
plays host to every kind of band from rock
to R&B, reggae, hip-hop, country, jazz
and, of course, blues. You can catch
anyone from B.B. King to Stevie Nicks
here. A Sunday Gospel Brunch features the
best of gospel music and a Southern-style
buffet with seating at 10am and 1pm. Live
blues Thurs–Sat. The 500-seater restaurant
serves everything from the casual to the
sublime including the classic Elwood
sandwich (named after Dan Aykroyd's
character in *The Blues Brothers*), Memphis-
style ribs with Jack Daniels sauce, cedar
plank salmon with watercress-jicama salad
and voodoo shrimp served with rosemary
cornbread.

BRITTIP

Don't hang around the bar at
the House of Blues if you want to
catch a good view of the band, as the
low-lying ceiling will obscure your view.

The Joint

Hard Rock Hotel, Harmon Avenue, 702
226 4650, hardrockhotel.com
Famous for its cracking live music in a
great rock 'n' roll environment. Phone for
live music updates. As Brandon Flowers,
front man of The Killers and Las Vegas
local said in *HRH* magazine, 'Before that,
it was dismal – there were a couple places
that nobody wanted to play at. Then I saw
Oasis play at The Joint when I was about
17 and my life was changed.'

BRITTIP

Generally gig tickets go for
$20–80, but can rise to a
staggering $1,000 a hit if you want to
see the Rolling Stones, for instance, at
The Joint!

Jazz

Napoleon's

Paris Las Vegas, 702 739 4111,
parislasvegas.com
One of the best champagne bars in the
city, with more than 100 varieties to
choose from, it also has a full-service bar.
So enjoy a glass of bubbly and sit back to
soak up the smooth live jazz. The bar also
has a fully stocked cigar humidor and a
carving station for fresh rolls piled high
with steak, mustard-rubbed roast turkey and
wine-braised pork loin. Open Sun–Thurs
4pm–2am; Fri and Sat 4pm–3am.

BRITTIP

Phone Napoleon's in advance
to check happy hour times, when
you get a complimentary carving
station roll if you buy a drink.

Stunning views from the House of Blues

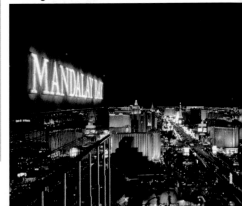

Onda Lounge

Mirage, 702 791 7111, mirage.com
Just outside the Onda restaurant (see page
117), this is where you can sip wines by
the glass or indulge in a cocktail while
enjoying the live jazz. Open nightly 5pm–
midnight.

Jazz Festival at the Fremont Street Experience

Downtown Las Vegas, 1 800 249 3559,
vegasexperience.com
Go to the city during the last weekend in
May and you'll enjoy the now annual free
jazz festival that takes place throughout the
5 city blocks that make up the Fremont
Street experience.

BRITTIP

Weird but true: women are
allowed to 'entertain' men, but
are not allowed entry to 'gentlemen's'
clubs unless they arrive with a man!

Burlesque

Ranging anywhere from sexy through
steamy and ribald to flat-out raunchy, sex
sells, and the Las Vegas tradition of
beautiful bodies reaches new levels as
dancers and strippers from both sexes peel
down to the very briefest of g-strings to
panting crowds. The main admission prices
may be reasonable, but guaranteed entry
and the best seats in the house come with
a hefty price tag.

Ivan Kane's Forty Deuce

Jazz at the Onda Lounge

Ivan Kane's Forty Deuce

Mandalay Bay, 702 632 9442,
fortydeuce.com
Modelled on a 1920s speakeasy and
popular with the celebrity crowd, the Forty
Deuce offers plush leather chairs, tiered
seating and cocktail tables with sweet little
lamps. The sultry atmosphere is created by
the low-level lighting and the dark red hues
and wooden decor. The club can hold just
300 people, so it pays to arrive early to
bag a prime-viewing seat. The burlesque
dancers strut their stuff magnificently before
defrocking to their sexy undies. Ivan Kane's
Forty Deuce is now producing the only
weekly male burlesque experience in the
country. Every Monday night 'Stormy
Monday' will feature professional male
burlesque dancers performing go-go, duets
and large-scale production numbers. The
club also has a boutique selling burlesque-
inspired clothing.

Admission is $20, front-of-line (queue)
admission $40, and a host of packages
range $400–850. The $400 Naughty
Package includes front-of-line admission for
4 guests, a guaranteed VIP table, 1 bottle
of vodka, mixers and a 10% discount at
Champagne Suzy. The $850 Premium
Scandalous Package includes front-of-line
admission for 8 guests, a guaranteed VIP
table, 2 bottles of premium vodka, mixers
and a 10% discount at Champagne Suzy.
Open Wed–Sun 10.30pm–dawn.

Pussycat Dolls Lounge

Caesars Palace, 702 731 7873,
caesarspalace.com
Inside Caesars' Pure nightclub, the famous
Pussycat Dolls of Hollywood lore have re-
created their sexy show in a bijou lounge
decorated with celebrity guest Dolls

Showgirls at Bally's

Charlize Theron, Christina Aguilera and Paris Hilton. Clad in fishnet tights and leather bustiers, the Dolls sing, dance and generally tantalise their audience from the stage and swings that hang from the ceiling. At just 3–5 minutes long, shows are relatively short, but take place every Tues, Thurs, Fri and Sat at 10.45pm and 11.45pm. The cover price varies constantly. Open Tues–Sat 6pm–4am.

Strip clubs

The sex industry is big business in Las Vegas and to prove it a raft of swanky new clubs has recently opened. Indeed the latest – Sapphire – cost $25m and is so upmarket you may even feel you've wandered into the lobby of a 5-star hotel. Kid yourself not though, the club is purely about titillation with a spot of elegance thrown in! The following are the major topless clubs.

Club Paradise

4416 Paradis Road, 702 734 7990, clubparadise.net
One of the older-style clubs, but extremely popular thanks to its lack of seediness (which in Las Vegas equals classy!). It consists of a large room with a nightclub atmosphere, 1 main stage and 2 other dance floors, plus go-go type dance stages near the ceiling. The club also has a restaurant and VIP room. Open Mon–Fri 4pm–6am, Sat and Sun 6pm–6am. Cover

prices: before 9pm $5 for women, $10 for men; after 9pm $10 for women, $20 for men; lap dance $20.

Sapphire Gentlemen's Club

3025 South Industrial Road, 702 796 6000, sapphirelasvegas.com
The newest, swankiest, largest club in town, at 71,000ft^2/6,600m^2, it is massive, and at peak times there can be up to 800 topless dancers entertaining the crowds. The huge, multi-layered central stage can be seen from any part of the club, while music includes a variety of dance and top 40 hits. The 3 main bars are the Martini Bar, which has an enormous Martini glass as its centrepiece, Pete's Bar and the Off Broadway bar, generally used for private parties. Other facilities include the Stake restaurant, serving steaks, which has its

BRITTIP

If you really want to get up close – but not personal – the going rate for a lap dance is generally $20. VIP rates, usually for 4 dances in a private room, start at around $100.

Burlesque dancers

Strip club etiquette

- First of all, in Las Vegas anyway, there is a distinction between a strip club and a gentlemen's club – the former offers full nudity and the latter topless only. Both have strict rules governing behaviour.
- While many strip clubs don't necessarily have a dress code, you won't get in if you look really scruffy or if you're drunk.
- If you try to touch one of the girls, you'll find yourself out on your ear pretty pronto.
- Have plenty of cash. The girls are not paid and work for tips only. It's a big no-no to take in the sights and not tip.
- Don't even think about sitting stage side without a wad for both drinks and tipping.
- While the dancers are working girls, they're not THAT kind of working girl. Prostitution is illegal in Las Vegas – ironic or what! – so forget it. It's also not on to ask for a date or even suggest dinner.

own separate entrance, and VIP sky boxes, which allow clients to overlook the main dance floor from a private room. Typical cover price is $30. Lap dances $20; VIP lap dances $100 for 3; an hour in the VIP area $400; sky box $250 an hour including drinks, plus $500 an hour for lap dances. Open 24/7.

Sapphire Gentlemen's Club

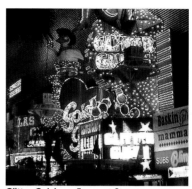

Glitter Gulch on Fremont Street

Other topless-only clubs

Cheetah's Topless Lounge

2112 Western Avenue between West Oakey Boulevard and Sahara Avenue, 702 384 0074, cheetahsnv.com
One of the friendliest clubs, it puts a big emphasis on providing coverage of major sporting events. It has 5 intimate little stages and is a favourite with locals. Open 24/7. Cover price: $10.

Crazy Horse Too

2476 Industrial Road at Sahara Avenue, 702 382 8003, crazyhorsetoo.com
Like Cheetah's, this club has been around forever, but is nowhere near as well laid out. There are only 2 stage areas and you'll have a long wait to get a ringside seat. Open 24/7. Cover price: $20 6pm–6am.

Girls of Glitter Gulch

20 Fremont Street between Casino Center and Main Street, 702 385 4774, vegas.com/ nightlife/stripclubs/glittergulch.html
Thanks to its location close to the Fremont Street Experience, this attracts a fairly touristy crowd. Open daily 1pm–4am. Cover price: $20.

Olympic Garden Cabaret

1531 Las Vegas Boulevard South at Wyoming Avenue, 702 386 9200, ogvegas.com
Once one of the largest topless clubs in Vegas – prior to the opening of Sapphire's – the main room has several stages, while the second has 2 stages and a catwalk. An exotic male dance revue takes place in the VIP lounge upstairs. Open 24/7. Cover price: free before 6pm; $20 after 6pm.

Spearmint Rhino

Play It Again, Sam

4120 Spring Mountain Road, 702 876
1550, playitagainsams.com
An intimate gentlemen's-style club with an
almost restaurant-like atmosphere, booths
and video poker machines. Features an all-
you-can-eat gourmet lunch buffet. Open
24/7. Cover price: $10 after 7pm.

The Spearmint Rhino

3344 Highland Drive, 702 966 2702,
spearmintrhino.com
Considered one of the best strip clubs in
town, it offers excellent dancers, seating

options and a choice of stages. Open
24/7. Cover price: $20 non-residents.

Total nudity

For classic dark and steamy, make for any
of these old-time strip clubs, which all
feature total nudity.

 BRITTIP

Strip clubs that offer total
nudity do not serve alcohol.

Can-Can Room

3155 Industrial Road, one block west of
the Stardust Hotel, 702 737 6846,
cancanroom.com
There are 5 stages and 7 fantasy theme
rooms. The club offers private dances in
VIP bedrooms – at a cost of $150 for 30
minutes. Open 4pm–5am. Cover price:
$20 non-residents (includes 2 drinks).

 BRITTIP

Some strip clubs do a big, hard-
sell number on private dances.
Do not feel you have to commit
yourself to something that could easily
cost $150 unless you are happy with
the quality of the dancer.

Leopard Lounge

3500 West Naples, a mile south of the Rio
All-Suite Hotel off Polaris Road, 702 798
6939, theleopardlounge.com
Open daily 2pm–4am. Cover prices: free if
arriving by personal transportation, $20 if
arriving by taxi or limo.

Las Vegas is a 24-hour city

Little Darlings

1514 Western Avenue, half a mile south of
Charleston Avenue/Interstate 15
intersection, 702 366 0959,
littledarlingsnv.com
Open Mon–Sat 11am–6am daily. Cover
prices: $10 for locals, $20 for non-
residents.

Palomino Club

1848 North Las Vegas Boulevard, 500m
south of the intersection with East Lake
Mead Road, 702 642 2984,
palominolv.com
Open daily 5pm–5am. Cover prices: $15
for locals and women, $30 non-residents.

Talk of the Town

1238 South Las Vegas Boulevard, one
block south of the intersection with East
Charleston Road, 702 385 1800,
talkofthetownlv.com
Open daily 4pm–4am. Cover price: free
with 1-drink minimum ($10).

BRITTIP

Make sure you have plenty of
singles ($1 bills) with you to tip
the dancers!

Palomino Club

||7|| GAMBLING

Everything you need to know about having a flutter without blowing all your cash

You've seen the erupting volcano, watched the fountains of Bellagio and witnessed amazing circus acts – all in the most opulent, best-that-money-can-buy settings. Now let's get down to the nitty gritty, the *raison d'être* of the city – the casinos.

Most of the Strip resorts have their casinos laid out in such a way that you can't fail to notice them even before you've got to your room. That is so you don't need to spend 5 straight hours taking a chance, but just hit a few dollars here and there to and from the show or dinner. It's no surprise really: you have to accept that there is only one reason for all the glamour and razzmatazz: the making of money – absolutely billions of it. Vegas's gaming revenue in 2008 was a whopping $6.1 billion.

⚙ BRITTIP

Remember the golden rules of gambling: stick to your own limits and always, always quit while you're ahead!

The casinos want people to have fun and to know when to walk away because they want them to return again and again and again. That way, they know, the odds are that they'll always get their money back – and more besides! High-roller baccarat players, the very latest slot machines, state-of-the-art video gambling machines and sports betting are the big money-spinners, and you'll also find everything else from roulette to craps and poker to blackjack.

To this end, the industry has been working hard to make casinos more user-friendly by providing free lessons in easy-to-find locations. A move to put 'comps'

In this chapter

Never let a small win dazzle you!

GAMBLING

Casino at Planet Hollywood

(see page 179) on a more straightforward footing has led to the creation of loyalty cards by many establishments where the amount of money you spend along with the time you spend gambling generates points to put towards free meals, free rooms and free shows.

Whether you intend to spend $20 or $2,000 gambling, or just sit in one of the many bars and watch the action, all these factors mean you can have a fantastic time in Las Vegas without parting with huge amounts of money – as long as you follow the rules: stick to your own limits and always, always quit while you're ahead!

Casino trends

As if the resorts and casinos weren't seductive enough, Las Vegas is putting a new spin on gaming, making it sexier and more exciting than ever before. The latest trend is the emergence of intimate, themed casinos within a casino.

The Pussycat Dolls Casino at Caesars Palace is located just across from The Pussycat Dolls Lounge inside Pure Nightclub. The casino features a mixture of sexy slot machines, blackjack, craps and roulette tables, a big 6 wheel and merchandise area, featuring the brand's sexy burlesque look. Playboy Enterprises, Inc., the Palms Casino Resort and N9NE Group opened Las Vegas's first **Playboy Club** atop the new Fantasy Tower at The Palms. The club and casino showcase the

iconic Playboy bunnies dealing high-limit table games, as well as a Diamond Bar built out of 10,000 diamond-shaped crystals.

While slot machines are the runaway favourite among gamblers in Las Vegas, table games have seen new additions and a tremendous resurgence in the popularity of poker. Some of the newer games, such as 3-card poker, and timeless favourites like pai gow continue to draw people to the tables. The increased exposure and popularity of poker, specifically Texas hold 'em, has prompted many casinos to re-open poker rooms that had been shuttered for a number of years. Las Vegas is featured regularly as the site of televised celebrity poker showdowns as well as professional poker tournaments.

High-rollers

The casinos like to keep all their customers happy, but they go to extraordinary lengths to accommodate high-rollers (big betters) – and I mean HIGH! Baccarat, the game they tend to play, accounts for a massive

High-rollers' area at Caesars Palace

The law

You must be over 21 to gamble in Las Vegas and under 18s are not allowed in arcades 10pm–5am during the week and midnight–5am at weekends. In a further move to appease the anti-gambling lobby, the city has passed a new law that bans under 18s from walking down or cruising the Strip after 9pm without a parent or guardian.

History of gambling in Vegas

It all began on 19 March 1931 when Governor Fred Balzar signed a bill that legalised gaming in Nevada. Since that day, Nevada, and especially Las Vegas, has become recognised worldwide as a premier gaming destination. From traditional card and dice games, to slot machines and race and sports book betting, the casino industry has flourished and evolved into an international phenomenon. Now, more than 75 years later, Nevada celebrates the very industry that has supported economic growth in the state.

Las Vegas has come a long way from its first legalised gaming establishment, Northern Club on Fremont Street, in 1931. Owned by Mayme Stocker and her family, the Northern Club and others like it on the infamous Block 16 in downtown Las Vegas pumped $69,000 into the state coffers during their first 2 years of operation. Today, gaming revenue in Clark County alone totals more than $10.9 billion per year.

In the early 1940s, Thomas Hull selected a plot along the 2-lane highway that led to Los Angeles as the site for the El Rancho. His themed resort – the first in Las Vegas – would become the first hotel along what is now known as the Strip. Five years later, Benjamin 'Bugsy' Siegel would open his lavish Flamingo Hotel, ushering in the era of celebrity glitz in Las Vegas. Some of the world-famous entertainers who became synonymous with Las Vegas included The Rat Pack, Elvis and Liberace.

Further development occurred in the late 1960s when business, aviation and movie mogul Howard Hughes introduced corporate financing to the Las Vegas resort landscape. In 1989 Steve Wynn opened the Mirage, the first of many mega-resorts now lining the Las Vegas Strip. Today gaming is still the centrepiece of Las Vegas, one of the world's most desirable destinations.

▶ BRITTIP

When in a casino always remember that Big Brother is watching you! Mirrors or dark glass in the ceilings house cameras to record almost every square inch of the casino. In the old days, similar mirrors hid people who stood on catwalks to watch casino action to stop cheating by players or dealers.

13% of casino takings. With its high-bet limits and liberal odds, baccarat is worth a cool $1b in gambling income worldwide and Las Vegas casinos have been working hard to cash in. Bally's casino on the Strip has hired a high-roller expert to weed out the big fish – gamblers willing to bet $300,000 to $1m each hand – from the 'whales', who only bet around $250,000 a hand!

High-stakes poker is big business, too, and Las Vegas has been home to the World Series of Poker (WSOP) title for the last 4 decades. For 35 years, Binions Casino in the Fremont Street area hosted this gathering of card sharks. However, in 2005 Harrah's bought the rights to the WSOP and eventually moved it to the Rio Suites and Casino. This came as internet poker sites began to explode in popularity, and the WSOP exploded in size, besides being moved from May to a June–July setting.

The move included an increase in the number of events, and what was once a single poker tournament has reached a stunning series of 51 poker tournaments held over 6 weeks. The main event, a no-limit Texas hold 'em tournament that costs a cool $10,000 just to enter, attracted over 8,200 contestants in 2007. The winner in 2006, Jamie Gold, took home a breathless $12,000,000 from a single tournament played over 7 days. A set of laws enacted by the US Government which cut into the ability to transfer gambling money from US-based credit cards and bank accounts cut down on the 2007 WSOP event. The 2007 winner, Jerry Yang, overcame only 6,358 players and won a 'mere' $8,250,000.

Have fun at the MGM Grand casino

Fun books and other freebies

Whether or not you intend to do any gambling, always check the casino cages for their free fun books. These will give free goes on slot machines, may entitle you to double a bet at the blackjack table or increase the value of a keno ticket. They will also be full of bargains on food and drink or offer discounts on souvenirs such as T-shirts. These books are also available from car rental agencies, hotels, motels and other locations in the city. Some tour operators – most notably Funway – have put together their own fun books, which include some fantastic deals on excursions and attractions.

The monthly *Las Vegas Advisor* gives subscribers lots of information on deals and freebies available in Las Vegas and sometimes includes valuable coupons or arranges special deals for subscribers. Write to the Las Vegas Advisor, Huntington Press, PO Box 28401, Las Vegas, Nevada 89126. Subscriptions are $54 a year, but you'll generally get back that cost in money-saving coupons on your first day in Las Vegas, let alone all the other tips! Also, check out their website at lasvegasadvisor.com for up-to-the minute top bargains and information.

How to get in on the action

I remember the first time I visited Las Vegas, the bright lights were so overwhelming and the sheer scale of everything so overpowering that it seemed far too daunting to go into the casinos and play a game or two. Removing some of the mystique surrounding these games of chance is not to remove the magic of the setting, but it will give you the right kind of edge.

When it comes to a weekend gambling spree, the average American will allow a budget of $200–500. When a touring Brit arrives in town, their budget of $100–200 is usually simply there to fritter away while downing complimentary drinks. If you do want to have a go, though, here is a guide to the different games, the rules and the best ways to place your bets, so that even if you don't win, you won't blow your entire budget straight away.

The aim of the game is to make your spending money last as long as possible while having fun – and, who knows, you may even come out a winner! Bear in mind that these tips are aimed at those people who are new to gambling as opposed to those looking for more detailed and advanced information. But I have included details of where you can go for further information and more in-depth advice.

The odds

There are 2 aspects to every game you play – the chance of you winning inherent in each game (the odds) and the rules designed to favour the house, including payoffs at less than the actual odds or predetermined payoffs, as in slot machines (the edge). It is because of this edge that, no matter how well you are playing or how much luck you seem to be having, the odds almost always favour the casinos, who will win everything back in the long run. That's why when you've come to the end of a winning streak you should always walk away.

Table games with the best odds on winning or on reducing your losses are baccarat and blackjack (in fact, you can expect to win money if you are an accomplished 'card counter' in blackjack). Craps is not good, roulette is terrible and in keno you have about as much chance of winning as you do with our National Lottery. Of course, a keno bet is usually $1 or less, so you may not care.

Beachside Casino at the Mandalay Bay

Blackjack is one of the easiest games

Gambling milestones

1931
Nevada Governor Fred Balzar signs a bill legalising gaming in Nevada

1955
Nevada Gaming Control Board is established

Mid-1950s
Gaming revenue tops $100 million

1964
Nevada Electronic introduces first electronic slot machine

2003
Non-gaming revenue surpasses gaming revenue in Clark County

2005
Nevada gaming revenue tops $11.6 billion

2006
Nevada celebrates 75 years of gaming

The 2 games on which you can actually expect to win money are blackjack (if you are a skilled card counter) and poker (if you are better than the other players). The other side of the coin, though, is that if you are not skilled, you will likely lose your coin quite fast.

As a general rule, the smaller casinos away from the Strip are what are known as the 'loosest' – they will offer the best returns on slot machines. For some time, the downtown casinos have been rated as the 'loosest slots in America' by the *Casino Player* magazine. For instance, slot machines will give 95–99% return on your play. That means if you bet $1, you'll get 95–99 cents back over the long term if you win. Downtown, you have more chance of finding machines with a 98–99% return. Sometimes, as part of promotions, a casino will offer a few slot machines that offer a 100–101% return! But then it is only one or two machines and they'll be available for only a short time.

The exception on the Strip is the Stratosphere, which has made a corporate decision to lure in punters with the promise of the best returns in town. Their deals include 100 times odds on craps, single-zero roulette, hand-dealt double-deck blackjack, double-exposure blackjack (where you see both the dealer's cards),

98% return on 100 $1 slots and more than 100% return on 100 video poker machines. But do bear in mind that there are only a certain number of the high-paying machines, so always check the returns on a machine before you play.

Limits

The table limits are an important consideration because the higher the minimum bet, the quicker you'll get through your money. Unless you're a serious gambler, you'll steer clear of baccarat. The minimum at most Strip resorts is $100! Cheapest, though, is New York-New York, which has games with minimum bets of $10. You can also play mini-baccarat at the Stratosphere with minimum bets of $5 per hand.

Table games at New York-New York

BRITTIP
Be careful of places that have gaudy signs that say 'Loosest Slots'. Often they will have only one or two 99% machines in some hard-to-find corner, while the rest of the machines are 95% money-eaters.

Card counters

You will probably have heard of card counters. These are people who basically keep a track of the low and high cards that are being played in blackjack to try to determine the likelihood of drawing a high or low card at a crucial moment – e.g. when they've got a 15, which is unlikely to be enough to win but they can't guarantee they'll get a 6 or under. There are many different forms of card counting, but the most simple is the one used with single-deck blackjack. Basically, 10, J, Q, K and Aces are worth minus one, while 2, 3, 4, 5 and 6 are worth one, and the other cards (7, 8, 9) have no value. Starting from zero, you count upwards and downwards according to the cards dealt. Generally you should bet the minimum when the score is negative (you're more likely to bust) and higher when the count is positive two or more.

It is not illegal to count cards but the casinos in Las Vegas frown on this misguided attempt by players to play the game well. They consider it an attempt to cheat them out of money and tend to refuse to let card counters into their casinos. This is why it's best to practise your technique in advance so you won't be noticed!

BRITTIP

Limits fluctuate. Minimum bets tend to be higher in the evening, at weekends and during special events. The Strip hotels all have higher minimums than downtown casinos.

Most Strip resorts have a minimum of $10 on blackjack. The cheapest are Circus Circus ($5), Excalibur ($5), Luxor ($5), Monte Carlo ($5), Stratosphere ($3) and Treasure Island ($3). In comparison, you'll find $2 blackjack tables aplenty and $1 roulette at casinos away from the Strip.

Table games

Baccarat

There is normally an aura of glamour surrounding this game as it tends to attract high-rollers and is usually played in a separate, often more refined, area, cordoned off and staffed by croupiers in posh tuxedos. But don't be put off by the

glamour of it all. The mega-bucks, high-roller games will be played in special VIP rooms, so the areas you see really are for mere mortals! What's more, it is an easy game to play and offers the best chance of you beating the casino.

Generally, up to 15 players sit around a table where 2 cards from an 8-deck shoe are dealt to each of the players and to the bank (see Gambling lingo, page 172). You can bet either on you winning, the bank winning or there being a tie, but you are only playing against the bank, not the other players. Each time you win, the casino takes a commission, though not if you lose.

The idea is simple: you're aiming to get to a total of either 8 or 9 and the value of the cards are: ace to 9 – face value; 10 and face cards – zero. If the cards add up to more than 10, only the second digit is counted. For instance, if your hand contains a 9 and a 4, it adds up to 13 but is worth 3 as you drop the first digit from the total. In this case you'd ask the dealer for another card.

The house edge in baccarat is very low, which is why it is such an attractive proposition. The edge when betting on a bank hand is 1.17% (though that is increased by the fact that a commission is always paid to the house on with-bank bets) and the edge on a player is 1.36%.

A version that is becoming very popular is mini-baccarat. Basically it is the same game, but it is played around a table

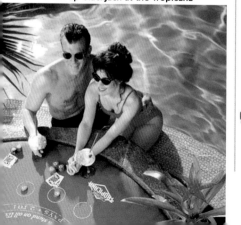

Swim-up blackjack at the Tropicana

BRITTIP

In blackjack, avoid high minimum/low maximum tables like the plague – they'll eat up your bankroll in a very short space of time.

Always stick to your limit

about the size of a blackjack table, with spaces for 6 or 7 players.

Blackjack or 21

After baccarat, blackjack (or 21) is one of the easiest games to play and the rows of blackjack tables in casinos reflect the huge number of gamblers who play the game. The object is to get as close to 21 as possible without 'busting'. There can be up to 6 people around a table, all playing against the dealer.

Bets are placed first, then the dealer gives 2 cards to each player and himself, the first face down (known as the hole card), the second showing (upcard). Numbered cards count as their face value, face cards count as 10 and aces are worth either 1 or 11. You can either decide to stand with the 2 cards you received or take a hit (another card from the dealer) until you're happy with your hand or you go bust.

When all the players have finished, the dealer turns over his hole card and takes hits until his total exceeds 17. If the dealer busts,

everyone around the table wins, otherwise only those whose hands are higher than the dealer's win. If the first 2 cards you are dealt total 21, then you've got what is known as a natural, i.e. a blackjack, and you automatically win. If both you and the dealer are dealt a blackjack, then it is a stand-off and no one wins.

As a general rule, if you have a hand without an ace against the dealer's 7 or higher, you should take hits until you reach at least 17. Against the dealer's 4, 5 or 6, you can stand on a 12 or higher; if against the dealer's 2 or 3, hit a 12.

With a soft hand (one which includes an ace), hit all totals of 17 or lower. Against the dealer's 9 or 10, hit 18.

What gives the house the edge is that you have to play your hand first, so even if the dealer busts after you have, you're still a loser. But there are 2 ways to help you even the odds – you can double down or split pairs. If you feel you may have a good hand and will only need one more card, you double down – i.e. you double your initial bet and accept one extra card to complete your hand.

If you are dealt a pair, you can opt to split them, thereby increasing your chances of winning. You separate the cards to create 2 hands, thereby doubling your bet, and draw extra cards for each hand. When splitting aces you are only allowed to take one extra card for each ace. If the next card is an ace, though, you can split again. The rule is always to split aces and 8s.

A word about 'insurance'. When the dealer's 'show' card is an ace, you will be offered the chance to insure yourself against the dealer getting a blackjack to win 2–1 if the dealer holds a blackjack, so you break even. But it is not a good bet to make because even if you end up with a blackjack, you'll only get 2–1 on a bet that should pay 9–4.

'Dealertainers' – celebrity impersonator dealers – at the Imperial Palace

GAMBLING

Gambling lingo

Acorn	Player who is generous with tips
Ante	Money you bet in card games
Bank	Inventory of coins and chips on all table games
Big digger	Ace of spades
Book	Place where bets are made on sporting events
Boxcars	When a gambler rolls two sixes for a point of 12
Boxman	Craps table dealer who sits over the drop box and supervises bets and payoffs
Bumble puppy	Careless or inexperienced card player
Bust	Exceed the maximum score allowed, for instance 21 in blackjack
Buster	Term used for illegally altered dice
Casino boss	Person who oversees the entire casino
Casino cage	Secure area within the casino for banking services and casino operations
Comp	Free meal, gift, etc. (short for complimentary)
Coupons	Redeemable for nearly everything from a free meal to a free pull on a slot machine
Crossroaders	Card cheats who travel across America in search of games
Dealer	Person who conducts table games
Drop box	Locked box on 'live' gaming tables where dealers deposit your cash
Eye in the sky	One-way mirror used for surveillance of the casino area
Flat top	Slot machine with a fixed jackpot, as opposed to a progressive slot machine where the jackpot increases according to the amount of play
Frog skin	Old-time gamblers' name for paper money
Gaming	Las Vegas euphemism for gambling
Green	Gambling chip worth $25, also known as a quarter
High-roller	Someone who bets large sums of money
Hit me	What you say when you want another card from the dealer in a blackjack game
In red	If you get a free meal, your name will appear in red on the maître d's reservation list
Ladderman	The person who supervises baccarat games and has the final say over any disputes
Limit	Minimum and maximum bet, as decided by the casino
Loose	Term used to describe slot machines that pay out at the best percentages
Marker	IOU
Nevada lettuce	$1,000 bill
Pit	Area of the casino containing gambling tables
Pit boss	Person who oversees a number of table dealers
Red	Gambling chip worth $5, also known as a nickel
RFB comp	If the casino is impressed with someone's credit rating, they will arrange free room, food or beverages (RFB) during a hotel stay
Shoe	Contains the packs of playing cards used in blackjack and baccarat
Shooter	Person rolling the dice in craps
Snake eyes	Craps term used when the dice holder rolls a point of 2
Soft hand	When you have at least one ace in your blackjack hand; it is counted as either 1 or 11 so you have two possible totals
Spoon	A device used by slot machine cheats
Stand	To refuse any more cards in blackjack
Stickman	Dealer who moves the dice around on a craps table with a hook-shaped stick
Table games	Everything from blackjack and baccarat to roulette
Toke or gratuity	Tip
Whale	Gambler who is willing to bet $250,000 a hand
Whip shot	In craps, the way of rolling the dice to hit the table in a flat spin so the desired numbers are on top when the dice stop rolling

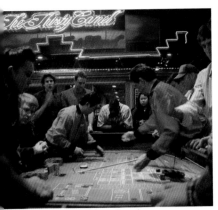

Craps at the Thirsty Camel

Another way the casino gets an edge is by using a shoe containing 6 packs of playing cards. This makes busts less likely, which helps the dealer, who is forced by the rules to take more hits than the player. And blackjacks are also less frequent, another drawback as you get paid 3–2 for those.

If you want to learn more, call into the Gambler's Book Club (1550 E. Tropicana Avenue, 702 382 7555, gamblers book.com, open Mon–Fri 9am–5pm) where you'll find copies of just about every book ever written about blackjack, and experts on the game – including card counters – who are happy to answer questions. Also, most gift shops have blackjack strategy cards, playing-card sized helpers that give the 'book' answer to when to hit and when to stand.

Craps

We've all seen this game played down New York alleyways in gangster movies, now here's your chance to give it a go! Sadly it is one of the most complicated table games on offer, but it is also the one that produces the most excitement.

You join a game by standing anywhere around the table, start betting any time and wait for your turn to shoot. When rolling the dice you have to do it hard enough for

BRITTIP

Carry a sweater – the air con is deliberately chilly to put you off facing the desert heat outside. Some casinos pump scented oxygen in to keep tired players pepped up so they carry on gambling.

them to bounce off the far wall of the table to ensure a random bounce. Basically, the shooter rolls a pair of dice that determine the outcome of everyone's bets. The first roll is called the 'come-out roll'. If it is a 7 or an 11, the shooter and all those who bet with him or her win. If the shooter rolls a 2, 3 or 12, that is craps and the shooter and all those betting with him or her lose. If the shooter rolls a 4, 5, 6, 7, 8, 9 or 10, he or she must roll the same number again to win. If the shooter rolls a 7 before that number, he or she 'sevens out' and loses.

There is a whole series of bets that can be made – with the most bizarre titles you could imagine – from 'pass lines' to 'don't pass', 'come' and 'don't come', 'field', 'big six' or 'eight', 'any craps', 'hard ways', 'bet the horn', 'any seven' and 'under or over seven'.

The odds on winning and payouts vary wildly.

BRITTIP

Many casinos have moving walkways that take you in but rarely take you out again!

Best bets: The **pass line**, where you are betting with the shooter, and the **don't pass line**, where you are betting against, pay even money. **Come** and **don't come** bets are the same as the **pass** and **don't pass** bets, with the same odds, but can only be placed after the first roll of the dice. The best bet of all is the **free odds**, which is only available to the above betters, but is not even indicated on the table. Once the point has been established by the first roll of the dice, you can make a bet equal to your original and get true odds (2–1 on the 4 and 10, 3–2 on the 5 and 9 and 6–5 on the 6 and 8) rather than even money.

Most casinos have a high-limit salon

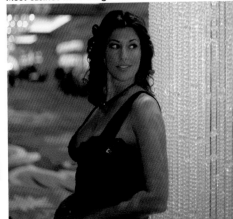

Poor bets: The **field**, where you bet that any number in the field, i.e. not 5, 6, 7 or 8, will be rolled. If the numbers mentioned come up, you lose. **Place bets**, where you bet the 4, 5, 6, 7, 8, 9 or 10 will be thrown before a 7, sound like a good idea but the casino edge is so great that you should not consider any bets other than placing the 6 and 8.

The downright daft bets!: Big six and **big eight** bets on either the 6 or 8 or both can be made at any time and either must appear before a 7 is thrown but the bet only pays even money so the casino's advantage is high. Worst bets of all are the proposition bets, which include the **hard ways** and **one-roll** bets. The casino's advantage is so great that you shouldn't even consider these.

BRITTIP

Exits from casinos are hard to find and even if you do see a signpost it won't be plain sailing getting there, as your way will be blocked by a maze-like arrangement of slot machines!

Roulette

This game has been growing in popularity in America since Europeans started visiting the city in greater numbers, but generally it does not carry very good odds even in the European version. The American roulette table has 36 numbers, plus a green zero and a green double zero – as opposed to the European wheel, which does not have the extra double zero (the only Strip exception is at the Stratosphere). This turns the roulette wheel into a game heavily tilted in the casino's favour.

You place chips on the game board, gambling that either a single number, any of a dozen numbers, a column of numbers,

The poker room at Beau Rivage

Roulette is an easy game to understand

corner of 4 numbers, red or black, or odd or even numbers comes up on the wheel. After all the chips have been put down, the dealer sends a small metal ball spinning around the roulette wheel, which spins in the opposite direction. When the ball drops into one of the slots, the owner(s) of the chips in that slot collect(s).

The lure is that if your number comes up you're paid at the rate of 35–1, but what makes roulette a poor game for strategists is that it basically involves blind luck. The best way to reduce the chance of losing is to stick to betting that the ball will drop on either a red or black number; and odd or even number of numbers 1–18 or 19–36. The worst bet is any one number. Other bets include groups of 12 numbers (2–1), groups of 6 numbers (5–1), groups of 4 numbers (8–1), groups of 3 numbers (11–1), groups of 2 numbers (17–1) and a group of 0, 00, 1, 2 and 3 (6–1).

Card games

Poker

For the real Wild West experience, this is a must! There are many variations, but most follow the same principles: all players play for themselves, paying a commission, or 'rake', from each pot (or a certain sum of money per half hour of play at high limits) to the casino, and a regular deck of cards is used. Before joining a game, always check with the dealer to find out the specific game being played.

In the past there were many different styles of poker games available. At the World Series of Poker tournaments, held at the Rio All-Suites, you can still play old-time poker games like 7 card stud, Omaha which is favoured in most European casinos, deuce to 7 and 5 card draw. But with the enormous increase in interest caused by the televised events of the World Poker Tour and the European Poker Tour, Texas hold 'em has become the game of choice in Las Vegas. In fact, it is almost impossible to find any other poker game.

Poker is a game that requires nerves of steel and the skill to know when to cut your losses and drop out. Professional poker players reckon that you'll have a pretty good idea of your chances by the time the first 2 cards have been dealt, and there are basic combinations that you need to have if you are going to continue.

Texas hold 'em: This is the game of the high-stakes World Series of Poker and is now the most popular poker game in the world. There are 2 types of game offered: limit hold 'em, where there are only set amounts that can be bet at each betting round, and no-limit hold 'em, where you can bet any amount during any betting round, up to and including your entire stack of chips.

In both limit and no-limit there is a 'dealer button' which advances round the table at the start of each hand. It indicates which 2 players, called the 'big blind' and 'small blind', are required to make forced bets before any cards are dealt, so that there is some money on the table to fight for. Everybody is then dealt 2 cards face down and a round of betting starts. Obviously, the first 2 cards you're dealt are the most important and should be either a pair of aces, kings, queens or jacks or 2 high-value cards.

After the first round of betting, the dealer places 3 cards in the middle of the table, called 'the flop'. These are community cards that all players use, with the 2 cards in their hand, to make their best 5-card poker hand. There is another round of betting. Then a fourth card is placed on the table by the dealer, 'the turn'. Another round of betting is made, then the last card is placed in the middle, 'the river'. There are now 7 cards, 2 in your hand and 5 on the table. You use the best 5 cards of the 7 to make your best 5-card poker hand. The last round of betting ensues and when the last bet is covered or called, the dealer calls for the showing of hands and the highest hand wins.

Most casinos now have poker rooms, where Texas hold 'em is offered. Most also hold a series of daily tournaments, where you play poker against other players. You keep playing until you have no more chips. Usually 10% of the top-placing players get cash prizes, and the top prizes typically run into the thousands of dollars.

There are other poker games that are offered with the other table games, where blackjack and baccarat are offered.

Pai gow poker: Played with a deck of 52 playing cards plus 1 joker, which can be used only as an ace to complete a straight, a flush or a straight flush. Players are dealt 7 cards which they arrange to make 2 hands – a low hand of 2 cards and a high hand of 5. The cards are arranged according to high-draw poker rankings, i.e. the highest 2-card hand is 2 aces and the highest 5-card hand is a royal flush. The object is for both hands to beat the banker's hands.

High-roller lounge at Treasure Island

Caribbean stud poker™: Played with a standard 52-card deck and no joker, it is the first casino table game to offer a progressive jackpot. You start by placing your bet in the box marked 'ante' and then have the option to bet $1 to enter the progressive jackpot, after which all the players and the dealer are dealt 5 cards. None of your cards is exposed, though one of the dealer's is, but you cannot draw any more cards.

BRITTIP

The average electricity bill for a large Las Vegas casino is around $3m a year!

Now you have to decide whether to play or fold; in the latter case your ante is lost. To carry on playing, you have to wager double your ante in the box marked 'bet' to see the dealer's hand. If the dealer's hand is less than ace-king high, then he folds and automatically pays the ante bets at even money. The bet wagers are considered 'no action' and returned to the player regardless of their hand. If the dealer's hand is ace-king high or higher, then he calls all bet wagers. If the dealer's hand is higher than yours, he takes both the ante and the bet. If it's lower than yours, he pays the ante at even money and the bet according to the signposted rates, based on your hand. Regardless of the dealer's hand, if your hand qualifies for the progressive jackpot, you will win the appropriate amount for your hand (shared if there is more than one winner).

Let it ride poker™: In this game, you are not playing against the dealer or the other players but simply trying to get a good poker hand. To play, you place 3 equal bets as indicated on the table layout and then get 3 cards. After looking at your

Loose slots offer the best return

Slots accept any kind of cash!

cards, you can ask for your first bet back or 'let it ride'. The dealer then exposes one of his cards, which becomes all of the players' fourth card. At this point you can either ask for your second bet back or again let it ride, after which the dealer exposes another card to complete the 5-card hand. Winning hands are then paid according to the payout schedule.

BRITTIP

Most of the newer slot machines have coloured lights on top to signify the machine's denomination. A red light means it's a 5-cent machine, green 10 cents, yellow 25 cents, orange 50 cents, blue $1 and purple $5.

Keno

This game originated in China more than 2,000 years ago but is basically a form of our lotto. You mark anywhere between one and 15 of the 80 numbers on the keno ticket, then place your bet with the keno writer. You then keep a duplicate ticket to match against the 20 numbers drawn by the casino at a set time. All the casinos have their own rules about winning combinations, so check before playing. The alternative to this game is throwing your money in a bin, but the lure is the massive payouts.

Slots

Las Vegas is home to the most sophisticated, state-of-the-art machinery in the world and gamblers get so mesmerised by the idea of their winning line coming up that they spend hours feeding money into these machines. But slot machines are such

The stylish casino at Monte Carlo

big business now that they account for around 60% of total casino earnings – and so fill a staggering amount of floor space in the casinos.

BRITTIP

Only play on machines that tell you the return and look for a 98–99% return on $1 slots.

Mechanical penny and nickel slot machines that took one coin at a time have been replaced by computerised dollar slot machines that can accept multiple coins simultaneously and now feature poker, keno, blackjack, bingo and craps. Some even accept credit card-style gambling and the linking up of machines has led to massive $10m-and-more jackpots. You can still play for as little as a nickel a go, but some slots now allow you to use $500-dollar tokens – usually in special VIP slot areas!

Progressive slots are machines that are computer-linked to other machines throughout the States and pay out incredible jackpots. One of the progressive slots is known as Megabucks, which is computer-linked to other machines in the state of Nevada. The CircusBucks progressives start the jackpot climbing at $500,000, but the most recent Super Megabucks starts climbing at $10m! What's more, gamblers can now phone a toll-free number to find out the current

jackpot total on Megabucks and 7 other progressive slot networks run by International Game Technology. The number is: 888 448 2946.

BRITTIP

The coin trays of slot machines are not anchored to the machine so that the money falls with a 'play-me' ting-ting-ting-ting!

Video games

These are basically interactive slot machines aimed directly at the new generation who grew up with computers and computer games. Multiple-use videos can offer up to 10 games with anything from poker to keno and blackjack, plus regular slot machines and are activated simply by touching the screen. Some machines even allow you to play for a $1m poker payout with a 25-cent bet! Another reason for the increase in popularity of video games is that you can play at your own pace, without pressure from dealers, croupiers or other players. The returns that you should be looking for on all the different games are as follows:

All-American poker: Also known as gator bonus poker. Go for machines that pay 8–1 on full houses, a flush and a straight.

Bonus deuces: Best machines are those paying 20–1 for a wild royal flush, 10–1 on 5 of a kind and straight flush and 4–1 on 4 of a kind and a full house.

Deuces wild: Look for a 5–1 payout on 4 of a kind, which is considerably better than 4–1 for 4 of a kind that you'll find on many of these video machines.

The race and sports book at the Mirage

Double bonus poker: Find a 10/7 machine – one that pays 10–1 on a full house and 7–1 on a flush.

Flush attack: Do not play on a machine that needs more than 3 flushes to go into attack mode, and look for one that pays 8–1 for a full house and 5–1 on flushes (known as an 8/5 machine).

Jacks or better: Look for 9/6 machines, which pay 9–1 for a full house and 6–1 on flushes.

Joker wild: Kings or better. Look for a machine that pays 20–1 for 4 of a kind, 7–1 for a full house and 5–1 on a flush.

Sports betting

The race and sports book, as it is known, gives you the chance to bet on horse races and major sporting events. For horse races you can bet on a win (first place only), a place (first or second) and a show (first, second or third). Further bets include naming the first 2 horses in any order, naming the first 2 horses in the correct order or the horses that will win any 2 specified races.

Details of races, the horses and odds are displayed or you can read local newspapers, racing sheets and other publications before making up your mind. Then watch the action on closed-circuit broadcasts live from race tracks across America. The latest innovation in sports betting is proposals for a progressive prize MegaSports jackpot, where the final payout is determined by the amount of betting over a certain period. The prize pools will start at $1m.

The surge in televised coverage of sporting events in America has also created a surge in sports gambling. During one Super Bowl weekend (held every February), nearly 200,000 visitors flocked to Las Vegas to bet more than $50m on their favourite team and spent a further $50m in the city in the process! At Caesars Palace Race and Sports Book – the first to open in Las Vegas – they have a total of

Playing the slots at the Bellagio

50 different ways to part with your cash, including betting on the number of quarterback sacks or the total field goals.

Internet betting

Online casinos have exploded in popularity, especially those sites offering poker. Many different sites often have more than 10,000 punters playing at the same time, all in the comfort of their own homes. The casinos also offer home access to gambling on blackjack, craps, video poker, roulette, bingo and three-dimensional, interactive slot machines. In fact, many industry experts credit much of Las Vegas recent explosive growth to the internet. It is estimated that over 100,000,000 people gamble on internet sites worldwide (62,000,000 in the US alone!) and soon get the urge to give the lights of Vegas a try!

Gambling lessons

For first-timers or for those who just want to brush up on their skills, many casinos in Las Vegas still offer complimentary gaming lessons. Rediscover classic Las Vegas at any of the famous casinos Downtown. The Golden Nugget offers free, daily gaming lessons for a variety of table games including craps, 3-card poker, Pai gow, Texas hold 'em, roulette and blackjack.

On the Strip: The Venetian and The Palazzo offer complimentary gaming lessons for blackjack, roulette and craps. The Venetian also offers 1-on-1 and group poker lessons for no-limit and limit Texas hold 'em. All gaming lessons are available 24 hours based on availability. The Sahara Hotel and Casino features a vast program of player education including an in-room television channel dedicated to gaming education. The 24/7 video tutorial teaches the basics of every major casino game including craps, blackjack, roulette, slots, keno and poker. Complimentary live gaming lessons are also available.

Off-Strip: The Gold Coast offers craps lessons every Fri, Sat and Sun in the casino pit. Its sister property, Suncoast, offers instructional handouts on table games. Dealers provide personal instruction and assistance on the floor even during live games.

BRITTIP

Floral fragrances are pumped around selected slot machines, which increases play by up to 50%.

Table games at the MGM Grand

BRITTIP

Savvy locals know that if they play at a slot machine that offers a 99% return on $1 slots, plus play with their slot club card to get comps from the casino (generally a 1–3% value), they can actually expect to beat the casino!

Many hotels are linked to the Players Network (playersnetwork.com), which you can access through the TV for tips on how to play different games, table etiquette and sports betting.

For tips on how to play all the different video poker machines, it is worth taking the trip to north-west Las Vegas for Bob Dancer's weekly lessons at the Fiesta Rancho Hotel & Casino (2400 North Rancho Drive, 702 631 7000, fiestacasino.com).

Comps

Many Vegas veterans are misty over the good old 'mobbed-up days' when the mob-owned casinos offered free drinks, cheap food and cheap or even free hotel rooms to draw in the punters. The new age of corporate casinos brought a waft of business managers who demanded all areas, including the hotel and restaurant sides, show a profit along with the gambling hall.

Most casinos still liberally hand out free drinks for gamblers. And you can still get comps on everything from free rooms to food, show tickets, front-row seats and limos, without being a high-roller. You just have to earn them. Casinos are looking for loyalty and consistent gambling.

To qualify for a comp, you'll need a player's card, which you can request from the casino as soon as you arrive. Blackjack used to be the fastest way to get comps. Over the last 2 decades casinos began to recognise that slot machines were more profitable so they now offer their best comps for slot players. In fact, the old players cards are now as often referred to as 'slot club cards'.

But while slots get the best comp values, some savvy blackjack players have learned some tricks to maximise their comps. As soon as you sit down at a table, ask to be 'rated', presenting your player's card to the pit boss. This effectively starts the clock on your play and so long as you keep

Beachside casino at the Mirage

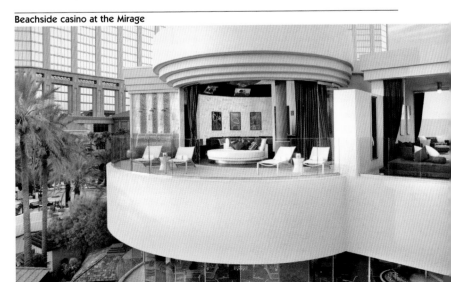

BRITTIP

Part of the fun of a visit to Las Vegas is to check out all the different resorts and attractions. However, try to do most of your gambling at one casino to maximise your freebies.

gambling, however slowly and gently, you'll be noted for comps. Another tip is to change all your money up front, don't do it in small increments as this makes you look like a small-time gambler. Big-time gamblers placing bets in the thousands of dollars get a casino host who will organise limos, money off room bills and so on. Whatever you've gambled, it's worth telling the casino when you check out. The more you lose, the bigger the comps!

Many of the casinos are so determined to foster good relationships with their customers that they have introduced loyalty cards – the amount of play gives you points that can be put towards meals, rooms, shows or even getting cash back. Ask at your hotel, but the following are a few of the best.

BRITTIP

If you're a regular gambler or plan to gamble a lot when in Las Vegas, join a slot club and see what deals you're offered. Apart from free drinks, you may get a comp room or even free show tickets.

Casino floor at the Excalibur

a-List Players Club: Available at Planet Hollywood Resort, the a-List Players Club gives you great rewards such as room nights, restaurant meals and show tickets. It also gives you access to PH Perks. This includes PH Award Play that lets you redeem your slot points for free slot play right at your favourite slot machines. PH Bonus Play allows you to earn extra rewards by participating in a-List Players Club promotions and special gaming offers sent to you based on your play.

Circus Circus Players Club: Players can earn dollars redeemable at Slots-of-Fun and Circus Circus for hotel stays, airport limousine transportation, meals and tickets to shows at other MGM Mirage properties in Las Vegas.

Club Palms: Earn 1 point for every $1 of coin-in on slot and video poker machines. Points can be redeemed at the rate of 400 points = $1 for comps or for Free Slot Play. Comps for your points can be redeemed at over 35 outlets including The Pearl Concert Theater, Simon at Palms Place, N9NE Steakhouse, Ghostbar, Drift Spa, Brenden Theatres, Playboy Club and Moon Nightclub. You can even get a tattoo at Huntington Ink or a palm reading at Cosmic Corner.

Island Winners' Club: At the Tropicana, this rewards slot, video poker and table-game players. Slot and video poker players can earn both comps and cash by inserting their club card into the slot machine. On average, about 2 hours of play on a dollar slot with maximum coins played on each 'pull' will earn about $10 cash back. Table-game players present their card to a floor person to earn comp credits at blackjack, craps or roulette tables. Credits are based on the average bets and length of time you play.

MGM Mirage Players Club: With just 1 card you can earn valuable rewards based on slot and table-games play, such as cash, complimentary rooms, show tickets and invitations to promotions and special events. The card is valid across the MGM Grand, Bellagio, Mirage, Treasure Island, New York-New York, Mandalay Bay, Luxor, Excalibur and Monte Carlo.

Play Rio Card: This card, at the Rio All-Suite Hotel and Casino in Valley View Boulevard at Flamingo Road, will allow you to earn points during both slot and table play towards reduced-price or comp suites, comp dining or tickets to a show. Sign up at the Play Rio Center.

Total Rewards: The new Harrah's card lets

Gambling fast facts

- In 2007, Clark County's casinos (Clark County includes Las Vegas, Laughlin, Mesquite, Primm and Jean) took in $10.9 billion in gross gaming revenue. Las Vegas casinos accounted for $8.4 billion.
- In 2007, the average gambling budget per trip was approximately $556 per visitor.
- The average visitor gambled 3.4 hours per day.
- 84% of visitors said they gambled during their stay.
- Slot machines reign in the casinos – 65% of visitors hit the slots during their stay. Blackjack came in a distant second at 14% with video poker rounding out the top 3 with 6%.
- The statewide Megabucks games experienced a first in September 2005 when a player hit the progressive jackpot for the second time. The 92-year-old winner took home $4.6 million in 1989 and then hit the jackpot again in 2005 for $21 million.
- Nevada's casino and gaming areas are off-limits to people younger than 21. When Bellagio opened on the Las Vegas Strip in October 1998, the hotel barred patrons from the premises who were under 18 years of age unless they were registered guests of the hotel; this policy was a first, although it is not strictly enforced today.
- Race and sports betting tops $2 billion per year. Some Las Vegas casinos treat gamblers to plush seating, free drinks and buffets in the race and sports book complexes where live racing and athletic events are viewed on giant, satellite-fed screens.

you build up points at all Harrah's properties; especially valuable at Caesars Palace.

The casinos

As much imagination has gone into the decor of the casinos as every other part of the resort-hotels.

Aria: arialasvegas.com The new resort at CityCenter brings gambling out of the dark ages, literally, with its use of natural light which streams through the gaming floor in pools of illumination. Unthinkable only a year or two ago!

Caesars Palace: caesarspalace.com At Caesars Palace Forum Casino you can take a break from gambling and have your photo taken with Caesar and Cleopatra as they stroll around with their royal entourage, while the west corridor is home to animatronic Atlantis statues!

Excalibur: excalibur.com/casino The Excalibur casino continues its theme with staff dressed in medieval costume and trumpet players blowing on horns straight out of Robin Hood.

Imperial Palace: imperialpalace.com If you're having trouble parking, then you can always place your bets at the new drive-up sports book at the Imperial Palace! In fact, more casinos would offer the same service but just don't have the space. The manager at the Imperial drive-up says business is always brisk – especially in summer when gamblers prefer to remain in their air-conditioned cars.

Las Vegas Hilton: lvhilton.com/casino The Las Vegas Hilton Casino is one of the most beautifully decorated, with marble, rich woods and tier after tier of crystal chandeliers. The largest race and sports book is also to be found at the Hilton.

Luxor: luxor.com/casino At the Luxor you'll find a sumptuous setting surrounded by the Nile.

MGM Grand: mgmgrand.com/gaming If you want to see how the other half lives, take a sneak look into the VIP high-limit area at the MGM Grand. Here high-rollers rub cheeks with celebrities in a setting based on the elegance and style of the grand old casinos of Monte Carlo. Tall, classic columns, rose-coloured curtains and cherry wood and suede tables embroidered with the gold MGM Grand monograms are a real sight!

The casino at New York-New York

The Palms: palms.com Gambling with the beautiful people and the high-rollers in the Mint Hi-Limit Lounge.

Planet Hollywood Resort & Casino: planethollywoodresort.com Nearly 3acres/1.2ha of action in typical slick PH style. The Pleasure Pit, for example, features blackjack and roulette dealt by women in lingerie as go-go dancers keep the guys playing with their moves.

SpaceQuest Casino: lvhilton.com The new pièce de résistance is the SpaceQuest Casino where gamblers board a futuristic space station that orbits the earth, with space windows that create the illusion of circling the globe from sunrise to sunset.

Tropicana: http://tropicanalv.com/casino You can beat the heat of the summer at the Tropicana by swimming up to the blackjack table, open daily 9.30am–5pm. In the indoor area of the resort's indoor–outdoor swimming pool, up to 14 players sit on marble stools up to their hips in water. They play with plastic cards and use either chips or cash. The paper money is kept in mint condition by specially heated rotating drop boxes that dry the cash in less than 60 seconds!

BRITTIP

Many of the casinos have information on how to play the games on their websites.

Downtown casinos

Now home to the last neon signs of what used to be Glitter Gulch city, the downtown casinos are generally more friendly and relaxed, have cheaper-play slot machines, better returns and more comps. Regular visitors to Las Vegas may like staying at the

Sam's Town

Tropicana casino

ritzy, glamorous Strip hotels, but often enjoy a trip downtown to play on the nickel slot machines.

Binion's Horseshoe: 128 East Fremont Street, 702 878 2452, binions.com Once home to the world poker championships, this casino is famous for its single-deck blackjack and liberal rules, single-zero roulette, great odds-on crap, loose nickel and quarter machines and loads of comps. Binion's is also known for its friendly atmosphere.

Four Queens Hotel: 202 Fremont Street, 702 385 4011, fourqueens.com You'll find the world's largest regular slot machine at the Four Queens Hotel downtown. It is the size of a small motorhome and allows 6 people to play at the same time!

Gold Coast: 4000 West Flamingo Road, 702 367 7111, goldcoastcasino.com The karaoke bar at the Gold Coast is excellent for entertainment (locals dressed as stars such as Roy Orbison, Dean Martin and Elvis) and cheap drinks.

Gold Spike: 40 East Ogden Avenue, 702 384 8444, goldspike.com About to relaunch at time of going to press.

Golden Gate: 1 Fremont Street, 702 385 1906, goldengatecasino.net Another friendly establishment, this still serves up its famous 99-cent shrimp (huge prawn) cocktail.

Sam's Town: 5111 Boulder Highway, 800 851 1703, samstownlv.com The favoured haunt of locals is Sam's Town on Boulder Highway (going out towards the Hoover Dam). The free light and laser show is excellent and you'll find great odds on slots and video machines, and good comps.

BRITTIP

Many people are rude, so the waitresses always remember the nice punters who tip in advance, and make sure they get their free drinks.

8 GOING TO THE CHAPEL

Getting married on any budget in the wedding capital of the world

Las Vegas has more chapels per square mile and more options on how you tie the knot than any other city in the world – and it's all so easy. Liberal state laws mean that Nevada is one of the few states that does not require a blood test, and to get you quickly on your way to the altar, the Marriage License Bureau is open 8am–midnight daily, including holidays.

If you do decide to go ahead, you'll be in star-studded company – this is where Elvis wed Priscilla, Frank Sinatra wed Mia Farrow, Jane Fonda wed Roger Vadim and Paul Newman wed Joanne Woodward. Others include Bruce Willis and Demi Moore, while Brigitte Bardot, Britney Spears, Bob Geldof, his daughter Peaches Geldof, David Cassidy, Richard Gere, Michael Jordan and Joan Collins all said 'I do' at a chapel in Las Vegas.

Getting married here is so simple that an amazing 100,000 get marriage licences here every year. The most popular day is Valentine's Day, closely followed by New Year's Eve, while the date 7 July 2007 (7/7/07) was considered lucky and it also happened to be a Saturday – 4,450 weddings were performed that day. On 8 August 2008 (8/8/08) 2,196 wedding took place in Vegas.

And you can do it all in such style. Dress up as a medieval prince and princess at the Canterbury Chapel in the Excalibur, allow an Elvis impersonator to wed you at Graceland Wedding Chapel, or try any of the other themes available from *Star Trek* to gangsters and rock 'n' roll. Then again, you could decide to make your vows before diving off a bungee-jump platform, soaring high above Las Vegas in a hot-air balloon or flying over the Grand Canyon. You can even stay in your car at the

BRITTIP

Avoid Valentine's Day unless you want to queue for 4 hours to get your licence!

world's first ever drive-up wedding chapel or try the Tunnel of Love chapel at A Little White Chapel on the Strip.

The stunning setting at the Excalibur

What you need to wed

- A marriage licence from one of 3 bureaus (see below). Once the licence has been issued it is valid for 1 year.
- Proof of age (driver's licence, passport or birth certificate).
- Minimum age for adults is 18. Those aged 16–17 must have either a parent present at the time the licence is issued or a notarised affidavit.
- If you have been divorced, you will need to specify the date when and the city and state/country where it became final.

It costs $55 for a marriage licence, which must be paid in cash, and $35 for the ceremony. A very basic package starts at $100, but the sky's the limit depending on where you wed, what you do and the accessories you choose.

License bureaus

Clark County Marriage License Bureau: 201 Clark Avenue, 702 671 0600. For recorded information: 702 455 4415, co.clark.nv.us/clerk/marriage_information. htm Open 8am–midnight daily.

Laughlin, Nev. Marriage License Bureau: 101 Civic Way, #2, 702 298 4622. Open Tues–Thurs 8am–4:30pm; Fri 8am–8pm; weekends 8am–5pm. Closed Mon and holidays.

Mesquite, Nev. Marriage License Bureau: 500 Hillside Drive, 702 346 1867. Open Wed 8am–3:30pm; Fri 3pm–9pm; Sat 9am–3pm. Closed Mon, Tues, Thurs, Sun and holidays.

Although many of the high-profile marriages have ended in the divorce courts, a Las Vegas wedding is not synonymous with one that ends in tears. People tend to opt for the wedding capital of the world because here they are free of family pressures and can make all their own choices. Furthermore, thanks to the raft of amazing accommodation, romantic restaurants, shows and nightlife, the city is also becoming a honeymoon mecca where the wedding can also be combined with a visit to the Grand Canyon and its surroundings.

Fascinating facts

Ancestry.com, the world's largest online family history resource, recently launched a collection of Nevada's marriage and divorce records of the more than 9 million people who said their 'I do's' and 'I don'ts' in Nevada between 1956 and 2005. A cross-section of the collection reveals some fascinating and fun facts on getting together, splitting up, celebrity sightings, most popular days of the week to get married, percentage of marriages that take place in Nevada versus nationwide, shortest marriages in Nevada history, repeat offenders and much more. And, in true betting fashion, the site also launched VegasWeddingOdds.com, an online marriage-predicting site which, based on your first name, will give you the first names of the people you're most likely to marry in Nevada.

Ceremonies

Like every other aspect of Las Vegas, the business of helping people to tie the knot is booming. Hotel ceremonies tend to be more ostentatious than those at ordinary chapels, but they have prices to match, too! One couple were taken to their wedding site at The Venetian's St Mark's Square in an oversized white gondola, with a host of actors cavorting about as if it were a renaissance fair. After the gilt ceremony, the reception was held in the gardens area, where champagne and caviar celebrated the blessed union. All for a mere $12,000.

Not quite as expensive, but definitely unusual, is a wedding on the roller-coaster at New York-New York Hotel & Casino (702 740 6607, nynyhotelcasino.com/entertainment/entertainment_therollercoaster). Ceremonies take place at 67mph/108kph and cost $600 in the morning and $700 in the evening. Or how about saying 'I do' at Chopper Chapel at the Harley-Davidson® Café (702 740 4555, harley-davidson cafe.com/chapel) on the Strip from $199?

Wedding queen of the West

Possibly the most famous wedding chapel in the world is the Little White Wedding Chapel (alittlewhitechapel.com) owned by Charolette Richards, dubbed the 'wedding queen of the West'. In her time, she has

Little White Wedding Chapel

You can even take your vows at Red Rock Canyon

married celebs including Joan Collins, Patty Duke and Bruce Willis. She is also a savvy business woman as well as a wedding planner and has an empire of wedding chapels and more exotic options:

- Little White Wedding Chapel
- Chapel l'Amour
- Chapel of Promises
- Crystal Chapel
- Gazebo Chapel
- Tunnel of Love Drive Thru: In 1991, Charolette noticed a disabled couple having difficulty getting out of their car to go into her chapel so she hit upon the idea of a drive-up window and opened it at the Little White Wedding Chapel on the Strip. It became such a novelty that couples began queuing up for the drive-through wedding. They come on motorcycles, roller-skates, in cars, limos, trucks, taxis and even boats! Now it includes a Tunnel of Love in which couples are surrounded by floating cherubs, twinkling stars, birds on ribbons and signs everywhere saying 'I love you, I want you, I need you and I can't live without you'.
- A Little White Chapel in the Sky for balloon weddings

Contact details are in the A–Z of major wedding chapels on page 186.

Contact details are in the A–Z of major wedding chapels on page 186.

BRITTIP

If you do get married in Las Vegas you need copies of your marriage certificate, which you can now order via the internet. Go to co.clark.nv.us.

At the Little White Wedding Chapel you pay anything from $229 for the Lover's Package, which includes a decorated chapel, traditional music, a witness (if required), a religious or civil ceremony, 12 digital photographs, a rose bouquet for the bride and a boutonniere for the groom plus a 'beautiful love recipe, keepsake rules for a happy marriage and a keepsake' to $829 for the Honeymooner Package, which includes all of the above plus 82 digital photographs and a photo album, a large bridal bouquet and bridesmaid bouquet, best man's boutonniere, a DVD of the ceremony, padded marriage licence

Happy day at the MGM Grand

A–Z of major wedding chapels

All Religions Wedding Chapel: 2855 Las Vegas Blvd South, 702 735 4179

Bally's Celebration Wedding Chapel: 3645 Las Vegas Blvd South, 702 892 2222

Chapel by the Courthouse: 201 East Bridger Avenue, 702 384 9099, achapelbythecourthouse.com

Chapel L'Amour: 1901 Las Vegas Blvd South, 702 369 5683, alittlewhitechapel.com

Chapel of Dreams: 316 Bridger Ave, Suite 103, 702 471 7729

Chapel of Love: 1430 Las Vegas Blvd South, 702 387 0155

Chapel of Promises: 1901 Las Vegas Blvd South, 702 369 5683, alittlewhitechapel.com

Chapel of the Bells: 2233 Las Vegas Blvd South, 702 735 6803, chapelofthebellslasvegas.com

Chaplain at Large: 3162 Cadbury Dr, 702 898 2694

China Town Wedding Temple: 4215 Spring Mountain Rd, 702 252 0400

Crystal Chapel: 1901 Las Vegas Blvd South, 702 369 5683, alittlewhitechapel.com

Cupid's Wedding Chapel: 827 Las Vegas Blvd South, 702 598 4444, cupidswedding.com

Divine Madness Fantasy Wedding Chapel: 111 Las Vegas Blvd South, Suite H, 702 384 5660

Drive-up Wedding Window: 1301 Las Vegas Blvd South, 702 382 5943, alittlewhitechapel.com

Elvis Chapel: 1205 Las Vegas Blvd South, 702 384 0771, theelvisweddingchapel.com

Emerald at Queensridge: 891 Las Vegas Blvd South, 702 242 5700, emeraldgarden.com

Flamingo Hilton Garden Chapel: 3555 Las Vegas Blvd South, 702 733 3232

Gazebo Chapel: 1901 Las Vegas Blvd South, 702 369 5683, alittlewhitechapel.com

Gothic Weddings: 1205 Las Vegas Blvd South, 702 384 0771, gothicweddings.com

Graceland Wedding Chapel: 619 Las Vegas Blvd South, 702 382 0091, gracelandchapel.com

Hartland Mansion: 1044 South 6th Street, 702 387 6700, lasvegashartlandmansion.com

Heavenly Bliss Wedding Chapel: 930 South 3rd Street, 702 444 5444, heavenlyblisschapel.com

Hitching Post Wedding Chapel: 1737 Las Vegas Blvd South, 1 800 572 5530, hitchingpostweddingchapel.com.

Las Vegas Helicopters Inc.: 3724 Las Vegas Blvd South, 702 736 0013, lvhelicopters.com

Las Vegas Villa: 4982 Shirley Street, 702 795 8119, lasvegasvilla.com

Las Vegas Wedding Chapel: 727 South 9th, 702 383 5909, lvchapel.com

Little Chapel of the Flowers: 301 Las Vegas Blvd South, 702 735 4331, littlechapel.com

Little Church of the West: 4617 Las Vegas Blvd South, 702 739 7971, littlechurchlv.com

Little White Chapel in the Sky: 1301 Las Vegas Blvd South, 702 382 5943, alittlewhitechapel.com

Little White Wedding Chapel: 1301 Las Vegas Blvd South, 702 382 5943, alittlewhitechapel.com

Long Fung Wedding Temple: 4215 Spring Mountain Rd, 702 252 0400

Mount Charleston Hotel and Restaurant: 2 Kyle Canyon Road, Mount Charleston, 702 872 5500, mtcharlestonhotel.com

Rainbow Gardens: 4125 West Charleston Blvd, 702 878 4646, ilv.com/rainbowgardens

San Francisco Sally's Victorian Chapel: 1304 Las Vegas Blvd South, 702 385 7777

Silver Bell Wedding Chapel: 607 Las Vegas Blvd South, 702 382 3726

Special Memory Wedding Chapel: 800 South 4th Street, 702 384 2211, aspecialmemory.com.

Speedway to Love Wedding Chapel: 7000 North Las Vegas Blvd, 702 644 3000

Sunset Gardens: 3931 East Sunset Road, 702 456 9986

Sweethearts Wedding Chapel: 1155 Las Vegas Blvd South, 702 385 7785, sweetheartschapel.com

Valley Outreach Synagogue: 1692 Long Horizon Lane, 702 436 4900, valleyoutreach.com

Victoria's Wedding Chapel: 2800 West Sahara, 702 252 4565, avictorias.com

Wedding Bells Chapel: 375 E Harmon, 702 731 2355, weddingbellschapel.com

Wedding on Wheels: 1301 Las Vegas Blvd South, 702 382 5943, alittlewhitechapel.com

The Wedding Room at the Cellar: 3601 West Sahara Ave, 702 362 6712

Wee Kirk o' the Heather: 231 Las Vegas Blvd South, 702 382 9830, weekirk.com

holder and bride and groom champagne glasses. All the packages include a courtesy limousine service from your hotel to the Marriage License Bureau, on to the Little White Wedding Chapel and back to your hotel.

The chapel fee is $55, drive-through weddings cost $40, hot-air balloon weddings start at $1,500 and helicopter weddings start at $995.

BRITTIP

A useful website for chapel hunting is las-vegas-weddings.co.uk.

Co-ordinators

In addition to the chapels there are several very good wedding specialists. Co-ordinators have no chapel themselves, but co-ordinate with a variety of vendors to make a memorable wedding for you, from themed to decadent.

Viva Las Vegas Weddings

702 384 0771, vivalasvegasweddings.com
This company arranges an extraordinary number of differently themed weddings from *Star Trek* to Elvis and rock 'n' roll. Here are some examples.

Bond: You can choose a Bond wedding ceremony for $1,100, which includes a limousine pick-up by Bond baddie Oddjob, 2 dancing Bond girls and a ceremony performed by a 007 impersonator who arrives by sports car.

Camelot: The Camelot theme includes Merlin or King Arthur as the minister, while you'll be treated like a king and queen. The basic package costs $700 and includes period music, knights, trumpeters and fair ladies. For an extra $100 you can have a soloist perform a medieval tune.

Elvis in Blue Hawaii: Here you have an Elvis impersonator and dancers from the Tropicana's *Folies Bergères* at your ceremony, which takes place in the Elvis Chapel. In addition to all the Elvis memorabilia, Hawaiian sets, showgirls and hula dancers, there will be theatrical lighting and fog, while 'Elvis' will sing 'Love Me Tender', 'Viva Las Vegas' and 'I Can't Help Falling In Love With You' ($700).

Gangster: Here you'll step back in time to a 1940s mafioso shotgun wedding where the Godfather/minister opens the door to wedded bliss accompanied by 2 bodyguards and a waiter/soloist singing in Italian ($650).

Getting married Elvis style

Intergalactic: Your special day is presided over by Captain James T Quirk or Captain Schpock in the Starship Chapel, surrounded by life-size cut-outs of your favourite characters. The package comes with a Minister Transporter, an illusion entrance, theatrical lighting and lots of fog for $700.

Las Vegas: This package includes showgirls, keno runners, cocktail waitresses, card dealers and a Las Vegas-style singer/minister, plus theatrical lights and fog. It costs $650 and for another $250 you can even have Elvis or Marilyn Monroe at your wedding. Other packages include the Victorian ($600), the Disco ($650) and the Beach Party ($650).

Rock 'n' Roll: This is all about rock 'n' roll, complete with memorabilia and an electric guitar version of the Wedding March, while a rock star impersonator will sing during the ceremony for $650.

Nevada Wedding Connection

702 236 8728, lvweddingconnection.com
Joni Moss can arrange anything from a wedding in a luxury 16-passenger coach while driving down the Strip, to vows on a Harley Davidson (in a private room, not on the road!). She also works with the following chapels (but can also assist with weddings anywhere throughout town): Chapel of the Flowers, Viva Las Vegas, Imperial Palace Wedding Chapel, Stained Glass Chapel, Vegas Chapel, Mon Bel Ami Chapel and Belleza Chapel.

Candlelight Wedding Chapel

BRITTIP

If you're coming to Las Vegas to propose, yourhandinmarriage. com is ready to assist. Services include a proposal written in the sky to finding the perfect engagement ring.

Las Vegas Weddings and Room Co-ordinators

2770 South Maryland Parkway, Suite 416, 702 737 6800, lasvegasweddings.com
This company can book your rooms and organise every aspect of your wedding.

Graceland Wedding Chapel

East Chapel at the Bellagio

Open 24/7, they arrange flowers, transport, clothes, reception and entertainments. They have 17 chapels and themes include Elvis and nature weddings. Or you can choose to take one of the packages arranged by tour operators from Britain.

Getting married at resort-hotels on the Strip

With all the resort-hotel websites, it's usually quickest to key in the main website address, then navigate via the menus. If you can't immediately see a weddings option, look under 'amenities' or sometimes 'meetings'.

Bellagio

702 693 7700, bellagio.com

East Chapel: The more intimate chapel holds a maximum of 30 guests, and is decorated in hues of cream, rose and peach, with antique green and bride's blue. The classy design allows you to say

BRITTIP

Most resort hotels are very willing to put together bachelorette parties for the bride and her maids.

your vows at the altar with a beautiful full-length stained glass window as the backdrop.

South Chapel: Holds up to 130 guests in an elegant and refined classic European-designed environment. Beautifully decorated in gold and muted colours with stained glass windows, it is also light and airy.

Caesars Palace

702 731 7110, caesarspalace.com
Caesars specialises in customising weddings to suit the most romantic tastes and a recent flurry of developments have led to the opening of some of the most attractive and varied chapel settings in any

resort-hotel. For something even more special, you can also hire ancient characters – Caesar, Cleopatra, Roman guards, handmaidens and sirens are the favourites – to attend your ceremony at any of the chapels. Packages cost $950–4,100 but the sky's the limit with extras.

Classico: Having opened in August 2005, this now offers the chance for 196 guests to enjoy a wedding ceremony in a classical environment. On a theme of beige, light blue and cream, it has chandeliers, stained glass windows and magnificent floral arrangements.

Romano: A more intimate affair for 35 guests, its décor is based on Rome of course!

Venus Garden: Small, beautiful and secluded, the Romanesque temple is surrounded by tropical palm trees, a blooming floral landscape, koi fish pond and fountains. Seats 114.

Tuscana: Based on the romance and charm of old world Tuscany, the colour scheme is creams and browns. Seats 80.

Circus Circus
702 794 3777, circuscircus.com

Chapel of the Fountain: One of the first and longest-running hotel-casino wedding chapels in town. Packages cost $281–901.

Excalibur
702 597 7278, excalibur.com

Canterbury Wedding Chapel: In keeping with the theme of the hotel, the chapel in a lovely gazebo has a medieval-gothic flavour with domed ceilings, stained glass windows and lots of dark wood. A large chandelier over the altar forms the perfect backdrop for photos and you can even look the part, too, by hiring period costumes. Now, where is that knight in shining armour …? Wedding packages from $199.

Four Seasons
702 632 5000, fourseasons.com/lasvegas

Fountain Terrace and suites: The Four Seasons offers the serenity and prestige of the city's most acclaimed hotel in an exclusive, non-gambling environment. In addition to an outdoor venue, the Fountain Terrace, the Four Seasons also offers the chance to get married in some of the most amazing suites available in Las Vegas. Normally reserved for those who like to pay up to $10,000 a night for their hotel accommodation, this is a wonderful way to experience how the other half lives, at $3,000 a night! The Presidential and Panoramic suites, on the 35th to 39th floors of the hotel, come with stunning views of the mountains and desert. They

The chapel at the Luxor

Wedding chapel at the Imperial Palace

are decorated in rich woods with floral and warm-hued upholstery and drapes. The Las Vegas Strip View suites feature floor-to-ceiling windows and – you guessed it – amazing views of the Strip. Prices on application.

Imperial Palace
702 967 0045, imperialpalace.com

Princess Wedding Chapel: The elegantly appointed chapel is on the fourth floor and is decorated in ivory and soft beiges with silk floral arrangements and crystal chandeliers. You can also have an Elvis wedding here, or the hotel will arrange for a wedding at Lake Mead or at the bottom of the Grand Canyon. Packages from $199.

Luxor
702 262 4444, luxor.com

Luxor wedding chapel: Surprisingly, given the strong theming throughout this hotel, the chapel is in keeping with the hotel, but not overtly Egyptian in feel. Elegantly decked out in creams and peaches, it seats 100 guests. Packages from $525. Themes include *Titanic*, cowboy, rock 'n' roll and Vegas, of course.

Mandalay Bay
702 632 7490, mandalaybay.com

Mandalay Bay chapels: There are 2 chapels within this resort, both set within an exotic island built on the shores of an 11acre/4.5ha tropical lagoon. The interiors are decorated in peaches and cream, while outside, the chapel fountain provides a superb photo backdrop. Many themed weddings are also available in different venues around the resort ranging

from a shark reef wedding to a cabana ceremony. Packages from $1,100.

Mandarin Oriental Las Vegas
702 590 8888, mandarinoriental.com/lasvegas/special_occasions

Intimate to ballroom: In true Mandarin Oriental style, weddings are tailor-made and can be as intimate or grand as you wish. Prices on request.

MGM Grand
1 800 646 5530, mgmgrandweddings.com

Forever Grand Wedding Chapel: A magnificent, cathedral-like archway announces your arrival at the lobby of this dual chapel. Lining the walls of the marble-floored area is a series of black and white photographs of movie stars in their wedding finery. Both chapels come in creams and blue with pretty domed ceilings. Other venues around the hotel include poolside, spa wall or the Terraza. Themes include Hollywood glamour. Packages from $800.

Cherish Chapel: Seats 45 guests.

Legacy Chapel: Seats 70 guests.

Mirage
702 791 7155, mirage.com

Customised ceremonies: The Mirage does not have a chapel, but can customise ceremonies to be performed in the banqueting space. You meet with their

Wedding chapel at the Mandalay Bay

Monte Carlo's beautiful chapel

design team to discuss your requirements and tailor-make your own fairytale wedding.

Monte Carlo

1 800 822 8651, montecarlo.com

French-Victorian-styled chapel: The upmarket resort offers a refined chapel,

Treasure Island's Enchantment Wedding

which is decorated in soft, neutral colours with hand-painted murals. It seats 100 guests. Packages from $385.

Palazzo Las Vegas

702 414 1013, palazzolasvegas.com
Upmarket weddings around the hotel including private use of the Palazzo Waterfall for 1 hour.

Paris Resort

1 877 650 5021, parislasvegas.com
In addition to 2 of the most romantic chapels in any resort hotel, you can also choose to get wed by the rooftop pool or on the observation deck at the top of the Eiffel Tower. Packages cost $800–10,000!

Chapelle du Jardin: An intimate chapel seating 30, it is decorated in pastel tones accented by charming garden murals.

Chapelle du Paradis: The cathedral-style setting of this beautiful chapel is enhanced by elegant columns, detailed gold-leaf designs, crystal chandeliers and angelic cherubs painted onto the blue-sky ceiling. Seats 90.

Planet Hollywood

702 702 785 5933,
planethollywoodresort.com

The chapel: The new Planet Hollywood is about cool lines and chic, designer flair and so is the chapel. Wedding packages cost from $899 for *Gone with the Wind* right up to $10,700 for 50 people minimum at *My Big Fat Greek Wedding*.

The Venetian wedding experience

Stratosphere

1 800 789 9436, stratospherehotel.com or chapelintheclouds.com

Bella Luna Salon – Chapel in the Clouds: The Stratosphere Tower holds the unique position of offering the highest chapels in all of America, sitting 800ft/240m above the ground and offering truly awesome views, especially at night. Couples can also get wed on the indoor observation deck and then use the outdoor patio overlooking the Strip for their reception. Prices from $99.09. Elvis impersonator (of course!) is also available at an extra cost.

Garden Chapel: The smaller chapel seats 20.

Terrace Chapel: This seats 100 and is decorated in orange and grey.

Treasure Island

702 894 7700, treasureisland.com

Elegant Wedding Chapels: White benches contrast with the terracotta hues of the décor to provide a romantic setting for your wedding. Packages from $599.

Tropicana

702 739 2451, tropicanalv.com

Gazebo: The outdoor island gazebo, an unusual and romantic chapel with a Polynesian theme, seats 20.

Island Wedding Chapel: This has been voted Best Wedding Chapel and Most Romantic Setting by the *Las Vegas Bride* magazine. Tucked away in the lush tropical foliage and tumbling waterfalls for which the hotel is famous, it seats 90. Packages start at $399.

The Venetian

866 548 1807, venetian.com

Chapels: This resort-hotel is themed around the ageless beauty and romance of Venice and the storybook charm of old-world Italy. There are 3 chapels, each holding 40–50 guests and overlooking the pool deck and lush gardens. Cleverly, all 3 chapels can be opened out to provide space for a larger event.

Ponte al di Piazza: Alternatively, couples can choose to say their vows on the bridge over the square, which is said to serve as the stairway to longevity and prosperity as man and wife. Afterwards, you can start married life by floating down the Grand Canal in a beautiful gondola while being serenaded. Packages from $800.

Wynn Las Vegas

702 770 7100, wynnlasvegas.com

In keeping with the standards for privacy that pervade all aspects of Wynn's mega-resort, each of the wedding salons has its own private foyer where guests can gather before the ceremony, and a private bridal room for last-minute touch-ups! Delicate tones, deluxe upholstery and beautiful lighting are the other hallmarks of each chapel. Packages for these glamorous venues cost $1,690.

Lavender Salon: Designed to be intimate, yet can accommodate 120 guests. Despite its name, back-lit rose murals and rose petals strewn along the aisle are the main features of this chapel.

Lilac Salon: This chapel is perfect for smaller wedding parties and seats 65. White, creams and terracottas run throughout the salon and are reflected in the choice of flowers that line the aisle and altar.

Style and romance at The Venetian

Primrose Courtyard: Think luxurious fabrics in genteel Caribbean colours draped over an exterior altar and you get a good idea of what this chapel is about. A private courtyard under a canopy of trees that is surrounded by 2 fountains, it can seat up to 40 guests. It also available for pre-event cocktails or post-wedding cake and champagne.

Getting married at resort-hotels off the Strip

Hard Rock Hotel & Casino

702 693 5000, hardrockhotel.com
Tailor-made weddings can be anything from a ceremony under billowy drapery to one surrounded by black roses at the hotel's rock 'n' roll wedding. Receptions can be a brunch buffet to a poolside party.

Terrace of Dreams at the Bellagio

Ritz-Carlton Lake Las Vegas

Las Vegas Hilton

702 732 5755, lvhilton.com

La Bella Wedding Chapel: Traditional cream chapel and a variety of packages available.

M Resort

702 797 1919, themresort.com
A variety of venues with stunning views over Vegas.

Rio All-Suite Hotel

702 252 7777, riolasvegas.com
Tie the knot in the Palazzo Gardens, on the 51st floor in the VooDoo Lounge or poolside.

Getting married at Lake Las Vegas

Ritz-Carlton Lake Las Vegas

702 567 4700, ritzcarlton.com
Chapel Fiorenza sits directly over the shimmering waters of 320-acre/130-ha Lake Las Vegas on the resort's landmark Ponte Vecchio-inspired bridge. Offering spectacular lake views and charming Tuscan design, the chapel lies within steps of the Ritz-Carlton. Other options include the Presidential Suite, on a white sand beach by the lake, in the Tuscany Courtyard or in the Pont Vecchio Park.

A full guide to restaurants, bars and clubs

Surprisingly, for a city that claims to be so adult, there is relatively little available for the gay community. Nevadan anti-sodomy laws were only repealed in 1995 and a decade later, the city now has its first openly gay nightclub on the Strip – Krave. Despite this, Las Vegas was ranked as one of the top 10 gay-friendly destinations in the US according to a survey conducted by the Travel Industry Association.

There may not be the gay areas you'll find in many other cities, but there is an active scene and the annual Gay Pride Parade in April or May (702 615 9429, lasvegaspride.org for details) is testimony to the presence of a gay community. For the most part, though, a lot of gay activity is immersed in the mainstream. Here is a guide to the specific amenities available to gay men and women.

Information

Gay and Lesbian Center

953 East Sahara Avenue between 6th Street and Maryland Parkway, 702 733 9800, thecenterlv.com
A good place to start is the Gay and Lesbian Center. It is open Mon–Fri 11am–7pm – call ahead for schedules. It is a relatively new building and a new meeting point for gays. The Center's website is very helpful.

BRITTIP

A leading gay newspaper, *QVegas*, maintains a great website, qvegas.com full of information for the gay community. gayvegas.com and outinlasvegas are useful websites.

The Gay Triangle

The Gay Triangle area around Paradise Road has several bars, Get Booked and the Mariposa coffee house. Pick up copies of the free *QVegas* at any of those locations. This area is also lovingly referred to as the Fruit Loop by local gay and straight residents, for the business signs that show the rainbow colours of gay pride. Hotspots include **Suede**, a piano bar and restaurant, and **Gipsy**, the city's original gay dance club. Popular among celebrities, **Piranha Nightclub** and **8½ Ultra Lounge** feature a second floor with a beautiful view

Pool fun is on offer at many hotels

of the Strip, VIP cabanas and sky boxes and a private bar. You'll also discover **Freezone** and, as the name implies, there is never a cover at this popular bar and nightclub. A favourite among lesbian visitors, Freezone offers daily drink specials, good times and an ever-friendly staff.

Get Booked: At Paradise Plaza, 4640 South Paradise Road, 702 737 7780, this is a bookstore at the heart of the Gay Triangle at the corner of Naples Drive and Paradise Road, just south of Hard Rock Café, and a great source of information. It is open Mon–Thurs 10am–midnight; Fri 10am–2am; Sat noon–2am and Sun noon–midnight.

Another great gay area can be found along and between East Sahara and Karen Avenue, just to the west of Maryland Parkway. Here you will find Apollo Spa, Pride Factory, Spotlight Lounge, Badlands, Rainbow Lounge and the Las Vegas Lounge.

🏴 BRITTIP

Nevada Gay Rodeo Association, ngra.com, is an all-volunteer, non-profit organisation dedicated to preserving the Western lifestyle and producing gay rodeos with a commitment to raise funds for charitable organisations.

Accommodation

Alexis Park

375 East Harmon, 702 796 3300, alexispark.com
The closest hotel to the Fruit Loop area and host to a number of gay events.

Alexis Park

Blue Moon Resort

2651 Westwood Drive, just off the Strip, 702 784 4500, bluemoonlv.com
The $3.1m Blue Moon Resort opened in December 2002 providing a full-service gay resort for men only with 45 rooms and suites. Amenities include a Jacuzzi Grotto with 10ft/3m waterfalls to relax and enjoy the sun, a lagoon-style pool and sundeck with a clothing-optional area, plus a steam room.

Parlour suites provide 800ft^2/74m^2 of space that are ideal for small meetings, entertaining guests or simply watching the TV and have large beds and armoires, large TVs, cable TV and electronic door locks.

Lucky You Casino & Hotel

3227 Civic Center Drive, 1 800 551 2409
An exclusively gay B&B just 2 blocks from the Strip within walking distance of gay bars. Well priced but no credit cards accepted.

Blue Moon Resort

Riviera

2901 The Strip at Riviera Boulevard, 702 794 9433, rivierahotel.com

The most openly gay hotel on the Strip, it is the home of *La Cage*, a top drag show starring Frank Marino as Joan Rivers.

Café

Garlic Café

Decatur Twain Shopping Center, 3650 South Decatur Boulevard, 702 221 0266

The only openly gay-owned café in town; you choose the strength of garlic. It's always busy and serves great food. Open daily 5–10pm.

Clubs and bars

Back Door Lounge

1415 East Charleston Blvd, 702 385 2018

Has a happy hour every night 5–7pm. Monday night a free poker party starts at 7pm and there is a free barbecue on Saturday nights at 6pm. Very popular with gay Latinos at the weekends.

Badlands Saloon

953 East Sahara Avenue, 702 792 9262

New home of the Gay Rodeo Association and probably the friendliest bar in town, the best times to visit are Sun around 4pm and Tues and Thurs around 7pm when the line-dancing classes get going.

Bar Code

5150 Spring Mountain Road, 702 221 5150

This is a trendy, alternative nightclub that puts on lots of sometimes kookie promotions most days of the week.

Charlie's Las Vegas

5012 South Arville Street, 702 876 1844, charlieslasvegas.com

Part of a popular chain of gay bars popular in Chicago, Phoenix and Denver. It sports a Country and Western theme with social events nightly.

Escape Lounge

4212 West Sahara Avenue, 702 364 1167, escapeloungelv.com

This is a new place designed for friends to have a quiet drink together and enjoy life.

Flex

4371 West Charleston Blvd, 702 878 3355

A great mixed club with drink specials, dancing and live music.

Krave

BRITTIP

Visit gaybar.com for up-to-date information and location maps for all the local gay bars.

Freezone Night Club

610 East Naples, 702 794 2300, freezonelv.com

All-round bar with restaurant. Tuesday is the Ladies 4 Ladies revue night, Thursday the all-male revue for Boys Night, and What a Drag! is held on Friday and Saturday. As its name implies: never a cover charge to enter.

BRITTIP

Some of the gay night spots are in quite out-of-the-way locations. For help finding them, look up addresses on mapquest.com.

Escape Lounge

Gipsy

4605 S. Paradise Road, 702 731 1919, gipsylasvegas.com
The city's original gay dance club with live music some nights. Expect go-go boys and drag queens. Open 9pm–dawn.

Good Time Bar & Grill

1775 East Tropicana, 702 736 9494
Happy hours 5–7am and 5–7pm. Monday is the most popular. No credit cards.

Krave

Miracle Mile, at the corner of Harmon Avenue and the Strip, 702 836 0830, kravelasvegas.com
The only gay nightclub on the Strip has been voted the best venue in town by many of the leading gay papers. There are events for men throughout the week – all starting at 11pm – with a GirlBar on Sat 9pm–3am. For dining, check out Lucky Cheng's inside Krave. This popular drag queen Chinese restaurant originally debuted in Manhattan's East Village to rave revues. True to its New York counterpart, Lucky Chen's serves Pan Asian cuisine as well as a nightly cabaret.

Las Vegas Eagle

3430 E Tropicana Ave, 702 458 8662, gaylasvegasfun.com
The true adventure-seeker will earn free drinks and beer every Wed and Fri at Las Vegas Eagle, but only under one condition: that bar patrons strip down to their boxers or briefs!

Good Time Bar & Grill

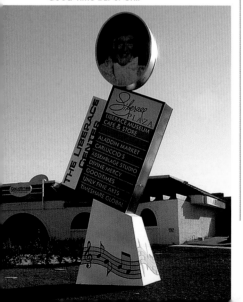

Piranha Nightclub & 8½ Ultra Lounge

4633 Paradise Road, 702 791 0100, piranhavegas.com
Popular among celebrities, this venue offers a beautiful view of the Strip from the second floor, VIP cabanas and sky boxes and a private bar. Thursdays is Comedy Drag Night. Open nightly 9am–dawn.

Snick's Place

1402 South 3rd Street, 702 385 9298, snicksplace.com
One of Vegas's oldest gay bars, and still going strong with happy hours Mon–Fri 2–4pm and 2–4am.

Spotlight Lounge

957 E Sahara Avenue, 702 696 0202, thespotlightbar.com
Over the last few years, the Spotlight has grown into a leader of the gay community, hosting a number of meetings and charity events to raise money for gay causes. It is also a great working class bar in which to relax.

Suede Restaurant & Lounge

4640 Paradise Road, 702 791 3463
Slick ultra-lounge and restaurant.
Wednesdays is Sheila's Karaoke at 9pm, Thursday is Sheila's Pajama Karaoke, Fridays is Queer as Food, a *Queer as Folk* themed evening, and Saturday is singles night. Open Wed–Sat 5pm–2am.

BRITTIP

There are no exclusively female bars in Las Vegas, but 2 of the most popular with women are Freezone and Charlie's.

Gay bath house

Entourage Spa & Health Club

953E Sahara Avenue, Suite A-19, 702 650 9191, entouragevegas.com
Located in the north-west corner of Commercial Center, this is a bath house that caters for men, with gym, steam room, dry sauna, 2 Jacuzzis, pool, video room and 60 private rooms all with video feed. The first Monday of each month is Manhunt Monday. For out-of-towners this is a great place to get clued up about the Vegas gay scene.

10 ATTRACTIONS

Thrill rides, children's attractions, museums and animal habitats

Yes, there really is more to Las Vegas than bright lights and gambling dens. There are a whole host of attractions that appeal to people of all ages, some amazing thrill rides and even a little – overpriced – culture in the form of art museums.

The high-tech wizardry that can be seen in so many nightclubs and production shows is also put to use in heart-thumping simulator rides and 3-D movies. And there is a raft of museums that celebrate aspects of the city's history and people – including Liberace and Elvis – and the Las Vegas Natural History Museum, while animals can be seen at several resort-hotels and the local zoo.

As in other chapters, to save keying in a long website address, you can go to the home page for the resort-hotel, then follow the entertainment or attractions links.

Chaos at the Adventuredrome is not for the faint-hearted

Conventional rides

Many resorts around the Las Vegas area
have added a number of thrill rides to get
the blood pumping before you hit the
gambling tables. Circus Circus draws top
hand for the most rides, while the
Stratosphere's sky-reaching thrillers are
some of the most wrenching. There are
more too, including great roller-coasters at
the Sahara and New York-New York.

Adventuredome Theme Park

**Circus Circus, 702 794 3939,
adventuredome.com**
The desert may be scorching hot outside,
but here in this 5acre/2ha, fully enclosed
elevated theme park – the largest space-
frame dome in America – the temperature
stays a comfortable 22°C/72°F all year
round. Grand Slam Canyon is designed to
look like a desert with a large rock canyon
that gives way to caverns, pinnacles and
steep cliffs, while a stream flows gently
through the lush landscape. But this canyon
is home to prehistoric creatures – well, life-
sized replicas of them at least! – that make
themselves known between two 140ft/43m
peaks, a fossil wall, archaeological dig
and a replica of an Indian cliff dwelling.

The 25 rides and attractions in the
Adventuredome divide into Premium Rides,
Large Rides, Junior Rides, Family Rides and
Featured Attractions. Below are some of the
most popular.

The **Canyon Blaster** is the only indoor,
double-loop, double-corkscrew roller-coaster
in America, and sends you careening
between canyon walls at 55mph/86kph.

The 2-minute long **Inverter** involves a
360-degree rotation in which you are held
upside-down with only a harness and a T-
bar separating you from the concrete floor
50ft/15m below.

Chaos twirls and whirls you anti-
clockwise, backwards and upside-down on
a circular platform amid the tracks of the

You know what to expect on the Inverter

Canyon Blaster. Lasting 2 minutes, it
creates a 3-D effect as you rise, tilt and
spin all at the same time, and due to the
variation in speed and motion, no 2 rides
are the same.

In the **Sling Shot** you are shot up a tower
at 4Gs of acceleration and then shot
straight back down again.

The **Rim Runner** is a more relaxing ride,
taking you on a scenic journey through
botanical landscaping before plunging
over a heart-stopping 60ft/18m waterfall.

BRITTIP

Save the Rim Runner thrill ride
until the end of your
Adventuredome visit as you will get
soaked!

Lazer Blast is where sharpshooters take
part in a high-tech war. There are also
bumper cars and a swinging ship, plus an
IMAX simulator thrill ride (see page 203).
Younger children are well catered for from
plane and train rides to bumper-mobiles,
plus strolling entertainers who juggle, mime
and do magic tricks.

One of the newer rides to try is **Disk'O**
which once you're strapped in, rocks and
spins you at the same time.

Open: Daily from 10am. It closes at 6pm
Mon–Thurs, midnight Fri and Sat and 8pm
Sun, though exact hours may vary
according to the seasons – in September it
opens at 11am for example, so do check.

Tickets: Entrance to the park is free; you
just pay for the rides of your life! The main

Slightly less scary is the Rim Runner

The Big Shot

thrill rides cost $4–7 each or you can buy an All Day Ride Pass at $24.95 for people 4ft/1.2m tall or taller and $14.95 for those under 4ft/1.2m. Children under 2' 9"/84cm ride free with an adult.

The Roller Coaster

New York-New York, 702 740 6969 or 866 815 4365, nynyhotelcasino.com/ entertainment/entertainment_theroller coaster.aspx
Based on the kind of roller-coaster that made Coney Island in the real New York so famous, the Roller Coaster twists, loops and dives around the perimeter and even through the New York-New York hotel, which can be a worry when you are sitting in 'Central Park' and hear a roar and rattling through the rafters. It has the world's first heart-line twist and dive that simulates the sensation felt by a pilot during a barrel roll in an aeroplane when the centre of rotation actually becomes the same as your centre of gravity! Incidentally, the Roller Coaster has been voted Best Thrill Ride in Nevada by *Nevada Magazine*'s reader survey.

Open: Sun–Thurs 10.30am–12am daily

Tickets: $14 per person; all-day Scream Pass $25 or Family Fun Flight for Four $60

Speed: The Ride and Cyber Speedway

Sahara Hotel, 702 734 7223 or 702 737 2111, saharavegas.com/nascar
Speed: The Ride is the fastest roller-coaster in Las Vegas and literally slingshots riders at speeds of up to 70mph/112kph. You go through breathtaking loops as you zip your way around the Sahara before halting and repeating the experience in reverse!

On **Cyber Speedway**, you really are in the driving seat. Driving an almost real-sized racing car, you speed around a track modelled on the Las Vegas Motor Speedway at speeds of up to 22mph/35kph doing 7 laps in all against up to 7 other drivers.

Open: Daily noon–10pm. Hours may vary, so call ahead for updated times

Tickets: $10 for 1 ride, $17.95 for both rides or $22.95 for an unlimited day pass

Stratosphere Tower Thrill Rides

Stratosphere Casino Hotel and Tower, 702 380 7777 or 800 998 6937, stratospherehotel.com/thrills
Three extreme thrill rides are found here. The **Big Shot** thrusts 16 passengers 160ft/50m into the air along the 228ft/70m spire at speeds of around 45mph/72kph, producing up to 4Gs with

The Manhattan Express

negative Gs on the way back down. What is so scary about the ride is not just the speed and force of it all, but the fact that you are so high up in the air in the first place as The Stratosphere Tower is 100 floors up and over 900ft/274m high.

Insanity, the Ride thrusts passengers 64ft/20m over the north edge of the tower at speeds that create forces of up to 3Gs, while at a 70-degree angle, providing a perfect view of nothingness beneath you – except a 900ft/274m drop to the Strip below (though no time for photos, folks!).

In **X-Scream** (i.e screaming to the extreme) passengers are propelled 27ft/8m over the edge of the tower at 30mph/48kph – again providing excellent views of the 900ft/274m drop.

Open: Sun–Thurs 10am–1am; Fri–Sat 10am–2pm. However, the rides are often not open on windy days

Tickets: $13.95 for admission to Stratosphere Tower. Tickets to ride X-Scream and Insanity are $12 each and the Big Shot is $13. Tower admission and 3 rides is $27.95, and an unlimited day pass $33.95

BRITTIP

For the best selection of thrill rides in town, the Stratosphere is the place to go. Thrill seekers with a car should head out of town to Buffalo Bill's Adventure Canyon in Primm.

Thrill Rides at Buffalo Bill's

Buffalo Bill's Resort & Casino, 31900 South Las Vegas Boulevard, Primm, 702 386 7867 or 1-800 FUN STOP, primmvalleyresorts.com For amazing thrill rides on a Wild West theme, head to Buffalo Bill's in Primm, which is just 35mls/56km south of Las Vegas on Interstate 15.

One of America's tallest and fastest roller-coasters, **Desperado**, has a top speed of around 90mph/145kph and creates a

X-Scream

Desperado at Buffalo Bill's

G-force of nearly 4. A high-speed dive down a 55-degree hill into a tunnel starts the ride and is then followed by a 155ft/47m second hill, which leads to a zero-gravity sensation – 2.43 minutes of heart-pounding fun.

Turbo Drop creates a similar sensation to flying straight towards the ground in a jet fighter. Riders are nestled in padded saddles and shoulder harnesses, lifted 200ft/60m up in the air and plunged to earth at 45mph/72kph, creating positive G-forces close to 4.5.

The **Vault** is the first 3-D, digital projection motor ride in America. Each of the 6 motion pads drops, twists and turns as the screen takes you on one of 10 different rides ranging from the turbulent waters of Aquaride to the seriously rickety mine car on the Haunted Mine Ride.

Other rides: The Adventure Canyon Log Flume starts as a classic flume ride with a 35ft/11m drop, but once you splash down, you continue through an electronic shooting gallery that follows the park's Wild West theme. You take out a pistol as targets are lit up along the way, then if you shoot a bad guy you get points and if you shoot a good guy you lose points! Other rides to make your visit worthwhile include the **Maxflight Cyber Coaster** and the **Froghopper** and there's also the **Attraction Zone Arcade** and the **Carolee Theatre**, showing big name movies.

Open: Mon–Thurs noon–6pm; Fri and Sat 10am–midnight; Sun 10am–7pm. Times can change, so best to call ahead for hours of operation

Tickets: The main rides cost $3–8 each or $30 for a full-day wristband, $22 for a half-day wristband. Little Wrangler passes for those under 4ft/1.2m are $12

Merlin's Magic Motion Machines

Simulator rides and 3-D movies

SimEx Theater

Adventuredome Theme Park, Circus Circus, 702 794 3939, adventuredome.com
Fans of the Nickelodeon cartoon will love **SpongeBob SquarePants 4-D Ride**, where they get the chance to dive into Bikini Bottom and join SpongeBob and co on a 4D adventure – wind, bubbles and scent are just a few of the 4D effects. For children over 3′ 6″/106cm only.

Open: Daily from 10am. It closes at 6pm Mon–Thurs, midnight Fri and Sat and 8pm Sun, though exact hours may vary according to the seasons, so do check

Tickets: $7 per ride. All-day passes for the Adventuredome are also available (see page 200)

BRITTIP
The website vegas.com/attractions lists free attractions, thrill rides, kids activities and more and sells tickets to top attractions online.

Excalibur rides

Excalibur, 877 750 5464 or 702 597 7777, excalibur.com/attractions
Here you'll find a series of hilarious rides produced by Iwerks Entertainment. In **Dino Island 2D** you get to explore a newly formed island where dinosaurs now roam. In **Speed Racer 4D**, Speed Racer takes on fierce competition on the race track in a high-speed, adrenaline-fueled charge to the finish. The newest ride is **SpongeBob SquarePants 4-D Ride**, also shown at The Adventuredome (see left). You must be 3′ 6″/106cm tall to ride.

Open: Mon–Thurs 11am–10pm; Fri 11am–11pm; Sat 10am–11pm; Sun 10am–10pm
Tickets: $9.99 per ride

The Froghopper

Fun rides

The Cloud Nine Balloon

3951 Las Vegas Boulevard South (directly across from the Mandalay Bay Resort & Casino), 800 585 8688, cloud9vegas.com
The largest tethered helium balloon in the world has taken to the skies above Las Vegas, offering visitors the chance to float almost 500 ft/150m above the Strip and take in stunning 360-degree views. The balloon's gondola can carry up to 30 people at a time. A flight lasts for 10 minutes.
Open: Sun–Thurs 10am–10pm
Fri–Sat 10am–midnight
Tickets: Adults $22.50 day and $27.50 night, children (5–12) $17.50 day and $22.50 night, children under 4 fly free with a paid adult.

Eiffel Tower Experience

Paris, 888 266 5687 or 702 946 7000, parislasvegas.com
You take a lift to about two-thirds of the way up the replica Eiffel Tower and then look out at the desert through an iron mesh. The hotel's tower is, in fact, only two-thirds of the height of the real Eiffel Tower, so your view is blocked by many of the tall buildings about. Although voted 'Best Place to View the City', it is hard to get a decent view of the entire Strip and impossible to take any worthwhile pictures through the grille.

A gondola ride at the Venetian

BRITTIP

The Eiffel Tower Experience is probably the most expensive elevator (lift) ride in the world. Save your money and enjoy Strip views from any one of the fab restaurants with views (see page 107).

Open: Daily 9.30am–12.30am, weather permitting
Tickets: $10 daytime, $12 at night

Gondola rides

Venetian, 702 414 4300, venetian.com/gondola.aspx
Supplying the full Venetian experience, the hotel puts on indoor gondola rides around the Grand Canal Shoppes. They're pricey, but still cheaper than gondola rides in Venice! Tours start from St Mark's Square. Better yet are the newest outdoor gondola rides by the main entrance of the Doge's Palace. These gondoliers are required to be Italian, or at least have travelled enough in Italy to be able to talk about it first hand. Plus, they must have great singing voices as they croon romantic melodies to their passengers. Many a wedding proposal has been made here. They even have a special wedding gondola, oversized and all in white, if you'd like to take your vows here.

Open: Sun–Thurs 10am–11pm; Fri–Sat 10am–midnight
Tickets: Adults $16, private 2-passenger gondola $64. Reservations must be made in person, same day

BRITTIP

The gondola rides are so popular that tickets sell out every day and the average wait for a ride is 1 hour.

Observation Deck Stratosphere Tower

Stratosphere, 800 99 TOWER or 702 380 7777, stratospherehotel.com/thrills
Take a ride up the Stratosphere's lifts to the top of the tallest free-standing observation tower in America, which has an indoor and outdoor observation deck where all the landmarks seen from different points of the circular deck are explained. The best time of day to see the Strip is just before sunset when you can make out all the landmarks before the town goes dark and

everything lights up. Better still, start at the observation deck, then move up to the Top of the World Restaurant for a romantic dinner.

Open: Sun–Thurs 10am–1am; Fri–Sat 10am–2am

Tickets: Adults $13.95, children 4–12 $8, senior and Stratosphere guests $10 (see page 201 for the details of the tower's thrill rides)

BRITTIP

The Las Vegas Power Pass is the passport to top attractions from the Stratosphere Tower to Hoover Dam for a fixed fee starting from a day pass for $77.50 adults and $45 children (888 527 8342, vegas.com).

Free shows

CBS Television City

MGM Grand, 800 646 7787 or 702 891 5752, mgmgrand.com
A research centre that allows audiences to view TV shows in production and comment on them.

Show times: Free screenings are conducted every half an hour daily 10am–8.30pm

Circus acts at Circus Circus

Circus Circus, 2880 Las Vegas Boulevard South, 702 734 0410, circuscircus.com/las_vegas_entertainment
World-renowned circus acts include African acrobats, a 14-year-old contortionist, a stilt-walking juggler and a blindfolded triple somersault, all in the world's largest permanent circus.

Show times: Daily from 11am

Fountain at Miracle Mile Shops

Planet Hollywood Resort & Casino, 3667 Las Vegas Boulevard South, 702 866 0710, miraclemileshopslv.com
This multi-million dollar popular water feature sees the fountain leaping 5 storeys high with effects such as colour-changing fog, bursts of light and surround sound.

Show times: Daily on the hour noon–11pm

Fountains of Bellagio

In the lake outside the Bellagio, 702 693 7111, bellagio.com/amenities/fountains-of-bellagio.aspx
An incredibly stunning visual and audio experience as the now world-famous

fountains set in an 8-acre/3-ha lake perform carefully choreographed movements in time to operatic, classical and whimsical music.

Show times: Mon–Fri 3pm–midnight; Sat–Sun noon–midnight. Shows every half hour until 8pm, then every 15 minutes until midnight

Fremont Street Experience

425 Fremont Street, 702 678 5777, vegasexperience.com
Towering 90ft/27.4m above 4 of the blocks of the Fremont Street Experience pedestrian mall in Downtown is a massive space-frame lit up by 12.5 million lights and 540,000 watts of sound.

Show times: Nightly, 8pm–midnight

Lake of Dreams

Wynn Las Vegas, 3131 Las Vegas Boulevard, 702 770 7000
This secluded 3-acre/1.2-ha lake surrounded by a lush forest is a tranquil idyll in the midst of the city and provides free vantage points to view the water and light show if you don't want to wander into one of the bars and restaurants.

Show times: Nightly every half hour after dark

The Bellagio fountains show at night

ATTRACTIONS

Live Runway Shows

Fashion Show Mall, 3200 Las Vegas Boulevard, 702 784 7000, thefashionshow.com
The fullest line-up of fashion on the Strip is on this 80-ft/24-m runway which rises out of the ground for 1,000 shows a year. Think Saks, Bloomingdale's and Macy's.

Show times: Weekends hourly midday–6pm

BRITTIP

If you are travelling with children, be warned that the Masquerade Show in the Sky includes topless showgirls during the evening performances.

Masquerade Show in the Sky

Rio All-Suite Hotel, 3700 West Flamingo, 702 252 7777, riolasvegas.com
A $25m Disney-esque spectacle in which dozens of Mardi Gras floats containing exotically costumed dancers literally 'float' about 20ft/6m above your head,

BRITTIP

For just $12.95 guests can ride in the float with the dancers at Masquerade Show in the Sky. Buy tickets at the Rio Hotel's box office.

accompanied by music. Different shows on different nights; on Mon–Wed, they're accompanied by hot live Latin rhythms.

Show times: Thurs–Sun hourly 7pm–midnight

Mirage Volcano

The Mirage, 3400 Las Vegas Boulevard, 702 791 7111, mirage.com/attractions/volcano.aspx
The newest free show on the Strip, this man-made wonder blasts fireballs 12ft/3.7m into the air with fiery lava flames flowing down its sides into the lagoon, close enough for spectators to feel the heat. The accompanying soundtrack was composed by Grateful Dead drummer Mickey Hart and Indian tabla virtuoso Zakir Hussain.

Show times: Erupts nightly, every hour 8pm–midnight, weather permitting

Sirens of TI

Treasure Island, 702 894 7111, treasureisland.com/shows/sirens_of_ti.aspx
A rowdy bunch of buccaneers do battle against alluring but treacherous Sirens in a spectacle full of singing, sword play, canon shots and, of course, at least one walking of the plank.

Show times: Daily at 5.30pm (winter only); 7pm, 8.30pm, 10pm and 11.30pm (summer only)

The Sirens of TI

Two dolphins at the Dolphin Habitat

Be a dolphin trainer

One of the most exciting – although expensive – attractions to hit Las Vegas is the chance to become a dolphin trainer for the day at Siegfried and Roy's Secret Garden and Dolphin Habitat at the Mirage. For a hefty fee of around $720 per person (with 2 people per family as a maximum, participants must be at least 13 years old), it is possible to learn how to feed and play with dolphins as you accompany real trainers 9.45am–3.45pm. Throughout the day, your activities and contact with the dolphins will be captured on camera and the photos put on a CD to take home. For further details or to make a reservation, phone 702 792 7889.

Sunset Stampede at Sam's Town

Sam's Town Hotel & Gambling Hall, 5111 Boulder Highway (less than 10mls/16km from the Strip), 702 456 7777, samstownlv/com/things-to-do/mystic-falls
This 8-minute show in Mystic Falls Park starts with the plaintive howl of a wolf and goes on to create a symphonic journey through the Wild West with water, laser, light and animation.

Show times: Daily 2pm, 6pm, 8pm and 10pm

Streetmosphere at the Grand Canal Shoppes

Venetian Hotel and Casino, 3555 South Las Vegas Boulevard, 702 414 4500, venetian.com
Street performers, Artiste del Arte – singers, actors and entertainers who put on shows throughout the day – Living Statues and The Venetian Trio – who offer elegant music in the evening – all adds fun to the shopping experience. Most of the action is around St Mark's Square.

Show times: Daily, at various times. Artiste del Arte 1pm, 2pm, 4pm, 5pm and 6pm; Living Statues 10am–6pm; The Venetian Trio 6–10pm; the Gondolier March 9.45am and 4.15pm

BRITTIP

Don't forget to get your picture taken below the 'Welcome to Fabulous Las Vegas' sign at 5200 Las Vegas Boulevard South – a must!

Streetmosphere happens at the Grand Canal Shoppes

Animal magic

Lion Habitat

MGM Grand, 800 929 1111 or 702 891 1111, mgmgrand.com/entertainment/lion-habitat.aspx

In this $9m multi-level lion habitat at the MGM Grand, visitors are encircled by lions and cubs via a see-through glass tunnel running through it. Out of 31 lions cared for on a ranch by a veteran animal trainer, up to 7 can be viewed here at any time. Three of the lions – Goldie, Metro and Baby Lion – are direct descendants of the MGM Studios lion, Leo.

Open: 11am–7pm. Feeding at 11.15am and 4.30pm daily

Admission: Free, though an 'official' picture costs around $10. There's a gift shop on the way out

Shark Reef

Mandalay Bay Hotel, 702 632 7777, sharkreef.com

An aquarium you walk underneath so you are completely surrounded by water giving you a 360 degree view of some of the world's most dangerous aquatic animals and fish from the world's tropical waters. More than 2,000 animals can be seen here in 14 exhibits from a 100-ft/30-m nurse shark to a tiny clown fish. Divers in

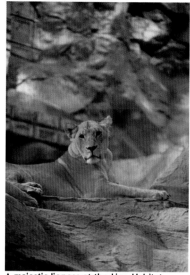

A majestic lioness at the Lion Habitat

the aquarium talk about the animals and answer questions via a high-tech underwater communications system.

The largest display of golden saltwater crocodiles outside Thailand can be seen here too. This is a seriously endangered species as there are only 12 left in the world. Other animals include moray eels,

Superb royal white tigers

Lions at the Southern Nevada Zoo

southern stingrays, angelfish, puffer fish, jellyfish and serpents and dragons featuring green tree pythons, known for their vivid green colour and razor-sharp teeth. A touch pool includes sharks, rays and horseshoe crabs. Certified divers staying at the Mandalay can dive with the sharks in the largest 'Shipwreck' exhibit.

Open: Daily 10am–10pm; last admission at 9pm

Admission: Adults $16.95, under-13s $10.95, under-5s free

Siegfried and Roy's Secret Garden and Dolphin Habitat

Mirage Hotel, 702 791 7111, mirage.com/attractions or themiragehabitat.com
Here is your chance to get a closer look at the rare breeds of animal that Siegfried and Roy used in their magical illusion show. The $15m, 2.5acre/1ha natural **Secret Garden** habitat was specially built to house their white tigers, lions, panthers, snow leopards and Asian elephants.

🇬🇧 BRITTIP

Make the most of the Mirage's free attractions by taking a look at the enormous tropical fish tank behind the resort's lobby during your visit to see the beautiful white tigers.

Next door is the massive **Dolphin Habitat**, which is home to a family of Atlantic bottlenose dolphins. Four connected pools, an artificial coral reef system and a sandy bottom replicate the dolphin's natural environment, which aims to provide a healthy and nurturing home for the marine mammals and educate the public about their role in the ecosystem.

Open: Mon–Fri 11am–7pm; Sat–Sun 10am–7pm

Admission: Adults $15, children (4–12 years) $10 includes entrance to both habitats. On Wednesday and after the garden closes $6. Tickets can be booked online. VIP 1-hour group tours run at 11am, 1pm and 2.30pm. Call 702 792 7889 for prices

Southern Nevada Zoo

1755 North Rancho Drive, 702 647 4685, lasvegaszoo.com
A small zoo committed to conservation, education and recreation, it houses more than 50 species of reptiles and small animals of the great south-western desert. It is also home to other animals including an African lion, Bengal tiger, Barbary apes, monkeys, wallabies, flamingos, king vultures and North America's only tigrina, an endangered tropical cat, as well as many species of plants.

Open: Daily 9am–5pm

Admission: Over-12s $8, 2–12s and seniors $6, under-2s free

The Tank

Golden Nugget, 702 385 7111 or 866 946 5336 for cabana reservations, goldennugget.com
While primarily for guests staying at the Golden Nugget in downtown Las Vegas, sometimes staff will let you slide in. The Tank is the new $30m swimming pool complex, including a 3-storey waterslide. But the coolest part is the shark tank – yes,

Walking through the Shark Reef tunnel

sharks! The Tank is designed in such a way that while going down the water slide you go through a tube through the middle of the sharks. It is the closest you can come to these cold-blooded killers without donning a mask and fins.

Open: Daily 10am–8pm. Jacuzzi and H20 bar open until 2am

Admission: Rent 1 of the 7 private cabanas for the day for $175 Mon–Thurs or $250 Fri–Sun

Wildlife Habitat at the Flamingo

Flamingo Hotel, 702 733 3111, flamingolasvegas.com
Surrounded by lush pines, palms and magnolia, this is the only place in town where you can see flamingos up close. Over 300 birds can be seen here, including Impeyn and silver pheasants along with Gambel's quails, a crown crane and ducks, as well as koi and turtles.

Open: 24/7

Admission: Free

Art galleries and exhibitions

Being but 100 years old, Las Vegas has a limited run of culture to draw on and what there is happens to be imported at a tidy cost. So it's perhaps no surprise then that the exhibitions have been dropping like flies since the onset of the credit crunch, due to poor ticket sales. Museums and galleries may be a bit pricey here, but they are a good way to avoid the searing heat!

One lovely counterpoint, though, is that several of the high-end shopping areas, including places like Grand Canal Shoppes

The Las Vegas Guggenheim

and Forum Shops, have some dazzling art galleries. And away from the resorts, there are some fascinating places to check out.

Bellagio Gallery of Fine Art

Bellagio, 877 957 9777 or 702 693 7871, bellagiolasvegas.com/amenities/gallery-of-fine-art.aspx
This originally opened to show off the previous owner Steve Wynn's masterpieces, which included Rembrandts, Monets and Picassos, but he took the paintings with him when he sold the hotel to the MGM Grand. Now it showcases travelling art exhibitions and is theoretically non-profit-making. The exhibitions are on a small scale, rarely more than 12–20 pieces or so, but the cost is steep, so you should

Wildlife Habitat at the Flamingo

The Tomb and Museum of King Tutankhamun

only come by if the current exhibition is particularly of interest to you. In 2009, the gallery was showing 'Classic Contemporary: Lichtenstein, Warhol and Friends'.

Open: Sun–Thurs 10am–6pm; Fri and Sat 10am–7pm

Admission: Adults $15, seniors $12, students $10. Children 12 and under go free

Luxor exhibitions

Luxor Hotel 800 557 7428 or 702 262 4400, luxor.com/attractions

Bodies – the Exhibition: Showcaseing 21 real bodies and 260 organs dissected – not for the squeamish but a fascinating look into our system and a wake-up call for a healthy lifestyle!

Titanic: The Artifact Exhibition: This tells the story behind the ill-fated journey of the 'Ship of Dreams' with more than 300 artifacts recovered from below the icy Atlantic – whose temperatures can be felt on the Promenade deck— and a full-scale recreation of the Grand Staircase as well as passengers' memories.

Open: Daily 10am–10pm. Last admission 9pm

Admission: Bodies: $31 adults, $29 seniors, $23 children (4–12 years). Titanic: $27 adults, $25 seniors, $20 children (4–12 years). Audio tours available for $6

The Wynn Collection

Wynn Las Vegas, 877 321 9966 or 702 770 3590, wynnlasvegas.com

Casino mogul Steve Wynn's private collection scattered around this resort includes Picasso's *Le Rêve*, (the painting that originally inspired him for Wynn Las Vegas), Matisse's *The Persian Robe* and *Pineapples and Anemones* and Manet's *Portrait of Mademoiselle Suzette Lemaire in Profile*. Oh, and there's also a portrait of Steve Wynn himself by Andy Warhol! Named one of the top 10 private collectors by US magazine *ARTnews*, Wynn has been collecting art for years and now has a collection that spans 400 years of art history. The one drawback? There are only 13–15 pictures on display at any one time.

Open: 24/7

Admission: free

The Wynn has a considerable art collection

ATTRACTIONS

Attractions

Bellagio Conservatory and Botanical Gardens

Bellagio, 702 693 7111, bellagio.com
This glorious display of exotic plants and flowers provides row upon row of blooms that create a unique tapestry to reflect each season and holiday. The combination of the fragrances, textures and colours are heavenly, while the inspirational conservatory with its glass-topped atrium and sweeping staircase is simply divine. This is a wonderful place to come and release the tension of otherwise intense Las Vegas.

Open: 24/7

Admission: Free

BRITTIP

Feel a photo opportunity coming on? Then the perfect spot to capture yourself in Vegas is at the gorgeous Botanical Gardens in the Bellagio.

The Cloud

Fashion Show Mall, 3200 Las Vegas Boulevard, 702 784 7000, thefashionshow.com
One of the most eye-catching attractions on the Strip hovers 128ft/39m above a pedestrian plaza right outside the Fashion Show Mall. Nearly 500ft/152m long, the steel canopy is called The Cloud and is a wonderful source of shade during the day. At night, giant images are projected on to its surface to highlight promotions and events happening at the mall, while a further 4 massive LED screens are used to broadcast videos and other live broadcasts from the city.

Open: Mall hours are Mon–Sat 10am–9pm; Sun 11am–7pm

Admission: Free

Ethel M Chocolate Factory

The Conservatory at Chinese New Year

CSI: The Experience

MGM Grand Hotel and Casino, 3799 Las Vegas Boulevard, 877 660 0660 or 702 891 7006, lasvegas.csiexhibit.com
This latest blockbuster show to hit the Strip opened in September 2009 and is based on the hit US show. Participants join forces with the team of investigators to crack crime cases in this interactive exhibit using forensic evidence.

Open: Daily 10am–10pm. Last admission 8.30pm

Admission: Adults $30 (12 years and up), children 4–11 $23. Book tickets in advance

Ethel M Chocolate Factory and Cactus Gardens

2 Cactus Garden Drive, Henderson, 888 627 0990 or 702 458 8864, ethelschocolate.com
This large American sweet-making factory, just 5mls/8km from the Strip, gives an insight into the entire process. The tour ends with a free sample, but as you'll also find yourself in the factory shop, you won't be alone in deciding to buy a box of chocolates. Afterwards, step outside to see the 2.5acres/1ha of cactus gardens with over 350 species of desert plants and the Living Machine, a revolutionary new waste water recycling plant – the first of its kind designed for treating industrial waste water.

Open: Daily 8.30am–6pm

Admission: Free

Imperial Palace Auto Collection

Imperial Palace Auto Collection

Fifth floor, Imperial Palace Hotel, 702 794 3174, autocollections.com
More than 600 cars make up this collection but only 250 are ever on show at one time. However, that still makes this the 'World's Largest Classic Car Showroom'. Some of the vintage, classic and special-interest cars include the Chaser, the world's fastest petrol-powered police car; a 1986 Ford Mustang, which was specially built for the Nevada Highway Patrol; President Woodrow Wilson's 1917 Pierce Arrow car and a 1961 Lincoln Continental that was once owned by Jacqueline Kennedy Onassis.

Open: Daily 10am–6.30pm

Admission: Adults $8.95, seniors and under-13s $5

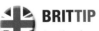 **BRITTIP**

Another fun outing is a trip to Laser Quest (see page 241).

Las Vegas Mini Grand Prix

1401 North Rainbow Boulevard, 702 259 7000, lvmgp.com
In the unlikely event that you do turn up in Sin City with children in tow, then this is the place to come to stop them feeling they have to spend their entire sojourn being kept out of all the adult activities. There are a few fun slides, but the real draw here is the fun mini-car races, which take place in Grand Prix-style cars of various shapes and sizes. To ride a Kiddie car you must be 4 years old or at least 4'6"/1.37m tall. To ride a Grand Prix car you must be 16.

Open: Sun–Thurs 10am–10pm; Fri and Sat 10am–11pm

Admission: $6.50 per ticket or $30 for 5 tickets

Madame Tussauds

Venetian Resort Hotel Casino, 702 862 7800, madametussauds.com/lasvegas
This is the Las Vegas version of the popular wax museum franchise. Five theme areas include the Big Night, a special VIP party with Whoopi Goldberg and Brad Pitt among others; the Sports Arena with Muhammad Ali, Babe Ruth and Evander Holyfield (who is missing part of his right ear!); Rock and Pop with Elton John and Tina Turner; Las Vegas Legends with Frank Sinatra and Marilyn Monroe; and the

Tiger Woods at Madame Tussauds

Finale, a state-of-the-art tribute to modern Las Vegas legends including Wayne Newton and Siegfried and Roy. The entrance is just off the Doge's Palace at the south end of the square.

Take the moving walkway until you see 2 wax figures standing guard at the entrance. These figures change regularly, rotating between basketball's Michael Jordan, Johnny Depp as *Pirates of the Caribbean*'s Jack Sparrow, Muhammad Ali and Don King (the wild-haired boxing promoter). It is a great photo opportunity! Inside are loads of other photo opportunities from staging a wedding with George Clooney to auditioning in front of Simon Cowell.

Open: Times vary but generally daily 10am–11.30pm

Admission: Adults $25, seniors and students $18, children $15 (children 6 and under go free). Book online to get 10% discount

Old Las Vegas Mormon Fort

State Historic Park, 908 Las Vegas Boulevard North, 702 486 3511, parks.nv.gov/olvmf.htm
This is the oldest surviving non-native-American structure in Las Vegas and dates back to 14 June 1855 when the Mormon missionaries arrived in New Mexico Territory. Their aim was to convert the indigenous inhabitants and provide a safe way-station between Mormon communities in Salt Lake City to the north and San Bernardino to the east. The 150ft²/14m² adobe-walled fort was still being built when the fort was abandoned in 1858 and subsequently was used by lead miners

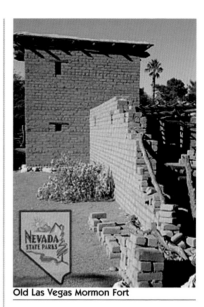
Old Las Vegas Mormon Fort

before becoming a ranch. To think, Sin City could have been a conservative Mormon haunt like Salt Lake City!

Open: Daily 8am–4.30pm; Tues–Sat 8am-4.30pm (closed Sun) in winter

Admission: Adults $3, under-13s $2, under-6s free

Planetarium and Observatory

College of Southern Nevada, 3200 East Cheyenne Avenue, North Las Vegas, 702 651 4759/4SKY, csn.edu
This is star-gazing with a difference. Escape from the glitz and glamour into

Atomic Testing Museum

Marine Gallery at the LVNH

Southern Nevada's only public planetarium and observatory which has multimedia shows on astronomy plus hemispheric motion pictures. Public observing sessions are held after the last showings.

Prehistoric Life Gallery at the LVNH

Open: Shows are on Fri 6pm and 7.30pm, Sat 3.30pm and 7.30pm. Public observing sessions are held at about 8.30pm, weather permitting. The shop is open Fri 5–8pm and Sat 3–8pm

Admission: Adults $6, under-12s and over-55s $4. It fills up fast

Museums

Atomic Testing Museum
Desert Research Institute, 755 East Flamingo Road, 702 794 5161, atomictestingmuseum.org
Once classified as top secret, the most chilling episodes in Nevada's history have been re-created at this museum. Tracing the history of the Nevada test site, which from 1951 until 1992 saw more than 900 nuclear weapons being tested for the US government, you enter an interactive bunker to witness bomb blasts. As the seats vibrate and gusts of air blow through the theatre, it is easy to get a feel for the power of the bombs. Exhibits include replicas of bomb shelters, offices and guards station from the Nevada test site and nearly 400,000 declassified documents. They include letters from Albert Einstein and the captain of a Japanese fishing boat caught in the fall-out tests carried out in the Pacific.
Open: Mon–Sat 9am–5pm; Sun 1–5pm
Admission: Adults $12, students and seniors $9, children 6 and under free

Las Vegas Natural History Museum
900 North Las Vegas Boulevard, 702 384 3466, lvnhm.org
Wildlife existed in the Las Vegas valley long before humans arrived and created casinos! Here you can take a walk on the wild side and discover the scenic and wild natural beauty of southern Nevada. It includes exhibits representing the many different habitats in the Las Vegas area with a diverse variety of plants and wildlife. The historical side is represented by animated dinosaurs, while there is an international wildlife room, small live sharks in the aquarium, and a hands-on exploration room for children. There is also an extensive wildlife art gallery with award-winning wood sculptures. There are travelling exhibits as well as changing exhibitions. The Egyptian Pavilion, its centrepiece a replica of King Tut's tomb, arrives in early 2010.

Open: Daily 9am–4pm

Admission: Adults $8, seniors and students $7, 3–11s $4, children 2 and under free

Las Vegas Natural History Museum

Marjorie Barrick Museum of Natural History

BRITTIP

A Mob Museum www.themob museum.org which pays tribute to the gangster life that made Las Vegas what it is today has been promised as a future attraction ... watch this space.

Liberace Museum

Liberace Plaza, 1775 East Tropicana Avenue, 702 798 5595, liberace.org
The man known as Mr Showmanship lives on in one of the most popular attractions in Nevada. One building houses 18 rare and antique pianos, including Liberace's favourite Baldwin grand piano, and others owned by Chopin and George Gershwin, plus Liberace's cars. Another building is

Singer Lynn Ross at the Liberace Museum

devoted to his famous stage wardrobe of multi-sequinned, bejewelled and rhinestone-studded costumes and famous rings that used to dazzle audiences around the world. The third contains an extensive collection of Liberace's memorabilia including hundreds of rare Moser crystals from the Czech Republic, a monogrammed set of dinner plates that once belonged to President John F. Kennedy, and Liberace's violin, made by the famous violin-maker George Winterling.

A portion of the proceeds from the museum, gift shop and café go to the Liberace Foundation for the Performing and Creative Arts, which has donated thousands of dollars to schools, universities and other organisations for music, dance, drama, film and visual arts.

Open: Mon–Sat 10am–5pm; Sun noon–4pm

Admission: Adults $15, and seniors and students and children over 12 $10. Children 11 and under free

Lied Discovery Children's Museum

833 North Las Vegas Boulevard, 702 382 5437, ldcm.org
Here children can touch, see, explore and experience more than 100 hands-on exhibits in one of America's largest – and most exciting – children's museums. Children crawl and slide through the Toddler Towers, become a star on the Performing Arts stage, pilot the Space Shuttle or Gyrochair, create colour computer prints and toe-tap a tune on the Musical Pathway. They can also stand in a

The Neon Museum

Marjorie Barrick Museum of Natural History

4505 South Maryland Parkway, 702 895 3381, http://hrc.nevada.edu/museum
Another genuinely fascinating offering at the University of Las Vegas campus, the real interest in this museum is its emphasis on the lives and traditions of the Paiute and Hopi Indians. A museum dedicated to the natural history of the region, one of the other main exhibits shows the reptiles that live in Nevada's deserts, including the venomous Gila Monster lizard, plus an open-air habitat for desert tortoises.

Open: Mon–Fri 8am–4.45pm; Sat 10am–2pm. Closed Sun

Admission: Free. Suggested donation: adults $5, seniors $2

Neon Museum

East end of the Fremont Street Experience, 702 387 6366/NEON, neonmuseum.org
Once the City of Neon, now all that remains of many of Vegas's most famous older hotels are their neon signs. Here you'll find the Hacienda Hotel sign before the building was imploded to make way for the Mandalay Bay, plus the original Aladdin's genie lamp and many other historical neon signs with their spectacular colours, intricate animation and sheer size. A small museum with big appeal!

While there are lots of exhibits inside, the best part is out the back at 'The

giant bubble, play at being a disc jockey at the KKID radio station or use their bodies to generate electricity.

Open: Tues–Fri 9am–4pm; Sat 10am–5pm; Sun noon–5pm. Closed Mon. 1 Jun–7 Sept: Mon–Sat 10am–5pm; Sun noon–5pm

Admission: Adults $8, children 1–17 and seniors $7, under-1s free. Children under the age of 11 must be accompanied by an adult

---

Duelling armadillo puppets at the Lied Discovery Children's Museum

Springs Preserve

Boneyard' where the massive signs are kept. This area is constantly being used by movies and TV shows for location shoots. Many of the best signs have been refurbished and mounted in the areas of the Fremont Street Experience and the East Fremont Street Entertainment District. You can download a free walking tour from the website.

Open: By appointment. Tours Tues–Sat 12pm and 2pm, advanced booking necessary

Admission: Free. Guided tour $15 per person

Ravine Walk at the Nevada State Museum

Nevada State Museum

700 Twin Lakes Drive, 702 486 5205, nevadaculture.org/museums
The history of southern Nevada from mammoths to gambling is presented in 3 galleries – Biology, Earth Science and History/Anthropology. There is also a display explaining how neon has been used in the city. The Springs Preserve will eventually also host the Nevada State Museum.

Open: Wed–Sat 9am–5pm except major holidays

Admission: Adults $4, seniors $3, under-18s free

Springs Preserve

333 South Valley View Boulevard, 702 822 7700, springspreserve.org
A recently opened 180-acre/73ha cultural and historical attraction situated on the site of the natural springs which encouraged the early settlers. Interactive exhibits include activities for kids – such as digging for fossils in the Mojave Desert Gallery, video games to learn about Las Vegas in the New Frontier Gallery and a playground resembling a desert canyon with wildlife replicas and a 'nature exchange' popular with little ones. There are Native American dwellings and a myriad of live animals here as well as trails through desert vegetation. Four hiking trails lead off through the picturesque Springs Preserve with interesting interpretative displays. The Springs Preserve will eventually also host the Nevada State Museum (see above).

Open: Daily 10am–6pm

11 OUTDOOR ADVENTURE

Every kind of fun from cowboy cook-outs to horseback riding

Las Vegas is a wonderful city, and practically everything you'd like to do in the great outdoors in America can be found in the stunning desertscape that surrounds it. Nearby are Red Rock Canyon, where ponderosa pines and Joshua trees grow out of towering cliffs of Aztec sandstone; the Valley of Fire, a Martian landscape of vivid red, pastel and white sandstone, and Mount Charleston, which looms 12,000ft/3,658m above sea level.

The biggest jewel in Las Vegas's crown of outdoor splendours, though, is the Grand Canyon. A whole raft of companies organise plane and helicopter flights to – and even down to the bottom of – the 10ml/16km wide and 1ml/1.6km deep natural wonder. Many of those companies also offer trips a little further north to the stunning Bryce Canyon and Zion National Park, famous for cascading waterfalls.

On top of that, there are a whole host of brilliant ways to experience this great

region, from white-water rafting and rock climbing, to horse riding and quad biking and following the cowboy trail. At certain times of the year, it is possible to go skiing in the morning at Lee Canyon on Mount Charleston, then head off to Lake Mead for a spot of water-skiing in the afternoon. Where else could you find such a dramatic mix of marvels? In Las Vegas you are just moments away from a world of beauty and adventure.

Hoover Dam from the South

Places to see

Hoover Dam

South on Highway 93 just past Boulder City, 30mls/50km south-east of Las Vegas at the Nevada-Arizona border. 702 494 2517, hooverdam.com and www.usbr.gov/lc/hooverdam/service

Visitor Center: Open daily, except Thanksgiving and Christmas Day, 9am–6pm. Tickets sold until 5.15pm

Admission: Visitor Center: adults, seniors, juniors $8, under-3s free; Powerplant Tour: adults $11, 4–16s $9, under-3s free; Hoover Dam Tour $30, not accessible to those on wheelchairs/crutches

BRITTIP

If you want to time your visit to tour Hoover Dam at the least crowded times, go between 9am and 10.30am and 3pm and 4.45pm.

This amazing construction – it's 726ft/221m high and 1,244ft/379m long – is filled with enough concrete to build a 2-lane highway from San Francisco to New York, and it literally changed the face of America's West. Blocking the Colorado River at the Black Canyon, which spans Nevada and Arizona, the dam put an end to centuries of droughts and floods caused by the mighty Colorado. Work began on the dam in 1931 and the $165m project was completed by 1935. Its offspring, Lake Mead, now produces drinking and irrigation water for the entire Las Vegas Valley, while the electric power plant creates enough energy to sell to Nevada, Arizona and California.

Hoover Dam near Boulder City

Spectacular view of the dam

BRITTIP

If you're touring in an RV (recreational vehicle, or camper van) you will have to park on the Arizona side of the dam as they have been banned from the parking garage at Hoover Dam for security reasons.

Discovery Tour: This gives you access to the Visitor Center, a 3-level, 110ft/34m diameter circular building, which stands 700ft/213m above the base of the dam. From the indoor and outdoor observation decks are stunning views of the dam, Lake Mead and the waters of the Colorado River re-entering the Black Canyon after passing through the dam's giant turbines.

BRITTIP

As you leave Boulder City and head for Hoover Dam, watch out for stupendous views of Lake Mead at the junction with Highway 93.

A gallery houses an environmental exhibit, technology exhibit and the story of the settlement of the lower Colorado River area. The rotating theatre is divided into 3 segments and you move between the 3 areas to see different films about the making and history of the dam.

Powerplant Tour: This tour includes presentations by reclamation guides, audio and film presentations, exhibits and other media to give a comprehensive view of the

The awe-inspiring Lake Mead

massive dam and its operations. Tours last around 2 hours and tickets can be bought 9am–4.15pm.

Hoover Dam Tour: The longest tour, this is a guided exploration of lesser known parts of the dam. It is offered from 9.30am every half an hour until 3.30pm, on a first come first served basis.

Boulder City/Hoover Dam Museum: At Boulder Dam Hotel, Boulder City, museum 702 294 1988, hotel 702 293 3510, bcmha.org, Mon–Sat 10am–5pm, Sun 12–5pm, admission adults $2, seniors/children $1. Here you'll see a free movie about the building of the dam plus historical memorabilia from the workers. While you're there, take a peek at the renovated home in the museum, which in its time has accommodated movie star James Cagney and reclusive billionaire Howard Hughes.

Other activities: While you're in the area you can also take a river raft trip (see page 230). An excellent stop-off point during your day trip is Harry's Café (512 Nevada Hwy, 702 293 1950, open 7am–8pm). Boulder's oldest diner, its 1950s-style environment makes for a fun pit stop.

Lake Mead

Visitor Center is 4mls/6km north-east of Boulder City, 702 293 8990, nps.gov/lame or lakemead.areaparks.com

Open: Year round, 24 hours a day. Visitor Center open daily 8.30am–4.30pm

Admission: $5 per vehicle; $3 others

Other useful numbers: Lake Mead Marina 702 293 3484; Park Information Desk 702 293 8906 (Mon–Fri)

The dazzling-blue Lake Mead, created by the construction of the Hoover Dam, is about 25mls/40km south of Las Vegas. It is 110mls/177km long and has 550mls/885km of freshwater shoreline. It is the Las Vegas outdoor retreat of choice and many permanent residents have boats here. Here you can try out anything from boating to swimming, scuba-diving, kayaking, water-skiing, camping, biking and fishing, while 6 marinas provide docking space for boats, plus restaurants and other services. Every December, a Parade of Lights is held at Lake Mead marina, with a flotilla of powerboats, houseboats and sailing boats covered in lights. A newer, annual event is the hydroplane race held in September.

The Visitor Center contains a botanical garden and exhibits on natural history. Here you will find details of a self-guided tour, with tape recording, of the lake's Northshore and Lakeshore roads, plus information about facilities and services.

Marinas: Two not-so-scenic roads – Lakeside Scenic Drive (Highway 146) and Northshore Scenic Drive (Highway 167) provide access to the marinas around the Nevada shoreline of Lake Mead, which include **Las Vegas Boat Harbor** (702 293 1191), **Calville Bay Resort** (702 565 8958) and **Echo Bay Resort** (702 394 4000). These are all full-service marinas offering houseboat and daily deck cruiser rentals, restaurants and gift shops. At night, Callville Bay provides a barbecue on the patio overlooking the lake. Lake Mead Cruises (702 293 6180, www.LakeMead Cruises.com) has sunset, dinner dance and breakfast cruises.

If you'd like to explore a little further afield, head off south to Lake Mohave and Cottonwood Cove Resort and Marina (1000 Cottonwood Cove Road, Cottonwood, 702 297 1464). It's a full-service marina offering luxury houseboats, small boats and personal watercraft rentals

Stunning scenery in the Valley of Fire

about one and a half hours south of Las Vegas. For a thrill, Forever Resorts (702 294 1414) offer The Black Canyon River Adventure – a smooth water-rafting trip in the Black Canyon.

Hiking: During the cooler months, from November to March, you can take a hike in the Lake Mead National Recreation Area on Saturday mornings to learn about the history of the people of the area, from the mining era onwards. Each hike is limited to 25 people and you can make reservations by phoning 702 293 8990.

Valley of Fire State Park

6mls/10km from Lake Mead and 55mls/88km north-east of Las Vegas using Interstate 15 and Highway 169, 702 397 2088, desertusa.com/nvval/index.html

Open: Year round, dawn to dusk; Visitor Center: Open daily 8.30am–4.30pm

Admission: $6 per vehicle

The park – the oldest in Nevada – gets its name from the red sandstone formations that were formed from great, shifting desert sand dunes during the age of the dinosaurs 150 million years ago. Complex geological movements and extensive erosion have created the spectacular wind carvings in the colourful rock formations. There are shaded areas with restrooms at Atlatl Rock, Seven Sisters, the Cabins, near Mouse's Tank trail head and White Domes. At the Visitor Center, there are exhibits on the geology, ecology and history of the park, plus the nearby region.

This whole area was extensively used by basket-making peoples and later by the Anasazi Pueblo farmers from the nearby Moapa Valley from 300BCE to 1150CE. It

was probably visited for hunting, food gathering and religious ceremonies, though the lack of water limited their stays. Wonderful reminders of the time these ancient tribes spent here can be seen in the extraordinarily detailed Indian petroglyphs that tell the stories of their lives. The fantastic scenery and fascinating history make it well worth a day's visit.

Nature's way: The whole area is dominated by creosote, burro and brittle bushes, plus several different types of cactus. Spring is a wonderful time to visit as this is the time to see desert marigold, indigo bushes and desert mallow in bloom. The park is visited by many species of bird, but those in residence include raven, house finch, sage sparrow and, of course, the famous road runner – beep beep!

The animals tend to be nocturnal, coming out to forage for food when the desert heat has begun to fade, and include many different types of lizard, as well as snakes, coyote, kit fox, spotted skunk, black-tailed jack rabbit and ground squirrel. The desert tortoise is now so rare it is protected by Nevada State law. Early mornings or late afternoons are the best time to see the wildlife, but keep your distance.

One of the best ways to explore the park is by hiking through it and maps of trails are provided at the Visitor Center.

Arch Rock: A 2ml/3km scenic loop road provides views of some of the valley's most interesting rock formations, for example Arch Rock and Piano Rock. You'll get a true wilderness experience at the secluded Arch Rock Campground with its primitive facilities!

Amazing rock formations in the Valley of Fire

Rock climbing at Red Rock

Atlatl Rock: Here you will find outstanding examples of ancient Indian rock art or petroglyphs, including a depiction of the atlatl (at'-lat-l), a notched stick used to throw primitive spears and the forerunner of the bow and arrow.

BRITTIP

Atlatl Rock is a great location for campers and the campsite is well-equipped with modern WC and shower facilities.

Beehives: Unusual sandstone formations weathered by the eroding forces of wind and water, there are 3 group camping areas nearby, available by reservation only.

Cabins: Now a picnic area, these historic stone cabins were built with native sandstone by the Civilian Conservation Corps in the 1930s as a shelter for passing travellers.

Mouse's Tank: Named after a renegade Indian who used the area as a hideout in the 1890s, this is a natural basin in the rock where water collects after rainfall, sometimes remaining for months. A half-mile/800m round trip trail leads to Mouse's Tank from the trail head parking area, passing numerous examples of prehistoric Indian petroglyphs.

Petrified logs: Logs and stumps washed into the area from an ancient forest about 225 million years ago are exposed in 2 locations.

Rainbow vista: A favourite photo point with a panoramic view of multicoloured sandstone.

Seven Sisters: Fascinating red rock formations, which are easily accessible from the road. Picnic areas provide a relaxing stop.

White Domes: Sandstone formations with brilliant contrasting colours, picnic area and trail head. White Domes is an 11ml/17.7km round trip drive from the Visitor Center. Duck Rock is a short hike.

Other sights: Clark Memorial, Elephant Rock, the deep red sandstone of Fire Canyon and the amazing Silica Dome.

Red Rock Canyon

17mls/27km west of the Las Vegas Strip on Charleston Boulevard (Highway 159), 702 515 5367 or 702 363 1921 (Visitor Center), redrockcanyonlv.org or sunsetcities.com/redrock.html

Red Rock Canyon is part of the Red Rock Canyon Conservancy Area and encompasses a large part of the Mojave Desert, the unearthly landscape where Steven Spielberg's sci-fi classic was filmed. Red Rock Canyon also includes the Spring Mountain Range, home of Mount Charleston and Bonnie Springs Old Nevada.

Once the home of ancient Native American tribes, this magnificent canyon was formed by a thrust fault – a fracture in the Earth's crust where one plate is pushed horizontally over another – 65 million years ago. It is home to feral horses and burros (donkeys), as well as native wildlife such as desert bighorn sheep and coyotes, which you can see on the 13ml/21km Scenic Loop Drive (see page 224).

The Calico Vista points are good stopping points, offering great views of the crossed-bedded Aztec sandstone. For easy

Cycling at Red Rock

access to the sandstone, stop at the Sandstone Quarry car park where you can see large blocks of stone and other historic evidence of quarry activity that took place during the turn of the last century. You can have a picnic at Red Spring and Willow Spring, where there's also a Petroglyph Wall Trail, while there are also great views of wooded canyons and desert washes at Icebox Canyon, Pine Creek Canyon and Red Rock Wash.

With 30mls/48km of trails, hiking, mountain-biking, horse-riding and rock-climbing tours are all available at Red Rock Canyon and cost from $69 per person.

Stop at the Visitor Center at the entrance to the Scenic Loop Drive for touring and adventure activities information, trail maps and tours. Open 8am–4.30pm November to March, and 8am–5.30pm April to October. Costs $5 which includes scenic drive.

⚓ BRITTIP

You need to stop at the Visitor Center before going into the park's Scenic Loop Drive to acquaint yourself with the park regulations, including where you can drive and park.

Scenic Loop Drive: Open daily, changing by season, but generally from sunrise to sunset; Nov–Feb 6am–5pm, Apr–Sep 6am–8pm and Mar–Oct 6am–7pm. Entrance to the loop costs $5 for motorists and $2 for motorcyclists; free for hikers and cyclists.

The 13ml/21km scenic drive is a one-way road. Cyclists are permitted to ride on the scenic drive, but must obey traffic laws. Sightseeing, photography and hiking trails are accessible from the designated pullouts and parking areas. If you would like to go hiking or rock climbing in Red Rock or Mount Charleston, see page 229.

Spring Valley

Sailing on Lake Mead

Pahrump Valley Winery: 3810 Winery Road, Pahrump, 775 751 7800, pahrumpwinery.com. Just north of Red Rock is Nevada's only vineyard and it regularly produces award-winning Chardonnay, Cabernet and Burgundy. In 2009, it released Nevada's first ever commercial red – a 2005 Zinfandel called Nevada Ridge. Free tours offered most days at 11.30am, 1.30pm, and 3.30pm; call to check schedule.

Bonnie Springs Old Nevada

16mls/26km west of Las Vegas, 702 875 4191, bonniesprings.com

Open: Wed–Sun 10.30am–6pm (summer), 10.30am–5pm (winter)

Admission: $20 per car (up to 6 people and includes a $10 restaurant coupon) or $3 per person on a bus. Price includes access to the zoo

Originally built in 1843 as a stopover for the wagon trains going to California down the Old Spanish Trail, Bonnie Springs has been used as a tourist attraction since 1952. Now this replicated old American West mining town includes gunfights in the street, hangings, an 1880 melodrama, miniature train, US Post Office, blacksmith display, wax museum and Boot Hill Cemetery.

A 1-hour guided horseback ride through Red Rock Canyon costs $55 (no children under 6) is offered 9am–3.15pm – and there is a petting zoo, duck pond and aviary for families. Breakfast, lunch, dinner – ranch food including Cowboy Toast and Bronco Burgers – and cocktails are also

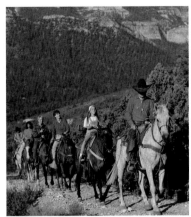

Riding at Mount Charleston

available. A shuttle service from Las Vegas gets you here in half an hour and is provided through Star Land Tours (702 296 4381) or for $90 by Bonnie Springs for groups of 6 or more.

Spring Mountain Ranch State Park

15mls/24km west of Las Vegas, via Charleston Boulevard (Highway 159), in the Red Rock Canyon National Conservation Area, 702 875 4141, http://parks.nv.gov/smr.htm

Open: Daily 9am–6pm. The main ranch house is open daily 10am–4pm

Admission: $5 per vehicle; walk-ins, bicycles and bus $1

The many springs in these mountains once provided water for Paiute Indians and later brought mountain men and early settlers to the area. This 520acre/210ha oasis was developed into a combination working ranch and luxurious retreat by a string of owners who have given the area a long and colourful history. Chester Lauck of the comedy team Lum & Abner, and millionaire Howard Hughes are past owners of the ranch.

In the mid-1830s a campsite was established along the wash that runs through the ranch. The spring-fed creek and grassy meadows formed a welcome oasis for travellers using this as an alternative route to the Spanish Trail through Cottonwood Valley. The use of the site by pack and wagon trains continued until their replacement by the railroad in 1905.

At the ranch house, you can find information about the ranch and surrounding areas and take a self-guided tour. Guided

tours throughout the historic area are available weekdays at noon, 1 and 2pm; weekends at noon, 1, 2 and 3pm.

🏴 BRITTIP

There are often fire restrictions in this area, so check the website for the latest information.

The remote trail was also perfect for outlaws and was used extensively by those involved in slave trading, horse stealing and raids on passing caravans. One of the most famous was mountain man Bill Williams, after whom the ranch was first named.

In 1876 it was taken over by 2 men and named Sand Stone Ranch. The name stuck until it was leased in 1944 to Chet Lauck, the Lum part of comedy duo Lum & Abner and renamed Bar Nothing Ranch. A ranch house was built as a family retreat and Lum created a boys' camp. In 1955, German actress Vera Krupp bought the property, expanded the ranching business side and renamed it Spring Mountain Ranch.

At 3,800ft/1,158m, it is usually up to 10°C/15°F cooler than Las Vegas with cold winters and thunderstorms and flash floods in summer. Visitors can see wonderful plants including the Joshua tree, Mohave yucca, indigo bush, desert marigold and globe mallow. Animals are harder to spot as many are nocturnal, but include lizards, snakes, antelope ground squirrels, kit fox, jackrabbits, coyote, rock squirrel, badger, mule deer and bighorn sheep.

What's on: The programme includes hikes by moonlight into Sandstone Canyon. A Living History programme re-creates the ranch's past in the spring and autumn, including demonstrations of pioneer skills. The Super Summer Theater puts on outdoor performances every June, July, August and

Watersports on Lake Mead

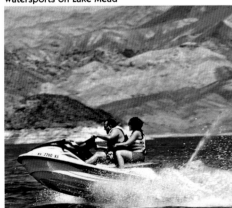

Further afield

Full details of the Grand Canyon, Zion, Bryce and Death Valley are given in Chapter 15 on pages 262–278 and details of air and bus tours are in this chapter on page 228.

Grand Canyon: nps.gov/grca. If you're planning to go on a bit of a tour, then you're bound to want to see the Grand Canyon close up and for real. But it is also possible to take plane and helicopter rides to this, the most spectacular canyon on earth – even landing on the canyon floor and having a spot of lunch on the banks of the Colorado. With Papillon Grand Canyon Helicopters you can land and have lunch inside the canyon and with Heli USA combine a flight to the Grand Canyon with a river rafting trip.

Zion National Park: 435 772 3256, zion.national-park.com. North of Las Vegas and the Grand Canyon in southern Utah is the majestic Zion National Park with its beautiful waterfalls cascading down red rocks, and its hanging gardens. Once home to the ancient Anasazi, its history and majesty are presented in an adventure film at the Zion Canyon Giant Screen Theatre (435 772 2466, zioncanyontheatre.com) along with Hollywood movies, some in 3D.

Bryce Canyon: 435 834 5322, nps.gov/brca. Nearby in Utah is the equally beautiful Bryce Canyon, once home to both Native Americans and cowboys of the Old West. Both Zion and Bryce offer hiking, biking, horse riding, rock climbing and bird watching and in winter, snow shoeing.

Death Valley: 760 786 3200, nps.gov.deva. West of Las Vegas in eastern California, this is the hottest place on earth, with average summer temperatures of 45°C/113°F. Here you will see miles of sand that has been hardened into a sea-like landscape by the heat of the sun, extinct volcanoes and wind-carved rock formations.

Many companies offer day trips to Death Valley and to break up the monotonous terrain on the way, you'll be taken through the beautiful Titus Canyon and some ghost towns and be shown Native American Indian petroglyphs. Once there, you'll be shown all the Death Valley highlights including Furnace Creek, Zabriskie Point, Bad Water and Scotty's Castle.

September while the Theatre under the Stars features musicals and plays for the whole family. Gates open at 6pm, shows start at 8pm (7pm in September). Tickets cost $10 in advance (children 5 and under go free). There is also a picnic area.

Extraterrestrial Highway

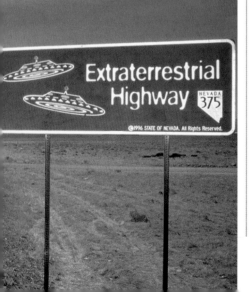

Mount Charleston

35mls/56km north-west of Las Vegas on Highways 95 and 157, 702 514 5400, sunsetcities.com/mt-charleston.html

Camping: 1-800 280 CAMP (2267). Six campgrounds are open from May to September. Cost is from $10 per night depending on campsite, picnic area and trail, for a maximum 5 days

Set in the lush Toiyabe National Forest, Mount Charleston looms nearly 12,000ft/ 3,658m above sea level. One of the most beautiful areas in the Las Vegas Valley, Lee Canyon Road, the Kyle Canyon section of Charleston Park Road and Deer Creek Road have all been designated Scenic Byways because of their extraordinary scenery and panoramic views. The area is about 17°C/30°F cooler than Las Vegas, making it a perfect escape from the city heat for a day.

Charleston Peak was the birthplace of the Paiute people, so for the Native Americans it is sacred land. To respect this, the scale and extent of the road system remains fairly limited.

Camping is popular here, along with horse riding, and in the winter you can ski at Lee Canyon (see Activities, page 230).

BRITTIP

Day trips to the Grand Canyon, Bryce Canyon and Zion Canyon from Las Vegas are available via helicopter, small plane or coach (see page 228).

Spooky sights

ET Highway

About 140mls/225km north of Las Vegas, 1 800 NEVADA 8

A 98ml/158km stretch of road on Route 375, a few miles north of the notorious Area 51 and the super-secret Groom Lake Air Force Base, this is where the American Air Force is believed to have tested the Stealth and U-2 aircraft and where numerous American TV shows have claimed aliens from outer space have undergone examinations at the top-secret Department of Defense site. UFO buffs often gather on ridges above Area 51 and use high-powered telescopes and binoculars to spy on the secret location. Their favourite meeting points are at the bars in nearby Rachel (rachel-nevada.com/ethighway.html), where they exchange tales about extra-terrestrials.

Now the road has been officially dubbed the ET Highway by the Nevada Commission on Tourism, which has even created a new programme called the ET Experience.

Pioneer Saloon

Goodsprings, south of Las Vegas, 702 874 9362

Founded in the old mining town, this has much historical memorabilia and is worth dropping into to soak up some old-Americana atmosphere. Sitting on top of the US Army Cannon Stove, once used to warm people up on cold winter nights, is a piece of melted aluminium from the aeroplane in which film star Carole Lombard died. The plane crashed into Double Deal Mountain in January 1942 and her husband Clark Gable sat in the bar for days after, hoping for a miracle. Open daily from 10am.

Bonnie and Clyde's 'Death Car'

Primm Valley Hotel, 702 386 7867, www.primmvalleyresorts.com

The original car driven by Bonnie Parker and Clyde Barrow in their final shoot-out with the FBI on 23 May 1934 is on display at Whiskey Pete's Hotel. The infamous duo who held up gas stations, restaurants and small banks in Texas, New Mexico, Oklahoma and Missouri were shopped by a friend. At a cost of $75,000, Clyde's bullet-ridden and bloodstained shirt is now on display too!

Ghost towns

The old gold and silver mining towns are the stuff of many a Western movie and it is possible to visit some of these abandoned sites.

Goldfield Ghost Town (4650 N Mammoth Mine Road, Arizona – on Interstate 95 north of Scotty's Castle, 480 983 0333, www.goldfieldghosttown.com) was once Nevada's largest city after gold was discovered in 1902. Known for its opulence, it was called the Queen of Camps and had 20,000 residents at its peak, with mines producing $10,000 a day in 1907. A flood in 1913 and a fire in 1923 destroyed much of the town, but still standing are the Courthouse and Santa Fe Saloon among others. Open 10am–5pm daily.

In 1904 gold was discovered in the Amargosa Valley and the town of Rhyolite (just outside Beatty on Interstate 95, then 374) was born. At its peak, it housed 10,000 people and had more than 50 saloons, 18 grocery stores and half a dozen barbers. But it became a ghost town in 1911 after losing its financial backing. You can still see the Cook Bank Building, school and jail, plus a house built in 1905 entirely of bottles. Visit ghosttowns.com to find other ghost towns in the area or see Creative Adventures in the A–Z of tour companies on pages 231–234.

BRITTIP

Take the 3-hour Haunted Vegas Tour in town, leaving at 9.30pm and costing $66.25 (hauntedvegas tours.com; tickets at www.vegas explorers.com or by calling toll free 866 218 4935).

Ghost town at Belmont

Flying to the Grand Canyon

The Maverick Helicopters' pilot looked the spitting image of Tom Cruise and the theme from *Mission: Impossible* was blasting down our earphones as we took off from McCarran Airport. Suddenly the helicopter banked steeply and we 5 passengers had an altogether too-close-for-comfort view of the ground. Then, just as suddenly as we'd banked to the right, the helicopter straightened up and we found ourselves inching over the 'matchbox' houses at what seemed to be a snail's pace. In reality, we were speeding out of the Las Vegas Valley at 130mph/210kph, heading east to the West Rim of the Grand Canyon.

Within minutes, we were flying over the $1m homes in the exclusive community of Lake Las Vegas and its 2 golf courses. Next came the 110ml/177km long Lake Mead, the largest man-made lake in America providing a beautiful blue contrast to the pale brown rocks, and then the Hoover Dam. My thoughts that the scenery had a volcanic look to it were confirmed when our pilot pointed out an extinct volcano.

It took half an hour to reach the Grand Canyon and after a brief flyover, we landed on its rocky floor. Our pilot immediately jumped out and started preparing our champagne drinks with light snacks. It seemed a perfect way to spend 40 minutes – quaffing champagne and looking around at this millions-of-years-old natural wonder.

All too soon, it seemed, we were taking off again, but before we started our return journey we were flown through the canyon. The half-hour ride back to Las Vegas sped by and we headed for our final treat – a flight down the entire length of the famous Strip for a bird's-eye view of all those amazing buildings. (For information on helicopter flights to the Grand Canyon see page 266.)

Tours

Air tours

You can fly to all the major sights mentioned in this chapter either in a small plane or by helicopter. Flight packages or helicopter flights are offered by many of the tour companies listed. Scenic Airlines is the largest. These tours may be pricey – anything up to $650 – but they offer a marvellous opportunity to see amazing scenery in a very short space of time.

Generally, a short flight will include the Las Vegas Strip, Western Grand Canyon, Hoover Dam and Lake Mead and will cost around $60. The next step up will be the above plus a complete aerial tour of the Grand Canyon for around $200. The more expensive prices will include extras such as a champagne lunch on the Grand Canyon rim or, in the case of a helicopter flight, on the Canyon floor next to the Colorado.

There's stunning scenery for hiking

Combination tours may include lunch with Native Americans, river rafting, hiking and canyon sunset/sunrise. Some companies offer an overnight stay at the Grand Canyon, Bryce Canyon or Monument Valley. Tour companies are listed on pages 231–234.

Bus tours

The prices are cheaper, but the days are longer as you get to see all the sights covered by the air tours – only on the ground, of course! Tour companies are listed on pages 231–234.

Activities

All the contact details for the various companies are in the A–Z on pages 231–234.

Bike tours

Bootleg Canyon Trails: With names like The Reaper, Dominatrix and Armageddon, the world-class downhill and cross country trails at Bootleg Canyon Mountain Bike Park near Boulder City are for real mountain bikers. The most extreme is Elavator Shaft – flying down a 22% degree hillside.

Escape Adventures: Runs mountain bike trips in Red Rock Canyon from a half day to a weekend for $499.

Las Vegas Cyclery: This professional outfit offers half, full and multi-day mountain,

Canoeing at Pyramid

road and multi-sport cycling adventures for casual to experienced cyclists. The Red Rock Scenic Loop costs from $99 self-guided and $109.99 guided.

Single Track Tours Las Vegas: Professionally guided mountain bike tours and road trips in Las Vegas, Red Rock and Lake Mead for both the beginner and professional at $115 per person.

Hiking

Escape Adventures: 6-day hiking adventures include Color Country Hiker – a moderate hike through Bryce, Zion and Grand Canyon National Parks ($1,390 camping) and Death Valley to Red Rock Canyon ($1,290 camping and inns).

Grand Canyon Tour Company: They do half-day trips to Red Rock Canyon ($119.99), a hike to the Hot Springs ($100) and full-day hikes of the Grand Canyon with guides who tell you all about the geology and human and natural history. You will be given drinking water, high-energy drink mixers and snacks.

HikeThis!: Moderate or moderately strenuous guided hikes start at $99 per person for 2–5 people and cover 4–6mls/6.5–9.5km (4 hours' round trip). The more popular, moderately strenuous to strenuous rock scrambling adventure deep in the canyons, over creek bed stones and massive sandstone boulders is 3–4mls/ 5–6.5km and takes up to 5 hours. Free pick-up and drop-off and lunch included.

Rocky Trails: You can hike just about anywhere with Rocky Trails, one of the largest dedicated hiking organisations, which specialises in providing geological tours of everywhere from Red Rock to Valley of Fire, Mount Charleston, Eldorado Canyon and even Death Valley. Tours cost $99–160 including lunch. Or you can hike

down the Grand Canyon – still the best way of seeing one of the most beautiful places on earth.

Horse riding

Available at Red Rock Canyon, Bonnie Springs Old Nevada, Mount Charleston and Valley of Fire.

Cowboy Trail Rides: You can go on horseback rides, custom and group trail rides and pack trips in southern Nevada, Utah and Northern Arizona. Trips are tailor-made and can last an hour or 7 days. They offer day rides for kids through to a sunset ride with a Western-style barbecue under the stars through Red Rock Canyon and a 5-hour Wow Ride through untouched Wild West wilderness. Rides cost $45–329 per person.

Wild Wild West Horseback Trail Rides: Both novice and experienced riders can choose from a Red Rock Canyon Breakfast Ride or an Old Spanish Trail Ride with lunch ($119 and 6 hours each) or the Wild West Sunset Dinner Ride ($149), bookable through LookTours.

Off-road adventures

ATV Action Tours: ATV has the sole licensing permits for many desert regions, mountains and other points of interest in south-west Nevada. They combine the off-road experience in Land Rovers, Jeep Cherokees, Wranglers and ATVs with short hiking excursions, climbing large rock formations and searching for petroglyphs. Definitely the most fun way to get back to nature without breaking into a sweat! Tours cost from $89, with free hotel pick-up and daily departures. Book online for the cheapest prices.

Awesome Adventures: Offers off-road ATV tours that explore the lives and trails

Amargosa is great for quad biking

travelled by pioneers and explorers of the past such as The Anasazi, a lost civilisation; Outlaws and Gunfighters of the Wild West and Gold Chasing Miners. The Eldorado Canyon tour takes around 5 hours (lunch included) and costs $189.

LookTours: This company offers ATV tours alongside the 6-hour Hoover Dam and Lake Mead. This 4x4 Off-road Hummer Adventure includes around 2.5 hours of 4-wheel, off-road adventure through the Mojave Desert, including Lava Butte, Rainbow Gardens and Lizard Eye Ridge, plus Hoover Dam and Lake Mead and costs $188.99 including lunch. It's the same price for a 6-hour Desert ATV Adventure, which includes 2.5 hours on an ATV through the Valley of Fire. Other off-roading experiences on offer include an Extreme Dirt Bike Adventure through the Mojave Desert ($278.99).

Pink Jeep Tours: The first independent company to set up in Death Valley, Pink Jeep's off-road adventures are in custom-designed Tour Trekkers that seat 10 people or 6-passenger SUVs, with 12 nature-based guided tours to choose from including a 6-hour Valley of Fire tour for $135 and a 4-hour Mt Charleston tour, for $89.

Other companies: Since ATV set the ball rolling, many other tour companies are now offering Hummer Tours – the term used to describe off-road adventures in 4x4 Hummers. Those companies include Grand Canyon Tour Company and Rebel Adventure Tours. The Hummer tours can be combined with other activities such as jet-skiing and rafting.

✚ BRITTIP

For excitement seekers the Grand Canyon helicopter, Hummer, jet ski from LookTours ($559.99 online) may be just the ticket.

Snowboarding at Mount Charleston

Rafting

Rafting the Grand Canyon's Colorado River is rated as America's top adventure. Two basic types of rafting are easily available from Las Vegas.

Black Canyon River Raft Tours: You can take a gentle ride in a motorised raft down an 11ml/18km stretch of the Colorado, starting at the base of the mighty Hoover Dam and stopping for lunch (and a cooling swim). Along the way you will see hot water springs bubbling out of cliffs, flora and fauna and the amazing desert bighorn sheep, who think nothing of living on the perilous slopes of the Grand Canyon. These rides usually last around 7 hours and cost $79–125 from February to November. Plenty of other tour companies offer similar tours.

Grand Canyon Tour Company: The other kind of rafting is a lot more expensive, but more authentic and involves rapids. One- or two-day trips on rapids with strengths of 4–7 (on a scale of 1–10) are available with Native Americans from the Grand Canyon area. The Grand Canyon Tour Company offers trips from Lees Ferry in Arizona (about 2.5 hours' drive from the South Rim of the Grand Canyon) that can also be combined with a hike down the Grand Canyon between April and October. A long day trip (children must be over 8) aboard a motorised raft with Hualapai Indian guide takes you across class 3–6 rapids with an optional hike before being lifted by helicopter to Grand Canyon West ($459 per person). Otherwise most of their trips start at 2 days and go up to 10, in an oar craft or motorised, on class 3–6 water, between April and September, costing around $250 per day. If you're coming in the off-season, you can take a day trip on the Colorado River from Diamond Creek to Pierce Ferry (about 3 hours from Vegas). Trips need to be booked well in advance as permits need to be arranged.

Skiing and snowboarding

Just 35 minutes away from Las Vegas in Mount Charleston's Lee Canyon, you can ski or snowboard from Thanksgiving to Easter. Beginner packages for skiing or snowboarding cost $90 for ski rental equipment, lift ticket and a 2-hour group lesson or the whole morning for kids (skiing lessons age 4–12, snowboarding age 6–12). Lift prices for those with experience are $50 a day for adults and $30 for under-12s. In summer (mid-June to October) ski-lift chair rides to the top of the ski runs are only $5 for adults and $3 for under-12s.

Water activities

Cruising, boating, fishing and jet-skiing are all available on Lake Mead.

Lake Mead Cruises: The largest provider of cruises and jet-skiing runs brunch, midday and dinner (Sun–Thurs) cruises on the glassy waters of Lake Mead on board the Desert Princess, an authentic 300-passenger paddle-wheeler, which is climate-controlled inside. Sunday brunch cruises cost $39 (under-12s $18), April to October; midday sightseeing cruises $24 (under-12s $12) daily 12pm and 2pm; dinner cruises $49 (under-12s $25) April to October. Under-2s go free and all prices include tax. You can either board at Hoover Dam or at Lake Mead Marina.

Lake Mead Jetski Tours: Rents powercraft from $200 per day. Package includes a 2-day orientation class and 90 minutes on the water. Each tour is accompanied by a guide who will narrate the trip via a hands-free, waterproof, 2-way radio on each personal jet-ski. Lunch is provided.

BRITTIP

Tight on time? Discover the diversity of the desert in style on the Fantastic 4 Mojave Desert Tour which takes in Hoover Dam, Lake Mead, Red Rock Canyon, Mount Charleston and The Valley of Fire (costs $199 per person from anniebananie.com).

Overton Beach Watercraft: Further north at Overton Beach Marina you can hire everything from personal watercraft to patio and fishing boats. Overnight packages are even available. Personal watercraft can seat 2–3 people and have storage compartments with a built-in cooler for your packed lunch. Patio boats for up to 10 people are perfect for fishing or cruising and come with a motor, radio/cassette, cooler, cushioned bench seating and an awning. Costs are $125 for 4 hours, $195 for 8 hours. Fishing boats hold 4 people and come with a Fish Finder and Pole Holder to increase your odds! Costs are $65 for 4 hours, $100 for 8.

A–Z of tour companies

As you can see, the outdoor options are numerous, so to make life a little simpler I have tried to list most of the major tour companies in this simple A–Z format. In many cases the companies have their own websites through which it is possible to book excursions and trips in advance. This is probably most useful for those planning to do something quite specialist, such as rock climbing or trying to go off the beaten track, as times and dates may be specific.

Adventure Photo Tours: 702 889 8687, adventurephototours.com. Private or semi-private photo safaris with professional and well-informed guides to Red Rock, Valley of Fire, Lake Mead and ghost towns in 7-seater Ford Expeditions, with pick-up from your hotel.

Adventure West Tours: 702 420 3211/3257, www.adventurewesttours. com. Day tours of the Grand Canyon include the Skywalk, and an optional helicopter ride to the floor of the canyon and a boat ride on the Colorado River.

All Las Vegas Tours: 1 800 566 5868 or 702 233 1627, alllasvegastours.com. A whole range of adventure tours available online and with testimonials from those who have done them.

Annie Bananie's Wild West Tours: 702 804 9755, anniebananie.com. Experienced 'cowboy' guides take you on a trip through ancient and western history and show the diversity of the desert landscape.

ATV Action Tours: 702 566 7400 or toll free 888 288 5200, actiontours.com. Get to the other side of Las Vegas Valley in a Jeep Cherokee or Wrangler off-roader and then take a short hike, or take an adventure by ATV, or go horse-riding or white-water rafting. Also offers custom tours – including overnight stays at a dude ranch (see page 267), in a mountain cabin or even camping under the stars.

Awesome Adventures: 702 257 7338, www.awesomeadventureguide.com. This company is a one-stop shop for outdoor adventure tours, offering ATV tours, ziplining at Bootleg Canyon, hiking, biking and horse-riding, white-water rafting and kayaking. It also offers combo-tours such as the Eldorado kayak, ATV and horse ride.

Black Canyon River Raft Tours: 702 294 1414 or toll free 800 455 3490, blackcanyonadventures.com.

BRITTIP

Watch out! Some tour companies offer 2-for-1 or other big discounts, making their prices appear very competitive, but they don't include taxes and other extras, which can bump up the cost.

Cowboys ...

You can't get away from them in Nevada – even the casinos are packed with Stetsons bobbing around among the slot machines. One of the most exciting festivals the city has to offer is the annual National Finals Rodeo held in the second week of December. Great contests include saddle bronco riding, bareback riding, bull riding, calf roping, steer wrestling, team roping, steer roping and barrel racing.

Annie Bananie's Wild West Tour: Here you can get the best of the Wild West in comfort and style at $60–199 per person. Experienced 'cowboy' guides take you to Lake Mead for lunch at the historical Calville Bay Marina, before your air-conditioned coach whisks you off to the Black Mountains, Rogers' Springs, the Valley of Fire and the Moapa Indian Reservation.

Bonnie Springs Old Nevada: A visit here (see page 224) will give you a real taste of the Wild West.

Cowboy Trail Rides: Offer a 1.5-hour sunset ride with Western-style barbecue under the stars through Red Rock Canyon ($169) and a 5-hour WOW ride that takes you through untouched wilderness, making you think you are in the 1800s Old West.

Grand Canyon West Ranch: You can get a taste for real-life ranch action at any of the many ranches dotted throughout Nevada, Arizona and California that allow non-cowboys on board for a bit of fun (see page 262 for a full description of the different types and how to get in). One of the nearest – just 45 minutes by helicopter from the Las Vegas Strip – is the new Grand Canyon West Ranch (1 800 359 8727, grandcanyonranch.com), which nestles in the mountainous area between the west end of the Grand Canyon and the 6,000ft/1,829m Music Mountains of Arizona. Heli USA (see page 233) offers VIP overnight packages, including helicopter flight, at this working cattle and guest ranch for $499 adults, $399 children, plus $50 fee each, other packages available. Accommodation consists of rustic 2- or 4-person cabins with authentic roll-top bathtubs and log fires. A herd of long-horn Corriente cattle roam the ranch along with the wild animals such as deer, mountain lion, bob cats, rattlesnakes and lizards. Self-drive packages with cabin stay and Western-style entertainment start at $99 per person mid week.

Oatman: About 20mls/32km east of Laughlin is Oatman, a ghost town in Arizona. Once a thriving mining town during the gold rush, wild burros now wander the streets of this popular TV and Western movie backdrop. At weekends you can take a trip back to the Old West with free cowboy gunfights and showdowns on Main Street. For details phone the Chamber of Commerce (928 768 6222 or 928 768 3839).

Wild Wild West Horseback Trail Rides: If time doesn't permit a stay, try these trail rides available through LookTours, including a free pick-up from your hotel to the Sage Brush Range on the Moapa Indian Reservation. Choose from a Red Rock Canyon Breakfast Ride ($119 for 6 hours), Old Spanish Trail Ride with lunch ($119 for 6 hours) or the Wild West Sunset Dinner Ride ($149). Including a hearty feast prepared by cowboys and cowgirls, the trails are designed to be user-friendly for both novice and experienced riders.

Bootleg Canyon Trails: 702 204 7810, bootlegcanyon.org. World-class downhill and cross-country trails at Bootleg Canyon Mountain Bike Park near Boulder City.

Coach America/Gray Line Tours: 702 384 1234, grayline.com. The big bus trip specialist, covering everywhere from Hoover Dam to Bryce Canyon and Death Valley. If you pay for your tour in advance, you'll get a free round trip transfer from the airport to your hotel or a free Laughlin Day Tour.

Cowboy Trail Rides: 702 387 2457, cowboytrailrides.com or redrockranch or mountcharlestonridingstables.com. Fun horse rides from day rides for kids and sunset rides through Red Rock Canyon to multi-day rides.

Creative Adventures: 702 893 2051, creativeadventuresltd.net. Specialists in the Ghost Town Tour, which takes you to the wild country along the Colorado to Native American country before touring Searchlight, once a bustling mining town at the turn of the last century. They also offer a Historic Spanish Trail through Red Rock Canyon, The Valley of Fire State Park and Lost City Museum Tour, which includes boating on Lake Mead and the Grand Canyon Adventure Tour.

Drive Yourself Tours: 1 800 724 7767 or 435 658 2227, driveyourselftours.com. Pop a tape in the cassette machine and take yourself off to the Grand Canyon, Bryce Canyon and Zion National Park

... and Indians

Three tribes have dominated Nevada's Native American history – the Northern Paiute, Southern Paiute and the Shoshone. Between them they have etched their stories in the rock petroglyphs of the Valley of Fire and other sacred places including Mount Charleston. The modern-day Native Americans still remain an important force in Nevada, with major Indian reservations at Moapa plus Fort Mojave Reservation in the southern-most tip of the state. They still live by their ancient codes and, even though they now run their own casinos and restaurants, maintain their heritage through traditional pow wows.

Originally, the pow wow was designed to bring various tribes together in a friendly way. It was a festive gathering where they exchanged gifts, heard the latest news and sold foods and crafts. Rodeos were an attraction, but the highlight was always the tribal dance competition for which they would dress in tribal regalia.

Bruno's Indian and Turquoise Museum: 1306 Nevada Highway, Boulder City, 702 293 4865. This promotes and gives information about the Native American artists of the south-west, of which 2,000 are represented by the museum. Open 9.30am– 5pm.

Grand Canyon West Ranch: (1 800 359 8727, grandcanyonranch.com). This company offers accommodation in Indian Tipis or pine cabins.

Great Venture Tours: (1 800 578 2643, greatventures.com) Another way to get the 'Indian' experience is to go on a rafting trip with a Native American river guide on the Colorado River. This company offers a 1-day rafting trip on class 2–4 rapids with Hualapai River Guides from Sedona for $549 (minimum age 8), Tues, Thurs and Sat.

Heli USA: See below. Offers overnight packages, including sunrise helicopter flight for $349 adults, $279 children, plus $50 fee each, or self-drive package for $259 adults, $199 children, plus $15 fee.

Hualapai Indians: Most of the major tour companies offer Grand Canyon flights or helicopter tours to the West Rim combined with a barbecue lunch with the Hualapai Indians, who will tell you about their legends and culture. The trips have been so successful that the Hualapai have even built a tiny village overlooking the Grand Canyon where you can shop for souvenirs or check out the small museum.

Lost City Museum of Archaeology: 721 South Moapa Valley Boulevard, Overton, 702 397 2193, sunsetcities.com/lost-city-museum.html. Another great place to go, this is just north of Red Rock Canyon. For $3 admission you will be able to see artefacts from the Anasazis who lived in the Moapa Valley from the 1st to the 12th centuries AD. Displays include a reconstruction of the basket-maker pithouse and pueblo dwellings. The museum is located 66mls/106km north-east of Las Vegas on Highway 15 and Highway 169 near Overton. Open daily 8.30am–4.30pm.

Moapa River Indian Reservation: Pow wows still take place today and are a wonderful way to experience the Indian culture. Of course, it cannot be guaranteed that a pow wow will be organised for your trip, but you can still get a taste of the Native American way of life by coming here, just east of the Valley of Fire off Interstate 15. The store at the entrance is famous for its duty-free tobacco, alcohol and fireworks. But be warned: fireworks are not allowed outside the reservation and police do stop and search cars periodically.

listening to information about points of interest. The tapes come with maps and take you on 2–7-day tours.

Escape Adventures: 702 596 2953, escapeadventurs.com. Runs mountain bike, road and multisport as well as hiking trips in Red Rock Canyon and beyond.

Grand Canyon Tour Company: 1 800 2 CANYON/1 800 222 6966 (UK) or 702 655 6060 (Las Vegas), grandcanyontour company.com. All kinds of tours by most methods of transport including self-drive.

Heli USA Airways: 01462 488227 (UK) or 702 736 8787 (Las Vegas), heliusa.com. Offers a comprehensive selection of flights to the Grand Canyon with overnight stays, plus exclusive stays at the Grand Canyon West Ranch (see Cowboys panel, left).

Hike This!: 702 393 4453, hikethislas vegas.com. Offers guided hiking and rock scrambling tours around some of the most spectacular scenery in southern Nevada. Costs from $99 (2 person minimum).

Keith Prowse: 0871 232425, keithprowse.com. For helicopter, aircraft and land tours. The West Rim Indian

Country Bus Tour includes lunch with the Hualapai Indians.

Lake Mead Cruises: 702 293 6180, lakemeadcruises.com. Cruises and jet-skiing on Lake Mead.

Lake Mead Jetski Tours: 702 558 7547, worldwidejetskis.com. Jet-ski tours and rental on Lake Mead.

Las Vegas Cyclery: 702 596 2953, lasvegascyclery.com This professional outfit offers half, full and multi-day mountain, road and multi-sport cycling adventures for casual to experienced cyclists as well as hiking tours in Red Rock Canyon.

Las Vegas Tour Desk: 1 866 GC Tours or 702 310 1320, lasvegastourdesk.com. Specialises in air tours to the Grand Canyon.

LookTours: 1 800 566 5868 or 702 233 1627, looktours.com. Winner of the 2005 Best Sightseeing Tour Company by the Nevada Commission on Tourism, the company offers every conceivable tour option and combination you could wish for – by aeroplane, bus, helicopter, raft and ATV or Hummer. It's worth checking out the website and booking directly to take advantage of the internet deals.

Maverick Helicopters Inc: 888-261 0007, maverickhelicopter.com. Custom charters and tours to Grand Canyon, Bryce, Zion, Monument Valley and Death Valley. Also offers personalised videos to take home.

Overton Beach Watercraft: 702 394 4400. Hire of anything from personal watercraft to patio and fishing boats.

Papillon Grand Canyon Helicopters: 0800 404 9767 (UK toll free) or 702 736 7243 (Las Vegas), papillon.com. Offers helicopter trips ranging from the Vegas strip at night to packages which plunge into the Grand Canyon.

Pink Jeep Tours: 702 895 6777, www.pinkjeep.com. Pink Jeep Tours have been operating here for 50 years and offer a choice of 12 nature and culture-based tours including Death Valley, Hoover Dam, Grand Canyon, Red Rock Canyon, Valley of Fire, Mt Charleston, Zion National Park and Eldorado Canyon.

Rebel Adventure Tours: 800 817 6789 or 702 380 6969, rebeladventuretours.com. Off-road Hummer tours to Lake Mead and Hoover Dam and Grand Canyon, also combined with jet-skiing, lunch with Native Americans and white water rafting. Rebel

also offer ATV, helicopter and horse-riding adventures.

Rocky Trails: 888 892 5380 or 702 425 3067, rockytrails.com. Run by a geologist, this company specialises in hiking tours that give you a real insight into the wonders of Red Rock, Eldorado Canyon, Valley of Fire, Mount Charleston and Death Valley. It also offers other adventure tours including ATV tours, horse riding, kayaking, white water rafting and mountain biking.

Scenic Airlines: 01992 463465, scenic.com. Since Eagle Airlines bought out Scenic, this is now the largest air tour company in Las Vegas. It offers every single destination you could think of – and every combination. In addition to the Grand Canyon, Zion Canyon, Bryce Canyon, Monument Valley and Lake Powell, you can also do overnight stops and get the Native American experience. Plus, of course, the night flight over the Strip.

Showtime Tours: 702 895 9976, showtimetourlasvegas.com. Tours include a Night on the Town, Grand Canyon Bus Tour, Colorado River Rafting and a Lake Mead Dinner Cruise.

Single Track Tours: 702 813 5730, singletracktours.com. Professionally guided mountain bike and road tours of the Las Vegas area.

Ski & Snowboard Resort: 702 593 9500. Las Vegas Ski & Snowboard Resort is a fully-serviced resort offering ski packages for adults and kids, in Mount Charleston's Lee Canyon, just 30 minutes from the strip.

Sky's the Limit: 702 363 4533. Hiking and rock climbing.

Stars and Stripes Air Tours: 1 888 779 0800, lvhelicopters.com. Offers a selection of helicopter flights from the strip at night to the Grand Canyon, including the skywalk and landing in the canyon. Tours cost $99–550.

Helicop-Tours: 702 736 0606, sundancehelicopters.com. Mostly helicopter trips to the Grand Canyon – landing on the canyon floor – but also do combinations with rafting, the Harley-Davidson® Café and Pahrump Valley Vineyard.

BRITTIP

Some tour companies offer free day-long trips to Laughlin, but these are just a classic way to get you to spend money at the casinos there.

12 GOLF AND OTHER SPORTS

Getting some golf action, plus spectator and extreme sports

Las Vegas is most famous for staging big-name fights between boxers, but its climate – especially in the spring, autumn and winter months – makes it perfect for golf. With a massive increase in courses built over the last decade, there are now an incredible 55 top-flight golf courses to choose from.

The irony is that the time when most Brits visit Las Vegas – the summer – is actually low season, so you should get some pretty good deals at golf courses then. The peak season is October to May, as the Americans consider the summer months far too hot to be playing golf! Fortunately, in the summer, golf courses are open early in the morning and later in the afternoon.

BRITTIP

If you want to arrange a round of golf, go for an afternoon slot as the early mornings tend to get very busy. It's also a lot cheaper at many places – ask about 'twilight' rates, which means any time after 1pm.

Many hotels are affiliated to different golf courses, which offer resort guests reduced-price tee fees. All the same, fees for those courses and others in central Las Vegas will be 2 to 3 times more expensive than those out of the city, although with more courses competing for business, fees came down in 2009, so I have given details of golf courses in Boulder City, North Las Vegas, Laughlin and Pahrump. A few Henderson courses are still well priced, but most of those in the sought-after Lake Las Vegas area are now very expensive. Generally, the prices given include a cart.

A full listing of golf courses open to visitors follows below, but several very

useful numbers are: **Stand-by Golf:** 1 866 224 BOOK or 702 597 2665 (7am–9pm), stand-bygolf.com. For same-day and next-day play at reduced prices (10–50% off) at many golf courses in the Las Vegas area. **Las Vegas Golf** 1 866 456 9912, lasvegasgolf.com is a newer site offering a similar service. **Golf Reservations of Nevada:** 702 732 3119, worldgolf.com/courses/unitedstates/nevada.html. For advance tee-time reservations for individuals and groups at major courses in the area.

There are plenty of golf courses

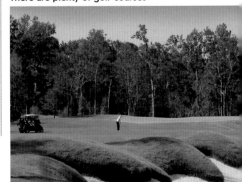

Golf courses in Las Vegas

Angel Park Golf Club

100 South Rampart Boulevard, 888 446 5358 or 702 254 4653, angelpark.com
Designed by Arnold Palmer, two 18-hole resort courses offer 36 holes of Championship golf with spectacular views of Red Rock Canyon. Rounds cost $55–119 depending on the season with very reasonable stay and play packages available. Twilight and reduced summer rates available. Reservations up to 4 months in advance, bookable online.

Badlands Golf Club

9119 Alta Drive, 1 800 675 1458 or 702 363 0754, badlandsgc.com
This 27-hole resort course designed by Johnny Miller is a true desert course experience. Rounds cost about $40 depending on season, if booked online. Twilight rates available. Reservations up to 60 days in advance.

BRITTIP

The Badlands is considered the golfing equivalent of an ultimate thrill ride. Carved through canyons, each of the 27 holes – the 3 nines called Desperado, Diablo and Outlaw – is known for dramatic shot values.

Bali Hai Golf Club

5160 Las Vegas Boulevard, 888 427 6678, bali-hai-golf-club.com
With 4,000 trees and 7acres/2.8ha of water hazards, this stunning tropical-themed course just south of the Mandalay Bay with a fabulous clubhouse was named

Bali Hai Golf Club

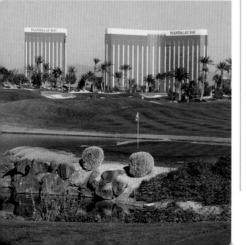

by *GolfWeek* as one of the 'Top 40 Resort Courses in America'. Rounds cost $89–325 depending on the season. Reservations up to 6 months in advance.

BRITTIP

The Bali Hai Golf Club is not only fantastically located just by the Four Seasons and Mandalay Bay hotels, but also has a divine restaurant, Cili, run by celebrity chef Wolfgang Puck.

Bear's Best Golf Club

11111 West Flamingo Avenue, 1 866 385 8500 or 702 804 8500, clubcorp.com
A collection of Jack Nicklaus's favourite 18 holes in a dramatic setting with a desert-style clubhouse. Rounds cost $55–125 booked online. Booking is up to 90 days in advance.

Callaway Golf Center/ Divine Nine

6730 Las Vegas Boulevard South at the corner with Sunset Road, 1 866 897 9500 or 702 896 4100, www.cgclv.com
Nine par-3 holes. Rounds cost $25–30. Driving range hits on to 12 greens with various hazards among grass and synthetic trees. Open 7.30am–9.30pm.

BRITTIP

The Callaway Golf Center is also home to the Danny Gans Junior Golf Academy that offers free golf instruction to children aged 11–16. Lessons cost $50 an hour with cheaper packages available.

Desert Pines Golf Club

3415 East Bonanza Road, 1 888 427 6678 or 702 388 4400, waltersgolf.com
Named after the thousands of mature pines that line the 18-hole public course, it also has covered hitting areas and an automatic ball delivery system. Just 15 minutes from the Strip, rounds cost $60–165 booked online. Reservations up to 6 months in advance.

Desert Rose Golf Club

5483 Club House Drive, 702 431 4653, desertrosegc.com
Palm trees, water and bunkers highlight the 18-hole county course, which has a wash between the holes. Rounds cost $49–69.

Desert Pines

Twilight rates available. Tee times 7 days in advance.

Las Vegas Golf Club

4300 West Washington Avenue, 702 646 3003, americangolf.com
The oldest golf course in Vegas, this 18-hole city course is also one of the busiest and a local favourite. Recently renovated, rounds cost $75–105. Reservations 60 days in advance.

BRITTIP
Don't forget your sun protection factor 30 and a hat when playing in summer. In autumn, take a sweater with you for late-afternoon games as it can get quite chilly when the sun goes down.

Las Vegas National Golf Club

1911 East Desert Inn Road, 1 866 731 4658 or 702 734 1796, lasvegasnational.com
An 18-hole public course less than 2mls/3km from the Strip. Rounds from $69. Twilight rates available. Floodlit driving range. Reservations 60 days in advance.

Las Vegas Paiute Golf Resort

10325 Nu-Wav Kaiv Boulevard, 20mls/32km north of city on the Snow Mountain exit near Mount Charleston, 1 800 711 2833 or 702 658 1400, lvpaiutegolf.com
Three 18-hole public courses designed by Pete Dye on the Las Vegas Paiute Tribe Indian Reservation. Green fees start at $59–199 depending on the season.

Twilight rates are available. Reservations up to 60 days in advance.

BRITTIP
The Snow Mountain course at Las Vegas Paiute Golf Resort is considered the best public access course in Las Vegas by *Golf Digest* magazine.

Painted Desert Golf Club

5555 Painted Mirage Drive, 1 800 468 7918 or 702 645 2880, painteddesertgc.com
This 18-hole public course was the first desert course in the area – expect holes shaped by desert landscape and cacti. Rounds cost $69–149 according to the season. Twilight rates are available. Reservations up to 60 days in advance.

Rhodes Ranch Golf Club

20 Rhodes Ranch Parkway, 1 888 311 8337 or 702 740 4114, rhodesranchgolf.com
This is a Ted Robinson-designed course tucked in the shadows of the Spring Mountain range, with tough, intriguing par-3s and numerous water features. Rounds cost from $45, varying according to the season. Reservations up to 60 days in advance.

Shadow Creek

3 Shadow Creek Drive, 1 888 778 3387 or 702 791 7161, shadowcreek.com
This 18-hole extraordinarily beautiful resort course is specifically for the MGM Mirage group, which includes the MGM Grand, the New York-New York, Bellagio, Treasure Island and the Mirage. One of the highest ranking courses in the world – accessible to MGM Mirage guests from a mere $500!

BRITTIP
When reserving your tee time, also check the cancellation policy and how much notice you need to give before forfeiting any money!

Badlands

Tournament Players Club (TPC) Las Vegas

9851 Canyon Run Drive, 1 888 321 5725 or 702 256 2500, tpc.com

This 18-hole resort course is the only public PGA course in Vegas and includes a meandering canyon. Rounds cost from $70 booked online depending on the season. Reservations up to a year in advance.

Golf courses north of Las Vegas

Aliante Golf Club

3100 East Elkhorn, North Las Vegas, 1 877 399 4888 or 702 399 4888, aliantegolf.com

Voted the Best New Course in Las Vegas by *Vegas Golfer Magazine*, this is a challenging tournament-quality course of 18 holes, with green fees running at $70–140 depending on the season.

Craig Ranch Golf Course

628 West Craig Road, 702 642 9700, http://thegolfcourses.net/golfcourses/NV/4123.htm

An 18-hole public course, with rates from $30, according to season. Reservations 7 days in advance.

North Las Vegas Golf Course

324 East Brooks Avenue, 702 633 1833, cityofnorthlasvegas.com

Nine-hole lighted city course (the ninth hole is on a hill and has a great view of Las Vegas) which is a bargain option for

Golf at Lake Tahoe

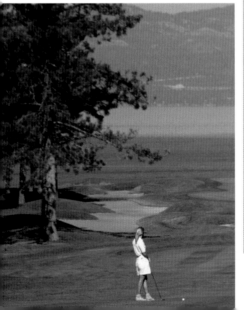

beginners. Rates from $13 for adults, according to season. Reservations 7 days in advance.

Golf course in Boulder City

Boulder City Golf Course

1 Clubhouse Drive, Boulder City, 702 293 9236, bouldercitygolf.com

This 18-hole city course near the Hoover Dam is shadowed by hundreds of large trees and has large greens, wide open fairways and two lakes. Rates from $50, depending on season, with twilight rates available. Reservations 1 week in advance.

Golf courses in Henderson and Green Valley

Black Mountain Golf and Country Club

500 Greenway Road, Henderson, 1 866 596 4833 or 702 565 7933, golfblackmountain.com

This 27-hole semi-private mature course catering to all levels in the Vegas Valley underwent a $2 million renovation in 2008. Rates from $75 depending on season, with twilight rates available. Tee times up to 4 days in advance.

DragonRidge Golf and Country Club

552 South Stephanie Street, Henderson, 1 877 855 1505 or 702 614 4444, dragonridgegolfclub.com

With great views of the Las Vegas Valley and bent-grass greens, this private 18-hole course will test even the best golfers and offers lessons from the Jack Nicklaus Academy. Cost $130–225. Reservations up to 30 days in advance.

The Legacy Golf Club

130 Par Excellence Drive, Henderson, 1 888 446 5358 or 702 897 2187, thelegacygc.com

This 18-hole resort Champion course is ranked by *Golf Digest* as one of the top 10 courses in Nevada. Cost $75–119 depending on the season with twilight rates available. Tee times up to 120 days in advance.

Reflection Bay Golf Club

75 MonteLago Boulevard, Lake Las Vegas, 702 740 4653, reservations 1 877 698 4653, lakelasvegas.com/golf_reflection.asp

Jack Nicklaus's prestigious course includes 5 holes played alongside 1.5mls/2.4km of

Lake Las Vegas shoreline, while other holes are decorated with water features. Green fees start from $150 but vary daily. Tee times up to 30 days in advance.

BRITTIP

Jack Nicklaus's nationally ranked Reflection Bay Golf Club is part of the exclusive MonteLago Lake Las Vegas Resort, which includes shops, restaurants, a casino and 2 waterfront hotels. For more details of the whole area, visit lakelasvegas.com.

Rio Secco Golf Club

2851 Grand Hills Drive, Henderson, 1 888 867 3226 or 702 777 2400, riosecco.net
This 18-hole resort course, which includes desert and canyon holes, is owned by the Rio All-Suite Hotel and is mostly for Rio's and Harrah's hotel guests. Rates from $60. Reservations 90 days in advance.

Wildhorse Golf Club

2100 Warm Springs Road, Henderson 702 434 9000, golfwildhorse.com
An 18-hole public course with rates from $62 that vary seasonally. Reservations up to 60 days in advance.

BRITTIP

The Wildhorse Golf Club's 18th hole is one of the most difficult in the Las Vegas Valley, thanks to the surrounding bunkers and 4 lakes!

Golf courses in Laughlin

Emerald River Country Club

1155 West Casino Drive, Laughlin, 702 298 0661
Demanding 18-hole resort course next to the Colorado including 5 holes along the river, 54 bunkers and plenty of changes in elevation. Rates from $79 through lasvegasgolf.com, depending on the season. Reservations up to 30 days in advance.

BRITTIP

The Emerald River Country Club has received a 3-star rating – the highest – from *Golf Digest*.

Mojave Resort Golf Club

9905 Aha Macav Parkway, Laughlin, 702 535 4653, mojaveresortgolfclub.com
An 18-hole course that hosts the Southern Nevada Golf Association Championships, this desert experience includes sand dunes and marshes and a GPS system on golf carts so you can't get lost! Rates are $54–94, depending on the season. Reservations 1 week in advance or 30 days with a credit card.

Golf courses in Summerlin and Pahrump

Sun City Summerlin Golf Club

0800 803 0758, golfsummerlin.com
Palm Valley: 9201 Del Webb Boulevard, 702 363 4373. 18-hole semi-private (preference is given to residents)
Highland Falls: 10201 Sun City Boulevard, 702 254 7010. 18-hole course
Eagle Crest: 2203 Thomas Ryan Boulevard, 702 240 1320. 18-hole course. Rates vary – check for web specials. Call for reservations

Willow Creek Golf Club

1500 Red Butte, Pahrump, 775 727 4653, lasvegasgolf.com
An 18-hole championship course surrounded by the Nopah and Spring Mountain ranges. Rates $20–60 depending on the season. Reservations 7 days in advance.

BRITTIP

The Willow Creek Golf Club – a pleasant 45-minute journey from Las Vegas – has a beautiful course famous for having the best rates in southern Nevada.

Reflection Bay

Spectator sports

Las Vegas has it all still to do in the sporting arena. It doesn't have a professional football or basketball team – both are university (or college, as they are called in America) teams, but sometimes NBA (basketball) friendlies are held during October, which are worth going to see.

The city is most famous for hosting major championship boxing events 2 or 3 times a year – and has done so since 1960, largely as a result of the fact that this was the only city in America where you could legally gamble on a winner. Most of the middle and heavyweight fights take place at Caesars Palace, the MGM Grand or the Mandalay Bay. Tickets start at $100 and rise to a steep $3,500 or more for ringside seats. The best place to do your homework is on ticketmaster.com.

American Football

Sam Boyd Stadium, Boulder Highway, 702 895 3900
The UNLV (University of Nevada, Las Vegas) team's season runs Sep–Dec. Tickets cost $15–25.

Baseball

Cashman Field, 850 Las Vegas Boulevard North at Washington Avenue, 702 386 7100
Home of the Las Vegas 51s, who play April–Sep as part of the Pacific Coast League.

Basketball

Hoop Hall Experience, Planet Hollywood Resort & Casino, 3667 Las Vegas Boulevard South, 702 785 5555, planethollywoodresort.com
Basketball fans can immerse themselves in interactive fun displays and exhibits in a celebration of the game and even give it their best shot at the 'dunk zone' to get in the mood.

Thomas & Mack Center, 4505 Maryland Parkway on the UNLV campus, 702 895 3761 or 1 866 388 3267 (box office), thomasandmack.com
The city's team is the UNLV Runnin' Rebels,

who play all their games here Nov–May. During October, NBA (National Basketball Association) teams sometimes play exhibition games here, and in 2007 the NBA's All-star Game was hosted here. There is a strong movement to move an NBA franchise to Sin City.

Ice hockey

Las Vegas Wranglers, 702 471 7825, lasvegaswranglers.com
Ice hockey is a big deal in America and desert-bound Las Vegas doesn't disappoint. For some fierce action try the local Wranglers' matches. Visit the website or phone for a schedule.

BRITTIP

For general sports events try UNLV Sports on 702 895 3761, unlvtickets.com.

Motor Sports

Las Vegas Motor Speedway, 7000 Las Vegas Boulevard North, 1 800 644 4444, lvms.com
Lying 17mls/27km north of the Strip, the 1,500acre/607ha speedway opened in 1996 at a cost of $200m and seats 107,000. Facilities include a 1.5ml/2.4km superspeedway, a 2.5ml/4km road course, a 0.5ml/0.8km dirt oval, drag strip, go-kart tracks and racing school. Check out Midnight Madness on Fridays and Saturdays for drag racing that starts at 10pm as part of the test-and-tune sessions that begin at 5pm. Phone ahead for schedules of upcoming events and tickets.

Wrestling

wwe.com
The city doesn't hold its own events, but does play host to several World Wrestling Federation and World Championship Wrestling events. Either check out the local paper when in town or look at the website in advance.

BRITTIP

Try Nevada Ticket Services on 702 597 1588 or lsvegas ticket.com to book anything from basketball to football, hockey, baseball, National Finals Rodeo, pro bull rides, Superbowl and Final Four.

Balloons over Laughlin

Major annual sporting events

March: NASCAR Winston Cup at the Las Vegas Motor Speedway, 1 800 644 4444

April: Big League Weekends (baseball) – Cashman Field Center, 702 386 7100; Spring Pro-Am Golf Tournament, 516 292 4055

September: NCAA College Football – UNLV Rebels – 1 866 459 9233; Pro-Am Golf Tournament – Sahara Country Club, 1 800 332 8776

October: Ice hockey season – a schedule is available in August for the Thomas and Mack Center, 702 895 3761, thomasandmack.com; Las Vegas Invitational PGA Golf Tournament – buy tickets from the Thomas and Mack Center; US Open of Supercross sees top supercross riders racing in and around the hotels on the strip, 1 866 459 9233; Professional Bull Riders meet for a 4-day competition at the Thomas and Mack Center

December: The first week kicks off with the Las Vegas Marathon which starts in front of Mandalay Bay, 702 731 1052; National Finals Rodeo at the Thomas and Mack Center, 702 895 3761; Las Vegas Bowl Collegiate Football Game at Sam Boyd Silver Bowl, 702 895 3761

For other events visit http://las.vegas.eventguide.com. The Event Channel has tickets for many of the above sporting events, 1 866 459 9233, http://tickets.eventchannel.net

Extreme sports

There are many ways to have fun in Las Vegas and if you are looking for extreme thrills, then you can do anything from racing at the Speedway to skydiving.

Laser Quest

7361 West Lake Mead Boulevard, Suite 100, 702 243 8881, laserquest.com
You wear a laser-sensing vest and shoot it out with other laser-wielding players in a maze of corners, turns, walkways and mirrored walls. Great for children up to the age of 80!

BRITTIP

Going to fight it out at Laser Quest? Remember that lasers are just like light beams and can ricochet off reflective spots throughout the Quest – a pretty neat way to do away with your opponents (or be done away with)!

Open: Mon–Thurs 2–9pm; Fri 2–11pm; Sat noon–11pm; Sun noon–6pm

Cost: Flat rate of $8 per person for 20 minutes of play. Book in advance to avoid the queue

Race Car Tours

The can mean anything from family fun in the Mini Grand Prix to the experience of riding or driving a racing car at high speed on the Las Vegas Motor Speedway, home to the city's NASCAR events and drag races.

Las Vegas Mini Grand Prix

1401 North Rainbow Boulevard, 702 259 7000, lvmgp.com
Take Exit 82a off US 95 for the family ride of a lifetime on sprint cars, go-karts and kiddie karts and adults' Grand Prix cars. This place also offers fairground style rides guaranteed to get little ones' hearts pumping. Try the new dip and glide Dive Bomber, fly and spin on the Tornado Twister and take a trip on the Dragon Roller Coaster. There is also a games arcade and snack bar.

Open: Sun–Thurs 10am–10pm; Fri–Sat 10am–11pm except Christmas Day and depending on the weather

Cost: $6.50 per ticket or $30 for 5. Cars available for from 4- to over 16-year-olds

Mario Andretti Racing School

1 877 722 3527 or 702 651 6317, andrettiracing.com
Billed as the World's Fastest Racing Experience, hold onto your seat as for $99 you race 3 laps as a passenger in a Champ Ride as a professional racing driver reaches speeds of up to 180mph/290kph. The Qualifier allows you to get behind the wheel of a full-sized,

Sam Boyd Stadium

600HP racing car yourself, where after minimal instruction you'll reach speeds of up to 150mph/241kph at a cost of $325. These costs reflect a 25% online discount.

Richard Petty Driving Experience

7000 North Las Vegas Boulevard, 800 BE PETTY
This offers a similar experience of driving a racing car at high speed (140mph/225kph) for $99–3,000. Try to go on a weekday or early at the weekend to avoid the crowds. If you're too nervous to drive, 'Ride Along' at 165mph/266kph!

Rocks & Ropes

Nevada Climbing Centers, 3065 East Patrick Lane, Suite 4, 702 898 8192, rocksandropes.com
This indoor climbing facility has more than 7,000ft²/650m² of sculpted and textured walls for climbing, 30ft/9m ceilings, top rope and lead climbing and a mega-cave with a leadable 40ft/12m roof so people can learn everything they need to know to go rock climbing for real!

Cost: $12 adults per day, $9 for children under 12, $12 first-time instruction (ages 12 and up), $6 equipment rental

Xtreme Zone

Adventuredome Theme Park, Circus Circus, 702 794 3939, adventuredome.com
A combination of rock climbing and aerial bungee jumping creates an interactive experience with multiple difficulty levels. The Zone's rock-climbing attraction combines traditional harnesses and handholds with cutting-edge belay technology to make it as safe as possible. The aerial trampoline combines a standard trampoline with a hydraulic system and bungee cords so you can climb up to 20ft/6m and then flip and spin yourself back and forth. You must weigh 40–265lb/18–120kg to climb the wall and 30–220lb/13.5–100kg to experience the bungee.

Skydiving

Skydiving has become big in Las Vegas and can be done indoors or outdoors, in tandem or solo, for those who dare.

Flyaway Indoor Skydiving

200 Convention Center Drive, 702 731 4768, vegasindoorskydiving.com
Learn how to fly in Vegas's only indoor skydiving simulator, where the vertical wind tunnel allows you to beat gravity and fly!

First-time flyers are given a 20-minute class in safety and body-control techniques. Experienced skydivers can also get valuable 'air' time to improve their skills without having to pack a rig and wait for the right weather. Video coaching programmes are also available in which your air tunnel flight is recorded to help you improve your style.

Open: Daily 9.45am–8pm. Classes every half hour from 11am to an hour before closing

Cost: $75 for single flight, $20.95 for same day repeat flight, $200 for 5 flights and $250 for learn-to-fly coaching package including 5 flights, video services and personalised coaching

Las Vegas Skydiving Center

Just behind the Goldstrike Hotel at Jean airport, 1 866 688 2378 or 702 997 4282 (south-west of Las Vegas)
Take a tandem skydive after a 30-minute lesson for $194.77 (including complimentary shuttle from the Strip). Daily 7.30, 10am and 12 noon; jumps that can be captured on camera or video for an extra fee, are by appointment only (minimum age 18).

Skydive Las Vegas

Boulder City Airport, 1401 Airport Road, Boulder City (near Hoover Dam), 702 759 3483, skydivelasvegas.com
You freefall for 45 seconds before enjoying a 7-minute parachute ride in a tandem jump. By appointment only.

Vegas Extreme Skydiving

23600 S Las Vegas Blvd, 702 303 3914, vegasextremeskydiving.com
View the Las Vegas strip from 2mls/3km up with the thrill of descending at 120mph/193kph before putting on the air brakes to savour views over the Hoover Dam, Lake Mead and the Colorado River. Vegas Extreme Skydiving offers tandem dives for first-time jumpers and solo dives for the experienced.

Open: By reservation only

Cost: From $199 for a tandem sky dive with instruction. Video and photographic services available

BRITTIP

Dress the part for your indoor skydive – make sure you're in comfy clothes with socks and trainers.

13 GETTING THERE

The tour operators, doing it your own way and specialist holiday planners

Of course, with Las Vegas your dream destination, you still have to get there. You have a lot of choices. After all, if you are going to fly across an entire ocean and most of a continent to get there, you might as well make it worth the trip! Do you use the city as a fantastically cheap base for visiting all the natural wonders on its doorstep? Maybe you head off on a fly-drive tour; or even start in Los Angeles and San Francisco and take in all the wonderful places that you can reasonably visit in the amount of time available to you?

Then there are the other factors, like how many of you are travelling, or whether you will be visiting friends in, say, San Diego or Phoenix. In that case you could take advantage of the incredibly cheap offers to Las Vegas that are advertised in the local papers and travel from there. If you have children and teenagers in your party, you'll probably be best with an airline/tour operator that caters well for the family market. You may even want to do a part fly-drive and add on a ranch or golfing holiday or an adventure trek.

The visitor figures show that Brits tend either to go on a long-weekend package to Las Vegas or do a combination of any of the above. It is for this reason that if you have ever picked up a brochure on visiting Las Vegas and California there seems to be so much information and so many options to wade through: multi-centre packages, fly-drives, coach tours, open-jaw flights (see page 246) and so on. It will take you some time to make sense of one brochure, let alone compare a few to see what suits you best. Then there is the other option – to organise your trip totally independently.

BRITTIP

When shopping around for flight prices, make sure the figure you are given includes all taxes and airport fees to make a proper comparison.

To try to make life easier, I've tried to outline the options available, what to look for and what to ask for.

Highway 50

HWY
50
The loneliest Road in America

Specialist tour operators

These are not your local travel agents, but those who specialise in organising holidays to Nevada and California and produce a brochure to display their products. This is important because Las Vegas in particular has quirks all of its own and someone with little local knowledge is unlikely to provide you with the best deals or choice of options.

What's good about the specialist North American tour operators is that the big outfits have massive buying power and so can offer some of the best prices available for both hotels and car-hire services. In many cases you can go for a 'land-only' deal for a nominal charge, which gives you the option to arrange your own flights through some of the cheap flight brokers who advertise in the weekend national newspapers (more about that in the independent travel section, page 253). Most do not advertise this, though, so you will have to ask.

All the main specialist North American operators provide tailor-made packages, which mean that you can take advantage of any special deals and arrangements they may have with, for instance, hotels, theme parks and local airline companies offering scenic flights around the Grand Canyon area and San Francisco.

The bigger guys – such as Virgin Holidays, Kuoni, Jetlife, Premier Holidays, Thomas Cook and Gold Medal – can pack in a lot of added-value extras, especially in these competitive, 'credit crunch' times. You can get room upgrades for honeymoon and anniversary holiday-makers, free transfers to the hotel (rarely part of a North American package), free accommodation and/or free meals for children, extra nights free, free flights to London from regional airports and so on. You may also like to know that out of the large tour companies operating in North America, Virgin Holidays, Kuoni, Travelsphere, Jetsave and

Page & Moy did particularly well in the 'would you recommend this tour operator to a friend?' stakes as part of a *Which?* tour operator survey.

Local knowledge

Big is not always best in this market, as good knowledge of the location is very important, along with the operator's determination to provide you with what is best for you (which may involve making alternative suggestions to your own best-laid plans) and offer a generally good level of service. Smaller outfits such as Just America (justamerica.co.uk) do not claim to be the cheapest, but with a high level of return custom and recommendation-to-friends business, they know their emphasis on getting things right for a slightly higher cost means all the difference between an okay holiday and a fantastic one. Their policy is based on not packing too much into one trip so that you travel to see destinations, not see destinations as you travel. Overall, it makes them very good value for money.

Another smaller UK operator, Funway Holidays (funwayholidays.co.uk), works alongside United Vacations, which sends more than one million people a year to Las Vegas, so they have tremendously good buying power and very good access to hotels in Las Vegas. More than 50 hotels are featured in the brochure (the average tends to be about 10 to 15), including all the recently opened resorts such as The Encore.

In addition, Funway's parent company is one of the largest in America, meaning they are likely to be able to get you into top resort-hotels when other tour operators may not – with the best choice and competitive rates and a whole raft of extras including discount vouchers. Overall, it makes them one of the best operators to Las Vegas. They also have some great arrangements for self-drive tours.

What to look for

Using a tour operator is great if you want to get everything sewn up before you go, but remember they're in business to make money and, while their brochures may be in one sense accurate, not all of them will point out any negatives. Also, it is useful to bear in mind that even if something is not included in the brochure, such as open-jaw tickets (see page 246) or air passes (see page 248), you should always ask your preferred operator if they can arrange those for you.

McCarran International airport

Arches National Park

The following sections will show you how to take the good, watch out for the bad and reject the downright ugly that tour operators have to offer.

Scheduled flights

Charter services to Las Vegas come and go – and are seasonal at best, so it really is down to scheduled flights. In the case of America generally, and Las Vegas in particular, this is a good thing as most of the airlines fly every day to a whole range of locations in North America – many at easy-to-catch times of the day – and from a range of regional airports in the UK.

Given the way most Brits tend to move around Nevada, Arizona and California during a holiday to the region, this provides the essential flexibility required when organising a trip. What tends to follow on from scheduled services is the ability to make a stop on the way to your final destination (stopover); fly into one city and out from another (open-jaw) and even fly between cities (using multi-centre packages or air-pass vouchers). And if you tend to do a lot of long-haul travelling, you can even arrange it so that you get frequent-flyer points. Most of the operators offer a minimum of 3 airline prices, some up to 6, except for airline-run operators, such as American Holiday (American Airlines); NorthWest Airlines; United Vacations (United Airlines) and Virgin.

Assessing flight choices

Flights to Las Vegas from Britain have multiplied at a happy rate. Direct service is with Virgin via London or Manchester, and in October 2009, a daily British Airways (BA) flight was added, from London Heathrow. Competition for passengers, though, has made going indirect through hubs much cheaper and you can save hundreds of pounds by waiting for change-overs in airports.

Indirect service is available through a host of airlines, including a partnership of British Airways/USAir, plus Continental, BMI, Virgin, American and United, although recently KLM Royal Dutch/NorthWest has consistently been having the lowest fares, with their London-Amsterdam-Minneapolis-Las Vegas route generally much cheaper than others, although you will spend at least 7 extra hours travelling.

So when comparing prices for flights, the first thing you need to look for is whether you are getting a direct flight with Virgin or BA or whether you are going via a hub city – which you will do with any of the other carriers – and how much longer that will add on to your travel time. When weighing up cost differences, bear in mind that flying into a hub city tends to involve changing planes to a less comfortable domestic plane, where you will also be charged for your drinks.

If you do opt to use a non-direct service, also remember that some tickets may provide better stopovers than others, which will make arranging a decent multi-centre deal easier.

The next thing is to take into consideration any differences between flying at the weekend or midweek – there is normally a surcharge for Friday and Saturday flights.

Finally, always ensure the price you are quoted includes all airport taxes and any

The Sphinx at the Luxor

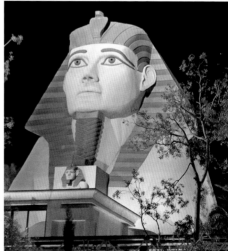

Frequent-flyer points

Did you know that every time you fly you could be clocking up frequent-flyer mileage points that will eventually give you free air travel or other perks such as last-minute availability, lounge access and free upgrades or discounts off attractions and excursions in the USA? Very often your holiday booking does give you free air miles, but you may not know about it. Even if you do not claim the benefits, your travel agent still has the right to do so and some like to keep this nice little perk under their hats! So, before you go on holiday, register with the airline for their loyalty scheme and keep your booking passes to prove that the flights were taken. Discounted flights may not qualify, but it's always worth checking. A useful site to browse is frequentflier.com which has links to many airlines.

Many of the North American specialists will automatically offer frequent-flyer points on American Airlines flights, though you may have to pay an additional fee for the privilege of collecting them. Having said that, AA give you one Advantage mile for every mile you fly, which is over 10,000 if you're flying from London to Los Angeles and back – enough to earn you one free ticket to certain European destinations (aa.com).

If you have a family, it is a good idea to register the whole family in the scheme so each person can build up their points. Some schemes, such as Virgin's Flying Club Frequent Flyer (0844 412 2414), expect their economy-class passengers to complete 3 return economy flights before qualifying, though upper class or premium economy passengers qualify immediately. British Airways offer both air miles – 1 mile per every mile flown – and travel points, the latter granting lounge facilities and even free travel insurance with enough credits. As most major airlines are members of alliances, you can collect air miles on different airlines, making it all the quicker to gain miles.

When arranging to join a frequent-flyer programme, ask if there is a bonus for joining at that particular time as different airlines offer bonuses. For instance, not so long ago Virgin was offering a bonus of 2,000 points on joining and Continental a special activation bonus of a whopping 5,000 miles when you take your first Continental Airlines holiday. The scheme offers free upgrades and free tickets.

Also, for those who have an American Express card, they have an excellent travel site (membershiprewards.com) where you can book everything you need, get frequent travel points for Amex and double up frequent flyer points for the airlines and hotels you use. These transcontinental trips can add up quickly when you are dipping twice.

Finally, following the lead of a partnership between MGM Mirage and American, most major resorts have teamed up with one airline's frequent-flyer programme or other to get points bonuses. So any time you spend money at the hotel you can earn even more points, or use your points for free shows, tours, or what have you.

non-negotiable fees – they can amount to a fair bit and you don't want those kinds of surprises!

Open-jaw flights

This means flying into one city and out from another. It's usually very simple to work out the cost – in most cases, you add the cost of flying to one destination to the cost of flying to the other, divide by two

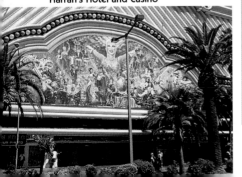

Harrah's Hotel and Casino

and add £1. Open-jaw flights mean you don't have to backtrack and can save you quite a lot of money on a touring trip. Very few operators advertise open-jaw so you will have to ask whether it can be arranged or shop around.

BRITTIP

Always check around for best flight prices before booking, as there may be good deals on offer. Check prices online at comparison sites such as cheapflights.co.uk and travelsupermarket.com.

Multi-centre packages

Fly into one city, look around, fly on to another, look around, fly on to another, look around and then fly home. This kind of package tends to be one of the most popular in the Las Vegas/California holiday market with the trio of Las Vegas, Los Angeles and San Francisco as the leading lights. It's a good idea if you don't want to spend time driving, or don't have enough time to drive, between all the main places you want to see, but it is a more expensive option, generally, than using your full quota of stopovers, or the open-jaw system.

Stopovers

The alternative to the above is to use the stopover system whereby you break your journey at various points. Most of the airlines offer this service, with the first stopover usually free and subsequent stopovers (up to a maximum of 3) being charged at around £70 a stop. Some airlines now offer 2 free stopovers.

BRITTIP

Do bear in mind that if you opt for the direct Virgin or British Airways flight there will be no stopovers to take advantage of.

If you want to use this system, you have to ensure that the route you are booking is the correct one for you as the first, free, stopover is usually limited to the 'gateway' city – the first place where the plane lands in the United States and where you'll go through American immigration. Watch this, as many of the American airlines use 'hub' cities as their gateway cities, such as Detroit or Minneapolis in the case of NorthWest Airlines, and you may not consider Delta's hub cities of Atlanta or Cincinatti to be as exciting a stopover point as New York or Los Angeles, for instance. As NorthWest is now allied with KLM, it may pay to route your trip via Amsterdam so that you get a more interesting 'gateway' city.

BRITTIP

To make best use of your free stopover, check your 'gateway' city is a reasonable destination, such as New York or Chicago, rather than Cincinatti or Atlanta!

Extra stops

These are similar to stopovers, except you'll pay an extra fee, usually £70. If you want to fly to more than one place not covered by your free stopover allowance, or if the place you want to go to isn't on the route, go for an air pass (see page 248).

BRITTIP

When booking flights, be sure to claim your free air miles or find out about the airline's loyalty scheme before you go, to be on track for free air travel or other benefits such as priority booking, lounge facilities and upgrades.

Child and youth discounts

Most airlines give child discounts (ages 2–11), usually at 50% off the published price during mid and low seasons and at 40% during peak season. The peak season does vary a little but a rough guide is July–August and the Christmas period around 15–27 December. Very few airlines offer youth discounts for 12- to 16-year-olds (a paltry 10%, which could be matched by shopping around the flight shops) but your best bets are tour operators who use United Airlines and Virgin.

Infant fares

The old days of tour operators publishing very cheap infant fares, but then adding on up to £70 of taxes are, thankfully, mostly gone, though some still continue this practice. Even BA charge £30 for infants with £70 tax – though £100 is a good fully inclusive price these days. Do check that the price you have been quoted includes all taxes.

Travelling with children

One point to stress is that many airline crews are being quite strict with child passengers. There have been numerous instances in recent years of children not being allowed to travel because of bad behaviour. It is quite a long trip, so make sure you bring enough things to keep your children merrily occupied.

Las Vegas from the air

Regional departures

More and more airlines are running routes directly from regional airports in the UK to Las Vegas and California, but in most cases you will have to pay a supplement to fly to London (from Newcastle or Glasgow, for example, this is around £60). However, United Vacations and US Airtours offer free connections from many regional UK airports, and Kuoni offers free flights in connection with transatlantic BA and United Airlines flights.

Air passes

If you plan to visit more than the one city covered by your free stopover or, for whatever reason, are likely to make quite a few flights between certain destinations, an air pass is the way to go. But you must buy before you go as North American residents are not permitted to buy air passes, so they won't be available once you get to the US.

Smoking

Virgin and most of the American airlines have a total non-smoking policy on their transatlantic flights; in fact, smoking is banned by law on all flights in US airspace, as it is on transatlantic flights, so you won't be smoking on your journey.

Code share

Many airlines enter into alliances with each other to share routes, which can offer you more choice of routes and fares. It means that your flight is marketed by one airline, with the airline's flight number, but when you board you find the service is operated by a different airline. Some tour operators will inform you in advance, but they may not always know as these alliances are constantly changing. Be careful of this if you have a particular dislike for one airline or know that you definitely want to fly with a certain company. A *Which?* survey of airlines found that Virgin was among the most highly rated, yet it currently has a code-share alliance with Continental, who came pretty near the bottom of the same report.

Circus Circus is popular with families

Kids stay free

Many operators offer this as an extra, but it is standard policy at many hotels to allow children to stay free in the same room as an adult. If you're not being offered this as an option, go elsewhere!

Length and type of visit

Fly-drive and tailor-made tours

Tailor-made tours are useful as there are so many options it would be daft for any tour company to force people into taking one particular tour. Fly-drives are popular and often combine LA and/or Phoenix with Las Vegas. Chapter 15 The Grand Canyon and Surroundings gives a good insight into great places to visit within easy striking distance of Las Vegas.

Coach and Tauck tours

If you don't want to worry about car hire, driving and all the other arrangements you will need to make, and you don't mind a coach-load of people crowding into an attraction at the same time as you, then this could be the way to go. Coach tours are not necessarily all-inclusive, though, and may not include meals so that you have the option of choosing where to eat.

Tauck tours are the posher version and usually include everything. They are run by an American company, and you will be greeted and treated as an individual, while the tours themselves tend to be shorter so you have more time to relax and explore sights by yourself. In addition, you are put up in first-class hotels with character.

⊞ BRITTIP

Don't try to see too much in too short a space of time – you don't want to spend your whole holiday driving and you may even want to leave time for an adventure tour or ranch holiday.

Extras

Grand Canyon flights

One of the added bonuses of visiting Las Vegas is that you can experience the amazing scenery of Arizona's Canyonlands, plus other natural wonders Bryce Canyon and Zion Park, without the long drive. A whole host of scenic flight operators work out of Las Vegas (details in Chapter 11 Outdoor Adventure), but if you want to make sure of your seat or tie up all loose ends before you go, many of the tour operators are offering these flights. Again, ask even if they're not advertised as they may be able to arrange a scenic flight for you.

Show tickets

You can buy these in advance to ensure you get a seat, but don't overdo it as you may miss out on cheap deals locally.

BRITTIP

If you are flexible and don't mind waiting until the last minute, you can save lots of money on show tickets. There are many half-price ticket stands along the Strip and Fremont Street and shows that aren't overbooked will sell tickets through these dealers at cut rates to put bums on seats. You can often get tickets for shows at 50% off by buying a ticket on the day of performance from one of these shops. But sorry, this won't do for hard to find tickets, so Cirque extravaganzas are rarely available this way.

Hotel vouchers

The 3 basic kinds of hotel vouchers are the Liberty and TourAmerica Hotel Passes and the North American Guestcheque. In all cases you buy vouchers at a certain price in advance that are valid for one night at a participating hotel – usually a chain hotel. You can book the hotel in advance and the room will accommodate up to 4 people. It can be a very good way of planning your holiday budget and pre-paying as far as possible. But one major drawback is that if you buy more than you need, there is usually a charge for redeeming any unused vouchers. Often it amounts to the value of one voucher and in some cases it can be one voucher plus an administrative charge of £25.

Another drawback is that you do not benefit from any promotions that participating hotels and motels may run locally. And do bear in mind that these chain hotels don't have much character and some may even seem a little soulless.

- Purchasing the vouchers does not automatically give you the right of accommodation, so it is always best to book as far in advance as possible, especially if you intend to travel in the peak seasons.

The Stratocoaster

- If you intend to arrive after 4pm, you will need a credit card to guarantee your reservation. If it is a hotel/motel in a particularly busy area, such as one of the major sights that is not near a big town or city, I'd recommend you ask them to send or fax the confirmation of your reservation.

- There are often many hotels of the same chain in the same town, so it is best to make a note of the full address so you go to the right one!

BRITTIP

To save money on everything from attractions to shows to wedding packages visit lasvegas-nv.com/las-vegas-coupons.htm.

Las Vegas showgirls

The American way

Motorbike hire

Okay, so you fancy yourself as a modern-day cowboy enjoying the ultimate touring experience of travelling along those wide-open roads on anything from a Harley Davidson Electra Glide to a Fat Boy or Road King. You can do this from LA and Las Vegas, but it'll be a lot more expensive than a car. The few operators that offer this include American Holidays and Jetlife.

Amtrak and Greyhound

Greyhound's Discovery Pass (greyhound.com) allows you to go where you want, when you want, travelling by coach day or night. It costs $199 for 7 days, $299 for 15 days, $399 for 30 days and a bargain $499 for 60 days. Greyhound will take you from Los Angeles to Las Vegas, for around $60 each way. The trip takes 5–7 hours. Amtrak rail passes start from $389 adults, $194 children (2–15 years) for 15 days; $579 adults, $289.50 children for 30 days and $749 adults, $374.50 children for 45 days. Amtrak covers all the major destinations and sights in California. Few tour operators advertise Amtrak travel, but others may arrange it for you if you ask. Take a look at amtrak.com.

BRITTIP

Hotel prices in America are for accommodation only and do not include breakfast.

Dirty South tour bus

Other things you need to know

The seasons

There are 4: low or off-peak, low shoulder, high shoulder and peak. Basically, the most expensive times to travel are Christmas, July, August, Easter and during the American bank holidays: President's Day (George Washington's birthday) – the third Monday in February; Memorial Day – the last Monday in May and the official start of the summer season; Independence Day – 4 July (in the middle of the high season); Labor Day – the first Monday in September and last holiday of summer; and Thanksgiving – always the fourth Thursday in November.

Low or off-peak season tends to be November, then January to the end of March excluding the bank holidays and Easter. May, June and October are low shoulder and all other times are high shoulder.

Best times to travel

Without a doubt, Monday to Thursday. Flights are cheaper, airports less crowded for departure and arrival, and hotels in Las Vegas, in particular, are far less busy. The very best days to arrive in Las Vegas are Tuesday to Thursday morning.

A–Z of specialist tour operators

visitlasvegas.co.uk

American Holidays

02890 511800, americanholidays.com
A Belfast-based operator with some excellent fly-drive packages.

American Sky

0870 9040 920, americansky.com
Tailor-made luxury holidays – everything from fly-drive to adventure tours.

Archers Direct

0870 460 3898, archersdirect.co.uk
Packages to California and Las Vegas that are very busy indeed.

Bon Voyage

0800 316 3012, bon-voyage.co.uk
One of the bigger operators, but surprisingly, offers very few extras.

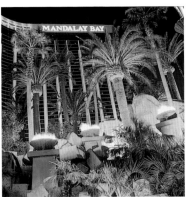

The tropical Mandalay Bay

British Airways Holidays

0870 243 3406, britishairwaysholidays.com
With the new BA flight launched in
October 2009, this operator should be
offering competitive direct deals.

Expedia

0871 226 0808, expedia.co.uk
Popular online travel agent offering cheap
flights, holidays, hotels and car hire.

Flight Centre

0870 499 0040, flightcentre.co.uk
With branches around the country, Flight
Centre is a travel agent offering all aspects
of a holiday at 'unbeatable prices'.

Funway

0844 557 0627, funwayholidays.co.uk
Funway offers the following at certain
hotels: free meals and breakfasts for
children, free children's clubs, free nights,
free shuttle bus service. Plus with every
booking: fun books, packed with money-
saving deals on sightseeing trips,
attractions, shows, shopping and dining;
free reduced rate phone card; free Rand
McNally Travel Planner and VIP shopping
discount card in conjunction with the Shop
America Alliance. Funway's parent
company has its own car rental and
sightseeing options that can be reserved
via its website.

Jetlife

0871 902 7877, jetlife.co.uk
Shop America discounts on stores offered
with every booking.

Jetset

08700 555 747, jetsetholidays.co.uk
Established operator offering tailor-made
packages with free accommodation for
children at certain hotels, Greyhound
Ameripass and Air Passes.

Just America

08448 806 802, justamerica.co.uk
Has the best value, easiest-to-use
arrangements for car hire. Also specialises
in a highly personalised, tailor-made
service.

Kuoni

01306 747002 (reservations), 0870 990
9905 (brochures), kuoni.co.uk
One of the UK's best long-haul tour
operators, Kuoni can offer extra nights free,
room upgrades, free sports, meals and
drinks and food discounts. There are also
special deals for honeymooners and those
celebrating silver or golden wedding
anniversaries (though you'll have to take a
copy of your marriage certificate with you!).

Lastminute.com

0871 222 5953, lastminute.com
Still one of the most popular sites for those
who are looking for a last-minute bargain –
offers everything from holidays to discount
deals in restaurants.

North America Travel Service

0845 122 8899,
northamericatravelservice.co.uk
Specialises in fly-drives but offers very little
information about flights and availability of
open-jaw and stopovers. Also offers some
free night deals at certain hotels, and has
separate brochures for coach, Tauck and
adventure tours.

Motorbikes in Laughlin

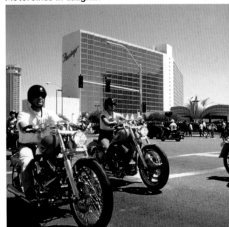

Premier Holidays

08444 937 531, premierholidays.co.uk
Premier Plus offers include extra nights free at certain hotels, free transport to attractions, breakfasts, upgrades for honeymooners, tea and coffee and use of health clubs.

Thomas Cook Signature

0870 443 4453, tcsignature.com
This is the only company offering chartered flights direct to Las Vegas.

Trailfinders

0845 058 5858, trailfinders.co.uk
The UK's largest independent travel agent, this is renowned for tailor-made itineraries and a good selection of discounted flights. One of the few tour operators still offering Amtrak passes.

United Vacations

0844 449 0033, unitedvacations.co.uk
No regional departures, unless you fly via Amsterdam, but free connecting flights from regional airports during off-peak times. Books of vouchers for cheaper dining and attraction entrance fees.

Virgin Holidays

0844 557 5825, virginholidays.co.uk
Virgin offer free kids' funpacks on flights, free breakfasts, free meals for children and extras for honeymoons and anniversaries at certain hotels. Don't forget to join the frequent-flyer programme if you qualify.

BRITTIP

To cut holiday planning call costs in the UK go to saynoto 0870.com to check if companies have a cheaper alternative local number.

Plus $50 discount at Virgin Megastores and better deals for single parents.

Escorted tour companies

Goldmedal

01772 251133, goldmedal.co.uk
Efficient and friendly large tour operator offering escorted and tailor-made holidays around the world.

Jetsave

0870 160 7324, jetsave.com
Jetsave give generous discounts for groups of 15 or more, plus free places depending on the number travelling. No supplements for single travellers if prepared to share a room.

Page & Moy

0800 567 7400, pageandmoy.com
Consistently rated highly by repeat-visit travellers.

Travelsphere

0800 567 7372, travelsphere.co.uk
National Express pick-ups to point of departure for £15–20; savings on hotel airports and regional departures.

You'll need formal clothes for restaurants such as Joël Robuchon

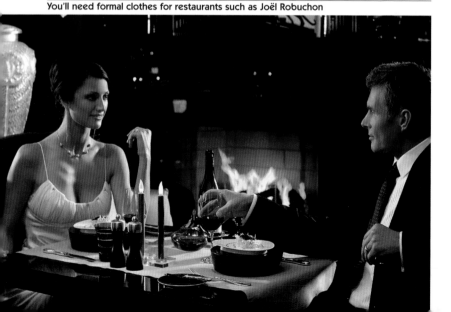

Airports

McCarran International airport

5757 Wayne Newton Boulevard, 702 261 5211, mccarran.com

Just 1ml/1.6km from the Strip and 5mls/8km from downtown, McCarran International airport is one of the slickest, most modern and easy-to-use airports in America. In a passenger survey of 36 major airports – which looked at speed of baggage delivery, ease of reaching gates, ground transport, cleanliness, quality of restaurants, attractiveness, ease of parking and following signs – McCarran came 6th.

The airport was ranked the 15th busiest airport in the world in 2008 and deals with over 800 flights a day and around 44 million passengers a year. The latest runway – opened recently at a cost of $80.5m – has given the airport the capacity to handle 60 million passengers a year. It has direct flights to 62 US airports and 9 international destinations and more than 5,000 cars a day use the parking facilities. It has more than 50 shops and nearly 30 restaurant, lounges and snack bars and more than 1,300 slot machines to start your gambling on arrival!

Like many other aspects of life in Las Vegas, the airport has the very latest technology. There is no need for departing passengers with tickets to go to ticket counters inside the terminals – they can check in their luggage at the ticketing/departure kerb. It is the first airport in America to use Common Use Terminal Equipment (CUTE). This allows airlines to use any gate as needed, which creates more efficient scheduling of gates and faster boarding for passengers. In addition, all facilities are accessible to the disabled and amplified phone sets are dotted throughout the terminal.

Los Angeles International airport

1 World Way, Los Angeles, CA 90045, 310 646 5252, www.airport-la.com

If you are planning a touring holiday or perhaps an open-jaw flight, you may want to come into or out of Los Angeles airport, the fourth busiest airport in the world with all the best facilities.

Independent booking

There may be many different reasons why you want to organise all or part of your trip independently. Some people (jammy dodgers, I call them!) fly to San Francisco or Los Angeles to visit friends and then decide to go off to Las Vegas and other parts of California or Arizona on trips. But by nature we Brits are an independent lot and one of the most appealing ideas for us is just to fly to the west coast of America and hit the open road. Whatever the reason, the following tips will help you to save money in all the right places so you have more to spend on enjoying the sights and buying those essential pairs of trainers, etc!

Flights

Competition in the transatlantic flight market is fierce, which is good news for us the customers. It also means that it makes sense to shop around for the best deal you can get. I recommend that you read the tour operators section (see pages 244–252) first, so you can acquaint yourself

The tram station at the new City Center

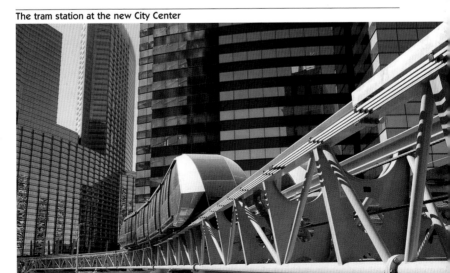

with all the terms and deals available.

Once you have worked out what your priorities are, then you have a pretty good chance of beating the prices quoted in the brochures by phoning round the transatlantic flight bookers that advertise in the weekend newspapers – *The Sunday Times* is particularly good. Remember, too, that the tour operators specialising in the North American market also have access to deals being offered by the airlines, so can often beat their own published prices! Low and low-shoulder seasons (see page 250) are particularly good for brilliant deals, such as flights to Las Vegas or Los Angeles for around £300 or even 5-night packages from £399.

You can even go for a totally no-frills, mega-cheap flight with 'consolidated' fares. These are the old-style bucket-shop fares which have now been legalised. The travel agent negotiates deals on your part, so you get very cheap fares and they're happy, too, as they earn better commission rates. The main restriction with these fares is that you can only use one airline and sometimes it may involve flying via that airline's 'home' country, for instance, somewhere in Europe. Also you won't get free or extra stopovers, but you can get around this by buying air passes for internal flights (see page 248). These air passes are not available in the States so you need to buy them before you go.

Hotels

If you're happy touring around Nevada, Arizona and California staying in the rather soulless chains such as Days Inn, Ramada and so on, you could take advantage of many of the special deals

Flying over LA International

that are advertised in local papers and find a room on an ad hoc basis. Generally this is no problem at all in cities and towns, but it may be worth booking a few days in advance for rooms at major sightseeing destinations, such as the Grand Canyon or Furnace Creek in Death Valley. Even if you'd prefer accommodation with a little more character, you can still find cheap deals through agents once you are in America (see opposite).

Las Vegas is one of the weirdest cities on earth for hotel prices. In most cities around the world, hotels tend to be busy during the week and offer incentives to fill their rooms at weekends. With Las Vegas, the reverse is true. So many Americans from Salt Lake City to Phoenix and Los Angeles use Las Vegas as a weekend destination that occupancy rates are a staggering 96% on Friday and Saturday nights (even with around 155,000 rooms to fill).

On top of that, the city hosts huge conventions and special events such as rodeos and prize fights that tie up hotels, restaurants, transportation, showrooms and traffic for a week at a time. For these reasons, although Las Vegas hotels have their rack (standard) room rates, prices vary wildly above or below that rate according to how busy it is and how much they think they can get away with! Having said that, the price of accommodation is probably cheaper than anywhere else in North America and given the class and quality of facilities on offer, you can live like a king or queen very cheaply at top resorts in Las Vegas.

McCarran International

BRITTIP

Good websites for booking Las Vegas Hotel rooms are lasvegasadvisor.com and hotels.com.

Cheap deals: If you happen to be in southern California in December or January and pick up a local paper, you may see promotional offers direct from Las Vegas hotels in which the rooms are practically being given away. On the basis that an empty room is a liability, they will be happy to do this just to get your foot in the door – and their casino! The deals often include not only incredibly cheap rooms, but also free shows and meals.

Also, the travel sections of the Sunday papers in the States – and at just about any time of year – are good for picking up fantastic deals to Las Vegas.

By far the best places to buy good Las Vegas deals from are southern California (Los Angeles and San Diego), Phoenix, Denver or Chicago. The package usually includes room, transport and possibly rental car and shows. Even if you've already got your transportation sorted, you can still take advantage of the special deals by asking for the 'land only' part of the deal.

BRITTIP

A smart way to find the cheapest hotel rate? First, check online or with booking companies for hotels at a good rate. Then check the hotel's website – they often have internet deals that are lower than anything else available.

In almost all cases, you will get a better deal on Las Vegas hotels once you are in the States (with the possible exception of Funway, which has access to so many hotels at great prices), especially if you are travelling at low or shoulder season.

In the unlikely event that you can't find deals for Las Vegas in the *LA Times* or other local papers, contact airline tour companies such as American Airlines Fly-Away (aavacations.com) and Delta Dream Vacations (deltavacations.com) and ask if they have special deals at particular hotels.

Other Las Vegas agents that will help not just with the price of a room, but actually get you in at the inn, so to speak, include Las Vegas Hotels and Casinos, toll free on 1 800 992 3059, LasVegasHotels-Online.com.

Wonder websites

Check out the following for up-to-date prices, the best deals and to book.

hotelanywhere.co.uk: A British-owned website providing discounts on hotels anywhere in the world.

quikbook.com: A service providing discounts on hotels from coast to coast in America. It promises there are no hidden cancellation or change penalties, and pre-payment is not required.

hotels.com: A great internet discount reservation service.

hotelconxions.com: Another good website for checking out availability at well-booked Las Vegas hotels and reserving a room.

BRITTIP

Most hotels in America work on a per-room price basis, though there may be a maximum number of adults allowed. In addition, the room usually consists of a double or 2 double beds – the latter can't be guaranteed, but can be requested. In some cases there may be a small extra charge if there are more than 2 adults, but this won't be much.

No room at the inn: It is also worth using one of the agents mentioned above if you're having trouble booking yourself into one of the top resort-hotels as they are more likely to have rooms. Once agents are given blocks of rooms to sell, as far as the reservations manager is concerned, those rooms are not available.

One word of warning: If booking a hotel yourself, always guarantee your first night with a credit card (even if you do not plan to arrive late). If you do, then sending a deposit is not needed. If you are booking by

McCarran is a first-class airport

phone, make sure you are given a reservation or confirmation number so you can verify the reservation. With a confirmation number, no written confirmation is needed. I have had reservations cancelled by a mistake at the hotel, but with the confirmation number, the hotel cannot turn you away. They must find you a room of at least the same standard or better than the one you reserved and at the same rate.

BRITTIP

Most hotels will allow children under a certain age to sleep for free if sharing a room paid for by one or more adults.

The internet

Take care when making bookings via the internet. As with all independent travel arrangements, you do not have a tour operator to complain to (and, possibly, get money back from) if things go wrong. Stick to bigger hotels and car-hire firms if you are booking some time in advance as you are not covered if the company goes bust before you arrive for your holiday.

Probably the biggest drawback to internet bookings, though, is that there have been concerns about the security of sending credit card details over the internet. Larger sites will use a secure server to process credit cards, and they are generally safe. If they do not, or for any reason you feel uncomfortable about giving the site your information, you can take details from the internet and make arrangements via the phone, fax or by letter. However, you are unlikely to get any special internet promotional rates by doing it this way.

The specialists

So you've seen the bright lights of the big cities, taken in the amazing natural wonders of the West and had a flutter in

Airport check-in at the MGM Grand

Las Vegas – what more could you want? Well, the truth is that we Brits not only have an independent spirit, we also have romantic notions of the rugged outdoors and cowboy lifestyle. The chances are that if you've gone all the way to the West, you'll want to add on a ranch holiday or 'soft' adventure tour such as rafting, cycling, climbing and motorbiking or perhaps go horse riding, bird watching, play a little golf, do the jazz thing or get a real taste of California wines. The following companies offer those services. See Chapter 11, Outdoor Adventure for further companies and suggestions.

Adventure

Exodus: 020 8772 3936, exodus.co.uk

Outlaw Trails: 0794 111 9785, outlawtrails.com

Ranch America: 0845 277 3306, ranchamerica.co.uk

Trailfinders: 0845 058 5858, trailfinders.com

Trek America: 0845 313 2614, trekamerica.com

Bird watching

Ornitholidays: 01794 519445, ornitholidays.co.uk

Golf

The American Golf Holiday: 023 8046 5885, americangolfholiday.com

Destination Golf USA: +353 59 913 36 3632, destinations-golf.com

Ranching

American Round-Up: 01798 865946, americanroundup.com
Jetlife: 0870 787 7877, jetlife.co.uk
Kuoni: 01306 747002, kuoni.co.uk
Ranch America: 0845 277 3306, ranchamerica.co.uk
Travelhouse of America (and NAR Ltd): 0870 777 8877, travelhouseofamerica.com/Home.aspx
United Vacations: 0844 499 00 33, unitedvacations.co.uk
Virgin: 0844 557 5825, virginholidays.co.uk

Wine

Arblaster and Clarke: 01730 263111, winetours.co.uk

Winetrails: 01306 712111, winetrails.co.uk

14 DRIVING AND CAR RENTAL

How to get out and about on the open road

It's the grand dream, isn't it – driving along the American highway, the only car on a stretch of road that goes on for so long you only lose it on the horizon, music blasting, shades on and not a care in the world? Believe me, it truly is an experience not to be missed. You cannot help but get a sense of being so much closer to nature when all around you is space, space, space on an unbelievable scale.

And while (thanks to the sheer size of America) you might on occasion feel as if you are driving through great swathes of nothingness, at least the skies are likely to provide some spectacular sights of their own, from multi-coloured sunsets to heavenly blue vistas and massive rainfalls that you can see from miles away. I once spent a whole day driving on a straight open road surrounded by Arizona desert landscape, with blue skies each side and a monumentally large downpour straight ahead – and not a drop fell on me until the night (when my tent almost got washed away!), which just gives you a feel for how vast the country is.

I tell you all this to help convey the scale of what you will encounter on a touring trip around the west of America, so be warned: unless you want to spend your entire time driving during your 2 weeks, don't try to tackle too much all in one hit.

The other point is that while you may have some reservations about your ability to drive on the wrong side of the road in a foreign country, it really is not a problem in America. In reality driving in America is both easier than driving in Britain and a great deal more fun, too. The whole system of getting on and off freeways and turning left and right somehow seems to me so much easier when driving on the right-hand side of the road.

Car rental

Now you must decide what type of car to hire and who to hire it from. Most of the tour operators have special deals going with Alamo, though one or two use Avis, Budget or Dollar. The prices have become pretty standardised since 2000, but the best deal can be found through the tour operator Just America (see page 251), which offers many extras included in the price – and at a lower rate than any other operator.

Costs

Many of the tour operators give the price of hiring the car separately from what it will actually cost you to walk away from

The Strip, looking north

Six steps to safe driving

Know your route: Before leaving home, check websites for route planning and general advice. When you arrive to collect your rental vehicle, ask at the counter for specific directions to your destination, including motorway entrance and exit numbers.

Know your car: Familiarise yourself with your car before leaving the rental branch and make sure you know where everything is, including headlights, hazard lights, horn, door locks, automatic window controls and the spare tyre. Also ensure that you have the number for Roadside Assistance.

See the light: Should you become lost, suspect you have a problem with your vehicle or another motorist gestures to suggest you have a problem, drive to the nearest well lit, populated, public place such as a service station or restaurant. If you need to leave your vehicle – even briefly – be sure to lock it and take the keys with you.

Locked down and rolled up!: Keep your car doors locked, even while driving. Always be cautious when windows are open – particularly in residential areas where traffic is moving slowly or stationary – and keep items such as purses, wallets, cases and valuables hidden from plain view in the glove compartment or in the boot. Always remember to close windows fully before leaving your vehicle.

No free rides: No matter how innocent or needy they may appear, hitchhikers can mean bad news. Avoid them.

Ready, check, go!: Park in well lit areas and make sure you have your keys ready in your hand when approaching your vehicle. Re-lock your car doors once in the car. Always fasten your seat belt.

the rental desk with your car keys, though others do now show all-inclusive prices. This makes sense as there are charges you must pay in addition to the car hire fees: extended protection, collision damage waiver (CDW), airport user fee, local/state surcharges and taxes. Additional items are priced per item and are exclusive of local taxes and paid locally if selected. These include under-age driver fees and child/infant seat, GPS and additional driver. In any case, when checking the price of hiring a car, make sure you look at the right area and right dates, as prices vary from place to place. Florida and California are cheaper than Western USA prices, which makes a big difference. Some rental companies consider Arizona and Nevada to be part of a region including California, while others consider them separate, and thus a higher rate.

BRITTIP

Pre-renting can help you avoid hard-sell tactics by car hire staff wanting you to take out personal insurance. If you have extended protection and travel insurance (see Chapter 16) you'll be well covered.

Additional driver fees: This is rarely required by most car hire chains, but when it is, it is around $10 per driver per day.

Airport user fee: This will cost you up to 14% of the total charge.

Cash deposit: Very few places will even accept a cash deposit, much preferring a credit card to act as deposit. For places that do take cash deposits, be ready for delays as the counterperson has to go through rarely used forms. The deposit tends to be around $100 per week. In addition, you will often be asked to provide a credit card in the driver's name to cover any additional charges you may incur. If you want to leave a cash deposit, you'll be asked to show 2 forms of identification, for instance passport, driving licence or other government-issued photo card.

Child seat and deposit: Children up to the age of 5 must, by law, travel in a child seat in America, and you should book these in advance. The cost will be $5–8 per day plus $50 deposit (on a credit card).

Collision damage waiver (CDW): At $20.99 per day, this covers you for $10,000–50,000 worth of damage to your hire car regardless of the cause, plus theft or loss.

Environmental tax: A further $2 per day if car rental is arranged in the UK.

Extended protection: Many Americans do not have any or enough insurance and if they caused the accident, you would have no one to sue for damage to your property or for personal injury (the car is covered by

Accidents and emergencies

If you have even a minor accident, the police must be contacted before the cars can be moved. The car-hire firm will also expect a full police report for the insurance paperwork. In the case of a breakdown, there should be an emergency number for the hire company among the paperwork they gave you. Always have your driving licence with you (remember an international driving licence is not valid) and your car-hire agreement forms in case you are stopped by the police at any time. If you are pulled over, keep your hands on the wheel and always be polite. If they find out you're British you could just get away with a ticking off for a minor offence (but not for speeding at 95mph/153kph!).

CDW, see above). This type of insurance covers all liabilities and costs about $8–14 per day.

One-way drop-off fees: Most companies charge if you want to pick up your car in one location and drop it off in another, which can easily add $100–300 on to your rental costs. The exceptions tend to be if you pick up and drop off in the same city, though always check.

Rental surcharges: During peak periods, you will be charged around a further £23 per week or £5 per day for your car rental. The peak seasons tend to be 15 July–31 August and 20–27 December.

State/local surcharges and taxes: 5–15% of the total cost depending on the exact location of rental and the rental company – some will include this in the overall fee.

Under-age driver fees: All the UK deals are for drivers with a minimum age of 25 and named drivers aged 21–25 will have to pay a further $20–25 per day.

Comprehensive Alamo rentals: The all-inclusive packages and comprehensive insurance cover schemes you take out in advance in the UK tend to cost £23–46 a day in Las Vegas/Nevada. They include extended protection, CDW, airport user fee and state/local surcharges and taxes, and generally work out cheaper than paying for all the above on arrival (which also saves a lot of time when you go to collect your car).

Documents and systems

Documents: You will need a UK driving licence or a driving licence (both paper and card) from your country of residence. An international driving licence is not acceptable.

Limits: You will not be allowed to drive your hire car in Mexico or off-road in America. Many Las Vegas car hire providers will further restrict your driving to Nevada, Arizona and California only.

Hiring cars locally: You may only wish to hire a car for a few days while you are on holiday, and this can easily be arranged when you arrive. You'll find phone numbers for all the major car-hire firms in a local phone directory, but remember that the prices they quote you will not include all the extras outlined above, so be sure to include those when you do your calculations. (For names and contact numbers of car-hire companies see page 17.)

Pre-rental: Some tour operators are now offering you the chance to fill out all the necessary paperwork before you leave home so when you arrive you can just pick up your car keys and go. Not only does this save you time, but it also means you can bypass efforts by the counter staff at American car-hire firms to give you the upgrade hard sell! In any case, you will generally get a better deal for bigger cars if you arrange this in advance. The possible exception is in Las Vegas where they practically give away upgrades on a quiet week. But be warned, if you arrive in Las Vegas when the city is packed, it may be difficult to find the car of your choice.

Choosing the right car

Sorry, but size *is* an issue! If your flight includes car rental, it will normally be for a small, economy-size car, which probably won't be much good for a tour even if there are only 2 of you. The biggest problem is the boot size – the boots of all American cars are much smaller than their European equivalents and you do have to take into account that you will need to accommodate your luggage.

This is what the different price brands will provide:

- **Economy:** Usually a Chevrolet Aveo or similar, equivalent to the UK's Vauxhall Corsa. Considered big enough for 2 adults.

- **Compact:** Usually a Chevrolet Cobalt or similar, equivalent to a UK Vauxhall Astra. Considered big enough for 3 adults.

- **Intermediate:** Usually a Pontiac G6, equivalent to the UK's Vauxhall Vectra.

Considered big enough for 4 adults.

- **Full size:** Usually a Pontiac Grand Prix or similar, equivalent to the UK's Vauxhall Omega. Again, large enough for 4 adults.
- **Convertible:** Usually a Chrysler Sebring or similar, equivalent to the UK's Vauxhall Astra Convertible. Large enough for 3 adults.
- **Luxury van:** Usually a Cadillac Escalade or similar, equivalent to the UK's VW Sharan. Large enough for 7 people.
- **SUV (sport utility vehicle):** Usually a Chevy Trailblazer or similar, no UK equivalent. Large enough for 5 people.

Automatics: All American hire cars will be automatics, unless you specifically get a high-performance car like a Maserati at a speciality car hire. Some things may confuse you at first if you are not familiar with automatics, for example you won't be able to drive until you put the car into D for drive and you probably won't be able to take the keys out of the ignition until you have put the car into P for park. D1 and D2 are extra gears, which you only need to use when going up or down very steep hills.

Most American cars have cruise control, which lets you set the speed at which you want to travel and then take your foot off the gas pedal (the accelerator). There are usually 2 buttons, either on the face of the steering wheel or on the switch that controls the car lights, for cruise control, one to switch it on and the other to set your speed. You take off cruise control by pressing the on button again or by simply accelerating or braking.

Air conditioning: In the California/Nevada/Arizona area it would be rare for a car not to have air conditioning but you must keep the windows closed to make it work.

Fuel/gas: You've hit the highway and need to fill up, but just bear in mind that for the most part interstates (the main roads) do not have gas stations – you will have to get off, though they are not usually too far away. Practically all gas stations are self service.

On the road
Rules and regulations

Here are a few things you should know.
Alcohol limits: The legal limit for blood alcohol in America is lower than in Britain and the police are very hot on drink-drivers (drunk-drivers in American parlance). Generally a single drink can put you at or over the limit if you are a smaller person! It is also illegal to carry open containers of alcohol in the car itself.

Parking: It is illegal to park within 10ft/3m of a fire hydrant or a lowered kerb and you should never stop in front of a yellow-painted kerb – they are for emergency vehicles and you will get towed away! Never park on a kerb either.

School buses: These cannot be overtaken in either direction while they are unloading and have their hazard lights flashing.

School zone: Flashing orange lights suspended over the road indicate a school zone ahead, so go slowly.

Seat belts: These are compulsory for all passengers. Babies and small children are required to be secured in child safety seats (available through most car-hire agencies).

Signposts and junctions: One of the most confusing aspects of driving around towns in America is the way they hang up road names underneath the traffic lights at every junction. The road name given is not for the road you are actually on, but the one you are crossing. Another thing to be wary of is that there is very little advance notice of junctions, and road names can be hard to read as you approach them, especially at night. So keep your speed down if you think you are close to your turn-off so you can get into the right lane. If you do miss your turning, don't panic, as nearly all roads in American towns are arranged in a simple grid system so it will be relatively easy to work your way back.

Sometimes you will meet a crossroads where there is no obvious right of way. This is a '4-way stop' and the way it works is that priority goes in order of arrival. When it is your turn, pull out slowly. If 2 come together at the same time, the one on the farthest 'right' has priority. If 2 cars stop facing each other, the one going straight has priority over any car turning.

At red lights, it is possible to turn right providing there is no traffic coming from the left and no pedestrian is crossing, unless specified by a sign saying 'No turn on red'. A green arrow gives you the right of way when turning left, but when it is a solid green light, you must give way to traffic coming from the other direction.

Speed: No speeding, please! The speed limits on the main Interstates are well signposted and tend to be 55–70mph/86–113kph and up to 75mph/121kph on some lonely stretches in Nevada and Arizona – while the MINIMUM allowed is 40mph/64kph.

U-turns: These are forbidden in built-up areas and where a solid line runs down the middle of the road.

15 | THE GRAND CANYON AND SURROUNDINGS

Must-see sights within easy reach of Sin City

Arizona and the Canyonlands

In California it's quite often the people and urban developments that make the state a truly remarkable experience. In Arizona it is the history and natural wonders that make it one of the most beautiful and thrilling of all of America's 50 states. This is the land of cowboys and Native Americans, of gold-mining and ghost towns, of movie-making and centuries-old history and of one of the 7 great natural wonders of the world: the Grand Canyon.

Without a shadow of a doubt it has some of the most spectacular landscapes ever crowded into such a compact area. On top of the Grand Canyon, there is the Petrified Forest, Walnut Canyon, Sunset Crater and Montezuma's Castle ... and that's just for starters.

Arizona is a massive state, encompassing the cities of Phoenix (its capital) and Tucson. Travelling to these destinations would require a big investment in time. Getting to the Grand Canyon and the Canyonlands, however, is feasible within a matter of hours from Las Vegas.

Going native

Arizona has the largest Native American population and more land devoted to reservations than any other state. In addition, the prehistoric Native American tribes, such as the Hohokam of southern Arizona, the Sinagua of the central, and the cliff-dwelling Anasazi (ancient ones) of northern Arizona provide some extremely old historical ruins (rare in America). These are a monument to their high degree of sophistication in dry farming, water management, plus their far-flung trade

routes and jewellery, pottery and textile-making.

And let us not forget, of course, that Arizona was the birthplace of possibly the best known Native American of them all, Geronimo. The Apache warrior engaged nearly three-quarters of America's military ground troops in his pursuit after the Civil War and up to 1886 when he surrendered – having never been captured – at Skeleton Canyon in Southern Arizona!

Native American artefacts

Ranching

Peeples Valley and Yarnell: On the cowboy front, even today mining and ranching are the most important industries of the small communities of Peeples Valley and Yarnell on Route 89 north of Wickenburg. The lush grasslands are home to a thriving cattle industry that has cowboys still riding the plains. The whole area down to Wickenburg is known as the Dude Ranch Capital of the World because of all the ranches that allow you to visit and participate in the activities.

Prescott: The old capital of Arizona, surrounded by Prescott National Forest, the pine-covered Bradshaw Mountains and the Yavapai Indian Reservation, is known for its boulder-strewn granite dells and grasslands. Stately Victorian homes are a reminder of its heyday, while the rowdier side of frontier life is remembered on Whiskey Row, where 26 saloons once attracted cowboys from far and wide. The annual Frontier Days celebration is held here at the beginning of July, complete with fireworks, dancing, rodeo performances, a parade and cowboy golf tournament.

Jerome: Further north on State Route 89A is Jerome, which sprang up during the gold-mining boom on Cleopatra Hill overlooking the Verde Valley. Once the ore diminished, Jerome became known as

The cowboy life

America's largest ghost city and is now home to a colony of artists and visitors who walk the steep, winding streets to see the historic buildings and browse through shops and boutiques.

The best historic sites are the town's 'travelling jail', which has slid downhill 225ft/69m since a dynamite explosion dislodged it from its foundations during the 1920s, and Jerome State Historic Park, once the mansion of mining developer 'Rawhide' Jimmy Douglas.

Campe Verde: This is to the south-east (along Route 260), and was established in 1864 as a cavalry outpost to protect Verde River settlers from Indian raids. The old fort still stands in the middle of the town.

Montezuma Castle National Monument: Just north, along Interstate 17, are these well-preserved cliff dwellings, a 5-storey, 20-room dwelling built in and under a cliff overlooking Beaver Creek. It was misnamed by early settlers who thought it had been inhabited by Aztecs, but it was actually built by Sinagua Indians in the 12th and 13th centuries.

Clarkdale: Further north is Clarkdale, where you can see the 100-room pueblo that housed 250 people from the 13th century until they mysteriously disappeared some time in the 15th century. Clarkdale is home to the scenic Verde Canyon Railroad, a renovated New York Metro Line train that transports passengers along a 40ml/64km route through cottonwood forests and the base of a desert mesa (table). En route you'll see bald eagles, great blue herons, deer and javelina.

Flagstaff: This is just a little further north and considered to be the gateway to the Grand Canyon.

The Grand Canyon

Grand Canyon National Park, PO Box 129, Grand Canyon, AZ 86023, 928-638 7888, nps.gov/grca

Open: The park is open 24 hours a day. National Geographic Visitor Center, 928 638 2468, explorethecanyon.com in Canyon View Information Plaza open 8am–5pm.

Admission: $25 per vehicle, $12 per person arriving by other means. The speediest way to pay is by credit card at pay stations at the south and east entrances or at the Visitor Center. Admission is for 7 days but does not cover fees for use of overnight campsites, which are extra. Under-15s free. Free planning guides are

BRITTIP

To avoid the crowds (around 5 million people visit each year) and searing heat, go in March, April, September or October either before 10am or after 2pm.

available in advance from the National Park Service. Download a Trip Planner, North and South Rim guides, Park Maps or Accessibility Guide.

Two billion years in the making, the majestic spectacle stands from between 4,500ft/ 1,370m and 5,700ft/1,740m high and twists for an amazing 277mls/446km with an average width of 10mls/16km. To geologists, it is like an open book, as they can immediately see that the bottom layer is 2 billion years old while the top is a mere 200 million years old, with the geological ages in between represented in the Canyon's colourful stony strata.

Viewing it from one of the many vantage points on the South Rim, you will see the myriad rock formations change colour according to the sun's position throughout the day. The best times to see it (and the quietest) are at sunrise or sunset. You can also walk out over the Canyon on the Skywalk – a $30 million dollar horseshoe-shaped glass bridge suspended over the West Rim at Eagle Point. It juts out 230ft/70m at 4,000ft/1,219m above the canyon floor, but in some ways you can only get a feel for its awesome, breathtaking hugeness by descending into its depths by mule. If you don't have the 1–2 days to spare needed for the trip, you can stop at the IMAX theatre at Tusayan and watch the *Grand Canyon – The Hidden Secrets* film.

Seeing the Grand Canyon

More than 5 million people a year flock to the South Rim to view the Grand Canyon. Closer to the Colorado River than the North Rim, it also provides better views of the canyon.

You can either drive straight to the Grand Canyon Village or head for the Canyon View Information Plaza and the Visitor Center and bookstore – where you can pick up a copy of the park's newspaper for up-to-the-minute information on facilities, activities and transportation options, and a map, if you haven't downloaded them.

From here you can walk to Mather Point, which gives wonderful views of the Canyon, before making use of the free shuttle service to the Grand Canyon Village for further views.

The film: The IMAX theatre, 928 638 2468, explorethecanyon.com, at the south entrance at Highway 64/US 180, Tusayan has shows at half past the hour 1 Mar–31 Oct 8.30am–8.30pm, 1 Nov–28 Feb 10.30am–6.30pm, daily, on a 70ft/21m screen with 6-track stereo sound. Adults $13.34, children (5–10) $10.14, under-6s free. For 25% discount, buy online.

Grand Canyon Skywalk: 702 220 8372, grandcanyonskywalk.com Adults $29.95, children (3–11) $22.46, seniors $26.96, plus 7% tribal tax. Advance booking reduces wait times.

By train: The Grand Canyon Railway, 800 THE TRAIN or 928 773 1976, thetrain.com, runs a 1920s Harriman coach steam train from Williams to the South Rim, travelling through 65mls/105km of beautiful countryside, complete with an authentic style western shoot out.

By bus: Open Road Tours (877 226 8060 or 928 226 8060, openroadshuttle.com) operates between Flagstaff and Williams/Grand Canyon Village which costs $54/$44 adults, $38/$34 children return trip. Guided coach tours are run by Xanterra Parks and Resorts (888 297 2757 or 303 297 2757, grandcanyon lodges.com) and include the Hermit's Rest Tour along the West Rim ($24), Desert View Tour travelling East ($42), Sunrise or Sunset Tour ($19) or a Combination Tour ($52) which can be taken in any order or on different days. Children 16 and under go free. The Trans-Canyon shuttle (928 638 2820, transcanyonshuttle.com) is the only public transport between the South and North Rim. It runs once a day each way mid May – mid October, taking 4.5 hours and costing $80 per person one way, $150 round trip.

Sunset over the Canyon

Helicopter view

By mule: Xanterra Parks and Resorts (888 297 2757 or 303 297 2757, grand canyonlodges.com) offer day-long and overnight mule trips from the South Rim year round – but these book up months in advance so book early. One-hour to half-day North Rim mule trips are offered mid-May – mid-October, starting from $40.

By foot: Hiking into the canyon is one of the best ways to see it and rim trail hikes on both the South and North Rim, often on paved paths, offer spectacular views. Alternatively, if you are fit and healthy, you can hike down into the canyon. A shuttle from the Grand Canyon Lodge to the North Kaibab trailhead is available twice daily in the morning ($8 for first person and $5 for additional people). As over 250 people are rescued from the canyon each year, it's a good idea to download a hike-smart podcast from nps.gov/grca or opt for one of the excellent ranger-led hikes on both rims (South Rim daily; North Rim, seasonally mid-May – mid October), a naturalist excursion from the National Geographic Visitor Center or one of 4 day hikes with Angel's Gate Tours (800 957 4557, angelsgatetours.com) for $159 adults, $139 children (aged 8–16).

Horseback rides: With the Apache Stables in Tusayan, adjacent to the park. Write to PO Box 158, Grand Canyon, AZ 86023, see apachestables.com or call 928 638 2891. Rides for adults and children include 1-hour rail rides through the pines ($45.50) to evening rides ending up round the campfire ($55.50).

Jeep tours: Head off into the back roads in an open-air safari vehicle to learn about cowboys, early settlers, native wildlife and local legend with Grand Canyon Outback Jeep Tours, 800 320 5337 or 928 638 5337, grandcanyonjeeptours. Choose from the Grand Sunset Tour, Grand Canyon Safari and Rim Walk departing at 9.30am (both tours adults $64, children 11 and under $49), Indian Paintings Tour at 3pm

(adult $45, children $35) or one of 2 Deluxe Combo Tours, a 4.5-hour trip costing $104 for adults, $84 for children. You can even combine a jeep trip with a scenic flight (adults $185, children $159). Newer operator, Pink Jeep Tours, 702 895 6777, pinkjeep.com, also offers trips in the Grand Canyon.

Rafting the Colorado: Explore Indian ruins, discover waterfalls, spot wildlife, take side hikes or ride rapids on a rafting trip down the mighty Colorado. Trips include half-day floating excursions, motor boat trips and 18-day expeditions on rowing boats. Most trips begin at Lee's Ferry at the eastern end of the Canyon. You need to book at least 6 months in advance and companies include:

- **Arizona Raft Adventures:** 4050 East Huntington Drive, Flagstaff, AZ 86004, 800 786 7238/RAFT, azraftcom
- **Arizona River Runners:** PO Box 47788, Phoenix, AZ 85068, 800 477 7238, raftarizona.com
- **Canyon Explorations Expeditions:** PO Box 310, Flagstaff, AZ 86002, 800 654 0723 or 928 774 4559, canyonexplorations.com
- **Canyoneers:** PO Box 2997, Flagstaff, AZ 86003, 800 525 0924 or 928 526 0924, canyoneers.com
- **Diamond River Adventures:** 916 Vista, PO Box 1300, Page, AZ 86040, 800 343 3121 or 928 645 8866, diamondriver.com
- **Hualapai Tribal River Runners:** 16500 East Route 66, Peach Springs, AZ 86434, 888 255 9550 or 928 769 2419, grandcanyonresort.com
- **Outdoors Unlimited:** 6900 Townsen Winona Road, Flagstaff, AZ 86004, 0800 637 RAFT or 928 526 4511, outdoorsunlimited.com
- **Wilderness River Adventures:** PO Box 717, Page, AZ 86040, 0800 992 8022 or 928 645 3296, riveradventures.com

Skywalk over the Canyon rim

Flightseeing: Flights by small aircraft or helicopter. Companies include:

- **Air Grand Canyon:** PO Box 3028, Grand Canyon, Arizona 86023, 800 247 4726 or 928 638 2686, airgrandcanyon.com
- **Maverick Helicopters:** 6075 Las Vegas Boulevard, Las Vegas, NV 89119, 888 261 4414 or 702 262 6199, maverickhelicopter.com
- **Heli USA Airways:** 245 E Tropicana Avenue, Suite 120, Las Vegas, AZ 89109. 01462 488227 (UK) or 702 736 8787 (Las Vegas), heliusa.com
- **Scenic Airlines:** 3900 Paradise Road, Suite 185, Las Vegas, NV 89169, 800 634 6801 or 702 638 3300
- **Papillon Grand Canyon Helicopters:** PO Box 455, Grand Canyon, AZ 86023, 928 638 2419. 0800 404 9767 (UK toll free) or 702 736 7243 (Las Vegas), papillon.com
- **Stars and Stripes Air Tours:** 500 E Cheyenne Avenue, Las Vegas. AZ 89030. 1 888 779 0800, lvhelicopters.com

Lodging: For full and up-to-date details of lodges near the rim, contact Xanterra Parks & Resorts, 303 600 3400, xanterra.com.

BRITTIP

The canyon is 10mls/16km across, but remember that 1.6-ml/2.6-km separate the North and South Rim, so make sure you allow for the 5 hours it takes to drive the 215 miles/346km from one side to the other.

The North Rim

Staying on the floor of the Canyon: Phantom Ranch, the only place to stay below the rim, offers separate-sex 10-bunk dorms with toilet and shower, plus 11 private rustic cabins. Book through Xanterra Parks & Resorts, 303 600 3400, xanterra.com.

North Rim

Through Jacob Lake on Highway 67, on the Utah side of the park, the North Rim is a lot quieter than the South Rim. It only receives 10% of the visitors to the Canyon and is open seasonally, from mid May to mid October. It is home to Canyon Trail Rides (435 679 8665, canyonrides.com), which runs 1-hour forest rides, half-day

Maverick Helicopters in the Grand Canyon

Spring Ranch near Las Vegas

trips from the North Rim into the Canyon and full-day trips to Roaring Springs where you can frolic in the natural pools. Here you can stay at the Grand Canyon Lodge late May – mid October. For reservations, contact Xanterra Parks & Resorts, 303 600 3400, xanterra.com. The Kaibab Lodge, 5mls/8km north of the park, is also open mid-May – early November. For reservations 928 638 2389, kaibablodge.com.

Howdy pardner!

Arizona is real cowboy country and if there is one way to see the stunning scenery, wide-open expanses and narrow gorges, it is on the back of a horse – as a cowboy. Nowadays, it is very easy to be a real 'city slicker' as a whole host of ranching options are available, depending on your riding abilities and need for luxury items, such as a bed. The types of ranches are:

Guest ranch: This is where you live as a 'guest' of the ranch owners in an environment that is designed to entertain you while providing plenty of horse-riding opportunities and Western activities. It's the soft option that will give you a feel for the way of life but no hands-on experience.

Dude ranch: Holiday-based rather than the seriously business-like working ranches, you'll do a lot of riding, while Western activities from Wild West shows to rodeo visits, square dances, barbecues and sports provide plenty of fun.

Resort ranch: These offer the Western experience but also have golf, tennis and ballooning, and the whole environment is much more luxurious than dude or working ranches.

Working ranch: Still in business to raise livestock and grow crops, these are home to the real cowboys. Depending on the time of year and the work that is necessary on the ranch, you'll be able to learn to drive cattle, brand and rope steers, eat around a camp fire and sleep under the stars. Round-ups take place in spring and autumn when the ranchers prepare their cattle to be moved to summer and winter ranges. It's a high-activity time at the ranches so the hours are long and the work is physically demanding. On the cattle drives you are likely to travel 6–12mls/10–19km a day, but ride at least 3 times as far as you bring in strays from the flanks. Evenings spent around the campfire hark back to bygone days in what is a truly wonderful, friendship-forming experience. Horse drives are a much faster version as the horses like to travel at speed. These are only for very seasoned riders with lots of cross-country experience, but the long-distance gallops are a real thrill. The following UK specialist tour companies offer ranching holidays:

- **American Round-Up:** 01798 865946, americanroundup.com. Offers the full range.
- **Ranch America:** 0845 277 3306, ranchamerica.co.uk. Also offers a range of holidays.
- **Equitour:** 0800 043 7942, equitour.co.uk. This specialist riding holiday operator is excellent for working ranches all over America's West and even provides riding clinics to bring you up to speed!

Joshua tree, southern Nevada

Watch the birdies!

You've seen them in cartoons, now you can see the birds of the Arizona deserts and mountains in real life. The south-eastern corner of the state is the most popular bird-watching area of North America and more than 400 species can be found here from migratory water fowl to native birds, nesting birds, grassland birds and mountain birds.

You can watch greater roadrunners chase lizards across the desert floors, black-chinned hummingbirds buzz around like bees, acorn woodpeckers drill holes in roadside telegraph poles and painted redstarts flit in the dappled light of oak woods with specialists such as **The Travelling Naturalist** (01305 267994, naturalist.co.uk) or **Sunbird** (01767 262522, sunbirdtours.co.uk). The Travelling Naturalist organises its 15-day trip in spring when the desert is comfortably cool and many birds are nesting while others are starting to migrate to their breeding grounds in the north. Sunbird's 2-week trip runs in September. Both offer spectacular views of the Grand Canyon.

Another favoured time of the year for birders to visit is August when the city of Sierra Vista has a birding festival complete with bat stalks and owl prowls.

Trail rides with Outlaw Trails: 0794 111 9785, outlawtrails.com. For horse-riding vacations with a difference try Outlaw Trails, which runs specially tailored, fully researched trips to the old trails used by the outlaws determined to avoid the long arm of the law. Closest to Arizona is the Robbers Roost trail in Utah on which you'll see the way stations and trail used by the Wild Bunch of Butch Cassidy and the Sundance Kid, the Hole in the Wall Gang and Robbers Roost Gang. Robbers Roost land is sprawled across 320mls²/830km² of high desert and you'll ride through pinyon, sage and cedar flats, a maze of rock gorges and canyons, plus long mesas, arches, pinnacles and high-shouldered buttes. If you attempt any of the 'climbs' used by the outlaws, you'll get a pretty good idea of what brilliant horsemen they were! The seasons and numbers are limited because of the weather and nature of the trips, but the trails are perfect for lovers of the historical West who want a great big chunk of adventure.

Sunset Crater

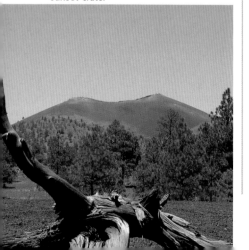

Other Arizona marvels

Once you've been there, done that at the Grand Canyon, don't miss out on the many other natural and historical wonders Arizona has to offer.

Sunset Crater: 928 526 0502, nps.gov/sucr. Leave the South Rim on Highway 64 and take the 89 south to Sunset Crater Volcano National Monument. An active volcano more than 900 years ago, it now rises to 1,000ft/305m and rangers here offer geology, seismology and other tours while the Visitor Center can provide you with maps for self-guided trails.

Walnut Canyon: 928 526 3367, nps.gov/waca. Further south, join the Interstate 40 going east and take in Walnut Canyon National Monument for an awe-inspiring view of how Sinagua Indians lived in homes built out of the limestone cliffs. The Visitor Center Museum displays artefacts that make it possible to imagine how they existed.

Meteor Crater: 800 289 2362, meteor crater.com. Nearby, this crater dates back 22,000 years when an enormous meteor travelling at 33,000mph/53,100kph plunged to Earth. Because of its resemblance to the lunar landscape, the 570ft/174m deep crater was used as a training site for Apollo astronauts and the museum displays a 1,406lb/638kg meteorite, the largest found in the area.

Petrified Forest: 928-524 6228, nps.gov/pefo. Further east is the Petrified Forest National Park and Painted Desert Visitor Center and Museum. There are more fossilised trees to be found here than anywhere else in the world with million-year-old agate logs lying in profusion on the ground.

Lake Powell

Canyon de Chelly: 928 674 5500, nps.gov/cach. Further north on Route 191, you can view the Indian cliff-dwelling ruins at Canyon de Chelly National Monument. At the base of sheer red cliffs and in canyon walls, the ruins date back to the 12th century and you can get to them on scenic rim drives, 4-wheel-drive vehicles, horseback or on foot. Phone the visitor center above for details. The area is rich with history, as the Anasazi Indians lived here until 1300 and the Navajo arrived in 1700, using it as a base to raid nearby Indian and Spanish settlements.

Monument Valley: 435 727 5874 or 928 871 6647, navajonationparks.org/monumentvalley.htm. Take Highways 59 and 163 to see one of the best-used locations for filming Westerns such as John Wayne's *Stagecoach*. To the left of this area is the Navajo Nation, the largest of all the Indian reservations – extending across 25,000mls^2/64,750km^2, it is bigger than the state of West Virginia – which is home to around 175,000 Native Americans, who welcome visitors for sightseeing and shopping – buy silver and turquoise jewellery, exquisitely woven rugs, intricate kachinas and other crafts.

The land encompasses mile upon mile of desert and forest land, interrupted only by spectacular mesas, buttes and rock formations. The Navajos provide hiking, horseback and 4-wheel-drive tours through some of the most popular sites such as Canyon de Chelly and Monument Valley.

BRITTIP

Did you know that more people have died of drowning in the desert than of thirst? It's all due to flash floods that are so violent and so sudden you have no time at all to react.

Lake Powell: 888 896 3829 or 928 645 2433, lakepowell.com. From this area, take Route 98 up to the shores of Lake Powell, a 25m acre/10m ha lake with more shoreline – 1,960mls/3,154km – than California, which was formed by the completion of the Glen Canyon Dam in 1963. Today it's a home for houseboats and pleasure craft that explore the 96 canyons discovered and mapped by intrepid, one-armed explorer John Wesley Powell in the 19th century.

Rainbow Bridge Natural Monument: 928 608 6200, nps.gov/rabr. A natural stone arch carved by the relentless forces of wind and water, the bridge only became easily accessible after the lake came into being. It is an amazing 290ft/88m high and 275ft/84m wide. Boat rentals, tours and accommodation are all available at the Wahweap Lodge and Marina on the lake's southern-most shore. For boat tour reservation to the bridge (marina is about 50m/65km away) phone 800 528 6154 or visit lakepowell.com.

Glen Canyon Dam: 928 608 6200, nps.gov/glca. Offers self-guided tours and day-long and half-day float trips along the Colorado River from the base of the dam, March–October. Phone for details. The town of Page, founded as a construction camp for crews building the dam, has plenty of restaurants and accommodation.

Cochise County: explorecochise.com (for a free visitors guide). This southeast corner of Arizona is an 1800s Old West museum all by itself. This area is just a 1–2-hour drive from Tucson and includes such historical areas as Texas Canyon and Skeleton Canyon, where Geronimo waged war against the American Army with no more than 42 men. There is the old mining town of Tombstone, infamous for the gun battle between the Earps and the Clantons in the OK Corral. Finally, in Fort Huachuca lies the old museum and remains of Camp Huachuca, home to the famous Buffalo Soldiers, 2 regiments of freed African American slaves who battled Puma and Apache native tribes for decades.

Glen Canyon Dam

Utah and the Wild West

Often overlooked thanks to the fame of the neighbouring Grand Canyon and Arizona, the south-western corner of Utah is home to an area known as the Grand Circle. Stunning national parks include Zion National Park, Kolob Canyons and Bryce Canyon. The Grand Circle also takes in Lake Powell and the Glen Canyon National Recreation Area, which straddles Utah and Arizona, and Nevada's Lake Mead National Recreational Area.

The beauty of Utah's natural wonders is matched by its sense of wilderness. Despite an increase in visitors, it is still an untamed environment with often only primitive facilities available, while the rich cowboy and outlaw history touches many sights and locations throughout the region.

Zion National Park

Within remarkably easy striking distance of Las Vegas, it takes just 2 hours to drive to the south-western end of the Grand Circle along Interstate 15 in the direction of St George. The entrance is on the south side just beyond the town of Springdale, where you will find the visitor center and 2 camping sites.

BRITTIP

Within Zion National Park is the Kolob Canyons area, which has its own Visitor Center.

Open: 435 772 3256, nps.gov/zion and zioncanyon.com. Park open daily. The Visitor Center is open year-round except Christmas Day, spring and winter 8am–5pm, autumn 8am–6pm and summer 8am–8pm, and provides everything from books, to information, maps, an introductory video and backcountry permits and even has a small museum.

Zion Canyon

Admission: 7-day pass $25 per car or $12 per person.

The natural rock sculptures and vividly coloured cliffs that tower above the floor of Zion Canyon pull in nearly 2.5 million visitors a year, making it one of the most popular sights in the region. To the Mormon pioneers who discovered it after the Paiute Indians had left, the beautiful rock structures so resembled natural temples they called it Little Zion. An early Methodist minister was so awe-struck that he gave many of the towers and cliffs that rise up 3,000ft/914m into the sky biblical names such as Three Patriarchs, Angels Landing and the Great White Throne.

Seeing the sights

Zion Canyon Scenic Drive: One of the easiest ways to appreciate its beauty is to take this 7ml/11km trek along the canyon floor – a narrow, deep gorge that is the centrepiece of the park, surrounded by wondrous monoliths that stand between 2,000ft/610m and 3,000ft/914m high. Along the bottom of the canyon flows the Virgin River. It may look small, yet it has the power of the once-mighty Colorado and is almost single-handedly responsible for carving the gorge – admittedly over a 13 million-year period! A round trip will take at least an hour and a half.

The Zion-Mount Carmel Highway: A 13ml/21km drive up steep switchbacks and through tunnels to Checkerboard Mesa. The road was considered an engineering marvel when it was completed in 1930 and cuts a swathe through rough up-and-down terrain to connect lower Zion Canyon with the high plateaux to the east.

Two narrow tunnels, including one over 1ml/1.6km long, were blasted through the cliffs to complete the job. As you travel from one side of the tunnel to the other, the landscape changes dramatically. On one side are the massive cliff walls of Zion Canyon, on the other is an area known as Slickrock Country. Here rocks coloured in white and pastels of orange and red have been eroded into hundreds of fantastic shapes and etched through time with odd patterns of cracks and grooves. It is followed by the mountains of sandstone known as Checkerboard Mesa – one of the best examples of naturally sculptured rock art.

Ranger-led shuttle bus tour: These 2-hour trips run both morning and evening provide an intimate look at the Canyon – reservations are free, but must be made a day in advance at the visitor center.

View across Zion Canyon

Seasons in the sun

Each season provides a spectacular array of colours in Zion. Spring sees the waterfalls cascading into the Virgin River. Summer – easily the busiest time of year – is the time to enjoy the striking sight of the deep red cliffs peeking out above the lush green foliage. Come autumn those leaves turn brilliant red and gold, while in winter a layer of snow adds a pristine cleanliness to the rugged landscape.

BRITTIP

The best times to visit Zion National Park are May and September, when the weather is at its finest and the crowds are at their smallest.

Things to do

You can cycle, take a tram ride or go on a horse ride through the park, yet most people agree that the best way to experience the full majesty is to hike. Hiking and other relevant information is found in the Zion Map & Guide downloadable from the nps.gov/zion website. For adventurers with a bit more time, the backcountry (downloadable planner from the site) offers more opportunities for adventure in the form of canyoneering and climbing as well as backcountry hiking trails.

Guided walks: These are offered along fairly easy trails – some of which are accessible by wheelchair. A huge range of other hikes, from moderate to strenuous and one day or more are available, although all are only accessed by shuttle bus, so plan ahead. True adventurers, though, will want to do the 16ml/26km hike through The Narrows, in the backcountry, which involves wading through the Virgin River. Be aware, though, that advance preparation and a permit are necessary to do this.

Guided horse rides: These are available from early March to the end of October. Call 435 772 3810 for information or book a trip with Canyon Trail Rides (canyonrides.com) who offer 1.5-hour rides here.

BRITTIP

It is not advisable to drink untreated water from streams or springs. Water can be bought at the visitor centre, campgrounds, Zion Lodge, Grotto Picnic Area and the Temple of Sinawa.

Bicycles: These are only permitted on established roads and the Pa'rus Trail, which leads from the campgrounds to the Scenic Drive junction.

Camping: This is allowed only in the campgrounds or in designated backcountry sites with a permit. The 3 campgrounds in Zion Canyon are South and Watchman, and Lava Point, which is about an hour's drive from the others. If visiting June–August, make sure you have a reservation.

Mountain biking in Austin

Climbing: Information is available at the visitor center. But many of Zion's cliffs are sandstone with much loose or 'rotten' rock and climbing tools and techniques used for granite are often less effective here.

BRITTIP

Kolob Canyons may be lesser known than Zion Canyon but is just as spectacular, and uncrowded.

Kolob Canyons

In the north-western reaches of Zion National Park, just off Interstate 15 at Exit 40 about 45mls/72km from the entrance to Zion.

Open: Visitor Center: 435 586 9548, nps.gov/zion open 8am–4.30pm daily, apart from 26 November and Christmas Day.

Admission: $25 per vehicle for 7 days.

Kolob Canyons Road is one of 2 scenic routes that provide stunning views of the spectacular finger canyons, carved out by springs along the edge of Kolob Terrace. It will take you 5mls/8km into the red rock, running perpendicular to the walled Finger Canyons and providing a high viewpoint at the end.

The Kolob Terrace Road overlooks the white and salmon-coloured cliffs at the left and right forks of North Creek. Both routes climb into forests of pinyon and juniper, ponderosa pine and fir, while aspen trees are found at Lava Point. In early spring the Kolob is still buried under thick snow, and in summer there is still a feel of mountain coolness to the air. Hikes and ranger-led activities are also available here. Visit

utah.com/nationalparks/zion/lolob_canyons.htm for ideas.

Lodging in Zion National Park

Zion Lodge: 303-297 2757, zionlodge.com. Open year-round and provides a choice of motel rooms, cabins and suites. It is the only lodge in the park and the only restaurant. There is also a gift shop and post office and access to hiking trails and horse riding.

Lodging in Springdale: The Zion Park City

Conveniently, the Zion shuttle leaves from Springdale where these lodgings are all located.

Bumbleberry Inn: 97 Bumbleberry Lane, Springdale. 800 828 1534 or 435 772 3224, bumbleberry.com. Large, spacious rooms with private balconies or patios overlooking wonderful scenery in a quiet, off-road location. Facilities include a heated pool, indoor Jacuzzi, indoor racquetball, games room, restaurant and gift shop.

Canyon Ranch Motel: 668 Zion Park Boulevard, Springdale 866 946 6276 or 435 772 3357, canyonranchmotel.com. Recently-built and remodelled cottages, some with kitchens, around a quiet, shady lawn with panoramic views of Zion characterise this motel just 0.5ml/800m from the park entrance. Amenities include a pool and Jacuzzi.

Cliffrose Lodge & Gardens: 281 Zion Park Boulevard, Springdale. 800 243 8824 or 435 772 3234, cliffroselodge.com. At the entrance to Zion National Park along the Virgin River. All rooms have excellent

Kolob Canyon

views, while there is also a large pool and 5acres/2ha of lawns, trees and flower gardens.

El Rio Lodge: 995 Zion Park Boulevard, Springdale. 435 772 3205, elriolodge.com. Claims to be the most affordable lodge in Springdale. Clean, quiet and friendly 14-roomed lodge with a green shady lawn, sundeck and fantastic views of Zion Park.

Lodging in Rockville

Hummingbird Inn B&B: 37 West Main, Rockville, 800 964 BIRD or 435 772 3632, infowest.com/hummingbird, on Highway 9, just 3mls/5km from the entrance to Zion National Park. All 4 guestrooms have private baths and a large country breakfast is included. The inn has a Jacuzzi plus an upstairs deck and a library/games room loft. Outside activities include croquet, horseshoes and badminton.

Lodging in Hurricane

Half-way between Zion National Park and St George. Visitor info 435 635 3402.

Pah Tempe Hot Springs: 825 North 800 East, 35–4 Hurricane, 888 726 8367 or 435 635 2879, infowest.com/pahtempe/ where.html. A tiny retreat where no smoking or alcohol is allowed, but where massage and therapy programmes are available, plus a relaxing hot mineral pool along the Virgin River.

Park Villa Motel 6: 650 West State Street, 435 635 2164. Luxury units with fridge and microwave, just 1ml/1.6km from mineral hot springs. Facilities include heated pool and spa, laundry, kitchen and cable TV.

Bryce Canyon

1 888 467 2757, nps.gov/brca and nationalparks.org

72mls/116km from Zion National Park. Follow Highway 89 towards Hatch, then turn into Highway 12 to Bryce village and the Visitor Center is just inside the entrance on Highway 63.

Open: Visitor Center 435 834 5322. Open 8am–8pm May–Sept, 8am–6pm Oct, 8am–4.30pm Nov–Mar, 8am–6pm April except Thanksgiving, Christmas and New Year's Day. Provides information, books and backcountry permits. The park is open 24 hours daily except as above.

A short introductory video on the park is shown on the hour and the half hour and short geology talks are given in the Visitor Center Museum.

Admission: 7-day pass $25 per vehicle, $12 per person. You can buy a National Parks Pass by phone or from the website.

BRITTIP

The best times to see large mammals in Bryce Canyon are summer mornings and evenings in roadside meadows.

Hoodoos and other formations

Bryce Canyon National Park consists of 37,277acres/15,085ha of scenic, colourful rock formations and wonderful desert and has been home to Indian tribes – including the Anasazi and Fremont – for about 12,000 years. The most recent tribe to inhabit the region was the Paiute, who were still here when explorers John Wesley Powell and Captain Clarence E. Dutton 'discovered' the area in the 1870s.

In 1875, Ebenezer Bryce settled in the Paria Valley to harvest timber from the plateau and neighbours called the nearby canyon Bryce's Canyon – a name that stuck!

The canyon is a geological wonder – home to a series of horseshoe-shaped amphitheatres carved from the eastern edge of the Paunsugunt Plateau. Erosion has shaped colourful Calron limestones, sandstones and mudstones into thousands of spires, pinnacles and fins that together provide unique formations known as hoodoos.

The Paiutes called the hoodoos Legend People who had been turned to stone by coyote because of their evil ways. In fact, they are fantastically shaped and incredibly tall pillars of rock that have been created by a series of massive land movements and river erosions.

Bryce Canyon

The result is a geological paradise filled as it is with wonderful examples of the effects of sedimentation from both fresh and sea water, erosion through wind, water and ice and earthquake and volcanic action over a period of millions and millions of years. The plateaux, staggering vertical columns, gullies and canyons are a joy to behold, while the high elevations – between 6,000ft/1,830m and 9,000ft/2,740m – provide panoramic views of 3 states and a perfect spot for stargazers.

Sights to look out for: The monoliths of Thor's Hammer, Deformation, Uplift and the Grand Staircase.

Nature's way

The diverse soil and moisture conditions throughout Bryce Canyon have allowed more than 400 species of wild flower to grow including rare gentian, bellflower, yarrow, gilia, sego lily and manzanita.

The meadows and forests are also home to many animals from foxes to deer, coyote, mountain lions and black bears. Elk and pronghorn antelope, reintroduced nearby, can also sometimes be spotted in the park.

On top of that there are more than 160 bird species who visit the park every year. Most migrate to warmer climates in the winter, but those that stay include jays, nuthatches, ravens, eagles and owls.

Scenic drives

A scenic drive along the 18mls/30km of the main park road affords outstanding views of the park and southern Utah scenery. From many overlooks you can see further than 100mls/160km on clear days.

Rainbow and Yovimpa Points: On crisp winter days, views from Rainbow and Yovimpa Points are restricted only by the curvature of the Earth. Driving south from

Rainbow Point

the Visitor Center to Rainbow Point, you gradually climb 1,100ft/335m. En route you will notice how the pines change to spruce, fir and aspen. Both points provide magnificent views of a large chunk of southern Utah. On most days you can see Navajo Mountain and the Kaibab Plateau, which is 90mls/145km away in Arizona. On the clearest day you can even see as far as New Mexico. In the foreground are the colours of the long-eroded slopes and remnant hoodoos. While you are here, search out The Poodle to the north west of Rainbow Point, and the Pink Cliffs behind it.

The park road ends at Rainbow Point with a road loop that turns you back towards the park entrance. In 2009, a free guided roundtrip shuttle bus tour was introduced along this route, 11am–3pm, 22 May–13 Sep.

Agua Canyon: This displays some of the best contrasts of light and colour in the park. Look for small trees atop a hoodoo known as the Hunter, while in the distance you will also be able to see the rims of southern plateaux and canyons.

Fairyland Canyon/Point: This offers stunning views of the Fairyland Amphitheater and its fanciful shapes, the Sinking Ship, Aquarius Plateau and Navajo Mountain in the distance. Because Fairyland Canyon lies between the entrance station and the park boundary, and 1ml/1.6km off the main road, many visitors miss this viewpoint, yet it has some of the most spectacular views in the park.

Farview Point: This provides a panoramic view of the neighbouring plateaux and mountains and far to the south-east even the Kaibab Plateau of the Grand Canyon's North Rim. The Natural Bridge is actually an arch that was formed by the combined forces of rain and frost erosion rather than the work of a stream.

Paria View: This looks out across hoodoos in an amphitheatre carved by Yellow Creek. The Paria River valley and Table Cliffs Plateau form the backdrop. To the south, the White Cliffs, weathered out of Navajo sandstone, can also be seen.

✠ BRITTIP

Picnic tables, water and WCs are available at Sunset Point, Yovimpa Point and the south end of the north campsites. There are also picnic tables along the road to Rainbow Point, but no amenities.

Thor's Hammer at Bryce Canyon

Ponderosa Canyon: This area reveals a series of multi-coloured hoodoos that are framed by pine-covered foothills and the Table Cliffs Plateau to the north.

Bryce Amphitheatre: The Sunrise, Sunset, Inspiration and Bryce Points ring Bryce Amphitheatre, the largest natural amphitheatre in the park. The Queen's Garden Trail begins at Sunrise Point. From Sunset Point, you can hike to Thor's Hammer and Wall Street. Inspiration Point offers the best view of the Silent City. The Under-the-Rim Trail begins at Bryce Point. From each point you can see as far as the Black Mountains in the north-east and Navajo Mountain in the south.

Things to do

You can avoid driving round the park by using the shuttle bus system, which has 3 different shuttle lines and leaves every 13–30 minutes depending on the time of day 22 May–13 Sep. The Visitor Center provides details of birding, camping, hiking, photography, star gazing, wildlife watching and trail rides. At the Visitor Center, you can see a film about the park and also get a schedule to join a National Park Service ranger to explore the Canyon's natural and cultural history and learn about the forces that shaped the landscape.

Cycling is only allowed on paved roads and there are no mountain biking trails.

Guided horse rides are available in the morning and afternoon April–Oct. For details contact Bryce Canyon Lodge (435 834 5361) or Canyon Trail Rides (435 679 8665, canyonrides.com). Easy to strenuous hikes and backcountry hiking (for which a permit is required) are detailed on the website. One of the most adventurous, and spectacular, is the 23-ml/37-km Under-the-Rim Trail, with camping en route, from Bryce Point to Rainbow Point. In winter, snowshoes or cross-country skis can be rented outside the park to tackle the plateau top.

Lodging in Bryce Canyon and Bryce

Bryce Canyon Lodge: 303 297 2757 or 435 834 8700, brycecanyonlodge.com. The only hotel accommodation inside the canyon, Bryce Canyon Lodge has 114 rooms including suites, motel rooms and cabins. The lodge also has a restaurant, gift shop and post office. There are also 2 campsites in the canyon itself, while backcountry camping is possible for a fee of $5.

Bryce Canyon Lodge

Best Western Ruby's Inn: 26 So Main, Highway 63, Bryce Canyon City, 866 866 6616 or 435 834 5341, rubysinn.com. Has 370 rooms including 2 suites and rooms for the disabled. All rooms are non-smoking. Facilities include in-room spa, cable TV, indoor swimming pool, spa, hot tub, restaurants, general store, gallery, internet access and gift shops. Also offers trail rides, scenic flights, mountain biking, chuckwagon cookouts, rodeo, ATV rides and cross-country skiing.

Bryce Canyon Pines Motel: Highway 12 Milepost 10, Bryce, 800 892 7923 or 435 834 5441, brycecanyonmotel.com. Has 51 rooms including cottages, 2 rooms with kitchenette and a room for the disabled. Facilities include a restaurant, swimming pool and spa, gift shop, campsite and day-long horse-riding trips with real cowboys.

Pink Cliffs Bryce Village Inn: 139 West State Highway 12, Bryce (at the junction of highways 12 and 63), 435 834 5300. The 53 rooms include 14 bunkhouses that are open seasonally. Amenities include a restaurant, café, swimming pool, trading post and barbecue dinners.

Death Valley National Park

From Las Vegas you can reach the park's southern end via Highway 95, which takes you to Amargosa Valley and Death Valley Junction. You can also get there by heading to Pahrump and then following the State Line Road to Death Valley Junction.

BRITTIP

Death Valley tours are not cheap but Rocky Trails (see page 234) do offer a great experience if you want to see it close up!

Death Valley

Furnace Creek Information Center

Furnace Creek Resort Area on California Highway 190, CA, 760 786 3200, nps.gov/deva

Open: daily 8am–5pm

Death Valley is the largest of all America's national parks outside of Alaska and covers more than $5,156mls^2/13,354km^2$. At the bottom of the 300-ml/483-km long Sierra Nevada mountain range that stretches to Lake Tahoe in the north, it is the hottest place on Earth. In summer the average temperature is 45°C/113°F and the rocks almost reach water-boiling point. The lowest point – 282ft/86m below sea level – in all of America is in the heart of the Valley.

Wimps can visit in March and April when it is just 18°C/64°F and admire the desert spring blooms that shoot out of the sculpted rocks. But let's face it, the whole point of going to Death Valley is to drive through it at the hottest time of year! I would, however, advise giving yourself – and your car – an even chance of making it across in one piece by setting off early in the morning and making sure both your car radiator – and you – have plenty of water.

The National Parks of California warn you not to stop your car in the heat of the day (it'll probably not restart until night-time) and don't drive too quickly, again to prevent overheating. Always ensure you have enough petrol as stations are thin on the ground, but can be found at Furnace Creek, Stovepipe Wells, Scotty's Castle and Panamint Springs.

BRITTIP

Death Valley may be the extreme when it comes to heat, but summer in all the regions surrounding Las Vegas is very hot, so always ensure you have plenty of water with you – dehydration is no fun.

Just bear in mind that if you do break down you'll be on your own for some time as there is no public transport in the Valley and not many Americans are daft enough (mad dogs and Englishmen and all that) to go through in the summer. However, if you're sensible you will survive and will be amazed by the breathtaking beauty of the miles and miles of sand and rocks that have been hardened into a sea-like landscape by the melting sun.

The main sights include Furnace Creek, the ruins of Harmony Borax Works, Zabriskie Point with its gorgeously golden hills that are best seen at sunrise or sunset, Badwater and the amazing heights of Dante's View where you get precisely that – a spectacular vista of the white salt lakes that stretch to the Panamint Mountains.

Other sights include Scotty's Castle, an incongruous mansion retreat built for American millionaire Albert Johnson in the 1920s; Ubehebe Crater, a 500ft/152m deep hole, which is all that remains of a volcano; the 700-ft/213-m high Eureka sand dunes and Racetrack Valley, so named because it is a dry mud flat covered in wind-blown boulders.

If you're mad enough to go hiking, try the 14ml/22.5km round trip to the top of Telescope Peak, which does at least get cooler as you get higher!

Some people opt to stay at Furnace Creek, though I can't see the point of being boiled alive for quite so long! However, if you do wish to stay, head for the rustic **Furnace Creek Ranch** (760 786 2345, furnacecreekresort.com) which has 224 rooms and a pool, stables, restaurant, bar, shop, tennis courts and even an 18-hole golf course – the lowest anywhere on Earth!

Mammoth Lakes

Mammoth Lakes Visitors Bureau: toll free in the US 888-466 2666, from elsewhere 760 934 2712, visitmammoth.com
A short 1.5-hour drive north of Big Pine in Death Valley National Park on Highways 190 and 136 is the majestic world of Mammoth Lakes. At the gateway to Yosemite, it is one of the best places in the Sierra Nevada for outdoor activities and is second only to Tahoe as a ski resort in winter. The magical setting and 50ml/80km trail make it popular with mountain bikers, while expert guides offer climbing, kayaking and hang-gliding.

The whole area is also good for golf, canoeing, swimming and searching out wildlife, gold mines and ghost towns. Recent investment in Mammoth Mountain mean there is now an 18-hole championship golf course and a pedestrian resort, Gondola Village, with shops, restaurants, a skating pond and gondola, which connects the centre of town to the heart of the mountain for unmissable views.

Lodgings include: Shilo Inn Mammoth Lakes (2963 Main Street, 0800 222 2244 or 760 934 4500); Mammoth Mountain Inn (1 Minaret Road, 800 626 6684 or 760 934 2581) and Sierra Nevada

Rodeway Inn & Suites (164 Old Mammoth Road, 800 824 5132 or 760 934 2515). Or you can write to the Mammoth Lakes Visitor Bureau at PO Box 48, Mammoth Lakes, CA 93546 (760 934 2712, visit mammoth.com) for a free vacation planner.

Good for food: Breakfast and lunch: Blondies (3599 Main Street, 760 934 4048). Dinner: Alpenrose Sierra Grill (343 Old Mammoth Road, 760 934 3077, alpenrosemammoth.com).

Good for getting around in town: Mammoth Shuttle on 760 934 2571 ext 9238.

Other useful contacts: Devil's Postpile National Monument (760 934 2289,

Ponderosa Pines

nps.gov/depo); Mammoth Museum (5489 Sherwin Creek Road, 760 934 6918); Mammoth Mountain Bike Park and Adventure Challenge Course (800 626 6684 or 760 934 0706, mammoth mountain.com); Mammoth Mountain Ski Resort (760 934 0745, mammoth mountain.com) and Tamarack Cross-Country Ski Area at Mammoth Lakes (760 934 2442, tamaracklodge.com/xcountry).

Yosemite National Park

This has to be one of the most stunning natural sights in America. Mile-high cliffs gouged out by glaciers thousands of years ago are topped with pinnacles and domes from which waterfalls cascade. Coyotes and black bears roam the valley floor, which is never more than 1ml/1.6km wide. In winter, roads in the park get blocked by snow and in summer by the thousands of visitors who flock to the area. It takes at least half a day to tour the Yosemite Valley, but would take 2 days to see all the sites and areas.

Open: The Park is open all day, every day during daylight hours although some areas are closed due to snow Nov–May. The Valley Visitor Center 209 372 0200, nps.gov/yose is the only visitor center open year round, 9am–5pm daily. It can give you all the latest information on park and surrounding road conditions (essential at all times except summer), transport, recreation, lodging, camping and dining options.

Yosemite National Park

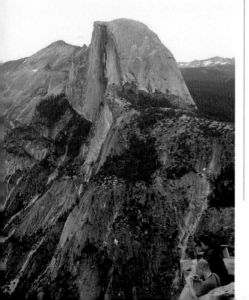

Admission: $20 per car or $10 per person, for 7-day pass

More info: yosemite.national-park.com; yosemite.com

Yosemite Sierra Visitors Bureau: 41969 Highway 41, Oakhurst 93644, 559 683 4636, yosemitethisyear.com. **Open:** 8.30am–5pm Mon–Sat; 9am–1pm Sun. Full details of mountain biking, fishing, boating at Bass Lake, steam train, the historic park and Native American museums are available here. Write to them for a visitors' guide. Guided tours, including trips around the valley and into the mountains, are bookable through most of the hotels in the area.

✦ BRITTIP

Fill up with petrol on your way into Yosemite as there are no petrol stations in the park.

Yosemite View Lodge: Yosemite Motels, 11136 Highway 140, El Portal, CA 95338, 888 742 4371 or 209 379 2861, yosemite-motels.com. Adjacent to the wild and scenic Merced River, Camp Grizzly opened early in 1999. Based on a theme of a 1950s summer camp, it provides educational nature trails, barbecue-style dining, country line dancing and other special events. Contact them to book and get more information on motels in the area.

✦ BRITTIP

Some roads close from late autumn to early summer – check in advance and have tyre chains at the ready for sudden falls of snow if driving in winter.

Other useful numbers: Yosemite Mountain Sugar Pine Railroad (559 683 7273, ymsprr.com) which runs steam trains through the Sierra National Forest near Yosemite Park; Yosemite Sightseeing Tours (559 658 8687/TOUR, yosemite tours.com); All-Outdoors Whitewater Trips (800 247 2387, aorafting.com) for half, 1-, 2- and 3-day rafting trips April–Nov; and Whitewater Voyages (800 400 7238, whitewatervoyages.com) for wonderful runs down the Merced with guides, food and equipment.

Safety, insurance, hints and tips on making the best of your holiday

N o one wants to think about anything going wrong with their dream holiday, but it is worth thinking about a few commonsense aspects of safety and security so that you can avoid any preventable problems.

General hints and tips

Don't allow your dream trip to Las Vegas and beyond to be spoilt by not taking the right kind of precautions, be they for personal safety or of a medical nature.

In the sun

Let's face it, most Brits tend to travel to America at the hottest time of the year – the summer – and most are unprepared for the sheer intensity of the sun. Before you even think about going out for the day, apply a high-factor sunblock, as it is very easy to get sunburnt when you are walking around, sightseeing or shopping. Reapply regularly throughout the day. It is also a

good idea to wear a hat or scarf to protect your head from the sun, especially at the hottest time of the day from 11am to 3pm, so you do not get sunstroke. If it is windy, you may be lulled into thinking that it is not as hot, but this is a dangerous illusion – especially in the desert valley of Las Vegas! If you are spending the day by the pool, it is advisable to use a sunshade at the hottest time of the day, and apply waterproof sunblock regularly, even when you are in the pool, as the UV rays travel through water. Always make sure you have plenty of fluids with you when travelling. Water is best. Try to avoid alcohol during the day, as this will have an additional dehydrating effect.

At your hotel

In America, your hotel room number is your main source of security. It is often your passport to eating and collecting messages, so keep the number safe and secure. When checking in, make sure none of the hotel staff mentions your room

Be safety conscious in your hotel

BRITTIP

Use a business address rather than your home address on all your luggage.

number out loud. If they do, give them back the key and ask them to give you a new room and to write down the new room number instead of announcing it (most hotels follow this practice in any case). When you need to give someone your room number – for instance when charging a dinner or any other bill to your room – write it down or show them your room card rather than calling it out.

When in your hotel room, always use the deadlocks and security chains and use the door peephole before opening the door to strangers. If someone knocks on the door and cannot give any identification, phone down to the hotel reception desk.

When you go out, make sure you lock the windows and door properly. Even if you leave your room just for a few seconds, lock the door.

Cash and documents

Most hotels in tourist areas have safety deposit boxes, so use these to store important documents such as airline tickets and passports. When you go out, do not take all your cash and credit cards with you – always have at least one credit card in the safe as an emergency back-up and only take enough cash with you for the day. Using a money belt is also a good idea. Keep a separate record of your travellers' cheque numbers. If your room does not have its own safe, leave your valuables in the main hotel safe.

Emergencies

For the police, fire department or ambulance, dial 911 (9-911 from your hotel room).

If you need medical help in Las Vegas, there are 3 main options, all of which are open 24 hours a day, 7 days a week: **Harmon Medical Center**, 150 East Harmon Avenue (702 796 1116, harmonmedical center.com); **Fremont Medical Center**, 4880 South Wynn Road (on the corner of Tropicana and Wynn, 702 871 5005, fmcnv.com); and **University Medical Center (UMC) Hospital**, 1800 W Charleston Boulevard (702 383 2000, umcsn.com).

Cars

Most of the advice is obvious, but when we go on holiday we sometimes relax to the point of not following our basic common sense. Never leave your car unlocked and never leave any valuable items on the car seats or anywhere else where they can be seen.

Travel insurance

The one thing you should not forget is travel insurance when travelling anywhere around America. Medical cover is very expensive and if you are involved in any kind of an accident you could be sued, which is very costly indeed in America.

If you do want to make savings in this area, don't avoid getting insurance cover, but do avoid buying it from tour operators, as they are notoriously expensive.

The alternative, particularly if you plan to make more than one trip in any given year, is to go for an annual worldwide policy directly from insurers. The worldwide annual policies can make even more sense if you're travelling as a family.

In all cases, you need to ensure that the policy gives you the following cover:

- **Actual coverage of the United States** – not all plans include America
- **Medical** cover of at least £2 million in America
- **Personal liability** cover of at least £2 million in America

Keep your winnings safe!

Check insurance for sports cover

- **Cancellation and curtailment** cover of around £3,000 in case you are forced to call off your holiday
- **Lost baggage and belongings** cover at around £1,500 – most premiums only offer cover for individual items up to around £250, so you will need additional cover for expensive cameras or camcorders
- **Cash cover** (usually around £200) and documents including your air tickets, passport and currency
- **24-hour helpline** to make it easy for you to get advice and instructions on what to do
- **Membership of the Financial Ombudsman Service** in case you are unhappy with the outcome of a claim.

Check and check again

Shop around: You do not have to buy your policy from your tour operator, so don't let them include it as a matter of course. You will almost certainly be able to get a better deal elsewhere.

Read the policy: Always ask for a copy of the policy document before you go and if you are not happy with the cover offered, cancel and demand your premium back – in some cases you will only have 7 days in which to do this.

Don't double up on cover: If you have an 'all risks' policy on your home contents, this will cover your property outside the home and may even cover lost money and credit cards. Check if this covers you abroad – and covers your property when in transit – before buying personal possessions cover.

Look at gold card cover: Some bank gold cards provide you with insurance

BRITTIP

Put away maps and brochures in the glove compartment, as these will be obvious signs that yours is a tourist's car.

cover if you buy your air ticket with the gold card, so it is worth checking, although there will be terms and conditions.

Check dangerous sports cover: In almost all cases mountaineering, racing and hazardous pursuits such as bungee jumping, skydiving, horse riding, windsurfing, trekking and even cycling are not included in normal policies. There are so many opportunities to do all of these activities that you really should ensure you are covered before you go. Backpackers and dangerous sports enthusiasts can try Insure & Go (0844 888 2787, insureandgo.com). Direct Travel Insurance (0845 605 2700, direct-travel.co.uk) is also an excellent place to look for travel insurance. It specialises in insurance for backpackers aged 18–35 and the cover includes walking holidays, sports and activities, skiing and scuba diving, bungee jumping and abseiling; as does Leading Edge (01892 836622, leadedge.co.uk).

Make sure you qualify: For instance, if you have been treated in hospital in the six months prior to travelling or are waiting for hospital treatment, you may need medical evidence that you are fit to travel. Ask your doctor for a report giving you the all-clear (you will have to pay for this) and if the insurance company still says your condition is not covered, shop around.

Get full coverage on car insurance

Insurance policies

This is a competitive market, so it pays to shop around to find the best policy for you. Some companies offer discounts if you already have another policy with them. These companies are worth checking out for annual-cover or single-trip travel insurance.

To compare deals, visit www.money supermarket.com or phone 0845 345 5708. It has cheap deals from more than 450 policies to compare online, with links directly through for purchasing. You can also compare leading providers of the most comprehensive deals at www.top4 deals.com/travel-insurance.

- **Atlas Direct** 0870 811 1700, atlasdirect.net.
- **Citybond Travel** 0845 618 0345, citybond.co.uk.
- **Clydesdale Bank** 0845 602 6917, cbonline.co.uk
- **CostOut** 0844 980 0271, costout.co.uk.
- **Direct Travel** 0845 605 2700, direct-travel.co.uk.
- **Egg** 08451 233 233, egg.com
- **Flexicover Direct** 0800 093 9495, flexicover.co.uk

- **James Hampden** 020 7398 8080, jameshampden.com
- **Leading Edge** 01892 836622, leadedge.co.uk
- **Marks & Spencer Financial Services** 0845 900 0900, money.marksandspencer.com
- **More Than** 0800 300 866, morethan.com
- **MRL Insurance Direct** 0845 676 0691, mrlinsurance.co.uk
- **Nationwide BS** 0800 756 8900, nationwide.co.uk
- **TravelPlan Direct** 0870 412 3110, travelplan-direct.com
- **Zurich Connect** 0845 603 1590, zurich-connect.co.uk
- **Worldwide Insure** 01892 833338, worldwideinsure.com

Other useful contacts

The Association of British Insurers (ABI) (020 7600 3333, abi.org.uk)
Financial Ombudsman Service (0845 080 1800, financial-ombudsman.org.uk)

Now how do you say that?

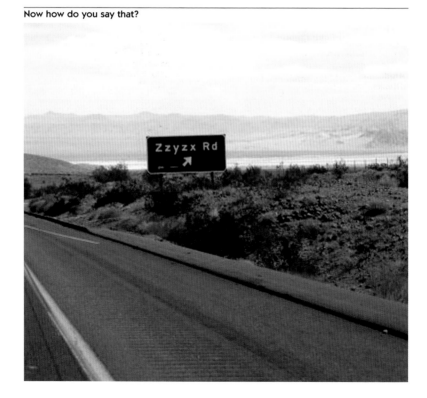

Major page references are in **bold**, illustrations are in *italics*. A=Attraction H=Hotel S=Show.

Acknowledgements

With thanks to everyone who supplied photographs for this book, in particular MGM Mirage.

Alexis Park 196 top; Blue Moon Resort 196 bottom; Bombadier.com 15; Caesars Palace 23, 85, 86, 88, 89, 153 bottom; Candlelight Wedding Chapel 188 top; Cherworld.com 66 top; Cirque du Soleil 63, 64, 65; City Center Land LLC 20, 26, 28, 37, 47, 80, 253; Comedy Club 73; Comedystop.com 20 bottom; El Cortez 58; Ethel M Chocolate Factory 212 bottom; Europebuyaasvegas.com 91 top; Fashion Show Mall 83 bottom ; Fitzgerald's 59; Flamingo 13 top, 67 top, 72 top, 210 bottom; Four Seasons, Mary Nichols 34, 132; General Growth Properties Inc. 82, 84; Golfamerica.biz 237, 239; Graceeland Wedding Chapel 182; Guggenheim 210 top; Hard Rock Café126; Hard Rock Hotel 51, 143 bottom, 150 bottom, 157 bottom; Harrah's 76, 138 top, 160 bottom, 166 bottom, 246 ; Ken Howard 67 bottom right; Imperial Palace 56 bottom, 68 top, 168, 191 top, 213 top; Las Vegas Natural History Museum 215; Las Vegas News Bureau 3, 7, 11, 12, 21 top, 61, 69 bottom, 87 top, 97, 137 bottom, 153 top, 156 bottom, 159 top, 173 bottom, 221 bottom,; Las Vegas Premium Outlets 98; Lasvegasadventurer.com 70 top; Lasvegaspropertiesblog.com 218 top; Lasvegasshow.com 66 bottom; Leonardo.com back cover, 52, 73 top, 155; Lied Discovery Children's Museum 217 bottom; Little White Wedding Chapel 184; Lvcasinoinfo.com 83 top, 202, 280; Marjorie Barrick Museum of Natural History 216 top; Maverick Helicopters 266 bottom; Tom Mescher 87 bottom, 140, 204, 27, 279; MGM Mirage 2, 10 top, 13 bottom, 16, 18, 19, 23, 29, 31, 33, 36, 38, 40, 41, 46 bottom, 74, 78, 79, 99, 100, 101, 103, 104, 108, 109, 110, 111, 112, 113, 114, 117, 119, 122, 123, 128, 129, 131, 133, 134, 135, 138 bottom, 135, 138, 141, 142 bottom, 143 top, 144, 145, 146 bottom, 147, 149, 150 top, 151, 152, 154 bottom, 156 top, 159 bottom, 160, 161 top, 167, 168, 169, 174, 176, 177, 178, 179,180, 181, 183, 185 bottom, 189, 190, 191 bottom, 192, 194 bottom, 199, 200, 201, 203, 205, 208, 211, 212 top, 245, 248, 251 top, 252, 256; Robert Miller 22; Miracle Mile Shops 91, 92, 136,; Nascar Café 127; Nevada Commission on Tourism 185, 219, 220, 221 top, 222–230, 236, 238, 240, 241, 243, 244, 245 top, 249, 250, 254 bottom, 261, 262, 266–278, ; Nevada State Museum 218; Painted Desert Golf Club 10 bottom; Palace Station 60 bottom; Palazzo Shops 93, 94, 139; Paris Las Vegas 40; Ian Parker 263; Planet Hollywood 44, 45 top, 145, 166; Planet99.com 197; Prnewswire.com 66 bottom; Rio All-Suite Hotel 55, 56 top, 115, 148; Ritz-Carlton 57 bottom, 194 top; Riviera 73 bottom; Lynn Ross 216; Sahara 60 top, 67 top, 121; Scott Hooper 164; Singletrack Tours 235; Spearmint Rhino 163 top; State Historic Park 214 top; Stratosphere 45, 46 top; The Palms 53, 54, 158, 146 top, 154 top; Lawrence Tierney 9, 14, 21 bottom, 24, 35, 42, 70 bottom, 137 top, 158 top; Tillerman 124; Town Square 95, 96; Treasure Island 120, 192; Tropicana 57 top, 170, 182 top, ; V – the Ultimate Variety Show 67 bottom left; Vdara 142 top; Vegastodayandtomorrow.com 62; Venetian 193; Wynn Las Vegas 49, 107, 116, 157 top